TURKEY AND THE EUROPEAN UNION

Can the Europeanisation of Turkey progress in the absence of a credible EU accession perspective? For a broad range of issues and policy areas, this volume shows convincingly how the EU's role has changed from direct impact to context factor for domestic politics. Recommended reading for anyone interested in the development of Turkish politics.

Frank Schimmelfennig, ETH Zurich, Switzerland

Nas and Özer have brought together some of the finest scholarship on EU-Turkey relations to produce the most comprehensive volume on the Europeanisation of Turkey to date. Building on the latest developments in Europeanisation theory, the contributors explore all relevant sectors of Turkish society and politics in a comprehensive set of rich empirical case studies with theoretical ramifications far beyond the case of Turkey.

Thomas Diez, University of Tübingen, Germany

Turkey and the European Union
Processes of Europeanisation

Edited by

ÇİĞDEM NAS
Yıldız Technical University, Turkey

YONCA ÖZER
Marmara University, Turkey

ASHGATE

Published by
Ashgate Publishing Limited
Wey Court East
Union Road
Farnham
Surrey, GU9 7PT
England

Ashgate Publishing Company
Suite 420
101 Cherry Street
Burlington
VT 05401-4405
USA

www.ashgate.com

British Library Cataloguing in Publication Data
Turkey and the European Union : processes of Europeanisation.
1. European Union–Turkey. 2. Turkey–Foreign relations–European Union countries. 3. European Union countries– Foreign relations–Turkey. 4. Turkey–Civilization– European influences. 5. Turkey–Politics and government–1980- 6. Turkey–Social conditions–21st century.
I. Nas, Çiğdem. II. Özer, Yonca.
327.5'61'04-dc23

Library of Congress Cataloging-in-Publication Data
Nas, Çiğdem.
Turkey and the European Union : processes of Europeanisation / by Çiğdem Nas and Yonca Özer.
    p. cm.
Includes bibliographical references and index.
ISBN 978-1-4094-4529-6 (hardback : alk. paper) — ISBN 978-1-4094-4530-2 (ebook) 1. European Union—Turkey. 2. Turkey—Relations—European Union countries. 3. European Union countries—Relations—Turkey. 4. Turkey—Politics and government—20th century. 5. Turkey—Politics and government—21st century. I. Özer, Yonca. II. Title.
HC240.25.T8N37 2012
341.242'209561—dc23

2012012809

ISBN 9781409445296 (hbk)
ISBN 9781409445302 (ebk)

Printed and bound in Great Britain by the
MPG Books Group, UK.

Contents

Notes on Contributors

Tanja A. Börzel is professor of political science and holds the Chair for European Integration at the Otto-Suhr-Institut for Political Science, Freie Universität Berlin. She is co-coordinator of the Research College 'The Transformative Power of Europe' and directs the Jean Monnet Center of Excellence 'Europe and its Citizens'. She received her PhD from the European University Institute in Florence, Italy in 1999. From 1999 to 2004, she conducted her research and taught at the Max Planck Institute for Research on Collective Goods in Bonn, the Humboldt-Universität zu Berlin and the University Heidelberg. Her research focus and teaching experience lie in the field of institutional theory and Governance, European Integration, and Comparative Politics with a focus on Western and Southern Europe. Her most recent publications include *Coping with Accession to the European Union. New Modes of Environmental Governance* (Palgrave, 2010, edited volume) and European Governance – Negotiation and Competition in the Shadow of Hierarchy, *Journal of Common Market Studies*, 48 (2), 2010.

Sevgi Uçan Çubukçu is Associate Professor at Istanbul University, Faculty of Political Sciences, Department of International Relations. She obtained her BSc in International Relations from Istanbul University, Faculty of Economics in 1988. She received her MSc in International Relations on the subject of 'Turkish Feminist Movement' at the Boğaziçi University in 1995. After studying for her PhD in LSE and SOAS in 1999 as a 'visiting research fellow', she completed her PhD in International Relations in 2002 with her dissertation on The Social Democracy in Post-Industrial Society: New Labour Party and The Third Way in Istanbul University. Sevgi Uçan Çubukçu teaches Feminist Theories, Gender and Democracy in Turkey, Globalism and Politics, Modern Political Theories, and The Theory of Democracy. Her interests include feminism, women's/gender issues, democracy, globalisation, and social democracy. She is member of the General Board of Women's Library and Information Center Foundation and member of the Collective of Purple Roof Women's Shelter Foundation. She is also vice director of the Women's Research and Education Center.

Rana İzci (BA and MA at Marmara University, Department of International Relations, PhD Marmara University, EU Institute, Jean Monnet fellow VGSP at University of Essex) is an assistant professor at the European Union Institute, Marmara University. She has written on a number of topics in environmental politics including climate change policies of Turkey and environmental security. She has been conducting a TÜBİTAK (The Scientific and Technological Research Council of Turkey) Project on the Impact of Pre-accession Financial Assistance

viii   *Turkey and the European Union*

on Institutional Structures of Universities and NGOs in Turkey since October 2010. Her recent publications include (co-authors İnce Z., Zengin S., and Tüzen, Z.) The impact of Turkey-EU relations on academic research agendas in Turkey: new research areas in European studies, in Ç. Nas and R. İzci (eds), *Changing Europe and Turkey: Current Debates*, İstanbul: Marmara University European Union Institute, 2010: 93–114; Turkey towards a New Development Path, *Turkish Politics Quarterly*, Summer 2009, 133–42.

Alper Kaliber is Assistant Professor of International Relations at İstanbul Bilgi University, Turkey. He completed his PhD in Political Science at Bilkent University, Turkey, and served as a research fellow at the University of Birmingham, United Kingdom and as an assistant professor at the Yaşar University, Turkey. His areas of interest include Critical Security Studies, European security, phenomenon of Europeanisation and European integration, Turkish foreign policy and the Cyprus conflict. Among his recent publications are: Conflict Society and the Transformation of Turkey's Kurdish Question, with Nathalie Tocci, *Security Dialogue*, 41(2), April 2010, 191–215; Re-imagining Cyprus: The Rise of Regionalism in Turkey's Security Lexicon, in *Cyprus: A Conflict at the Crossroads*, T. Diez and N. Tocci (eds), (Manchester: Manchester University Press, 2009): 105–23. He received an award of honourable mention in Sakıp Sabancı International Research Award 2011 with his article entitled Reorganization Of Geopolitics: Understanding The New Activism In Turkish Foreign Policy. His project, Europeanisation of Civil Society in Turkey (EUROCIV) was awarded the Marie Curie Career Integration Grant for 2012–14 by the European Commission.

Catherine MacMillan completed her doctorate in European Studies at the European Union Institute, Marmara University, Istanbul in 2008 with a dissertation on the EU's Justice and Home Affairs policies. She is Assistant Professor in the department of English Language and Literature at Yeditepe University, Istanbul. Her research interests focus on discursive attitudes to Turkish accession in the EU member states as well as the EU's Justice and Home Affairs policies. Her main publications include; The Application of Neofunctionalism to the Enlargement Process: The Case of Turkey, Journal of Common Market Studies 47(9) and Privileged Partnership, Open Ended Accession Negotiations and the Securitisation of Turkey's EU Accession Process, Journal of Contemporary European Studies, 18(4).

Çiğdem Nas is associate professor of international relations at the Yıldız Technical University of Istanbul. She received her BA in political science at the Bosphorous University, her Master's degree at the London School of Economics and her PhD degree at the Marmara University. Her research interests are the political system of the EU, Turkey-EU relations, democratisation, minority rights and identity questions. She also works for the Economic Development Foundation which is a non-governmental organisation specialising in the field of Turkey-EU relations. She has taken part in several EU projects and has published on the EU. Her recent publications include; Turkey and the EU: A Stumbling Accession Process under New Conditions, in Ö.Z. Oktav (ed.), *Turkey in the 21st Century: Quest for a New Foreign Policy*, Surrey: Ashgate, 2011; Changing Dynamics of Turkish Foreign Policy and the EU, *Turkish Policy Quarterly*, 9(4), 2010.

Bertil Emrah Oder is full professor of constitutional law at Koç University Law School. After receiving her LLB from Istanbul University Law School, she obtained an LLM degree from Marmara University European Union Institute. She received her PhD degree in law with distinction ('summa cum laude') from University of Cologne (Germany). She served as a full time faculty in the law schools of Istanbul University and Galatasaray University. She worked as associate director and executive member of various centres for EU law, human rights law, international relations and gender studies. Currently, she serves as Dean of Koç University Law School. Among others, her major publications include: *Constitution and Constitutionalism in the EU*, Istanbul: Anahtar Publishing, 2004, 544 pp.; Übertragung von Hoheitsrechten im Spannungsverhältnis zur nationalen Souveränität – Verfassungsrechtliche Vorgaben und verfassungspolitischer Änderungsbedarf, Otto Depenheuer (ed.), *Deutsch-Türkisches Forum für Staatsrechtslehre III*, Münster/Hamburg/Berlin/Wien/London: LIT Verlag, 2004, pp. 75–100; Militant Democracy in Turkey, in Markus Thiel (ed.), *Militant Democracy in Modern Democracies*, Ashgate Publishing, 2009, pp. 263–310.

Selcen Öner is currently working as Assistant professor Dr at Bahçeşehir University at the Department of EU Relations. She finished her PhD at Marmara University at the Department of EU Politics and International Relations of the EU Institute in 2008. Her PhD thesis was on 'Construction of European Identity within the EU'. She finished her MA at Marmara University at the department of Political Science and International Relations in 2002. She wrote her master's thesis on 'The Triadic Relationship between the EU, Nation-state and Sub-national Regions: The Cases of Basque Country, Catalonia and Corsica'. She received her undergraduate degree from Istanbul University, department of International Relations in 1999. Her research interests are Turkey-EU relations, European identity, EU politics, civil society in Turkey, Turkish foreign policy and Europeanisation. Some of her recent publications include *Turkey and the European Union: The Question of European Identity*, Lanham, Maryland: Lexington Pub., 2011; The External Identity of the EU in Terms of Common Foreign and Security Policy and the Possible Impacts of Turkey, in Lukasz Donaj and Marek Sempach (eds), *Turcja w Stosunkach Miedzynarodowych*, Poland: Lodz International Studies Academy, 2011.

Yonca Özer is an assistant professor at the Marmara University European Union Institute since 2008. Dr Ozer received her BA in political science and international relations at the Marmara University, her Master's degree at the Marmara University EU Institute and the London School of Economics, and her PhD degree at the Marmara University EU Institute. Her main research interests are EU-Turkey relations, international political economy and external relations of the EU. She wrote various articles on these subjects. She also supervised MA and PhD theses on European studies and teaches courses on EU-Turkey Relations, and International Political Economy. She edited a book titled *Living in a Unipolar World: Facts, Misconceptions and Expectations* for the Social Democracy Foundation in Turkey. Among her recent publications are The Influence of the Stalemate in the WTO on the EU: 'Global Europe's New Trade Policy', *Journal of US-China Public Administration*, 8(5), 2011, 497–511 and Kıbrıs Meselesinin Türkiye–Avrupa Birliği İlişkilerindeki Rolü (Role of the Cyprus Issue in Turkey-European Union Relations) in Cüneyt Yenigün and Ertan Efegil (eds), *Türkiye'nin Güncel Dış Politika Sorunları* (Turkey's Current Foreign Policy Problems), Ankara: Nobel Publishing, 2010.

Özlem Terzi is associate professor at the Department of International Relations, Istanbul University. She is the author of *The Influence of the European Union on Turkish Foreign Policy*, published by Ashgate in 2010. She received her PhD in International Relations from the Middle East Technical University (METU) in 2003. She studied at the London School of Economics European Institute between 1998–99, where she received her MSc in European Studies in 1999. She also has an MSc in International Relations from the Department of International Relations (1997), METU, where she worked as a research assistant between 1995–99. She completed her BSc in International Relations at Ankara University in 1995. Her research interests include EU foreign policy, European integration, EU-Turkish relations and Turkish foreign policy.

Dimitris Tsarouhas is Assistant Professor Dr in the Department of International Relations, Bilkent University. He is the author of *Social Democracy in Sweden* (IB Tauris 2008) and co-editor of *Bridging the Real Divide: Social and Regional Policy in Turkey's EU Accession Process* (METU University Press 2007). His research on Europeanisation, social policy, labour politics and Greek politics has been published in journals such as *Public Administration*, *Social Politics*, *Social Policy & Administration* and *European Journal of Industrial Relations*.

Gözde Yılmaz is a PhD candidate in Berlin Graduate School for Transnational Studies (BTS), Free University Berlin. She has recently been a visiting student at the London School of Economic and Political Science. Yılmaz has a BA in International Relations from Hacettepe University and an MA in International Studies (European Integration) from the University of Birmingham. In her PhD project, she explores external Europeanisation theories with the case of minority rights in Turkey. Her further research interests are Europeanisation and domestic change, external Europeanisation theories, EU enlargement policy, European Neighbourhood Policy, EU-Turkey Relations, EU-Ukraine Relations.

Preface

The idea for this book emerged at a workshop held by the Marmara University EU Institute in Istanbul in 2010. The workshop was titled 'Re-conceptualising Turkey-EU relations'. A common theme of most papers presented at the workshop was related to the process of Europeanisation that was engendered by Turkey's developing relations with the EU. Our editors at Ashgate Publishers and anonymous referees that evaluated our book proposal had a major role in shaping further the main framework of the publication. We would like to thank all contributors to this book as well as our colleagues who took part in the organisation and implementation of the workshop mentioned above. We would like, above all, to express our gratitude for the support and encouragement we received from our families. We would like to dedicate the book to Yiğit and Levent.

List of Abbreviations

APD	Accession Partnership Document
AKP	Adalet ve Kalkınma Partisi (Justice and Development Party)
ANAP	Anavatan Partisi (Motherland Party)
CEDAW	Convention on the Elimination of All Forms of Discrimination against Women
CEE	Central and Eastern Europe(an)
CEECs	Central and Eastern European Countries
CFSP	Common Foreign and Security Policy
CHP	Cumhuriyet Halk Partisi (Republican People's Party)
CTP	Cumhuriyetçi Türk Partisi (Republican Turkish Party)
CoE	Council of Europe
CSOs	Civil Society Organisations
CSI	Civil Society Index
DSP	Demokratik Sol Parti (Democratic Left Party)
ECHR	European Commission of Human Rights
EEC	European Economic Community
EU	European Union
FSP	Foreign and Security Policy
Habitat	United Nations Conference on Human Settlements
IPA	Instrument for Pre-accession Assistance
İKV	İktisadi Kalkınma Vakfı (Economic Development Foundation)
İTO	İstanbul Ticaret Odası (İstanbul Chamber of Commerce)
JHA	Justice and Home Affairs
KAGİDER	Türkiye Kadın Girişimcileri Derneği (Women Entrepreneurs Association of Turkey)
KSSGM	Turkish Republic Prime Ministry Directorate General on the Status and Problems of Women
MHP	Milliyetçi Hareket Partisi (Nationalist Action Party)
MLSS	Ministry for Labour and Social Security
MÜSİAD	Müstakil Sanayici ve İşadamları Derneği (Independent Industrialists' and Businessperson's Association)
NGOs	Non-Governmental Organisations
NEAP	National Environmental Action Plan
NP	National Programme for the adoption of *acquis*
OECD	Organisation for Economic Cooperation and Development
OIC	Organisation of Islamic Countries
OMC	Open Method of Coordination
PKK	Kurdistan Workers' Party

REC	Regional Environmental Centre
RoC	Republic of Cyprus
SHÇEK	Social Services and Children's Protection Institute
SME	Small and Medium Sized Enterprises
TAF	Turkish Armed Forces
TEMA	The Turkish Foundation for Combating Soil Erosion, for Reforestation and the Protection of Natural Habitats
TOBB	Türkiye Odalar ve Borsalar Birligi (Union of Turkish Chambers and Stock Exchanges)
TESEV	Türkiye Ekonomik ve Sosyal Etüdler Vakfı (Turkish Economic and Social Studies Foundation)
TUSKON	Türkiye İşadamları ve Sanayiciler Konfederasyonu (Confederation of Businessmen and Industrialists of Turkey)
TÜSİAD	Turkish Industrialists' and Businessmen's Association
TÜSEV	Third Sector Foundation of Turkey
TAV	Türkiye Avrupa Vakfı (Turkey Europe Foundation)
UN	United Nations
UNFCCC	United Nations Convention on Climate Change
YARSAV	Yargıçlar ve Savcılar Birliği (Association of Judges and Prosecutors)
WB	Western Balkans

Introduction

Çiğdem Nas and Yonca Özer

Europeanisation has emerged as a valuable approach with explanatory power in European studies since the 1990s as a response to the insufficiency of traditional European integration theories to analyse the EU's domestic impact. It aims to analyse and discover the effects that the EU process engenders on not only member states but candidate or other associated countries. The EU generated a whole body of law, institutions, norms and discourses over the area of Europe. Its effect is greatest in the member states which are by the force of the founding Treaties required to implement EU law. They also have the privilege of taking part in the institutions and decision-making structures that create and shape EU policies and legislation. This effect is not confined to the member states however. Countries that have various degrees of relations with the EU and above all the candidate countries are in interaction with the EU process. This interactive relationship is generally led by the EU in an asymmetrical fashion in the case of non-members since those countries cannot be represented in the decision-making structures of the EU. Nevertheless, they are required to implement certain conditions such as democracy and human rights standards or adhere to and adapt EU rules and regulations. The adoption of the EU regime may be easier or more difficult, it may bring certain benefits to some groups while disadvantaging others, it may influence values, open up the economy, increase welfare etc, depending on the respective country's specific conditions.

In the case of candidate countries, Europeanisation process brings about new adaptational pressures in almost all policy areas. Most importantly, the struggle to fulfil the Copenhagen criteria for membership brings about the pressure for change under the EU anchor. The EU leverage empowers those groups that are willing to act as the agents of change and disadvantages those groups that wish to preserve the *status quo* or resist change in the direction of the EU criteria. This process involves not only a technical and administrative process of adaptation but also a social learning process whereby these values and norms are internalised and implemented. All these are complex and multifaceted processes that may show variations, may lead to adaptational pressures, stamina, backlash etc. Any study of Europeanisation in candidate countries would need to address the adaptations and changes made possible as a result of the implementation of EU conditionality, the degree of fit/misfit between the country and the EU system in specific policy areas or institutional arrangements, the existence of inertia in some areas and/or resistance to change, obstacles and other related global, regional or domestic factors.

From the perspective of the external incentives model developed by Schimelfennig and Sedelmeier (2004, 2005), the reward of EU membership may exert a strong pressure for change by altering the cost-benefit calculations of domestic actors. The credibility of the EU perspective, the clarity of the EU model, and the clear delineation of the timing of EU rewards in response to the candidate country's fulfilment of EU criteria facilitate a successful adoption of EU norms, legislation and policies. The social learning model on the other hand focuses on the role of norm adoption of domestic actors through socialisation processes. Here the EU acts as a legitimisation device empowering those groups that are able to internalise and act in line with EU norms and values. Viewing the recent history of EU enlargement, it may easily be observed that the above-mentioned independent variables have differed in the case of enlargement to Central and Eastern Europe, Turkey and the Western Balkans.

The present volume concentrates on the case of Turkey as a candidate country to join the EU and aims to explore the extent, direction, nature and impact of Europeanisation since Turkey's declaration as a candidate at the 1999 Helsinki European Council. Turkey's relations with the European Union present a quite interesting area of research in the field of European studies. Turkey showed an interest in association with the European Economic Community early on in 1959. Despite the fact that relations go back to this date and the Association Agreement that was signed in 1963 envisaged a close relationship embodying the possibility of eventual membership, several difficulties and setbacks prevented rapid progress. Consecutive waves of entrants acceded to the EC/EU in the subsequent years, while Turkey is still a country negotiating accession to the European Union. Turkish governments carried through the Parliament constitutional amendments and reform packages especially between 2001 and 2004 with the aim of fulfilling the political aspects of the Copenhagen criteria. Those reforms were well appreciated by the EU leading the way to the opening of accession negotiations as of 3 October 2005. Optimism in Turkey-EU relations was not long-lived however due to the 2006 decision of the European Council not to open eight chapters of the negotiations and not to provisionally close any chapter as a reaction to Turkey's declaration of its continuing non-recognition of Greek Cyprus and not opening its ports and airports to Greek Cypriot vehicles.

This was not the only 'cold shower' for Turkey. Germany's Angela Merkel noted her opposition to Turkey's EU membership even before she formed the government in Germany while Nicholas Sarkozy after coming to power in 2007 made his opposition to Turkey's membership a pinnacle of his EU policy. Both advocated 'privileged partnership' for Turkey while especially Sarkozy noted at different occasions that he opposed Turkey in principle due to his understanding that Turkey cannot be considered as a European country. France under Sarkozy unilaterally vetoed the opening of five more chapters in the negotiations – one of them coinciding with the already blocked eight chapters – with the allegation that these chapters were only needed to be opened with a country that was to become a member of the EU. In the case of Turkey negotiations could continue but towards a form of special relationship not membership. Greek Cyprus further blocked the opening of six chapters protesting Turkey's non-recognition of the country as the legitimate representative of the island. So far 13 chapters could be opened to negotiations while only one could be provisionally closed. The latest chapter was opened in June 2010. Since then a stalemate is blocking further progress. No significant change can be discerned in the positions of the parties. In Turkey the EU-induced reform policy seemed to run out of steam. Coupled with the recent financial and economic crisis dominating the Euro-area, the EU, to an extent, seems to have lost its relevance and transformative power on Turkish politics and society. Recent EU policy towards Turkey led to disillusionment in Turkish society and political elites and a sense of being unjustly treated leading to a decline in the credibility of the EU perspective. Moreover, the economic performance and dynamism of Turkey, foreign policy activism and governmental stability since 2002 led to a generally-acclaimed perception that Turkey does not need the EU anchor. This observation needs to be tempered by adding that the recent democratic record of Turkey shows imperfections and failures regarding the development of a consensual democracy with full respect for rights and freedoms. Thus it may not be a strong argument that the EU has lost all relevance in guiding and driving reform in Turkey since EU norms and values still has a role to play in triggering change in Turkey by way of social learning of domestic actors if not directly by way of providing strong incentives.

While exploring the trajectory of Europeanisation in Turkey, one cannot but note that this process started early on at least since the entry into force of the customs union in 1996. Turkey adopted a constitutional package beforehand with the aim of allaying the concerns of several member states and political groups in the EU about political conditions. In addition Turkey also adopted a competition law in line with the EU *acquis* and harmonised its external trade and customs regime much before candidacy to the EU. Although several parallels may be drawn between Turkey and previous candidates to the EU, the Turkish case also presents some special factors, Turkey being the only current candidate state in a customs union with the EU. Paradoxically the customs union chapter in the negotiations cannot be opened due to the decision of the European Council in addition to the overall stalemate in the negotiations. The EU places further demands on Turkey like the conclusion of a re-admission agreement despite the continuing ambiguity regarding the final target. Negotiations are not formally suspended and Turkey is still a candidate country. Throughout this process, Europeanisation influenced Turkish politics and society despite the problems and setbacks outlined above. Europeanisation may be observed in the constitutional and legislative system, in the institutional structure, relations between State and society as well as between political elites, in the positioning, values and discourses of domestic actors and what defines acceptable behaviour and legitimate values. While the credibility of the EU perspective declined since 2006, the EU may still impact on the ideational preferences of domestic actors, power configurations in the political system, definition of legitimacy, as well as direction of policy change and legislative reform.

The aim of the book is to explore this process in the case of Turkey with respect to the relations with the EU that have taken on a new turn with the start of accession negotiations in 2005 in a thematic perspective. It aims at offering a coherent and focused account of Turkey's candidacy to the EU and its accession negotiations. The main conceptual framework will rest on Europeanisation as an explanatory tool to understand EU-induced change, lack of change or backlash in Turkey concentrating on the last decade. After an introductory chapter on the Europeanisation literature as implemented mainly to candidate countries, each of the chapters will discuss certain policy areas, actors or issues in Turkey with a view to the EU membership perspective since 1999 and the process of Europeanisation induced by that. Europeanisation as applied to certain policy areas or issues will involve a discussion of politics of conditionality and how it influenced norms, attitudes, rules and expectations in Turkey.

Each of the chapters involves an analysis of external incentives determined by the EU, credibility of EU conditionality and its legitimacy, processes of rule adoption and implementation and mechanisms of social learning and resistance. The three models of EU external governance, i.e. the external incentives model, social learning and lesson-drawing models developed by Schimmelfennig and Sedelmeier (2004, 2005) have been employed by the contributors to assess the differential impact of EU candidacy on Turkey. The issue areas concern the political system, foreign policy, civil society and selected policy areas. Almost all contributors start their chapters with a conceptual analysis of Europeanisation and apply it to the issues under consideration. Regarding Europeanisation Radaelli's definition (2004) is subscribed to in addition to references to Olsen's (2003) and Börzel and Risse's (2003) definitions:

> Europeanisation consists of processes of a) construction, b) diffusion and c) institutionalisation of formal and informal rules, procedures, policy paradigms, styles, 'ways of doing things' and shared beliefs and norms which are first defined and consolidated in the EU policy process and then incorporated in the logic of domestic (national and subnational) discourse, political structures and public policies (Radaelli 2004: 3).

Chapter 1 by Tanja Börzel elaborates on external Europeanisation with special reference to Turkey. Börzel argues that the transformative power of Europe on Turkey have been quite restricted owing to the high costs of adapting to the membership criteria, decreasing incentives offered by the EU and the limited reform capacity of the government. However, this situation does not mean that there has been no Europeanisation at all in the case of Turkey. Börzel poses the following question in this regard: 'The real puzzle is why there is Europeanisation despite these unfavourable conditions and why the domestic impact of the EU has been differential, i.e. varies across policies and institutions.' Börzel then goes on to discuss research findings on Europeanisation in the case of Central and East European countries and the Western Balkans and compares these with the case of

Turkey. While Turkey is mostly seen as a case of differential empowerment it is not a *sui generis* case. Europeanisation exerts a transformational impact on institutions and policies in Turkey. Börzel aims to apply rational choice institutionalism and sociological institutionalism to explain the differential impact of the EU on Turkish institutions and policies. Börzel finds that Europeanisation in Turkey is bottom-up and indirect mostly having to do with the political calculations of domestic actors to use the EU as a 'legitimisation device'. While the Turkish governments may make use a greater state capacity to induce EU-related change when compared with the Western Balkans, the costs of change may also be substantial as exemplified in the case of the Cyprus policy.

Chapter 2 by Çiğdem Nas approaches Europeanisation in the issue-area of identity. She largely draws on Thomas Risse's approach to the Europeanisation of identity and argues that Turkey's identity is indeed being Europeanised in a quite contradictory way. While Turkey more and more finds itself closer and more relevant to the regions surrounding it, above all the Middle East, it can no longer be described as an introverted state on the margins of Europe. The EU candidacy process has indeed helped Turkey to transform its international standing by becoming a more assertive international player that aims to influence the normative dimension of international politics. Nas mostly employs the social learning approach by focusing on the valid and legitimate norms and values of Turkish political class and the widespread internalisation not only by already westernised segments of the population but also political groups that traditionally took a counter-position to the EU. Nas does not neglect the external incentives model as well and includes in her analysis the role of domestic actors that made use of the EU as an external support mechanism.

Chapter 3 by Yonca Özer is on democratisation in Turkey and approaches the issue through the perspective of political conditionality. She approaches the issue from the perspective of rationalist institutionalism and regards political conditionality as an 'engine of Europeanisation of Turkish democracy and human rights regime'. Aiming to explain the slowdown and virtual halt of reforms in this sector recently, Özer also draws upon the social learning model and focuses on the internal conditions and level of internalisation of EU norms that would facilitate or impede democratisation. The chapter explains the stalling of reforms in Turkey after the opening of accession negotiations by the declining effectiveness of EU political conditionality and the loss of credibility of the EU membership perspective.

Bertil Emrah Oder in Chapter 4 views Constitutionalism in Turkey and analyses constitutional amendments in Turkey since the 1980's. She asks the question whether a Europeanisation of constitution-making may be discerned in this period. Oder notes that the EU emerged as an external factor firstly in the making of the 1982 constitution with regard to the issue of transfer of sovereignty in the case of membership to an international organisation. She analyses consecutive constitutional amendments starting with the one in 1987 and followed by 17 constitutional amendment packages between 1987–2011. Oder notes that even EU harmonisation packages adopted after 2001 have provided only a partial revision in sub-constitutional laws and in their well-established patterns of application noting the misfit between the EU criteria and Turkish constitutional order due to insufficient adoption and implementation. Oder traces the impact of the EU in the major constitutional amendments and their implementation so far by referring to a variation between a consensual and a confrontational approach.

Selcen Öner in Chapter 5 explores the transformative impact of the EU on Turkish civil society at both legal and practical levels. The chapter is based on interviews conducted with representatives of civil society organisations in Turkey to analyse the extent to which their behaviour was influenced by Europeanisation since the 1999 Helsinki European Council. Öner argues that Turkish civil society has been quite weak due to the existence of a state-centred polity and traces its increasing dynamism in response to several developments. Europeanisation influenced Turkish civil society organisations mostly by way of social learning involving the dissemination and internalisation of norms. Europeanisation impacted on the civil society organisations mostly by way of engendering legal reform and changing the legal environment they operated in, by facilitating interaction with their European counterparts, and by providing financial support. Öner notes the impact of Europeanisation in civil society organisation in Turkey by drawing conclusions with regard to the effects of legal reforms by changing the environment they operate in, by facilitating their activities through financial support and by engendering a socialisation process through increasing cooperation with their European counterparts.

Gözde Yılmaz in Chapter 6 explains Europeanisation of minority rights in Turkey by applying EU conditionality and domestic choice for change approach conceptualised by the external incentives and lesson-drawing models. She traces minority-related policy change in Turkey both regarding legal reforms and implementation after 1999 and aims to account for the variation between different time periods. Yılmaz notes the importance of the credibility of external incentives, power of veto players, adoption costs of reform, and domestic factors including change in political values of the government as explanatory factors regarding minority rights policy in Turkey.

Chapter 7 by Sevgi Uçan Çubukçu explores the field of women's rights from the perspective of Europeanisation. Çubukçu asks the question whether the Europeanisation process since the 1990s had a transformative impact on gender equality in Turkey. She discusses legislative changes that expanded the scope of women's rights and liberties. She particularly focuses on the independent women's movement within the current of second wave feminism in Turkey. In Çubukçu's understanding, women's movements that emerged in Turkey in the post-1980 era are agents of change and grasped the value of Europeanisation as a facilitating device for women's emancipation.

Dimitris Tsarouhas in Chapter 8 analyses the Europeanisation effect with reference to social policy. His research attests to a weak Europeanisation effect on Turkish social policy reform. As in many of the other chapters Tsarouhas also notes the contextual nature of Europeanisation whereby the EU is used as a legitimisation device in the area of social policy. This limited Europeanisation may be explained not only by the unwillingness of domestic actors but also by the weak development of social policy at the EU level. The EU does not present a well-structured, coherent and developed social policy model to candidate countries like Turkey. Tsarouhas notes the low level of expenditure allocated to social policy, continuing risks of poverty and social exclusion, and the fragmented nature of the policy field in Turkey as factors underlying the misfit with EU norms and standards.

Chapter 9 by Rana İzci studies whether, how and to what extent any change can occur in Turkish Environmental Policy, particularly in terms of the perception and practice of sustainable development through EU conditionality. İzci firstly explains how the sustainable development as a policy principle was evolved and then investigates the main dynamics of the prevailing sustainability discourse in Turkey. Subsequently, she tries to analyse the impact of EU-Turkey relations on Turkish environmental policy with special reference to sustainable development. Turkey's position to international environmental regimes is also explored to understand both how and under which conditions EU-Turkey relations can affect internationalisation of Turkish environmental policy and whether and how internationalisation of Turkish environmental policy can facilitate the EU-induced change in Turkey. She lastly makes a brief examination of civil society participation in Turkish environmental policy-making to analyse whether the accession negotiations can induce any change with regard to the policy-making process in Turkey.

Özlem Terzi in Chapter 10 discusses Europeanisation of Turkish foreign policy. She notes the change engendered by the EU candidacy in Turkish foreign policy but adds that this change did not lead to resolution of the major foreign policy problems despite successful incorporation of EU norms by policy-makers. Terzi finds that although the second and third AKP governments after 2007 lost interest in the EU membership process, foreign policy after 2002 have become more 'European' on the basis of a social learning model. According to Terzi, EU candidacy altered Turkish foreign-policy method and style and sets on to explain Europeanisation in foreign policy on a case-by-case basis. Terzi questions to what extent Europeanisation influenced the self-perception, norm adoption and composition of foreign policy-makers in Turkey and whether the recent 'shift-of-axis' argument regarding Turkey's international role may lead to a de-Europeanisation of Turkish foreign policy.

Alper Kaliber in Chapter 11 studies Turkey's Cyprus policy as a case of contextual Europeanisation. Kaliber notes the shift in Turkey's Cyprus policy in the 2000s as well as the persisting elements of this policy talking about a 'radical reorganization' of the issue-area between 2003–2005. Kaliber's approach is centred on Europeanisation as a political/normative context employed by domestic actors. According to Kaliber, 'Europeanisation penetrates into domestic politics, if and when these actors use the European context as a mobilising political instrument.' Kaliber also makes a distinction between EU-isation and Europeanisation: EU-isation denoting the more technical adoption of EU norms and convergence towards the EU *acquis* while Europeanisation is taken as a socio-political and normative process. According to Kaliber, Europeanisation has weakened as a driving factor influencing Turkey's Cyprus policy.

Chapter 12 by Catherine Macmillan dwells on Turkey's migration and asylum policies and questions the degree of Europeanisation. Macmillan also employs the external incentives and social learning models to explain 'the lag in the Europeanisation of Turkey's migration and asylum policies'. The chapter focuses on the lack of goodness of fit in these policy areas in Turkey comparing with the case of Central and East European countries and points out the quite high costs of rule-adoption. Turkey is mostly viewed as one of the main transit roads for irregular migration to the EU and the EU places much pressure on Turkey to align its *acquis* with that of the EU, as may be seen in the case of the EU demand to sign a readmission agreement. Macmillan concludes that Europeanisation in this policy area has been slower in Turkey compared to the central and East European countries mainly owing to lack of credible conditionality. She also highlights that Turkey was indeed able to toughen its migration policy and soften its asylum policy in line with the EU's expectations and accepts the role played by socialisation in this regard. At the end of the day however, the external incentives model may better explain the slow progress in this issue area due to the dimming of the membership perspective.

References

Börzel, T.A. and Risse, T. 2003. Conceptualizing the Domestic Impact of Europe, in *The Politics of Europeanization*, edited by K. Featherstone and C. Radaelli, Oxford: Oxford University Press, 55–78.

Olsen, J. 2003. Europeanisation, in *European Union Politics*, edited by M. Cini. Oxford: Oxford University Press, 333–48.

Radaelli, C. 2004. Europeanisation: solution or problem? *European Integration Online Papers (EIoP)* [Online], 8(16). Available at: http://eiop.or.at/eiop/texte/2004-016a.htm [accessed: 29 January 2012].

Schimmelfennig, F. and Sedelmeier, U. 2004. Governance by conditionality: EU Rule transfer to the candidate countries of Central and Eastern Europe. *Journal of European Public Policy*, 11(4), 661–79.

Schimmelfennig, F. and Sedelmeier, U. 2005 (eds). *The Europeanisation of Central and Eastern Europe*. Ithaca, NY: Cornell University Press.

Chapter 1
Europeanisation Meets Turkey.
A Case *Sui Generis?*

Tanja A. Börzel

Introduction

Research on Europeanisation and domestic change is thriving. With the borders of the European Union (EU) having moved south-eastwards, we have been given yet another real-world experiment on the domestic impact of the EU. Together with the Western Balkan countries, Turkey obtained an accession perspective. Whether the 'golden carrot' is big enough, however, to draw Turkey closer to Europe, is still an open question as EU demands for political and economic reforms are greater than they were in the case of Central and Eastern European Countries (CEEC). The EU has exerted much less pressure for adaptation on the Turkish government and the accession perspective granted in 1999 is losing credibility. Moreover, like in case of the Western Balkans, both the willingness and the capacity of the Turkish government to implement the *acquis communautaire* are more limited.

The contributions in this volume clearly show that the transformative power of the EU has indeed been limited in Turkey as in the Western Balkans (Elbasani 2012a). For students of Europeanisation, this should not come as a surprise given the combination of high costs, decreasing incentives and limited reform capacities. At the same time, the various chapters do find instances of EU-induced domestic change. Thus, the real puzzle is why there is Europeanisation despite these unfavourable conditions and why the domestic impact of the EU has been differential, i.e. varies across policies and institutions.

Can Europeanisation approaches account for the differential impact of the EU on Turkey we find in this edited volume? The chapter explores whether the Europeanisation literature travels south east. I will start by summarising the main findings of research on 'External Europeanisation' focusing on factors that have limited or at least qualified the domestic impact of the EU in the Central and Eastern European (CEE) and Western Balkan (WB) accession countries. The second part of the chapter will discuss to what extent the Europeanisation approaches need further qualification when applied to Turkey, which squares even on democracy with the WB (with the exception of Croatia) but whose statehood is less limited. As a result, Turkey has greater capacities to introduce domestic reforms required by the EU than most of the WB candidates. With regard to its willingness, the size and credibility of EU incentives have become insufficient to reward Turkey for its progress. I will argue that the selective and differential domestic changes the contributions to this edited volume find are largely related to the extent to which EU conditionality helps domestic actors gain or hold political power. The Europeanisation literature has identified differential empowerment as a key scope condition for the EU to induce domestic change (Cowles et al. 2001, Börzel and Risse 2003, Schimmelfennig and Sedelmeier 2005, Vachudova 2005). The case of Turkey shows that it is not only pro-Western, liberal reform coalitions that can use the EU to advance and legitimise their political agenda. The chapter will conclude with summarising the major implications Turkey has for Europeanisation approaches and discussing why Turkey is not a case *sui generis*.

Reaching Out? From Membership to Accession Europeanisation

Membership Europeanisation works to a large extent through legal coercion. EU member states are subject to policies and institutions diffused by the case law of the European Court of Justice or European directives harmonising national legislations (Börzel and Risse 2012a). Yet, the shadow of hierarchy cast by the supremacy and direct effect of EU Law also provides incentives, e.g. in the form of legal sanctions (Börzel 2003) and arenas for socialisation and persuasion (Panke 2007). For the new member states in Central and Eastern Europe, EU infringement proceedings and the Control and Verification Mechanism substitute accession conditionality as major incentives for post-accession compliance (Sedelmeier 2012, Spendzharova and Vachudova 2012). During the accession process, the EU casts at best a weak shadow of hierarchy and largely relies on positive and negative incentives for making candidate countries adopt and implement the *acquis communautaire*. The current candidate countries are even more subject to such accession conditionality than their CEE predecessors (Schimmelfennig and Sedelmeier 2004). Yet, accession credibility is declining given the EU's enlargement fatigue and the enormous changes many of the Western Balkans and Turkey still have to undergo in order to qualify for the next steps in the accession process – so far, Croatia is the only candidate that will join the EU in the near future (Noutcheva and Aydın-Düzgit 2012, Elbasani 2012a). While Turkey's capacities to implement domestic reforms are less limited than in most of the WB candidates, its perspective as well as its own enthusiasm for membership has been fading.

The literature on Accession Europeanisation has identified misfit and membership conditionality as two factors that decisively shape the effectiveness of the EU's transformative power in the Central and Eastern European accession countries (Kelley 2006, Lavenex 2004, Schimmelfennig and Trauner 2010). If low and non-credible conditionality combines with high policy or institutional misfit, EU-induced domestic change is unlikely to occur because costs are high and the EU offers little to pay them off (Schimmelfennig and Sedelmeier 2004). Yet, despite high misfit, substantial costs and few incentives, the chapters in this edited volume find ample evidence for the EU's influence on both institutional and policy change. The domestic impact of the EU on Turkey may be patchy, often shallow but certainly not spurious. While the EU is usually not the only game in town and Turkey is not merely down-loading EU policies and institutions, this edited volume demonstrates that the EU has influenced domestic change even where its shadow of hierarchy and conditionality is weak or non-existent. At the same time, the various chapters find significant variation. To what extent can existing approaches of Europeanisation and domestic change account for the differential impact of the EU on Turkey?

Beyond Misfit and EU Pressure for Adaptation: Factors Mediating Accession Europeanisation

The misfit between European and domestic policies, institutions and political processes is a necessary condition for domestic change. To what extent such misfit translates into change depends on domestic institutions, which mediate or filter the domestic impact of Europe (on the following see Börzel and Risse 2003, Börzel and Risse 2007).

Rational choice institutionalism argues that the EU facilitates domestic change through changing opportunity structures for domestic actors. In a first step, misfit between the EU and domestic norms creates demands for domestic adaptation. It takes agency, however, to translate misfit into domestic change. In a second step, the downloading of EU policies and institutions by the member states is shaped by cost/benefit calculations of strategic actors, whose interests are at stake. Institutions constrain or enable certain actions of rational actors by rendering some options more costly than others. From this perspective, Europeanisation is largely conceived as an emerging political opportunity structure which offers some actors additional resources to exert influence, while severely constraining the ability of others to pursue their goals. Domestic change is facilitated, if EU incentives discourage domestic actors to veto adaptation to EU requirements (*veto players*) or if, on the contrary, they empower domestic reform coalitions by providing them with additional resources to exploit the opportunities offered by Europeanisation (*formal supporting institutions*).

Sociological institutionalism draws on a normative logic of appropriateness to argue that actors are guided by collectively shared understandings of what constitutes proper, socially accepted behaviour. Such collective understandings and intersubjective meaning structures strongly influence the way actors define their goals and what they perceive as rational behaviour. Rather than maximising their egoistic self-interest, actors seek to meet social expectations in a given situation. From this perspective, Europeanisation is understood as the emergence of new rules, norms, practices, and structures of meaning to which member states are exposed and which they have to incorporate into their domestic rule structures. If there is such a misfit, it also takes agency to bring about domestic change. But the ways in which domestic actors engage with reforms are different. Norm entrepreneurs such as epistemic communities or advocacy networks socialise domestic actors into new norms and rules of appropriateness through persuasion and learning, a process through which they redefine their interests and identities accordingly. The more active norm entrepreneurs and EU allies are and the more they succeed in making EU policies resonate with domestic norms and beliefs, the more successful they will be in bringing about domestic change. Moreover, collective understandings of appropriate behaviour strongly influence the ways in which domestic actors download EU requirements. For example, a consensus-oriented or cooperative decision-making culture helps to overcome multiple veto points by rendering their use for actors inappropriate. Such consensus-oriented political culture allows for a sharing of adaptational costs which facilitates the accommodation of pressure for adaptation.

How do these two approaches fare in accounting for the differential impact of the EU on accession countries? In the accession process, misfit combines with conditional incentives in the *pressure for adaptation* the EU exerts. For the CEE, 'reinforcement by reward' (Schimmelfennig et al. 2003, cf. Schimmelfennig and Sedelmeier 2005) was strong enough to overcome the resistance of veto players against the substantial costs entailed in compliance with the Copenhagen Criteria and the adoption of the *acquis communautaire* (Jacoby 2006, Vachudova 2005, Andonova 2003, Grabbe 2006, Pridham 2005). Europeanisation has empowered CEE reformists and moderates over nationalist forces to push through domestic reforms. If domestic veto players have mattered, they delayed rather than forestalled compliance with EU requirements (Vachudova 2005, Schimmelfennig and Sedelmeier 2006). At the same time, formal veto players helped lock-in institutional changes induced by the EU if these changes no longer fit government preferences (Sedelmeier 2012). Hence, the mediating effect of both informal institutions and veto players is more ambivalent since they may facilitate as well as impair Europeanisation.

While the rationalist mechanisms of 'differential empowerment through conditionality' have dominated Accession Europeanisation, socialisation and social learning have played a role, too (Schimmelfennig and Sedelmeier 2005, Kelley 2004, Kubicek 2003). Next to financial and technical assistance and the substantial reward of membership, the EU provides elites in accession countries with the necessary legitimacy to enact domestic change. The strong domestic consensus in favour of EU membership in their 'return to Europe' allowed CEE decision-makers to silence domestic veto players inside and outside government, despite the considerable costs incurred by EU policies. Moreover, the Copenhagen Criteria strongly resonated with the ongoing reform agenda and large parts of the societies in the CEE countries supporting political and economic transition started by the 'velvet revolution' of 1989. The legitimacy of the EU generated sufficient diffuse support through the identification with Europe that often trumped cost/benefit calculations in the adoption of and adaptation to the package of enlargement conditionality. It also facilitated access and influence of (trans-) national norm entrepreneurs who had little difficulties in invoking the resonance of

EU requirements with domestic norms and values as to increase their acceptance and promote their internalisation. While it did not forge completely new identities and beliefs, EU accession reinforced the identification with Europe (Risse 2010).

Existing Europeanisation approaches did a fairly good job in accounting for the differential impact of Accession on the CEE. They require some serious adjustments when applied to the Western Balkans. While the CEE had made steady progress towards becoming consolidated democracies with functioning market economies, the Western Balkans remain 'borderline cases' of transition (Elbasani 2012b). Albania, Macedonia, Bosnia Herzegovina and Kosovo are still only partly free and their statehood is either weak or contested. Secessionist movements, unsettled borders, ethnic tensions, deficient state capacity and/or strong clientelistic networks have severely mitigated the transformative power of the EU (Börzel 2011b).

The EU certainly empowered domestic reform coalitions *vis-à-vis* nationalist and post-communist parties. By late 1990s, the EU willingness to withdraw support and shun the Tudjman regime has emboldened democratic opposition in Croatia. The leverage of EU was also crucial for the democratisation of the nationalist HDZ, who made EU membership the primary goal after 2003 and ousted hard liners from top positions in the party leadership (Boduszynski 2012). Similarly, EU strong stance against the Milosevic regime as much as the use of coercive instruments strengthened support for the opposition forces and facilitated their electoral victory in 2000 elections (Stojanovic 2012). At the same time, however, liberal reform coalitions have been too weak *vis-à-vis* nationalist or post-socialist forces to get empowered by the EU in the first place (Vachudova 2005, Spendzharova and Vachudova 2012). Moreover, informal institutions and practices of rent-seeking and clientelism provide domestic actors with viable possibilities to block domestic institutional change (Noutcheva and Aydın-Düzgit 2012). Finally, empowering domestic reformists is not enough if actors lack the necessary resources to introduce domestic change. The limited administrative capacities of the CEE candidate countries already mitigated the domestic impact of EU accession in CEE countries (Noutcheva and Bechev 2008, Börzel 2009b). In the Western Balkans, the lack of state capacities is even more pronounced and exacerbated by the contentedness of borders and political authority (Elbasani 2012a).

Public support for EU norms and values and EU membership more broadly speaking is more fragile in the WB candidate countries, too. While Europeanisation and democratisations are clearly linked, there is public resentment whenever EU demands for compliance with the Copenhagen Criteria clash with nationalist beliefs, e.g. regarding the role of minorities and the extradition of war criminals to the International Criminal Tribunal for the former Yugoslavia (Boduszynski 2012, Stojanovic 2012). The legacies of the past resonate less with the EU's reform agenda and undermine its legitimacy (Elbasani 2012b).

While socialisation takes time, the dominance of the 'external incentive model' and 'differential empowerment through conditionality' has given rise to 'shallow Europeanisation' (Goetz 2005: 262) or 'Potemkin harmonization' (Jacoby 1999) as we have found in the CEE. The CEE countries formally adopted a massive amount of EU legislation, which, however, is still often not properly applied and enforced and thus, has not changed actors' behaviour (Falkner, Treib and Holzleithner 2008, Börzel 2009) or fostered internalisation and long-term rule consistent practices. In the Western Balkans, history seems to repeat itself. EU accession results in rhetorical and often also formal rule adoption, but only scarce rule-consistent behaviour (Elbasani 2012a).

In order to explore such problems of 'decoupling', which also appear to abound in Turkey, Europeanisation research has started to go beyond formal adaptation and systematically study the practical implementation of and behavioural compliance with domestic reforms identifying additional scope conditions mitigating the transformative power of Europe.

It's the Domestic Structures, Stupid! Scope Conditions for Domestic Change

The mediating factors identified by the early Europeanisation literature are less relevant (norm entrepreneurs, formal supporting institutions) or more ambivalent in their impact (veto players, informal institutions) in South-East Europe than in Central and Eastern Europe. Studies on the Europeanisation of current candidate states and neighbourhood countries have therefore identified further scope conditions for EU-induced domestic institutional change focusing on *power (a)symmetries*; *regime type* (democracy vs. autocracy); *domestic incentives* for change; and *degrees of statehood* (consolidated vs. limited).[1]

Power (a)symmetries

The distribution of material and ideational resources between the EU, on the one hand, and accession or neighbourhood countries, on the other, is likely to matter in explaining the variation in domestic change. The degree of interdependence crucially shapes the pressure for adaptation the EU is able to exert and the power of the target country to resist such pressures. The economic and political power of the EU renders its external relations with accession and neighbouring countries rather asymmetrical. In principle, they have much to gain by closer relations with the EU which then increases the EU's ability to exert pressure. However, some states possess resources (gas, oil) the EU is interested in, are of strategic importance and/or have the potential to create substantial negative externalities for the EU (illegal immigration, cross-border crime). Strategic or economic goals can seriously undermine the consistency of the EU in pushing for domestic change in its neighbourhood (Börzel and Pamuk 2012, van Hüllen 2012).

Turkey's size, economic strength and self-understanding as a regional power render its relations with the EU far less asymmetrical than in case of the Western

---

1   The following draws on Börzel and Risse 2012a, Börzel and Risse 2012b, see also Ademmer and Börzel 2012.

Balkan accession candidates and the European neighbourhood countries. With the membership perspective ever losing credibility, its economic and political power makes Turkey a least likely case for Europeanisation among the current candidate countries.

Regime Type

The democratic quality of a regime influences the willingness of state actors to promote domestic change in response to EU influence (Schimmelfennig et al. 2005). The costs of adaptation to EU demands for domestic change are lower for incumbent governments of democratic states with market economies than for authoritarian regimes, which have a firm grip on economy and society as a result of which compliance with EU requirements threatens their hold on power. At the same time, the latter are less likely to face pressure from below since domestic actors lack the political autonomy to mobilise in favour of compliance with EU demands for reform. Thus, we should expect the EU to be less likely to influence domestic change in authoritarian regimes. This scope condition applies particularly to EU demands for domestic reforms with regard to human rights, the rule of law, democracy, or market economy. These EU demands directly threaten the survival of authoritarian regimes, as a result of which they are unlikely to lead to institutional reforms, unless other conditions are met (e.g. mobilisation of domestic opposition with regard to human rights, see Risse, Ropp and Sikkink 1999).

The early Europeanisation literature could not deal with regime type, since the EU 15 are all consolidated democracies. Accession Europeanisation still deals with mostly democratising countries, including Turkey (Pridham 2005, Morlino and Sadurski 2010). Yet, Europeanisation should meet greater resistance in areas, such as minority rights or freedom of expression, where democratic institutions are less consolidated or change is still wanting.

Domestic Incentives

The Europeanisation literature argues that the misfit between EU and domestic institutions, policies and political processes affects the domestic balance of power among different actors. Misfit may lead to the differential empowerment of societal as well as political actors. Those who profit from or are normatively aligned with the policies and rules emanating from Brussels will promote domestic institutional change. Yet, the literature on member state and CEE Europeanisation has overlooked that, first, the EU can empower not only liberal but also non-liberal forces and, second, that EU empowerment hinges on certain domestic conditions. In order to have an impact, EU incentives or socialisation and persuasion efforts have to align with domestic incentives, political preferences or survival strategies of ruling elites, so that the latter can use EU policies and institutions to push their own political agenda, please their constituencies, and regain or consolidate their power (Spendzharova and Vachudova 2012, Börzel and Pamuk 2012, Ademmer and Börzel 2012).

If these findings hold, we should expect parties, such as the *Adalet ve Kalkınma Partisi* (Justice and Development Party, AKP), which do not necessarily fall into the pro-Western, liberal camp, to be empowered by the EU, too – even if the EU's liberal policies and institutions impose significant costs and are not necessarily compatible with their overall political orientation. EU demands for domestic change are likely to have an impact in Turkey, even if they are costly and even if the membership perspective is no longer credible, if EU policies align with the political preferences and survival strategies of political elites.

Degrees of (Limited) Statehood

States vary considerably in the degree to which they are able to adopt, implement, and enforce decisions. While failed, failing, and fragile states are rather rare in the international system, 'areas of limited statehood' are ubiquitous (Risse 2011). Many countries lack the capacity to implement and enforce the law in large parts of their territory or with regard to some policy areas. Yet, state capacity is a decisive pre-condition for governments to adopt and adapt to EU demands for domestic institutional change. First, the legal adoption and implementation of EU norms and rules requires significant state capacity. The Copenhagen Criteria, therefore, require accession countries not only to transpose EU law into national legislation, which is less resource-intensive since staff, expertise and money can be concentrated at the central level. They also need to have the administrative infrastructure in place to put EU laws into practice (cf. Elbasani 2012a). Likewise, non-state actors (civil society and business) equally require the capacity to push the reform agenda at the domestic level by exerting pressure on state actors, talking them into domestic change and/or providing them with additional resources (Sissenich 2007, Börzel 2009a). Finally, the EU might be less inclined to push for domestic change in states whose institutions are already fragile (Youngs 2001, Börzel 2011a). Thus, the institutional and administrative capacity of states and degrees of statehood in general play a crucial role in mitigating the transformative power of the EU.

Turkey suffers less from problems of limited statehood than most of the WB candidate countries. In principle, the government should have sufficient administrative capacities to adopt and implement the *acquis communautaire*. At the same time, challenges to its statehood by Kurdish nationalist terrorism may seriously impair EU induced reforms, particularly with regard to the rule of law (Noutcheva and Aydın-Düzgit 2012). Europeanisation should be more likely in areas in which Turkish statehood is the least limited, i.e. necessary resources are available and national sovereignty is not challenged.

Turkey – A Case *Sui Generis*?

Approaches to (pre-CEE) Accession Europeanisation give rise to a series of hypotheses with regard to the domestic impact of on accession countries, which appear to largely hold for Turkey, too.

Like in the Western Balkans, the formal adoption of the *acquis communautaire* is selective and often decoupled from behavioural practices. At the same time, we also find instances of 'reversed decoupling', where Turkish laws and practices are changed in line with EU requirements but without formally adopting EU policies. This could be cases of 'spurious Europeanisation', in which either external actors other than the EU, such as the UNHCR, the US, or the Council of Europe, induce the Turkish government to initiate domestic change, e.g. in area of migration and asylum (Chapter 12 in this volume, Kirişçi and Aydın 2012). Or Turkish policy-makers introduce domestic reforms that conform to EU demands but are driven by their own political agenda as in case of the constitutional reform in 2010 (Noutcheva and Aydın-Düzgit 2012).

Rather than spurious, however, Europeanisation in Turkey appears to be often 'bottom-up' (Jacquot and Woll 2003) or 'indirect' (Börzel and Risse 2012a). Domestic actors are not merely downloading EU policies nor do they simply ignore them. Rather, they (ab)use the EU as 'legitimisation device' (Chapter 8 in this volume) to push their own political interests (Ademmer and Börzel 2012, Börzel and Pamuk 2012). The AKP government instrumentalised the promotion of EU accession to widen its support base towards the centre and to anchor its political reforms aimed at rolling back the influence of Kemalist forces and the military. Only when the AKP gained electoral support and the membership perspective became less credible, the EU has lost relevance for domestic institutional change (cf. Noutcheva and Aydın-Düzgit 2012). The declining support for EU membership in the Turkish public further undermines the potential for using EU accession as a legitimisation device (Chapter 3 in this volume).

The 'external incentive model' certainly accounts for the selective and overall moderate degree of Europeanisation in Turkey. Since the credibility of accession conditionality declines over time, however, it cannot explain why we do find instances of domestic change that conforms to EU demands in some areas and not in others. Like in case of the CEE and the Western Balkans, the role of formal and informal institutions appears to be marginal. Domestic veto players and (trans-) national change agents have mitigated and facilitated the introduction of reforms, respectively (Kirişçi and Aydın 2012). Civil society has been empowered in Turkey, not least by the legal, financial and technical support of the EU (Chapter 5 in this volume). Yet, domestic change is still largely driven by the political agenda of the Turkish government. Unlike some of the WB candidates, Turkish policy-makers have the necessary capacities to introduce reforms. Their willingness, however, is less influenced by EU incentives but by their preferences for consolidating their political power. Europeanisation appears to be most effective, where domestic policy choices, e.g. to roll-back the Kemalist legacy, align with EU demands for change.

These findings clearly show that there is nothing special about Europeanisation in Turkey. Its relations with the EU are more symmetrical than it is the case of the WB countries and its membership perspective is less credible. This significantly weakens the EU's transformative power in Turkey. At the same time, Turkey's statehood is less limited than in some of the Western Balkan countries, thus increasing its capacities for reform. Like in the CEE and the Western Balkans, Turkey has made progress towards complying with the Copenhagen criteria but the process appears to be mostly driven by endogenous dynamics (Börzel and van Hüllen 2011). Where Turkey may differ from the other candidate countries, is the impact of accession on its statehood.

While the EU has strengthened rather than weakened the state capacity of member states, candidates, and neighbourhood countries (Börzel 2011a, Börzel and van Hüllen 2011), introducing and fortifying minority and civil rights, restricting the power of the military, or changing the status of Cyprus might arguably challenge or even undermine Turkish statehood weakening both its willingness and capacity to comply with EU reform requirements. Together with the fading support for EU membership in Turkey, this may seriously constrain the potential of differential empowerment, curbing the EU's transformative power even more than the waning credibility of Turkey's accession perspective.

References

Ademmer, E. and Börzel, T.A. 2012. Migration, energy and good governance in the EU's Eastern neighbourhood. *Europe Asia Studies*. Forthcoming.

Andonova, L.B. 2003. Transnational Politics of the Environment. The European Union and Environmental Policy in Central and Eastern Europe. Cambridge: MIT Press.

Boduszynski, M.P. 2012. The unbearable weight of structure and state-building? The trials and triumphs of Europeanisation in Croatia, in *European Integration and Transformation in the Western Balkans: Europeanisation or Business as Usual*, edited by A. Elbasani. London: Routledge. Forthcoming.

Börzel, T.A. 2003. Guarding the treaty: the compliance strategies of the European Commission, in *The State of the European Union VI: Law, Politics, and Society*, edited by T.A. Börzel and R. Cichowski. Oxford: Oxford University Press, 197–220.

Börzel, T.A. 2009a (ed.). Coping with Accession to the European Union. New Modes of Environmental Governance. Houndmills: Palgrave Macmillan.

Börzel, T.A. 2009b. New modes of governance and accession. The paradox of double weakness, in *Coping with Accession to the European Union. New Modes of Environmental Governance*, edited by T.A. Börzel. Houndmills: Palgrave Macmillan, 7–31.

Börzel, T.A. 2011a. When Europe hits … across its borders. Europeanisation and the near abroad. *Comparative European Politics*. 9,(4), 394–413.

Börzel, T.A. 2011b. When Europe hits limited statehood. Europeanisation and domestic change in the Western Balkans. *KFG Working Papers*, 30. Research College 'The Transformative Power of Europe'. Freie Universität Berlin.

Börzel, T.A. and Pamuk, Y. 2012. Pathologies of Europeanisation. Fighting corruption in the Southern Caucasus. *West European Politics*, 35(1), 79–97.

Börzel, T.A. and Risse, T. 2003. Conceptualising the domestic impact of Europe, in *The Politics of Europeanisation,* edited by K. Featherstone and C. Radaelli. Oxford: Oxford University Press, 57–82.

Börzel, T.A. and Risse, T. 2007. Europeanisation: the domestic impact of EU politics, in *Handbook of European Union Politics,* edited by K.E. Jorgensen, M.A. Pollack and B. Rosamond. London: Sage, 483–504.

Börzel, T.A. and Risse, T. 2012a. From Europeanisation to diffusion: introduction. *West European Politics*, 35(1), 1–19.

Börzel, T.A. and Risse, T. 2012b. When Europeanisation meets diffusion. Exploring new territory. *West European Politics* 35(1), 192–207.

Börzel, T.A. and Van Hüllen, V. 2011. Good governance and bad neighbours? The limits of transformative power Europe. *KFG Working Papers*. Research College 'The Transformative Power of Europe'. Freie Universität Berlin.

Cowles, M., Caporaso, J.A. and Risse, T. 2001 (eds). *Transforming Europe. Europeanisation and Domestic Change*. Ithaca: Cornell University Press.

Elbasani, A. 2012a (ed.). European Integration and Transformation in the Western Balkans: Europeanisation or Business as Usual? London: Routledge.

Elbasani, A. 2012b. Europeanisation travels to the Western Balkans: EU enlargement, domestic obstacles and institutional change, in *European Integration and Transformation in the Western Balkans: Europeanisation or Business as Usual,* edited by A. Elbasani. London: Routledge.

Falkner, G., Treib, O. and Holzleithner, E. 2008. *Compliance in the Enlarged European Union: Living Rights or Dead Letters?* Aldershot: Ashgate.

Goetz, K.H. 2005. The new member states and the EU: responding to Europe, in *The Member States of the European Union,* edited by S. Bulmer and C. Lequesne. Oxford: Oxford University Press, 254–83.

Grabbe, H. 2006. The EU's Transformative Power – Europeanisation through Conditionality in Central and Eastern Europe. Houndsmills: Palgrave Macmillian.

Jacoby, W. 1999. Priest and penitent: the EU as a force in the domestic politics of Eastern Europe. *East European Constitutional Review*, 8(1-2), 62-67.

Jacoby, W. 2006. Inspiration, coalition and substitution. External influences on postcommunist transformations. *World Politics*, 58, 623–51.

Jacquot, S. and Woll, C. 2003. Usage of European integration – Europeanisation from a sociological perspective. *European Integration online Papers (EIoP)*, 7(12).

Kelley, J.G. 2004. International actors on the domestic scene: membership conditionality and socialization by international institutions. *International Organization*, 58(3), 425–57.

Kelley, J.G. 2006. New wine in old wineskins: promoting political reforms through the new European neighbourhood policy. *Journal of Common Market Studies*, 44(1), 29–55.

Kirişçi, K. and Aydın, U. 2012. With or without the EU: Europeanization of asylum and competition policies in Turkey. Manuscript.

Kubicek, P. 2003 (ed.). *The European Union and Democratization*. London: Routledge.

Lavenex, S. 2004. EU external governance in 'Wider Europe'. *Journal of European Public Policy*, 11(4), 680–700.

Morlino, L. and Sadurski, W. 2010 (eds). Democratization and the European Union: Comparing Central and Eastern European Post-Communist Countries. London: Routledge.

Noutcheva, G. and Bechev, D. 2008. The successful laggards: Bulgaria and Romania's accession to the EU. *East European Politics and Society*, 22(1), 114–44.

Noutcheva, G. and Aydın-Düzgit, S. 2012. Lost in Europeanisation? The Western Balkans and Turkey. *West European Politics*, 35(1).

Panke, D. 2007. The European Court of Justice as an agent of Europeanisation. Inducing compliance with EU law. *Journal of European Public Policy*, 14(6), 847-866.

Pridham, G. 2005. Designing Democracy. EU Enlargement and Regime Change in Post-Communist Europe. Basingstoke: Palgrave Macmillan.

Risse, T. 2010. A Community of Europeans? Transnational Identities and Public Spheres. Itahaca, NY: Cornell University Press.

Risse, T. 2011 (ed.). Governance without a State? Policies and Politics in Areas of Limited Statehood. New York: Columbia University Press.

Risse, T., Ropp, S.C. and Sikkink, K. 1999 (eds). *The Power of Human Rights. International Norms and Domestic Change*. Cambridge: Cambridge University Press.

Schimmelfennig, F., Engert, S. and Knobel, H. 2003. Costs, commitment and compliance. The impact of EU democratic conditionality on Latvia, Slovakia and Turkey. *Journal of Common Market Studies*, 41(3), 495–518.

Schimmelfennig, F., Engert, S. and Knobel, H. 2005. The impact of EU political conditionality, in *The Europeanisation of Central and Eastern Europe,* edited by F. Schimmelfennig and U. Sedelmeier. Ithaca: Cornell University Press, 29–50.

Schimmelfennig, F. and Sedelmeier, U. 2004. Governance by conditionality: EU rule transfer to the candidate countries of Central and Eastern Europe. *Journal of European Public Policy*, 11(4), 661–79.

Schimmelfennig, F. and Sedelmeier, U. 2005 (eds). *The Europeanisation of Central and Eastern Europe*. Ithaca, NY: Cornell University Press.

Schimmelfennig, F. and Sedelmeier, U. 2006. Candidate countries and conditionality, in *Europeanisation. New Research Agendas,* edited by P. Graziano and M.P. Vink. Houndsmill: Palgrave Macmillan.

Schimmelfennig, F. and Trauner, F. 2010. Post-accession compliance in the EU's new member states. *European Integration Online Papers (EIoP)*. Special Issue 2(1).

Sedelmeier, U. 2012. Is Europeanisation through conditionality sustainable? Lock-in of institutional change after EU accession. *West European Politics*, 35(1).

Sissenich, B. 2007. Building States without Society: European Union Enlargement and the Transfer of EU Social Policy to Poland and Hungary. Lanham: Lexington Books.

Spendzharova, A. and Vachudova, M.A. 2012. Catching-up? Consolidating liberal democracy in Bulgaria and Romania. *West European Politics*, 35(1).

Stojanovic, J. 2012. EU political conditionality towards Serbia: membership prospects vs. domestic constraints, in *European Integration and Transformation in the Western Balkans: Europeanisation or Business as Usual,* edited by A. Elbasani. London: Routledge.

Vachudova, M.A. 2005. Europe Undivided: Democracy, Leverage and Integration After Communism. Oxford: Oxford University Press.

van Hüllen, V. 2012. Europeanisation through cooperation? EU democracy promotion in Morocco and Tunisia. *West European Politics*, 35(1), 117–34.

Youngs, R. 2001. The European Union and the Promotion of Democracy: Europe's Mediterranean and Asian Policies. Oxford: Oxford University Press.

Chapter 2

Europeanisation of Identity: The Case of the Rebuffed Candidate

Çiğdem Nas

Introduction

Identity is one of the main concepts that define our existence in the world. Our identity as a member of several social groups helps us to situate ourselves in the world and organise our existence and regulate our relations with the outside world. It also defines the nature, character and extent of our values, norms, attitudes, and behaviour. According to Tajfel, social identity is defined as 'that part of the individual's self-concept which derives from his knowledge of his membership of a social group (or groups) together with the value and emotional significance attached to that membership' (Tajfel 1981: 255). Similarly, collective identities define the overall vocation of a group in the social plane by bringing out commonalities and accentuating differences from other groups. These identities are shared with the other members of the group and produce a sense of well-being and loyalty which stems from being a member of a collectivity. This chapter concerns the case of Turkish identity as a form of collective identity in a world of states. For the purposes of the chapter, Turkish identity is a political concept that is related but not confined to cultural identity. It includes all citizens of the State of Turkey and their relation to and understanding of their collective state identity. The chapter traces the Europeanisation process with regard to Turkish identity on the basis of adoption of norms and values propagated by the EU under the following headings: adherence to democracy as an overriding political norm embodying a system of checks and balances and moderation of power, respect for human rights and fundamental freedoms, non-discrimination for disadvantaged groups such as women, respect for minorities.

European Identity and Europeanisation

Despite the above assertion about Turkish identity in a world of states, the concept of European identity reflects a source of collective identity on a regional scale above or existing side by side with national identities. While different notions of Europe existed throughout the ages, the initiation of European integration at an institutional level dates back to the end of the Second World War and is related with the attempt not to ever experience the horrors of the world wars. The EU is thus based on a liberal and peaceful understanding and a desire and determination of the founding and participating nations to tie their fates together. Europe was defined in this era as an antithesis of and an antidote to fascism, wars, and crimes against humanity. Faced with the spectre of the Second World War, other conceptions of Europe, i.e. Europe as an area of the superior race and civilisation, were subdued. The rise of extreme right wing groups and parties in the 1990s and 2000s however challenge this notion of Europe as an open and liberal area of freedom and democracy. An alternative and essentialist notion of Europe excluding non-white immigrants and based on a racist understanding of Europeanness is now even contesting the EU project itself.

Discussing the Europeanisation of identities however, we refer to a change of national identities under the influence and interaction with the processes, exchanges, institutions, values and norms engendered by European integration. The values of European integration translated into the Copenhagen criteria would be the guiding post in this respect.

According to Risse, 'it is wrong to conceptualize European identity in zero-sum terms, as if an increase in European identity necessarily decreases one's loyalty to national or other communities' (Risse 2010: 40). Rather than discussing whether national or European identity prevails as the primary source of allegiance, Risse proposes to focus on 'the Europeanisation of national identities' (Risse 2010: 45):

> Europeanisation means that Europe and the EU are integrated into core understandings of one's national (or other) sense of belonging. It means that core understandings of what it means to be German, French or Polish change and that Europe and the EU become part and parcel of these understandings. We do not cease to be Germans, French, or Polish, but become European Germans, French Europeans, or Polish in the EU.

This should be a rather natural result of a country's membership to the EU since the EU is not any international organisation but entails a significant degree of supranational/transnational integration which cannot be limited to the political or economic spheres. As pinpointed by Risse, mutual trust levels among EU member states have shown a considerable increase among the original member states over time (Risse 2010: 44). Membership creates a process of shift in allegiance which does not amount to one replacing the other but changes in the definition and inner substance of identity among citizens of the EU. According to Mayer and Palmowski (2004: 591), European identity makes the differences between national identities less significant, highlighting similarities rather than differences: 'A European identity does not resolve the exclusivity of nationalism, but it moderates it ... National identities still matter, but within the EU the barriers between them have become permeable.'

The situation may be quite different when one studies processes of Europeanisation in identity in a candidate state, and especially in one which is constantly being questioned regarding its 'Europeanness'. For the purposes of this chapter, I would argue the following: With the politicisation of the EU in the 1990s, all enlargements after this date entails a considerable degree of convergence to European norms and values even before membership takes place and necessitates a considerable degree of identification with 'Europe'.[1] This convergence is not only about adoption of legislation or harmonisation of administrative structures, but necessitates an extensive social learning and internalisation process. Without a concomitant 'Europeanisation of identity' it would be very difficult if not impossible for this process towards membership to be achieved successfully. In the case of the Central and East European states, this process concerned the argument of 'return to Europe'. Without this basic understanding and attachment to Europe, justifying Eastern enlargement in the EU, and acquiring support and managing the process of preparation for EU membership in the candidate states would have been very difficult.

Turkey's case is different than Central and Eastern European countries, Malta or Cyprus or the Western Balkan states that are in a process of integration to the EU. Turkey's candidacy and accession to the EU is not justified but contested on the ground of Europeanness. Replacing the identity-related argument of inclusion into Europe, Turkey's membership is generally justified on the basis of benefits and rational cost-benefit calculations. Those supporters of Turkey's EU membership put forth arguments stemming from how much Europe needs Turkey and what kind of benefits Turkey's membership would bring that would outweigh the costs. While all these are true, my argument is that despite the rejections of Turkey's EU membership credentials, the most outspoken of which is the President of France, Turkey has been undergoing a significant change for a time now owing to the EU process. This started early on with Turkey's preparations for the transition to the last stage of the association, the customs union. It later intensified after the Helsinki decision proclaiming Turkey as a candidate state 'destined to join the EU on the basis of the same criteria as applied to the other candidate states'. The struggle to fulfil the Copenhagen criteria for membership necessitates a process of identification with Europe and a change in identity definition which would entail a degree of Europeanisation of identity even in the case of Turkey. I would suggest that this process is continuing despite some developments which may be seen on the contrary. The chapter will trace this process on the basis of the effects of the fulfilment of the Copenhagen criteria on identity definition in Turkey by helping the consolidation of a democratic system respectful of human and minority rights.

---

1   This does not mean to suggest that all enlargements before this date did not embody a similar identification process. A typical case in point is the case of Britain which was rejected by Charles de Gaulle on the grounds that it was different in nature from the six founding members.

Sites and Processes of Europeanisation of Identity: Where and How?

The process of European integration no doubt intensified homogenisation among the member states by bringing about a common system of legal rules, policies and joint action in many areas. At the same time, the existence and gradual strengthening of EU institutions and policy-making competences without a sufficient development of democratic channels at the EU level fed resentment to supranationalisation in many member states, both in the left and right of the political spectrum. Thus while a European identity is contested both as a shallow market-oriented source of identity and as an intrusion into national spheres, a Europeanisation process regarding identifications of the member states of the EU may be observed.

This Europeanisation is much different than a Europeanisation of policy-making, administrative structures or legal systems however. Public spheres, education systems, and media are still dominated by national priorities. Symbols and references that may have an effect on the construction of identity are also shaped by national figures, such as national days of commemoration, memories of war, great losses or victories, statues and other visual symbols, national heroes, popular national icons, and the like, while European symbols such as the Euro, EU citizenship, passport, Europe day, EU anthem are relatively less effective in forging emotive bonds of allegiance. When we speak of Europeanisation of identities, it would be more appropriate to refer to a process whereby national identities are being reconstructed on the basis of a Europeanised understanding of what they are composed of and a reinterpretation of the relation between national and European identity rather than a replacement of national identities with an overarching European identity. According to Risse 'Europeanised identities come in national colours in so far as they resonate with and are connected to respective national symbols and historical and cultural memories in different ways' (Risse 2010: 85). Thus while the understanding of and relation to Europe may differ to a great extent in the French and German contexts, a mutually-shared process of Europeanisation would bring the two national identity constructions closer to each other on the basis of a Europeanisation of each identity space. The boundaries between different national identities would become less conflictual, and more 'fuzzy' due to the common source of identity construction that European integration would present. According to Mayer and Palmowski (2004),

> A European identity does not resolve the exclusivity of nationalism, but it moderates it. Rights such as consular protection in third countries by any MS consulate or embassy to any EU citizen do not level national distinctiveness but create a sense in which EU nationalities are less exclusive in relation to each other than they are to outside nationalities. … National identities still matter but within the EU the barriers between them have become permeable.

Though the relation and perception of Europe would differ in various national contexts, a convergence and orientation towards Europe as an area of common values, 'shared beliefs and norms', and 'ways of doing things' (Radaelli 2004: 3) would bring national identities closer to each other.

Rather than the French and German identities othering each other and accentuating their differences while constructing and re-constructing their national identities, the incorporation of Europe in each identity group would diminish the importance of differences and conflicts that may depend on earlier periods of rivalry or confrontation and bring about a convergence towards a Europeanisation of identities. While the French would consider Europe in terms of an area where the French influence is preponderant, for the Germans, Europe may be associated with a rebirth and a rupture with the notoriety of the Nazi era. It should also be emphasised that this relationship and how Europe is incorporated into national identities may also change in the course of the integration process. The French or the German positions within the EU are no longer the same as during the Cold War era or before the big-bang enlargement of 2004 and 2007, while the same may be said for the case of the newly-acceding countries pre- and post-accession. Thus as collective identities are quite resistant to change and show resilience throughout time periods, they are also constantly being constructed and reconstructed each day. As the EU is a dynamic process without a fixed target, how it impacts on national identities and how member states relate to Europe may show change over time.

Europeanisation of national identities would imply a shifting of loyalties to a new centre which would accompany or maybe eventually override national capitals. While national differences diminish in importance and similarities are more accentuated, common elements already existing or that are more easily incorporated in national identities become markers of national identity that form the basis of a European identity. According to Mayer and Palmowski (2004),

> European identity is closely linked to national identity but it can and does move beyond it in two ways. First European identity is obviously common to all Europeans; it complements national and regional identities. As a composite identity made up of a large number of national identities it is both the same as and more than each national identity.

Throughout European integration, collective identities are reconstructed and are adapted to being part of this process by reinterpreting their relation to Europe and redefining the role of Europe within national identity. Thus Europeanisation alters how national identities are constructed and how they are related to Europe. The demands and expectations related with the European integration process lead to adaptational pressures that may or may not be accommodated by national identity. For example, the demands associated with being a member to the EC/EU could not be reconciled with Norwegian identity as may be concluded from the results of the referenda held in that country. However despite the apparent discordance with national identity, British identity was reappraised in the 1960s culminating in the country's membership in 1973. The extent of Europeanisation is influenced by the degree of fit/misfit between factors shaping national identity and the demands from and perception of Europe. High levels of adaptational pressure may lead to incompatibility and rather than highlighting similarities may accentuate differences. Visions, ideas, norms, values, meanings involved in European order and identity construction interact with collective nation-state identities producing change, inertia, backlash or similar reactions.

Here, the answer to Thomas Risse's question 'how much space there is for Europe in nation-state identities' may hold the key to understanding the different relations between the EU and European countries (Risse 2001: 202). According to Risse,

> Such political visions and identity constructions are the more likely to impact upon and to be incorporated in collective nation state identities the more they resonate with the ideas about the nation and political order embedded in these collective understandings. The degree of resonance resembles the goodness of fit ... the resonance of ideas and visions about Europe with given collective nation state identities explain which ideas and identity constructions are considered legitimate and appropriate in a given political setting.

While some national identities may more easily incorporate Europeanness without much tension since being part of Europe already has an association in the national self-concept, for others, the degree of incongruence may be so high that it may lead to resistance or backlash against being part of Europe. For yet other national identities, incorporation of Europe into national identity may be quite problematic since it necessitates a shift in the older association with Europe which is already existent in national self-definition. This latter case may be the closest to the case of Turkey.

While Europe does not hold an entirely negative connotation in the national self-definition, it is beyond doubt that a quite problematic relation with Europe complicates this process of what may be called a Europeanisation of Turkish identity. The demands of the EU and necessities associated with the accession process created important challenges regarding adaptation for Turkish identity. In addition to the Copenhagen criteria, which had an important defining role of the state and state-society relations, other requirements such as resolving the Cyprus issue and resolution of border disputes especially with Greece, had important repercussions in terms of identity. Resolution of the Cyprus issue would also mean that the Turkish state would have to make concessions and accommodations with the other related parties and would need to significantly alter its official position which was based on an unfaltering resolve about holding onto the *status quo*. Such demands created adaptational pressure not only for Turkish foreign or internal policies but also regarding the understanding of Turkish identity which included codes about acceptable behaviour. Although one of the official conditions for EU membership did not involve Turkey's recognition of the 'genocide' of Armenians, the inclusion of this statement as a condition in the EP's resolutions starting from 1987 upset many Turks and were condemned by all political leaders. If this were an official condition for membership demanded by the EU as a whole, most probably it would not be acceptable for Turkey.

Turkey attributed great importance to being justly treated by the EU throughout the process of candidacy. The Turkish government's reaction to the 1997 Luxembourg European Council conclusions which did not recognise Turkey's candidacy status was mostly based on the EU's unfair treatment and perception of being discriminated against compared to the other candidate countries. This significance attached to fair treatment may also be explained by how Europe resonated in national identity and may be traced back to the retreat of the Ottomans *vis-à-vis* major European powers after the seventeenth century. The association with Europe in Turkish national identity had a lot to do with recognition, equality and acceptance. While being a member of the EU and progressing on the road to membership would place a high level of adaptational pressure on Turkish identity, it would also be rewarding and reinforcing in the sense that incorporation into Europe would heal some deep-lying uncertainties and confidence problems associated with Turkey's relations with Europe.

Turkish identity is a construct which involves multiple relations. This relates to Turkey's status between different regional constellations and its historical legacy of an empire which had its borders in three different continents. The shrinking of borders and being confined to the current borders after the Balkan wars and the First World War led to a sense of insecurity in the newly founded Republic. Moreover, countries such as Greece and Bulgaria on Turkey's borders had the fight against the Ottomans as a prominent part of their national identity construction. This, together with the deterioration of the relations with the Arabic peoples of the Ottoman Empire after their collaboration with the British during the First World War, led to a sense of being encircled by 'enemies'. The early years of the Republic that coincided with the inter-war years led to turning inwards, and further exacerbated a sense of insecurity.

Until recently, Turkish identity oscillated between disengagement from external affairs to a wide extent except for issues judged to be of concern to the sense of national unity and integrity such as the Cyprus issue and a sense of engagement and commitment as a regional actor to regional affairs after the ending of the Cold War. Thus Turkish identity was squeezed between two alternatives: being the lonely wolf and rekindling the spirit of the Ottoman Empire by redefining historical, cultural and political ties with neighbouring countries. The first state of Turkish identity more or less continued into the Cold War era despite the fact that Turkey was part of the Western camp. It may be said that Turkey's inclusion into the Western camp was mostly based on security considerations and interest-based calculations. It lacked an affective link and communication with the West in terms of values or living standards. Even though Turkey became a member of NATO in 1952, it could only become an associated country of the EEC. The second alternative could be implemented only after the creation of the necessary geopolitical conditions with the ending of the Cold War. Former prime minister and president Turgut Özal talked of the 'Turkish century' while many-times prime minister and former president Süleyman Demirel portrayed the Turkic world from the Adriatic to the Great Wall of China. One of the former ministers of foreign affairs, the late Ismail Cem, of social democratic background, mentioned the new understanding of geopolitics even before AKP came to power in the following words (Cem 2000):

> Turkey's specific historical development – its cosmopolitan characteristics, its civilization melding Western and Eastern values, a multitude of beliefs and ethnicities – bestowed on Turkey a unique identity. We consider ourselves both European (which we have been for seven centuries) and Asian and view this plurality as an asset. Our history was moulded as much in Istanbul, Edirne, Tetova, Kosovo and Sarajevo as it was in Bursa, Kayseri, Diyarbakır and Damascus.

Turkey while redefining its role in the new global order also intensified its relationship to Europe through EU candidacy in this era. Incorporation of Europeanness in its identity was a necessary and indispensible component of a reconstruction process involving an adaptation to the changing international conjuncture and internal structure of the country. A Europeanised Turkey would have a real opportunity to redefine its role in its neighbourhood and the world by incorporating values and norms that would contribute to Turkey's soft power both in a material and immaterial sense.

Turkey and Europe: Shadow of the Past, Promises of the Future

Turkish identity cannot be understood without recourse to its relations with Europe. With the gradual demise of the Ottoman Empire, Europe came to mean an adversary that was ahead of the country in its rapid advancements in science, technology and economy, what we may collectively term as modernity. While European powers established global preponderance, the Ottoman era in the Near East and Eastern Europe was coming to an end. Europe was no longer an adversary that could be defeated but now a model of global civilisation that had to be taken as a model of advancement and lifestyle. Westernisation at the end of the Ottoman era and the Republican era aimed to adopt the European lifestyle and worldview. In terms of institutions, the rupture with the Sultanate and Caliphate with the formation of the Republic meant a quite fundamental transformation to Western political institutions and an underlying continuity with the old era in terms of political behaviour and understandings of state-society relations. While the source of legitimacy and site of sovereignty changed during this period, this was more in the direction from the monarchy to a republican oligarchy than to the people as a whole.

Social construction of Turkishness embodies an interpretation of historical memories, the mythical journey of Turkic tribes from Central Asia to Anatolia, the conversion to Islam, the controversial Ottoman heritage, the experiences of the wars of independence, nation-state building during the Republican era and Ataturk's legacy as well as the perception of how Turks are viewed by the outside mainly by the West and Europe. Like other identities, it is a relational concept and is embedded in societal structures, state-society relations, mode of citizenship and public institutions. Turkey's relation to and status regarding Europe is both a factor influencing and influenced by identity construction. While Turkey's early interest in the European Economic Community founded in 1957 was based on considerations of economic benefit and political necessity, it was also related with the ages-old historical and cultural relations with European countries and peoples. While the triggering factor was interest-based, it was possible to observe the influence of psychological factors throughout the process that were closely related to the association with Europe in Turkish identity.

The Turkish government at the time of the formation of the EEC showed an early interest in this process. The reshaping of the world in the aftermath of the Second World War situated Turkey in the Western camp next to the EEC member states. Thus it may be quite understandable that Adnan Menderes raised the matter during the proceedings of the Turkish Parliament and referred to the importance of the formation of the 'common market' which may have political aims in the future (Ministry for EU Affairs 2011). Security concerns as well as economic considerations of development were related to Turkey's search for closer ties with the EC in its application for association. The prime minister of Turkey during the signature of the Ankara Agreement, İsmet İnönü, mentioned Turkey's ties with the EC in the government programme and talked of a 'union of fate with the Western world' and a Turkey that was also related to Turkey's economic reality (Turkey-Europe Foundation 2011). Rapprochement was mutual however. Commission President Walter Hallstein also welcomed this association with Turkey by expressing that 'Turkey is part of Europe' (Rehn 2008).

The relation to Europe in Turkish identity gained a more political character after the 1980s. While Europe mostly connoted a cultural sphere with distinct 'civilised' life patterns previously, after the 1980s and 1990s, the idea of freedom and democracy that Europe implied gained an increasing appeal in Turkey. Leftist and Kurdish intellectuals who had to flee to Europe after the military coup of 1980, the recognition of the right of appeal to the European Court of Human Rights in 1987 for Turkish citizens, the breakdown of the Berlin wall, the intensification of political integration in Europe with the Maastricht Treaty, and the 1993 declaration of the criteria for membership to the EU at the Copenhagen European Council may be evaluated as milestones that reinforced the significance of Europe and the EU as an area of freedom and democracy. Closer relations with Europe would bring about an expansion of politics and extend the scope of rights and freedoms. This also implied a distancing from Europe in the eyes of the Kemalist establishment since association with Europe would inadvertently support anti-establishment groups who were in search of greater access to state structures and leeway to voice their own ideas (Diez 2005). Thus the relation to Europe in Turkish identity, being also politically determined, embodied political values of democracy and human rights.

The acceptance of candidacy status, while bringing obvious advantages for Turkey, also brought about substantial pressure for change in the country's foreign policy domain, most notably reflected in the need to convert the Cyprus policy towards a more conciliatory stance and an urgency to start a process of resolution of bilateral disputes with Greece. At the same time, the Helsinki conclusions 'Europeanised' those issues by integrating them into the EU process. The acceptance of candidacy status by the then Turkish government ruled by Bülent Ecevit spurred a process of reforms starting with important steps such as the reduction of the pre-trial detention period, reformulation of the consultative role and composition of the National Security Council, abolishment of the death penalty, and extension of remit of cultural rights. The following period witnessed the adoption of two major constitutional amendments in 2001 and 2004 coupled with eight harmonisation packages between 2002 and 2004 (General Secretariat for EU Affairs 2007).

In the meantime, Turkish identity was also being opened to question with the increasing freedom of expression in the public space. While Islamists focused on the role of Islam in defining Turkish identity and questioned the secular nature of the republic, liberals questioned the ethnic background to Turkish identity and put forward that the republican idea of Turkish identity was based on a Sunni, Turkic homogenising ethos. Liberals further criticised this understanding of Turkish identity for being assimilationist for minority groups, illiberal and repressive. While Ataturk's reforms and revolutions in the 1920s took Europe as a model, it was thought that this model of the nation-state emulated the fascistic regimes of the interwar era in Europe and did not embody the ideal of Europe as freedom and democracy (Parker 2009: 1090–91). Europe provided a common point of reference for those groups that felt alienated from the establishment and wanted change. This included Islamists in the form of the globalist AKP, liberal intellectuals, Kurdish nationalists and supporters of the Kurdish cause.

Thus Europeanisation of Turkish identity cannot be thought separately from these parallel processes of liberalisation and demystification of the republican version of Turkish identity. It is also a still ongoing process under the rule of the AKP part since 2002. While for some, the redefinition of Turkish identity, and its Europeanisation would mean the end of the Turkish nation and state (Oğuzlu and Kibaroğlu 2009: 586) for others it would mean welfare and freedom for all groups living in Turkey and who feel that they are not part of this Turkish identity.

During the last decade, while state identity in Turkey evolved by way of Europeanisation, the change in Turkey's Cyprus policy after 2003, the start of exploratory talks with Greece with a view to settling the border-related dispute over the Aegean, the adoption of 'zero problems with neighbours' approach, the lifting of visas with several countries enabling freedom of movement, the attempt to reach a settlement with Armenia and the attempts to establish a free trade area with the southern neighbours may be noted as manifestations of a Europeanisation effect whereby the civilian power understanding of Europe that emerged with the

EU came to dominate Turkish foreign policy. The worsening of relations with Israel especially after the Davos and flotilla incidents was mostly interpreted as a divergence between Turkey and the West. However, in that case also the arguments against Israeli policy were mostly centred on the rights of the Palestinians. Turkey successfully applied values and norms of Europeanisation with respect to interstate relations to its neighbourhood. The warnings made to the Syrian leader Bashar Assad were the latest sign of the normative dimension of Turkish foreign policy. Turkey's joint attempt with Brazil to reach a compromise on the Iranian nuclear question was also interpreted as an unwelcome and unrealistic intrusion into western policy towards Iran. However, the attempt to prevent the use of force or other compelling measures and strive to reach a compromise may be again seen as a sign of civilian diplomacy. This may be evaluated as Turkey's internalisation of European norms and the result of a socialisation process.

It should also be noted that candidacy to the EU and Turkey's quest to fulfil the political aspects of the Copenhagen criteria had a direct bearing on internal political developments in Turkey. The EU membership perspective acted as a powerful stimulus for the government and opposition to work together in the parliament to pass the necessary reforms. It also altered the political landscape by influencing the sources of legitimacy and power configurations determining what would be considered as appropriate behaviour according to European norms and standards. In this way, the candidacy process supported those groups in Turkey that criticised the system and desired change. What would determine their chances of success would be their adaptability to the EU conditions, such as advocacy of democracy and support for human rights added to the strength of their local constituencies.

It is also possible to discern a Europeanisation effect in terms of how Turkish identity was shaped and defined by politicians and opinion leaders. While the highly security-conscious idea of Turkey and the Turks, surrounded by enemies and with deep-running problems of internal divisions and faced with the threat of dissolution began to show signs of change, the Europeanisation effect that went hand in hand with a desecuritisation process became more discernable in the last decade. This was related both to the global shifts that contributed to the redefinition of Turkey's geopolitical positions and its relations *vis-à-vis* the outside world as well as its EU process. The change instigated by the EU process and the demands and expectations of the EU laid emphasis on democratisation, respect for human rights and minority rights and rule of law. One of the priority areas to take action according to the EU was the area of civil-military relations which envisaged civilian control of the military, and a curb on the intervention of the military into politics. What may be summarised as the confinement of the army into strictly the military sphere with civilian oversight was a process that involved the redefinition of the role of the National Security Council, and the establishment of a new *modus vivendi* between the government and the military staff. Another critical turning point had been realised with the September 2010 constitutional referendum which made it possible for the 12 September generals to be tried for the military coup. This process continued in parallel with the series of trials such as the Ergenekon and Balyoz cases where several retired and currently serving members of the staff were detained and tried for their alleged attempts to bring down the democratic order and the AKP government. The relegation of the role of the military bureaucracy in Turkish politics and the criticism of the military for its past takeovers, current coup attempts and more recently some military mistakes in the fight against the PKK led to a realignment in the understanding of Turkish identity towards a more democratic and civilian approach. The often referred understanding of Turkey as the military nation (Altınay 2004) encountered a rapid change and evolved towards a new understanding which may be interpreted as the trading nation akin to the words of Kirişçi (2009). This was related to an upsurge in the volume of trade in goods and services since the 1980s, where the EU emerged as a major trading partner especially since the entry into force of the customs union in 1996.

The EU process also influenced the vitalisation of civil society in Turkey by way of promoting and encouraging the activities of non-governmental organisations. Liberalisation of the constitution with consecutive amendments, and the relevant harmonisation packages extended the scope of individual rights thus empowering the individual citizen *vis-à-vis* the state and expanding the opportunities of getting organised within NGOs. This redefinition of state-society relations again had major effects on the idea of Turkish identity as primarily moulded by the State presided over by a hegemonic State ethos.

Other areas figuring prominently in analysing the Europeanisation effect are the areas of gender relations, minority rights and cultural rights. Change in these areas is also related to the Europeanisation process, whereby EU norms and values were adopted as a standard of conduct and model despite national variations. Whenever a political solution to the Kurdish issue is being pondered, examples from Ireland or Spain come to the fore. Similarly, issues with regard to gender and the problems of women in society are usually compared with the European standards such as the discussion about whether or not to apply quotas for women in parliament. More concretely, the progress reports prepared by the European Commission regularly note problems in these areas and call for improvements in line with the Copenhagen criteria and the *acquis communautaire*. Major improvements in the area of minority and cultural rights can be summarised as the right to broadcast in and learn 'languages traditionally used by Turkish citizens in their daily lives' and the new law on foundations which extended the liberties enjoyed by minority foundations. Such legislative reform was paralleled with a more conciliatory approach on the part of the government that recognised the existence of minority groups and cooperated with minority groups or ethnic groups in resolving their grievances. Although significant pitfalls continue to exist in this area, a new understanding seems to permeate the public bodies as well as the general public opinion.

Europeanisation of Turkish Identity within a Regionalisation Process?

While the above-mentioned developments may attest to a Europeanisation process in terms of the defining characteristics of Turkish identity, the political rhetoric with regard to where Turkey stands in the world tended to take a different turn since the mid-2000s. The era following the Helsinki European Council witnessed a reform period in Turkey where legislative reform followed the trajectory of candidacy to the EU. Turkey participated in the activities of the convention for the future of Europe and the Prime Minister Recep Tayyip Erdoğan signed the 'Treaty Establishing a Constitution for Europe' in 2004. Turkey was actively participating in the debates about the future of Europe as a potential member state. The constitutional amendments and harmonisation packages went through the parliament based on a consensus between the major political parties, AKP and CHP.

The AKP's quest for EU membership seemed contradictory at the outset looking at the party's Islamic roots. However, the EU card was a precious leverage for the party especially against criticisms and doubts that it was a religiously-oriented party that aimed at Islamising Turkey and severing the country's relations with the West. It was also a political strategy used by the party to gain leverage in the political system and outweigh and weaken its opponents, above all the military. The government programme made references to the EU as a source of legitimacy and emphasised the 'acceleration and conclusion of the process of membership to the EU as a priority of the government' (Programme of the 59th Government 2002). Europeanisation could be seen as a way of becoming an actor in the globalising world. For the AKP what was important was to emphasise the contemporary nature of today's Turkey symbolised by the country's candidacy to the EU, without undermining its Islamic and Eastern character (Çağlıyan-İçener 2009: 606). Turkey's being one of the co-sponsors of the Alliance for Civilisations Initiative since 2005 is a further sign of the resurfacing of the Islamic/Eastern character of Turkey that has been accelerated under the AKP rule.

The EU dimension tilted the balance in favour of the democratically elected to the detriment of the civil and military bureaucracy. What could be characterised as a tutelary regime in Turkey slowly declined with the limitation of the political role of the military. The government expanded its legitimacy together with its electoral base and made use of its support for EU membership to reach out to liberal groups and intellectuals. Secondly the EU criteria also had an effect on the traditional understanding of the state as a force over and above the government and the relations between the citizen and the state by expanding the scope of rights and civil liberties. Although demands for greater rights and democracy were made by different groups since the return to civilian politics after the 1980 coup, the EU factor had a triggering effect and exerted leverage in favour of reformists. It should be emphasised at this point that the process of democratisation still continues and the question of a viable democratic system is not yet resolved. The country is struggling with the evolution of a democratic system based on an unfaltering respect for rights and freedoms, checks and balances between different organs of the state, independence of the judiciary and effective democratic scrutiny of the executive.

While the former President of France, Nicholas Sarkozy and several other prominent figures in Europe such as Valery Giscard d'Estaing, an other former President of France, employed Turkey as the other in defining their understanding of European identity, this othering mechanism created a backlash against the European target among Turkish political elites and society. Prime Minister Erdoğan and Chief EU negotiator Egemen Bağış displayed a critical approach and an incriminating discourse against the EU and EU leaders. For example, while Erdoğan mainly criticised the EU and its leaders for failing to apply a just and non-discriminatory policy towards Turkey, he also dwelled on bonds and identifications that could not replace the European dimension but at least could compensate for the rejection by the EU and help Turkey in its quest for regional and ultimately global influence. In his recent speeches, he emphasised the common bonds, mutual sympathy and brotherhood in bilateral relations especially in his addresses to Muslim Middle Eastern, and Balkan countries, aiming to gain sympathy and extend the scope of Turkey's soft power by highlighting commonalities between those countries. (*T24* 2011) This contrasting attitude may be evaluated as a policy preference to give the message to the EU that Turkey may have other choices and need not indefinitely wait at the EU's door, while at the same time the EU is also operating such 'other'ing mechanisms on Turkey.

Judged on the basis of the dominant discourse of governmental figures in Turkey, Turkey's international identity is being constructed on the basis of a regional orientation emphasising Turkey's links with the Ottoman geography, sharing an Islamic civilisation with the Middle East and its unique standing in its region as a democratising country with a thriving economy. While cultural affinities, religious bonds, solidarity and brotherhood are being highlighted in Turkey's relations with especially Middle Eastern countries, accusations, and differences are mostly heard with regard to Europe. While this is partly a reflection of the EU's exclusionary Turkey policy, it is also a sign of a reorientation of Turkey's international status. The growing resentment felt towards the EU is also reflected in a new understanding and vision which is critical of the idea of Europe itself. This proceeds concomitantly with a new identity orientation based on Turkey's culture, and Ottoman heritage and portrayed in terms of a country as a role model in its region particularly with regard to the Islamic world, heir to a multicultural Empire, while the EU is increasingly being perceived as an inward-looking continent in decline, which is becoming xenophobic and defensive.

The growing rift between Turkey and the EU is best illustrated by the words of the Minister of State and Chief Negotiator for the EU, Egemen Bağış. During a ceremony to commemorate the Holocaust at Auschwitz, he said that 'the EU … is today under the risk of being overtaken by a racist mentality that cannot internalize its own values and emulates the fascist methods of 1930s' (*Euractiv* 2011a). While criticising this 'racist mentality', he also added that the best remedy would be Turkey's EU membership. Put differently, Bağış's words reflect the negative atmosphere towards the EU among the policy-makers in Turkey who have been continuously bringing up the idea both in domestic politics and in its relations especially with Middle Eastern neighbours that the European Union has been excluding Turkey not because of rational reasons but due to Turkey's belonging to a different culture and religion and therefore following 'racist' policies.[2]

While relations with the EU have entered a cooling phase since 2005 and especially 2006, Turkey's international standing has been displaying signs of a major transformation in the meantime. Turkish foreign policy has been under increasing scrutiny in recent years due to a rising activism in terms of foreign policy initiatives, an expansion of the scope of foreign policy, an assertiveness in the discourse employed, a noticeable autonomy especially from Western foreign policy stances, an opening to non-European regions such as the Middle East, emphasis on trade, economy and culture as instruments of soft power rather than hard power instruments or use of coercive diplomacy.

This overall change is sometimes linked with the identity and worldview of policy-makers and is denoted with the term, neo-Ottomanism. Although an increasing appreciation of Turkey's Ottoman heritage and a growing interest towards regions that formerly formed parts of the Ottoman Empire may be discerned in Turkey especially since the 1990s, the use of the term neo-Ottoman may be flawed. It may be more apt to argue that Turkish foreign policy is adapting itself to the changing global and regional circumstances in a world where USA leadership became more controversial in the aftermath of the Iraqi invasion and where the EU excludes Turkey from its plans for the near future.

In this context, the minister of Foreign Affairs, Prof. Ahmet Davutoğlu's foreign policy vision which places Turkey at the centre of a region including many adjacent basins of historical and strategic significance is of vital importance with respect to understanding his realistic vision towards the EU and Europe (Davutoğlu 2009). According to him, Turkey has to develop alternative land basin policies with the aim of preventing Turkey's isolation *vis-à-vis* an EU which is completely integrated with Eastern Europe strategies without disregarding the special importance of the EU and Europe for Turkey. Moreover, Davutoğlu (2009: 550) certainly did not base his foreign policy on the assumption that EU membership would be possible in the near to medium term and adopted a strategy based on a more balanced approach to foreign relations with a broader focus while aiming to give due consideration to the EU process.[3]

---

2   Such an exchange of words is reminiscent of an earlier controversy between former prime minister Mesut Yılmaz and former German chancellor Helmut Kohl about the EU's double standards, and Germany still implementing a policy of 'lebensraum' after the 1997 Luxembourg European Council excluding Turkey from the enlargement process.

3   'In the twenty-year period in front of us, the necessity to establish an area of maneuver that is prone to any kind of alternatives by developing alternative land basin policies with the aim of preventing Turkey's isolation *vis-à-vis* an EU which is completely integrated with Eastern Europe will be one of the most fundamental strategic parameters

This realistic vision contemplates the future of Turkey not defined only by its links with the EU but connected with regions surrounding it. Davutoğlu's warning to heed and neutralise the influence of 'historical/psychological mental parameters' (Davutoğlu 2009: 550) could be a defining factor for Turkey's future status *vis-à-vis* the EU. Since integration to the EU is not solely a foreign policy act but involves deeper understandings about identity and perceptions of Europe, divorcing this process from such psychological or affective dimensions would curb the driving force behind Turkey's search for membership. In the meantime the affective element would be introduced in Turkey's relations with other regions especially the Middle East and Arab world as well as parts of the Balkans. As argued by Öniş and Yılmaz (2009: 7), change in the AKP government's policies from 'commitment to deep Europeanisation', to 'loose Europeanisation and a parallel shift to … soft Euro-Asianism' should not be evaluated as a shift of foreign policy orientation in a direction focusing more on the former Soviet space and the Middle East. Rather, it should be seen as a foreign policy activism which is 'pursued with respect to all neighbouring regions, but with no firm EU axis as was previously the case' (Öniş and Yılmaz 2009: 12). The insertion of such a firm EU dimension to Turkey's foreign policy would be dependent on the revitalisation of Turkey's negotiations with the EU with a view to accession.

It should be borne in mind that Ankara tried to justify its amicable relations with Syria before the recent emergence of problems with the Assad regime, opening to Hamas and rapprochement to Iran over the nuclear issue which were cited as proving Turkey's slide away from the West and the EU with the argument that it is in fact acting in line with EU norms by forming relations with the democratically-elected Hamas, and engaging to bring peace to the region with its efforts at international mediation. In a way, Ankara utilised its EU links as a facilitator in pursuing relations with the actors isolated from the international society and enhancing its prestige and soft power in the region.

While Turkey's membership negotiations to the EU lost its pace after 2006, Turkey's identity began to show increasing signs of its Eastern dimension displayed by an increasing importance of religion and cultural and historical bonds to the region encompassing the Balkans, Caucasus and the Middle East. This development is concomitant with the growing importance of especially the Middle East in global politics, Turkey's need to adapt to fast-moving changes in the region and the ideological predisposition of decision-makers in Turkey. Together with the internal crises of the EU, i.e. the economic crisis related with the debt problem and the rising xenophobia, cultural essentialism and racism displayed by some events

---

for Turkey in the near future. Turkey cannot break away from Europe geographically or historically. However, the start of a new era in relations with Europe depends on the condition that historical/psychological mental parameters should not influence rational diplomatic processes. The primary condition to come out of this vicious cycle … is to re-evaluate Turkey's foreign relations strategy that encompasses the EU but does not in any way reduce it to only the EU factor.' Translated by the author (Davutoğlu 2009: 550).

like the expulsion of the Roma from France, the *burqa* ban, and the massacre in Norway, severely impacted on the image and perception of Europe in Turkey. The process of Europeanisation that started earlier with the reforms during the late Ottoman and early Republican era and continued with the relations with the EC took a new turn with the EU membership process. However, the stalling of the negotiations after 2006 and the above-mentioned deterioration in the perception of the EU and Europe led a questioning of Turkey's increasing integration to Europe.

It would, however, be misleading to argue that Turkey's changing foreign policy orientation towards non-European regions and closer relations with Muslim countries mean that Turkey is turning away from Europe. It does not also attest to a 'de-Europeanisation of identity'. While Turkey's identity has acquired a more regional quality and aimed to encompass the cultural diversity, historical richness and geopolitical potential of Turkey's identity sources, it continued to adhere to the target of EU membership. Turkey's policies in the international arena, which may be seen as reflections of identity construction, also embodied the values, norms and patterns of Europeanisation by adopting a policy of reconciliation with neighbours, opening of borders with a liberal visa policy and basing political relations on economic cooperation and integration. The increasing soft power and model-country image that Turkey has accumulated in recent years especially in its vicinity, is also very much tied to the Europeanisation of its identity embodying democratic ideals, peaceful international relations, economic potential with an emphasis on culture and history. It is possible to discern a Europeanisation of identity while at the same time the regional component in identity construction is taking a new turn under the AKP.

Prime Minister Erdoğan in a visit to Egypt following the fall of the Mubarek regime made a reference to the important role that secularism plays in democracy and displayed a vision of secularism that could be adapted as a model by Muslim-majority states: '... Secular state is at the same distance to all beliefs. It is not the people but the state which is secular' (*Sabah* 2011). This approach is quite interesting given the fact that Erdoğan himself was accused of undermining secularism in Turkey. Erdoğan's advocacy of secularism in the Middle East may be evaluated as a sign of successful adoption of European values by a sizeable majority of the Turkish population not only by Westernised segments.

The words of Egemen Bağış may be helpful in understanding this seeming dichotomy between a Europeanisation of identity which is at the same time becoming regional (*Euractiv* 2011b):

> [Referring to the 17 December 2004 European Council] Then Turkey had many problems in its democracy, many flaws that it had to overcome. People were afraid of talking in their own language; they could not freely express their opinions. Turkey began to observe the positive effects of the EU in every area of life...While people are being packed into wagons and deported in Europe [referring to the deportation of the Roma in France] Turkey is instigating new openings, coming to a point whereby it is a source of inspiration for others. We

made several reforms in education but the EU does not open the related chapter in negotiations. Why, because the Greek Administration of Cyprus is blocking. That is their concern. The EU is a dietician but its health is not in good shape these days. It cannot follow its own recipe. We are going to implement the recipe and finally full membership will be realized.

This kind of seemingly contradictory development may be peculiar to the case of Turkey. Turkey may be one of a few countries that started an accession process to the EU but was rebuffed by two leading EU States on the basis that it is not European. This denial of Europeanness which may be concomitant to the EU's own identity construction has spurred Turkey to be more active elsewhere. Still, while Turkey may be increasingly critical of the EU, and looking to establish a more active role in regional and global affairs this cannot be interpreted as an end to Europeanisation of identity. The recent evolution of identity in the case of Turkey displays signs of Europeanisation in the sense of adoption and successful incorporation of values, norms and ways of doing things. At the same time, Turkey may be turning away from Europe as a centre of allegiance which could be explained by the exclusionary approach displayed by the EU and the problems that emanated during the accession process. In terms of socio-economic development and modernisation Europe continues to pose as the main reference point and the EU membership aim is still on the table as evidenced by the recent establishment of a ministry for EU Affairs.

Conclusion

Recently, it is possible to discern a growing criticism of Europe's hypocrisy and double standards and a resentment of the way leading EU countries such as France and Germany treat Turkey with regard to EU membership. Especially after the declaration of candidacy and emergence of the possibility of Turkey's membership of the EU, mostly conservative and right-wing political parties, groups and eminent figures in Europe began to openly challenge Turkey's European character, the most vocal and noticeable figure being the outgoing President of France, Nicolas Sarkozy in this regard. This definition of Turkey as non-European or out-of-Europe influenced the identity perception of both Turkish elites and masses. It may be considered as a new phase in Europe's construction of Turkey's identity evolving from being defined as a 'liminal' identity in the door step of Europe to being definitely out of Europe. It may also be a continuation of the condescending attitude to Turkey based on continual criticism of political and economic conditions in the 1980's and 90's. While previously Turkey's exclusion from the EU was allegedly based on objective facts about Turkey's insufficiency to be a member, it was only a matter of time before Turkey would fulfil the necessary conditions for EU membership – mostly taken to be realised in a distant future. However, the discourse adopted by the likes of Sarkozy amounted to a total othering whereby the 'doors' of the EU are shut to Turkey since the EU means Europe and Turkey does not belong there. Here the identity construction within the EU proceeds concomitantly with the othering of Turkey and its construction as non-European.

Turkey's self-perception at the same time was in a state of flux. While Turkey continued to stay as a member of NATO and Council of Europe, and a candidate to join the EU, the Turkish public began to increasingly question the EU's sincerity towards Turkey. 'They will never have us as a member' became an expression used from time to time at both elite and mass levels. The tectonic changes taking place at the level of international and regional systems also influenced identity construction in Turkey by prioritising the regions surrounding the country. Increasing economic and commercial ties, social and cultural exchange with countries with which Turkey shares common historical references and religion had a role in this process. While Europe began to lose its legitimacy and attractiveness for Turkey, the importance of especially the Middle East or roughly the old Ottoman geography resurfaced in parallel with the search for new economic opportunities, political clout and need to fend off threats to regional stability.

The coming to power of the AKP also had a major role in identity construction. AKP's identification with Islam and conservative social values coupled with its popularity among the electorate meant that the agency shaping Turkey's identity also evolved on these lines, emphasising and bringing to the fore the traditional and 'oriental' characteristics of Turkish identity. At the same time, however, AKP was also associated with neo-liberal globalist ethics, a rupture from the old, reactionary Islamic understanding. The AKP's seizing of the globalist agenda as a source of legitimacy and power base also meant that it adopted a pro-European approach with a view to realising EU reforms. The accelerated pace of EU reforms and the existence of the EU as a 'disciplining' mechanism and an anchor contributed to fundamental changes in Turkish society and politics.

The application of the Europeanisation approach to Turkey's identity construction especially after the declaration of EU candidacy presents a quite contradictory and complex picture. Since 2006 and more so after 2009, Turkey's identity construction began to turn away from Europe as an area of allegiance and contest Europe as a source of legitimacy and belonging. It was very much reflexive of the dichotomy in the EU's approach to Turkey – starting official accession negotiations and then questioning Turkey's eligibility for membership. While a growing awareness of Turkey's links with and relevance for new geographies such as Central Asia and the Middle East began to emerge after the ending of the Cold War, the AKP era showed a definitive preference and emphasis on a 'regional' identity for Turkey, aiming to place the country in a central location with influence over surrounding regions.

While the above analysis may undermine a Europeanisation of identity in the case of Turkey, such a process has already been going on since at least the Helsinki European Council declaring Turkey as a candidate country. The adoption of the EU as a model for reforms went hand in hand with a concomitant internalisation and socialisation process concerning the underlying norms, values and methods.

Although it is a criticism voiced both in Europe and Turkey that most reforms are only on paper and have not permeated lower echelons of the administrative system and society, it would not be possible to pass those reforms through the Parliament unless there was already a basic acceptance of European norms and values. The Copenhagen criteria and reforms needed to proceed on the way to EU membership were based on underlying premises, value judgements and conceptions about what is just, right and appropriate. Most significantly, the EU process influenced and Europeanised ideas about the limits of State power, democratic representation, role of the military, gender equality, and minority rights.

Europeanisation in the case of a candidate country mostly involves a top-down mechanism of the EU influencing and acting as an agent of change by providing external incentives and/or sanctions guiding the behaviour and internal reform process of candidate countries. Europeanisation is and should be also domestically driven. Political actors instrumentalise the EU as a power base and source of legitimacy which empowers them to act in a way that would have been impeded by other actors in the absence of the EU factor. Moreover, the mindset, values and expectations of political actors also change as they take the EU as a reference point. They increasingly take their cues from the EU and define what is appropriate and legitimate with reference to the EU model. This kind of effect may weaken with the diminishing rewards the EU offers or with a changing perception of the EU as a source of legitimacy. It is possible to observe this development in the case of Turkey as the allure of the EU weakens and as Turkey's self-confidence grows. Nevertheless, the adoption of the goal of EU integration as a permanent policy preference even during times of military rule or interim regimes and the all-party support to EU reforms after 1999 shaped Turkey's general identification with the European model, instigating a slow but steady social learning process in the political system.

Even as the EU enlargement process loses credibility in the eyes of Turkish elite and public, the norms and values symbolised and preached by the EU – though EU countries may not always be perfect examples – continue to influence the expected normative understanding, value judgements and mindset of political and societal actors. Thus a Europeanisation of identity is not contrary to a 'regionalisation' of Turkish identity since Turkey's value as a model country in the Middle East is related to its Europeanisation. Turkey, despite its ongoing shortcomings in its democracy, is a better-than-most symbol of a country which is able to integrate the European dimension with its Near-Eastern heritage, a blend of Islam, democracy, secularism and market economy. Recent changes in its foreign policy, whereby Turkey became a 'benign' power in its region espousing democracy, secularism and human rights to countries such as Syria or Egypt stems from its growing soft power which is again based on a process of Europeanisation of foreign policy. Above all, Turkey's identity in the world in terms of what it stands for and represents in the mind of the international community is a product of Europeanisation, EU and domestically-driven. As a final point, it could be appropriate to ponder whether this could amount to a process of 'Europeanisation of the Middle East' conditional upon the continuing deepening of the EU by way of a stronger economic and monetary union and successful integration of Turkey to the EU's decision-making structures.

References

Altınay, A.G. 2004. *The Myth of the Military-Nation: Militarism, Gender and Education in Turkey.* New York: Palgrave Macmillan.

Cem, İ. 2000. Turkey and Europe: looking to the future from a historical perspective. *Perceptions*, 5 (June/August). [Online]. Available at: http://www.sam.gov.tr/perceptions/Volume5/JuneAugust2000/-VolumeVN2IsmailCem.pdf [accessed: 9 September 2010].

Çağlıyan-İçener, Z. 2009. The Justice and Development Party's conception of 'conservative democracy': invention or reinterpretation? *Turkish Studies*, 10(4), 595–612.

Davutoğlu, A. 2009. *Stratejik Derinlik* (Strategic Depth). 34th edition, İstanbul: Küre Publications.

Diez, T. 2005. Turkey, the EU and security complexes revisited. *Mediterranean Politics*, 10(2), 167–80.

Euractiv. 2011a. Bağış: AB ırkçı zihinlerin kuşatması ile karşı karşıya (The EU is faced with the siege of racist minds). [Online, 2 February]. Available at: http://www.euractiv.com.tr/yazicisayfasi/article/-bagis-ab-irkci-zihinlerin-kusatma-tehlikesinde-015392 [accessed: 12 October 2011].

Euractiv. 2011b. Bağış: AB diyetisyen ama sağlığı bozuk (Bağış: EU is a dietician but its health is poor). [Online, 24 February]. Available at: http://www.euractiv.com.tr/3/article/ba-ab-diyetisyen-ama-sal-bozuk-015967 [accessed: 9 September 2011].

General Secretariat for EU Affairs 2007. *AB Uyum Yasa Paketleri (EU Harmonisation Packages).* Ankara: M&B Tanıtım Hizmetleri ve Tic. Ltd.

Kirişçi, K. 2009. The Transformation of Turkish foreign policy: the rise of the trading state. *New Perspectives on Turkey*, 40, 29–57.

Mayer, F.C. and Palmowski, J. 2004. European identities and the EU: the ties that bind the peoples of Europe. *Journal of Common Market Studies*, 42(3), 443–62.

Ministry for EU Affairs website. 2011. Türkiye-AB İlişkilerinin Tarihçesi (History of Turkey-EU Relations). [Online]. Available at: http://www.abgs.gov.tr/index.php?p=111&l=1 [accessed: 29 November 2011].

Oğuzlu, T. and Kibaroğlu, M. 2009. Is the Westernization process losing pace in Turkey: who's to blame? *Turkish Studies*, 10(4), 577–93.

Öniş, Z. and Yılmaz, Ş. 2009. Between Europeanisation and Euro-asianism: foreign policy activism in Turkey during the AKP era. *Turkish Studies*, 10(1), 7–24.

Parker, O. 2009. 'Cosmopolitan Europe' and the EU-Turkey question: the politics of a 'common destiny'. *Journal of European Public Policy*, 16(7), 1085–101.

Programme of the 59th Government. 2002. [Online]. Available at: http://www. belgenet.com/-hukumet/program/59-1.html [accessed: 3 October 2011].

Radaelli, C.M. 2004. Europeanisation: solution or problem? *European Integration Online Papers (EIoP)*, 8(16).

Rehn, O. 2008. *45 Years from the Signing of the Ankara Agreement: EU-Turkey Cooperation Continues*. SPEECH/08/581. Conference on EC Turkey Association Agreement, 4 November. [Online]. Available at: http://www.eulib. com/-45-years-from-3021 [accessed: 2 October 2011].

Risse, T. 2001. A European identity? Europeanisation and the evolution of nation-state identities, in *Transforming Europe: Europeanisation and Domestic Change*, edited by M. Green-Cowles, T. Risse and J.A. Caporaso. Ithaca, NY: Cornell University Press, 198–216.

Risse, T. 2010. *A Community of Europeans: Transnational Identities and Public Spheres*. Ithaca, NY: Cornell University Press.

Sabah. 2011. Başbakan Erdoğan'dan laiklik açılımı (Prime minister Erdoğan's secularism opening) [Online, 15 September] Available at: http://www.sabah. com.tr/Gundem/2011/09/15/basbakan-erdogandan-laiklik-acilimi [accessed: 2 November 2011].

T24. 2011. Erdoğan: Katar-Türkiye 2.5 saat (Erdoğan: Qatar-Turkey 2.5 hours) [Online, 12 January] Available at: http://www.t24.com.tr/haberdetay/121824. aspx [accessed: 5 August 2011].

Tajfel, H. 1981. *Human Groups and Social Categories*. Cambridge: Cambridge University Press.

Turkey-Europe Foundation. 2011. [Online]. Available at: http://www. turkiyeavrupavakfi.org/-index.php/avrupa-birligi/tarihce/1601-1963.html [accessed: 5 November 2011].

Chapter 3

The EU's Impact on Democratisation in Turkey: Europeanisation through Political Conditionality

Yonca Özer

Introduction

Europeanisation is an essentially contested concept, which does not have a single definition. However, the literature generally employs the concept to demonstrate or to explain 'influence' or 'domestic impact' of the EU, which usually results in change. Although the study of Europeanisation has long been confined to analyses of the member states of the EU, the impact of the EU on domestic change also takes place in the candidate countries. Europeanisation is applied, in this chapter, in its top-down version, implying transformation at the domestic level activated by the dynamics of European integration since Europeanisation of candidate countries occurs through the adoption and implementation of EU rules and regulations.

Conditionality is a prominent strategy that is placed at the centre of the Europeanisation of candidate countries. The idea that membership, the eventual reward, is made conditional to the adoption and implementation of EU rules and regulations lies behind conditionality. It is obvious that accession to the EU is a process of massive rule adoption and necessitates transposition of the full *acquis communautaire* by the candidate countries. Also, the EU has set political criteria in the fields of democracy and human rights as the *sine qua non* conditions for the opening of accession negotiations and finally membership itself although they are not part of the EU *acquis*. Therefore, political conditionality is regarded by this chapter as an engine of *Europeanisation* of Turkish democracy and human rights regime. In other words, the chapter analyses the domestic impact of the EU on the candidate countries mainly from the perspective of *rationalist institutionalism*, which focuses on the use of conditionality by the EU to influence the countries concerned.

Turkey underwent dramatic democratic reforms after reaching candidacy status in the Helsinki European Council in December 1999. It is argued that the prospect of the launching of the accession negotiations generated a strong impetus on the part of Turkey to comply with the Copenhagen political criteria and to undertake radical reforms for this purpose. Therefore, rationalist institutionalist external incentives model appears to be well-suited for explaining the dramatic improvement in Turkish democracy in this period. However, after the launching of accession negotiations Turkey has drastically lost its momentum in this respect and the process of Europeanisation in Turkish democracy and human rights regime has nearly come to a halt. Turkey has faced important problems particularly regarding implementation of the adopted rules. In addition to the main emphasis on the rationalist institutionalist analysis of ineffective conditionality in explaining this severe slowdown the chapter also resorts to the *sociological institutionalist* social learning model particularly to account for the implementation problems. In other words, it tries to explain the recent deceleration in political reform process by questioning the recent (in)effectiveness of the political conditionality of the EU on the one hand and also how the (in)effectiveness of EU's persuasion and socialisation impacts appear relevant to understand implementation problems on the other hand. This reflects that the chapter considers these two alternative approaches which present analytically separate mechanisms as to a certain extent complementary in the recent period.

The comparative literature on democratisation suggests that external influences *per se* cannot generate democratic transition or consolidation in a country. It can play a significantly positive role provided that the underlying conditions for democratic transformation are also favourable (Whitehead 1996). Accordingly, this chapter analyses not only the extent of the impact of the EU political conditionality on the domestic change in Turkey but also the conditions and factors that determine the extent of that impact. The extent of the EU's influence, which implies whether or not the EU has an influence on domestic change or whether the EU's influence is strong or weak, is the *dependent variable* of this analysis while the conditions and facilitating factors that determine the effectiveness of the EU's influence form the *independent variables*. The chapter analyses both the international and the domestic level regarding independent variables and asks which conditions and facilitating factors at the EU's and the domestic level account for effectiveness of the EU's conditionality.

Europeanisation and Candidate Countries

The literature addressing especially the transformation of candidate countries makes extensive use of the term of Europeanisation. The term has been employed in different ways in diverse social science disciplines. From the perspective of political science, it mainly refers to the process of change at the domestic level due to the pressures generated by the EU. Political scientists studying European integration have renewed their interests in Europeanisation since the 1990s because the EU agenda was preoccupied with deepening. Europeanisation represented a new research field for these scientists in order to understand the dynamics of European integration both at the supranational and domestic levels. Mustafa Aydın and Sinem A. Açıkmeşe (2007) offered three conceptualisations of Europeanisation.

The first conceptualisation, which focuses on the generation of a European centre, constitutes bottom-up approach. In this approach, Europeanisation is the evolution of European institutions as a set of new norms, rules and practices, which formalise and regularise interactions among the actors (Börzel 2002: 193). The second conceptualisation signifies top-down approach which reflects Europeanisation as a process of domestic change that is ensured by the European integration. This Europeanisation-from-above process reorients the direction and shape of politics to the extent that EU political and economic dynamics become part of the organisational logic of national politics and policy-making. The domain of change is not only seen in politics, policies and polity, but also in a wider spectrum covering styles, informal rules, ways of doing, shared beliefs and norms (Radaelli 2000: 3). The third conceptualisation is a merger of top-down and bottom-up approaches that depicts Europeanisation as an ongoing, interactive and mutually constitutive process of change linking national and European levels, where the responses of the member states to the integration process feed back into the EU institutions and policy processes and *vice versa* (Major 2005: 177). This approach regards Europeanisation as a cycle of interactions and change at all levels and assumes that Europeanisation comes up through the coexistence of centre-building and domestic change in a vicious circle.

This merger approach, due to its cyclical nature, blurs the lines between cause and effect, dependent and independent variables (Major 2005: 177). Therefore, one should select one dimension of this process, either top-down or bottom-up, in order to ensure methodological clarity (Aydın and Açıkmeşe 2007: 265). Accordingly, Europeanisation is applied, in this chapter, in its top-down version, implying transformation at the domestic level activated by the dynamics of European integration. Since Turkey is a candidate country, not a member state, top-down process is more relevant than bottom-up process. Therefore, the chapter conceptualises the term Europeanisation as 'covering the consequences of fulfilment of EU requirements and of voluntary orientation towards EU standards in candidate countries' (Major 2005: 178). Accordingly, it generally defines the term as both the adoption (formal change) and implementation (behavioural change) of EU rules and regulations.[1]

One key difference between the Europeanisation of member states and candidate countries is related to the instruments and strategies through which the EU engenders pressure for change. Conditionality is the prominent strategy that the chapter places at the centre of the Europeanisation of candidate countries. In other words, the chapter analyses the domestic impact of the EU on the candidate countries from the perspective of *rationalist institutionalism*,[2] which focuses on the use of conditionality by the EU to influence the countries concerned. As Ulrich Sedelmeier (2011: 9) pointed out, since the EU's application of conditionality

---

1   Chapters in the edited book by Schimmelfening and Sedelmeier (2005a) differentiate change that the EU induces as formal change (the legal transposition of rules) and behavioural change (implementation, application and enforcement).

2   For a detailed analysis of alternative institutionalist approaches to the EU's impact (rationalist institutionalism versus constructivist institutionalism) see Sedelmeier (2011).

varies across issue areas, target countries and over time (as in the case of Turkey), this strategy – and its effectiveness – is not uniform and homogenous. That is why this chapter primarily identifies factors – at the level of the EU – that account for effectiveness of EU conditionality.

Conditionality and Its Effectiveness for Democratic Change in Candidate Countries

Conditionality can be defined as an instrument which entails 'the linking, by a state or international organisation, of benefits desired by another state to the fulfilment of certain conditions' (Smith 2003: 108). Asking for some conditions to be fulfilled by the recipient state before it can actually receive what it was promised supposes that this state will be deprived of foreseen reward if it does not comply with external actors' requirements (Ethier 2003: 100). In other words, the donor actor pays the reward if the recipient actor complies with the conditions and withholds the reward if it fails to comply. Economic conditionality long used by financial international institutions was later transformed into a political conditionality by other international actors (Pridham 1999: 62). Conditionality has also been increasingly used by international actors to enhance democratic capacities of a variety of countries in need of external aid (Spendzharova 2003: 146). Political (or democratic) conditionality implies that domestic actors or governments are required by external actors to introduce democratic structures or consolidate their democratic regime before receiving a promised reward.

As argued by Frank Schimmelfennig, Stefan Engert and Heiko Knobel (2002), the EU, from the beginning, has made financial and technical assistance and institutional ties (in the form of concluding various agreements of trade, cooperation, association and even accession as well as forging other mechanisms of relationship through political dialogue and common strategies) first informally and then formally conditional on the fulfilment of democratic and human rights standards. The EU is now one of the major international actors employing conditionality as a standard foreign policy tool to enforce democratic reforms and protection of human rights and minorities in its relations with the third countries. However, conditionality having a membership perspective, which draws together a wide range of policy fields and put them under a comprehensive accession strategy with a particular focus on democracy, is a far more influential tool.

Facing new potential applicants in the early 1990s, the democratic preconditions and the principle of the protection of fundamental rights were incorporated to the Treaty of European Union and also further elaborated by the Copenhagen European Council in 1993 to be strictly applied in the EU's next enlargements. That means that certain preconditions have to be met by applicant states before membership reward is granted by the EU (Pridham 1999: 65). Membership conditionality generally embodies *Article 49 of the Treaty on the EU* focusing on Europeanness and adherence to the main values of the EU,[3] the infamous *Copenhagen criteria*,[4] the *Madrid criterion*, as determined in the 1995 Madrid European Council, of effective implementation of adopted norms through appropriate administrative and judicial structure as well as the *Helsinki criteria*, as determined in the 1999 Helsinki European Council, of good neighbourliness and higher standards for nuclear safety[5] (Açıkmeşe 2010: 135–6). The 1997 Luxembourg European Council put the Copenhagen political criteria at the top of the conditionality hierarchy by deciding that compliance with the Copenhagen political criteria is a prerequisite for the opening of any accession negotiations[6] (Açıkmeşe 2010: 136).

The prospect of membership to an exclusive club of democratic societies is seen as a major strength of the EU and often distinguishes it from other similar international organisations in that specific race to be the vanguard of democracy promotion in the international arena. Linking membership to the establishment of a functioning democratic regime definitely entails much more than a simple expectation for a grand scale democratic transformation in recipient countries in return for economic and aid packages. In fact, so far the conditionality employed within the comprehensive membership perspective has proven successful first in Southern European countries and then in East European countries.

Heather Grabbe (2002) offered a detailed analysis of the relationship between conditionality and the transformation of former candidate countries from Central and Eastern Europe. She explained the levers that the EU uses to ensure conditionality and, therefore, to effect institutional and policy transformation in CEECs. She also underlined the unequal nature of the relationship in which accession would come up only when member states are actually ready for it. In her analysis, focus is more on the supply side of conditionality and the problems that are associated with the manner in which conditionality is applied by the EU. However, she also drew attention to the need to examine how conditionality is received by the candidate countries and what drives its reception and implementation.

Schimmelfennig and Sedelmeier (2005b: 10–17) analysed the actual influence of conditionality on the policy-makers of candidate countries. According to their

---

3   For example, respect for human dignity, freedom, democracy, equality, the rule of law and respect for human rights of persons belonging to minorities.

4   The Copenhagen criteria consists of three parts as political criteria (stability of institutions guaranteeing democracy, the rule of law, human rights and respect for and protection of minorities), economic criteria (the existence of a functioning market economy as well as the capacity to cope with competitive pressure and market forces within the Union) and adoption of EU *acquis* (ability to take on the obligations of membership including adherence to the aims of political, economic and monetary union).

5   For Helsinki criteria see paragraphs 4 and 7 of the Helsinki European Council Presidency Conclusions.

6   See paragraph 25 of the Luxembourg European Council Presidency Conclusions.

external incentives model[7] which is based on rationalist institutionalism, 'size and speed of rewards', 'credibility of conditionality' and the 'size of domestic adoption costs' are the most critical independent variables (or mediating factors) in explaining the dependent variable, which is 'rule adoption'. In other words, how conditionality is received by the candidate country will be a function of the interaction between these factors. Schimmelfennig and Schwellnus (2006) pointed out with a reference to the external intensives model that conditionality is effective – in other words, commitment of the conditionality recipient is higher – if the benefits (for example, the prospect of financial and institutional rewards by the EU) are sufficiently conditional, determinate, credible and high that they exceed the domestic costs of compliance with EU conditions.[8]

The study by Schimmelfennig, Engert and Knobel (2005: 33) on political conditionality showed that the 'credibility of threats and rewards is a core prerequisite of any effective bargaining process' even if this cannot on its own explain the success of conditionality. They underlined that a credible and conditional membership perspective is a necessary, although it may not be sufficient factor for the adoption of initially contested political rules and regulations. Conditionality cannot work effectively without credibility which means both the promise of membership, which will actually be wielded if the rules are adopted and the threat of exclusion from the accession if the rules are not adopted.[9]

If candidate countries are provided with determinate and credible membership conditionality, the external incentives model argues that the size of domestic adoption costs and their distribution among domestic actors determine if they will accept or reject conditions (Schimmelfennig and Sedelmeier 2004: 674). In order to have influence, the EU needs to have domestic allies in target countries. In other words, the preferences of the government and those of other 'veto players' are a mediating factor of the effectiveness of conditionality at the domestic level. The costs of adopting and implementing EU rules for target governments and other veto players must not be prohibitively high. In this model difficulty for a significant change of the *status quo* increases not only with the number of veto players but with the number of veto players with significant net costs of rule adoption (Schimmelfennig and Sedelmeier 2004: 674–5).

---

7   For a comparison between 'external incentive model', which is based on rationalism, and 'social learning model', which is based on social constructivism, please see Chapter 11 in this volume.

8   This is a rationalist bargaining model in which the actors involved are assumed to be strategic utility-maximisers interested in the maximisation of their own power and welfare. Actors involved exchange information, threats and promises and the outcome of the bargaining process depends on their bargaining power.

9   This definition of 'credibility' belongs to Schimmelfennig and Schwellnus (2006: 3).

Democratic Change in Turkey

Turkey applied for full membership to the then European Community in 1987. The application was not welcome due to Turkey's problems in its democracy, inadequate human rights records and its economic problems. The Commission emphasised Turkey's eligibility for membership in its *Avis*, but it did not present any motivating incentives to Turkey. The relations were redirected from membership perspective towards association path in the framework of the association agreement of 1964. Accordingly, the Customs Union between Turkey and the EU came into effect by 1 January 1996. In the 1997 Luxembourg European Council, Turkey was again granted candidacy status although the other applicants from Central and Eastern Europe were declared as candidates for EU membership. Although the eligibility of Turkey for membership restated, the European Council did not again present a motivating incentive like candidacy status.

The 1999 Helsinki Summit was a turning point for the relations in this respect. Turkey was declared as a candidate on the basis of the same criteria as applied to the other candidate states. Whereas a membership perspective was already included in the association agreement, it only became more concrete when the EU granted Turkey candidacy status at this summit. As in the case of CEECs, Turkey was promised that screening process would be opened and accession negotiations would begin as soon as it performed the Copenhagen political criteria. Thus the Helsinki Summit provided pressure for a series of radical reforms regarding Turkey's compliance with the Copenhagen political criteria. As a candidate state destined to join the Union, Turkey had to sufficiently meet the Copenhagen political criteria for the next step towards membership, namely the opening of accession negotiations. With its recognition as a candidate state in 1999, the EU introduced a strict conditionality mechanism and linked the improvement of Turkey's institutional ties with the EU to compliance with the Copenhagen political criteria . In other words, the declaration of its candidacy status, which offers a credible membership perspective, constituted an important incentive for Turkey to transform its democracy. Indeed, an extensive political reform process to redress shortcomings *vis-à-vis* the Copenhagen political criteria started to take place in Turkey: Firstly, the coalition government formed by Democratic Left Party (DSP), Motherland Party (ANAP) and Nationalist Action Party (MHP) approved constitutional amendments in 2001 and three harmonisation packages in 2002. The new government formed by Justice and Development Party (AKP) after the elections on 3 November 2002, followed this trend of reforms and adopted four more harmonisation packages in 2003 and two in 2004.

After the Helsinki Summit, the EU actively stimulated these reforms through the publication of its Accession Partnership Document (APD), which was announced in November 2000 and approved by the December 2000 Nice European Council. Just like the other APDs with the other candidate countries, the APD for Turkey constitutes the key instrument of the pre-accession strategy. It identifies short- and medium-term priorities aimed at the transformation of Turkey in line with the Copenhagen criteria. The APD, through which a road map was drawn up to prepare Turkey for EU membership, has been updated periodically by taking into consideration the progress that Turkey makes in the process of its candidacy. In response to the APD for Turkey, the Turkish government prepared 'the Turkish National Programme for the adoption of the *acquis*', which was submitted to the European Commission in March 2001. This was a major attempt to express how Ankara intended to perform the political and economic requirements laid out in the APD. Turkey's democratisation accelerated with these steps, which set the political ground for the reforms. The short-term incentive of the opening of accession negotiations was clear and credible.

Since then, Turkey has concentrated on the political aspects of the National Programme and taken a number of significant steps to address the EU's concerns during the period of 2001–2004. Firstly, an extensive and sweeping series of amendments particularly in the areas of democracy and human rights were made to the 1982 Turkish Constitution in October 2001.[10] The constitutional reforms, *inter alia*, included the shortening of pre-trial detention periods, a limitation on use of the death penalty to times of war or to imminent threat of war together with terrorist crimes, changes that made the prohibition and dissolution of political parties more difficult, an expansion of freedom of association, the strengthening of civil authority in the National Security Council and the abolition of Article 15 of the Constitution, which had banned the constitutional review of acts passed during the National Security Council regime established after the 1980 *coup* (Aydın-Düzgit and Keyman 2004: 15).[11] After the constitutional amendments, the new Civil Code entered into force in January 2002. It introduced significant changes in the areas of gender equality, protection of children and vulnerable persons and established new practices and institutions in Turkish Law, such as pre-nuptial contracts for the management of family assets (Aydın-Düzgit and Keyman 2004: 15). These amendments were followed by harmonisation laws designed with a view to not only converting the constitutional amendments into concrete action by bringing Turkish laws in line with the *acquis communautaire* but also introducing further reforms particularly in the areas of human rights, protection of minorities, freedom of expression and freedom of association.

The impressive measures relating to the first constitutional reform package in October 2001 and the first three harmonisation packages were engineered by a relatively weak coalition government of three different political orientations.[12] A number of critical areas, which were contested between the EU and Turkey, such as the abolition of the death penalty, the extension of cultural rights of minorities and the role of the military in Turkish politics, were on the agenda. Although

---

10   The first constitutional reform package includes 34 constitutional amendments.

11   See also Leyla Boulton (2001).

12   This coalition government was formed by the ultra-nationalist MHP, the nationalist-leftist DSP and the liberal centre-right ANAP.

the coalition government was clearly fragmented on these sensitive issues,[13] the Turkish Parliament, on 3 August 2002, abolished the death penalty, increased civilian representation in the National Security Council and granted the right to minority groups to be educated in their mother tongue and to broadcast in it (Eralp 2004: 80). These radical legislative changes on the democratisation front surprised most observers.

On the eve of the Copenhagen European Council in December 2002, these radical decisions paved the way in Turkey for a strong expectation regarding declaration of a date by the EU for the opening of accession negotiations by the end of April 2004 at the latest. The decision taken by the December 2002 Copenhagen European Council did not meet Turkey's expectation regarding a direct date for the launching of accession negotiations and led, at the beginning, to an important sense of disappointment on the Turkish side. However, it also fostered the sense of certainty in EU-Turkey relations by including a date, even indirect. The certainty and perceived strength of conditionality regarding that accession negotiations can be opened only if the Copenhagen political criteria are sufficiently fulfilled overcame the feeling of disappointment and paved the way to the acceleration of efforts of the government in the democratisation process. Indeed, the new government, which rationally wanted to reap the political benefits of the opening of accession negotiations, displayed a determined attitude to satisfy the political criteria.

The Turkish Parliament continued to address the EU's concerns in the areas of democratisation and human rights, between January 2003 and the end of 2004, with the adoption of six legislative reform packages aimed at improving the most-criticised aspects of the Turkish democracy, such as limits to freedom of speech and expression, freedom of association, torture and ill-treatment and the strong influence of the military on domestic politics. The parliament also abolished the provision that had allowed the nomination of a member of the High Audio-Visual Board by the Secretariat-General of the National Security Council. In addition to the two constitutional reform packages in October 2001 and in May 2004[14] and nine legislative reform packages between 2001 and the end of 2004, Turkey adopted, in September 2004, a new Penal Code which has positive effects on a number of areas

---

13   The two dominant parties of the coalition government, the DSP and the MHP, which were both characterized by a heavily nationalistic outlook, resisted the political reforms demanded by the EU in these sensitive areas. Only ANAP, a minor member of the coalition government, appeared to be more supportive of the EU-related reform agenda (Keyman and Öniş 2004: 183).

14   The second constitutional reform package in May 2004, which includes ten constitutional amendments, addresses a number of issues related to democracy and human rights: eradicating all remaining death penalty provisions; strengthening gender equality; broadening freedom of the press; aligning the judiciary with European standards and establishing the supremacy of international agreements in the area of fundamental freedoms over internal legislation.

related to human rights, particularly women's rights, discrimination and torture. A new Press Law in June 2004, a Law on Compensation of Losses Resulting from Terrorist Acts in July 2004, a new Law on Associations in November 2004 and a new Code of Criminal Procedure in December 2004 were also adopted. A number of regulations were also issued by the authorities in order to enable the implementation of legislation (European Commission 2004: 187). As a result, all these important measures in the form of constitutional and legislative reform cumulatively paved the way to the European Council decision for the opening of accession negotiations.

Since the EU was convinced that Turkey had sufficiently satisfied the Copenhagen political criteria, the European Council decided in its Brussels Summit of December 2004 to open accession negotiations with Turkey on 3 October 2005. The EU welcomed the decisive progress made by Turkey in its far-reaching reform process both in the Presidency Conclusions of the Brussels Summit and in the Negotiating Framework Document, which was prepared and issued on 3 October 2005 in the same line with the conclusions of this summit. However, it also underlined that this process was not completed and had to be sustained by Turkey. Additionally, it emphasised its expectation regarding Turkey's efforts to consolidate and broaden legislation and implementation measures specifically in relation to the zero tolerance policy in the fight against torture and ill-treatment and the implementation of provisions relating to freedom of expression, freedom of religion, women's rights, ILO standards including trade union rights, and minority rights.[15]

Effectiveness of Political Conditionality in Turkey's Europeanisation Process

Turkey's Europeanisation under the influence of the EU's political conditionality or, in other words, effectiveness of political conditionality can be analysed in two succeeding periods as the period between 1999 and the end of 2004, when radical reforms took place, and the period after the opening of accession negotiations until recently, when the performance of Turkey regarding democratic transformation has dramatically decreased. The chapter explains this differentiation in the performance of Turkey with the varied application, and therefore, effectiveness of conditionality by the EU. External incentives model of Schimmelfennig and Sedelmeier (2004, 2005b) helps one to understand and explain the radical transformation that Turkish democracy went through during the former period and the shift to the drastic slowdown in the transformation process during the latter period. At the international level the critical condition or facilitating factor of this model is 'credibility' of EU conditionality. It is a necessary, albeit may not be sufficient, factor for an effective conditionality in adopting initially contested political rules and regulations. Since this critical factor has been undermined after

---

15   See European Council (2004) and Council of the European Union (2005).

the opening of accession negotiations, the capacity of conditionality to induce rule adoption has been greatly weakened. In other words, incredible conditionality has negatively influenced the cost-benefit calculation of Turkish policy-makers who are responsible for the assessment of whether domestic costs of compliance with EU conditions exceed the benefits. This, in turn, led to the process of Europeanisation in Turkish democracy and changes to the human rights regime slowing down.

Size, clarity and credibility of the incentive, which have proven to be central to the effectiveness of the EU conditionality, have varied over time in the Turkish case as in the case of former Central and East European candidates.[16] The credibility of membership promise was low during the association relationship in the framework of the Ankara Agreement. Although the Agreement mainly depends on a customs union, it envisages closer and deeper economic integration than only a free movement of goods. More importantly, Article 28 of the Agreement states the possibility of Turkey's membership and, therefore, has an ultimate membership objective. However, this did not provide a certain membership perspective since it just says that 'whenever Turkey can fully assume the membership obligations, the possibility of its accession will be examined'. The 1993 Copenhagen European Council did not even mention Turkey's membership in spite of its long-lasting associate country status and its membership application in 1987 while it decided in favour of Eastern enlargement in principle without membership applications being made by the countries concerned yet. Again in 1997 Luxembourg European Council Turkey was not granted candidacy status while all the other applicants from Central and Eastern Europe were declared as candidates and accession negotiations were decided to open with some of these countries.

In the pre-Helsinki period the EU's criticisms regarding Turkey's human rights violations and anti-democratic practices could not be sufficiently effective in improving Turkey's democracy and human rights records. Turkey made just some amendments to the 1982 constitution and a number of legal codes[17] in order to consolidate its democracy under the influence of the Customs Union incentive. The EU's stance in respect of Turkey's desire for membership remained unclear. It neither totally excluded Turkey from Europe nor provided a clear membership perspective. The EU did not provide a clear democratisation programme in line with which Turkey could have realised necessary political reforms although its institutions, particularly the European Parliament, made progress in EU-Turkey relations conditional on improvement in Turkey's democracy and human rights situation. The EU's conditionality during this period was not clear and certain which decreased its own effectiveness. Just the Agenda 2000 and the first Regular Report in 1998 provided some degree of clarity about what the EU's demands

---

16   See Frank Schimmelfennig and Guido Schwellnus (2006) regarding how size and credibility of the incentive varied over time in the case of former Central and East European candidates.

17   Turkey made some changes to Article 8 of the Anti-Terror Law and the Criminal Procedure Code and the Association Law.

were. But the Turkish decision-makers did not take these demands seriously since they did not see the light at the end of the tunnel (Usul 2011: 97–9, 104).

Effectiveness in 1999–2005 Period

After the 1999 Helsinki Summit at which Turkey's membership application was clearly accepted, EU-Turkey relations gained 'certainty'. From 1999 onwards a fully-fledged credible accession conditionality was in place since the EU on the one hand decided to give candidacy to Turkey (and therefore provided a full membership perspective to Turkey) and on the other hand did not open accession negotiations with Turkey on the grounds of non-compliance with the Copenhagen political criteria. This credibility has forced the political and state actors to focus on democracy, since candidate country status required Turkey to comply with the Copenhagen political criteria[18] with a view to getting to the next stage of the accession process.

Indeed, Turkey experienced an unprecedented transformation process in its history in terms of political criteria. Before 1999 it was difficult even to imagine that Turkey would improve its democracy as much as it could start accession negotiations with the EU. Certainly, the EU's political conditionality has played a vital role in this transformation. In other words, the condition of complying with the Copenhagen political criteria in order to launch accession negotiations was central to the packages of reforms that were adopted. Some leading EU officials and politicians like Gunter Verheugen, the commissioner responsible for enlargement, and Romano Prodi, the president of the European Commission, persuaded Turkish policy-makers that if the conditions were met accession negotiations would indeed start. As Sinem A. Açıkmeşe pointed out, the EU seemed to be committed to Turkish accession, member states were not designing alternatives to EU membership (which means an intra-EU consensus on rewarding compliance) and Turkey did not relatively perceive double standards in the application of accession criteria and strategies (2010: 141). Turkish policy-makers also believed that Turkey would receive the reward only if it indeed fully met the requirements. This credible and certainly conditional incentive induced policy-makers to take radical steps towards Turkey's democratic transformation.

Another important point regarding the post-Helsinki period is that political reforms did not take place immediately after the 1999 Helsinki decision which was, as pointed out by Nathalie Tocci (2005: 76), initially mainly a symbolic, albeit important, gesture. Turkey had waited for the formal framework to be created and therefore the candidacy process to acquire more tangible characteristic by 2001 with the adoption of Turkey's Accession Partnership as a road map for accession and the increase in EU financial assistance. Indeed the 2001 constitutional amendments

---

18   The EU has set political criteria in the fields of democracy and human rights, which are not part of the *acquis*, but nonetheless were regarded as the *conditio sine qua non* for the opening of accession negotiations and finally membership itself.

which constituted the breaking point in the democratic transformation process and the first reform package which paved the way towards eight other packages were agreed shortly thereafter. This situation is an important indicator of how important and functional is certainty and credibility of the conditionality for consolidating the Turkish democracy. The more the EU is committed to accession, the more credible its conditionality is and therefore the more effective it is in transforming Turkish democracy. 'This commitment is only apparent in time-tables, calendars, temporal rules, roadmaps etc. in which candidacy, start of negotiations as well as their progress and final destination of membership are designated' (Açıkmeşe 2010: 138).

Regarding domestic level, external incentives model specifies size of domestic costs of compliance with EU rules and their distribution among domestic actors as mediating factors that mediate the EU's influence. If governments expect benefits in domestic politics from adopting and implementing EU rules then domestic adoption costs (or costs of compliance) are low. This was the case for the AKP government during the first period after the Helsinki Summit since EU rules regarding greater religious freedoms and civilian control over the military were parallel to its preferences. The AKP appeared as the political party that displayed a strong commitment to the EU accession and political reforms that was not apparent in the case of any other political party on either the right or the left wing.[19] It claims to be a moderate, centre-right party different from its 'Islamic' predecessors (the Welfare Party and the Virtue Party). To support this claim it has advocated not only religious freedoms but also personal freedoms in other areas. Accordingly, it may be argued that influence of EU conditionality on successful Turkish compliance with EU democratic rules in the first period was also mediated by a liberally-oriented government whose costs of complying with the EU's demands are not prohibitively high. However, it is obvious that without a credible EU membership incentive the government would not have been able to realise the reforms reflecting its liberal preferences in the existing Turkish domestic political setting. Therefore, the EU's conditionality played a causal role in Europeanisation of Turkish democracy. As Kıvanç Ulusoy (2008: 60) rightly pointed out, 'without a clear membership prospect, properly designed incentive structures and a time schedule tied to that, the hands of the reformist forces are extremely weakened'.

Evidently, even during the period of the coalition government which were heavily characterised by a nationalist position with the two dominant nationalist parties (the nationalist-rightist MHP and the nationalist-leftist DSP) and a minor liberal centre-right party (ANAP) even for which a significant gap may be specified between the leader and the rank and file of the party regarding the EU-related reforms, impressive measures relating to the constitutional amendments in October 2001 and the first three harmonisation packages were endorsed. The reforms regarding the abolition of capital punishment and an essential extension

---

19   The AKP government's commitment to the EU membership process and democratic reforms can be explained by both its interests and ideology. For these interest and ideology-related explanations see Nathalie Tocci (2005: 80).

of cultural rights for minorities, which would have been unimaginable only a few years ago, became a reality in August 2002 with direct implications for the Turkish citizens of Kurdish origin (Keyman and Öniş 2004: 185). This fact is another indicator of the causal role of strongly credible conditionality in the Turkish case even in the absence of low political costs of compliance for the coalition government as a mediating (or facilitating) factor.

Both in the case of the coalition and of the AKP, the government were convinced that the benefit (getting to the next stage on the way towards membership or, more correctly, membership perspective which is clear and credible) would be more than the political and the economic costs of compliance with the political conditionality. The credibility of the EU's sanctions and rewards also deeply influenced the Turkish public opinion, parts of the civil society and the market. This generated additional pressure on the government to break its resistance to the adoption of important reforms in politically quite costly areas like abolition of capital punishment, broadcasting and education in minority languages, decriminalising adultery (Kirişçi 2007: 6).

In view of rationalist approach to international socialisation effectiveness of conditionality depends not only on preferences of government but also those of other veto players whose agreement is necessary for a change in the *status quo* (Schimmelfennig and Sedelmeier 2004: 674). Some domestic conditions which were favourable during this period also contributed to veto players' (including the government's) preferences particularly in the above-mentioned politically sensitive areas to take part in line with the EU's demands. In other words, the number of veto players with significant net costs of compliance was significantly low. For instance, in the case of the abolition of capital punishment Turkey already had a moratorium in its application since 1987 and in the case of the extension of cultural rights (broadcasting and education in mother tongue) to Kurdish people the Kurdistan Workers' Party (PKK), in the early part of 1999, had abandoned armed conflict.

Effectiveness in the Period after the Opening of Accession Negotiations

From the opening of negotiations a massive reversal occurred in EU-Turkey relations and this situation has negatively influenced transformation of Turkish democracy. Support of the Turkish public for EU membership has drastically and unprecedentedly fallen.[20] The Turkish government seemed to lose its commitment and drive in support of reforms. Turkey has entered a process which is difficult to reconcile with a candidate country that is in the stage of accession talks where rule adoption and implementation regarding political criteria are critical. For example, the accusation and conviction of journalists and intellectuals for expressing their

---

20   According to the Fall 2008 Eurobarometer survey, only 42% of Turkish citizens supported Turkish accession as a good thing (−7 points since summer 2008; −19 points since 2005).

opinions; widespread accounts of excessive use of force, torture and ill-treatment on arrest and while being held in police custody and overly broad and vague anti-terrorism laws[21] that have resulted in countless unfair trials and prosecutions of those expressing peaceful dissenting opinions as well as recent plans by the government to curb abortion which will amount to a virtual ban and restrict women's rights[22] are all incompatible with the Copenhagen political criteria.

During this period the Turkish public and policy-makers have perceived that certainty regarding the realisation of eventual membership has severely weakened. This is not only because of the fact that the negotiations constitute a long and difficult process that necessitates compliance with not only the political criteria but also all of the Copenhagen criteria. But, more importantly, the policies of the EU towards Turkey have led to decrease in trust regarding ultimate membership in Turkey towards the EU. The negative nature and content of the discourse on Turkish membership which reflect the historical Turco-sceptic ideas in some of the member states like Austria, France, the Netherlands and Denmark have also contributed to the loss of trust.

Considering the previous enlargements of the EU, an accession process once it started was always completed with membership unless candidate countries themselves chose not to join the EU. For example, the membership perspective of the lastly acceding countries was never questioned. The European credentials of these countries were never in question. Studies of Europeanisation of these countries have been based implicitly or explicitly on the premises that these countries would one way or another eventually become members of the EU (Kirişçi 2007: 2). A similar situation is also true for Croatia which is set to become the 28th member of the EU on 1 July 2013 and Iceland with which the EU started the accession negotiations on 27 July 2010.

However, the situation for Turkey is different. It is widely known from the surveys which are regularly run by Euro-stat and a number of other agencies that a high proportion of European public opinion is against Turkish membership. The prospect of Turkish membership has led to a debate in which a noisy group of political figures particularly from Christian Democratic or Conservative parties in Europe resists ultimate membership due to Turkey's different culture and religion.

---

21   The Turkish Parliament has made amendments to anti-terrorism laws and therefore ended the prosecution of children under these laws solely for taking part in demonstrations. Amendments to the law mean that all children previously convicted under anti-terrorism legislation will have their convictions quashed. However, the new law will not prevent the prosecution of adult demonstrators under anti-terrorism laws allowing unfair trials of people aged 18 and over to continue.

22   The government is reportedly working on legislation to ban the operation after 4 weeks from conception, except in emergencies. Abortion is presently legal in Turkey up to 10 weeks from conception. Gynecologists agree that most women don't learn they are pregnant until after four weeks since it is difficult medically to determine pregnancy during that period.

The constant emphasis on *cultural and regional differences* and a *privileged partnership* instead of full membership generated a general belief in Turkish public onion that the EU is a *Christian Club* and that Turkey will not become a member whatever it does. On the other side, some other EU actors have, in relation to the Turkish accession, stated their concerns which are non-Copenhagen criteria-based concerns like Turkey's size, demographic growth and level of economic development reflecting the concerns over Turkish immigration to the EU countries, and its location as neighbour of the unstable regions. This ongoing debate on the desirability of Turkey's accession is naturally perceived by the Turkish government as the lack of a clear, credible and consistent EU conditionality which reduces the perceived value of the promised rewards (Tocci 2005: 77).

The credibility of the membership regarding whether it will actually be wielded has decreased also due to the EU policies such as linking accession to some other issues like Cyprus, which cannot be solved just by Turkey's effort. Indeed, the Cyprus issue which is not directly related to the Copenhagen criteria has almost blocked the course of the accession negotiations since the European Council decided in December 2006 that the negotiation chapters relating to the operation of the customs union between the EU and Turkey would not be opened and no chapter would be provisionally closed until Turkey performed the requirements regarding the extension of the customs union to the new members. The agenda of the EU-Turkey relations which has been heavily occupied by the problem of opening of Turkish sea ports to Greek Cypriot vessels and Turkish airspace to Greek Cypriot air carriers shows that the reward is made dependent on compliance with specific conditions. That the EU has stressed some other issues other than the Copenhagen criteria also shows that its conditionality has weakened. The Turkish side has started to think that compliance with the political conditions will not play a relevant role for the enlargement decision of the EU. This weak conditionality has tempted Turkey to avoid not only economically but also politically costly reform process.

In the case of the former Central and East European candidates, Schimmelfennig argued that, the EU pursued a meritocratic policy of enlargement, that is, it invited those countries to enter into accession negotiations on the same political preconditions. It did not discriminate against individual countries due to their strategic, economic or cultural features (2004: 15). When it comes to the Turkish case, the public is highly convinced that Turkey is treated differently than the countries from the previous round of enlargement and the current candidate countries. The negotiating framework document, which is the governing document of accession negotiation process, has contributed to this mistrust since it includes an ambivalent provision regarding membership that was not explicitly used in the previous enlargement rounds: 'the negotiations are an open-ended process, the outcome of which cannot be guaranteed beforehand. ... if Turkey is not in a position to assume in full all the obligations of membership it must be ensured that Turkey is fully anchored in the European structures through the strongest possible bond.' The last statement of this provision regarding being anchored in the EU through the strongest possible bond has been perceived as an offer of a *privileged partnership* instead of full membership and has created high displeasure in political and state circles. Additionally, the fact that the document also includes a renewed emphasis on the EU's *absorption capacity* further aggravated the credibility problem. Although the absorption capacity had actually been part of the Copenhagen criteria, it had never been invoked until the question of Turkish membership. Moreover, inclusion of such a clause in the Negotiating Framework Document to be used as a justification for Turkey's rejection to the Union was perceived as a sign of unwillingness of the EU for Turkey's accession. The statements of the Document on the possibility of suspending the negotiations and the prospect of 'permanent' restrictions in areas such as agriculture, structural policies and free movement of persons for Turkey were again almost unique in the enlargement history of the EU (Açıkmeşe 2010: 146). That is why the document has been regarded as the evidence of double standards towards Turkey and of reluctance on the EU side for Turkish membership. This ever more stringent and non-meritocratic nature of accession negotiations combined with ambiguity about the end result of the negotiations has played an important role in loss of motivation on the part of Turkish domestic actors.

The EU, probably for the first time in the history of its enlargement, has come to the point of losing its credibility with respect to delivering the ultimate membership. Turkey as a candidate country with which the EU started accession negotiations constitutes a unique case in terms of uncertainty over eventual membership. This situation has negatively influenced cost and benefit analysis of the Turkish policy-makers. When calculating the size of adoption costs they have taken into consideration the fact that ultimate membership was in question. This, in turn, led to a drastic slowdown in the process of Europeanisation in Turkish democracy and human rights regime and, therefore, displays the ineffectiveness of the political conditionality in ensuring adoption and implementation of the EU rules and regulations.

The Turkish policy-makers have finally begun to doubt that the EU is capable or willing to give the eventual reward even if conditions are complied with. That is why concentration and commitment of the Turkish government on the political criteria has been lost although the reform process regarding democracy and human rights has not yet been completed and has to be sustained.[23] This situation has also increased the number of veto players and strengthened the existing ones with significant costs of rule adoption and implementation. Due to the lack of a credible membership incentive the hands of genuinely reformist forces have been extremely weakened and, therefore, reforms have remained limited, superficial and more importantly on paper. Since the EU linked its conditionality to the Cyprus issue that always fosters nationalist sentiments as a sensitive question of the statehood, the military, political parties and even civil society organisations whose costs for

---

23   For the instances in which the government's lack of enthusiasm and commitment for the EU project was apparent see Açıkmeşe (2010: 146).

complying with EU conditionality increased have started to take a rather nationalist position and questioned legitimacy of the EU demands. '*The costs of compliance* involved in the Cyprus issue not only shaped the government's commitment to reform process to a certain extent, but also transformed the elitist positive stance towards the EU integration to a sceptical one' (Açıkmeşe 2010: 147).

The Problem of Implementation of the Adopted Norms

In addition to the slowdown of the reforms in terms of upgrading existing rules and legislation in line with the EU's norms Turkey also faced important problems particularly regarding implementation of the adopted norms. The 1995 Madrid European Council determined effective implementation of adopted rules through appropriate administrative and judicial structure as a critical element of membership conditionality. Transformation of domestic politics of a candidate country necessitates not just formal compliance as a show-off for obtaining membership, but also effective implementation of the adopted rules as well as the acceptance and internalisation of the adopted norms by society at large (Kubicek 2005: 362). Indeed the European Commission in its regular reports particularly highlighted the implementation problems of Turkey regarding the adopted norms.

The problem of implementation regarding the transferred norms in the Turkish case should not be explained just by the external incentives model. It needs also to be addressed in reference to the social learning model since, as Amichai Magen and Leonardo Morlino assume, only when *internalisation* gradually takes place the implementation which is relevant for democratisation actually takes place as well (2009: 41). Since most domestic actors in Turkey have not sufficiently internalised the adopted EU values and norms, they do not have motivation to implement them properly. Rules and norms that are adopted through social learning, in other words through internalisation, are much less contested domestically. Implementation is more likely to result in behavioural rule adoption and sustained compliance while external incentives lead to formal rule adoption as the least costly form of rule adoption. Rules and norms adopted under the influence of external incentives are more likely to suffer domestic resistance to be implemented in the absence of continued effective conditionality (Schimmelfennig and Sedelmeier 2004: 682).

In the same vein, Turkey has been suffering implementation problems regarding EU's democratic rules since it adopted those rules under the influence of membership incentive rather than social learning. Formal rule adoption motivated by membership incentive has caused domestic resistance and poor implementation in the absence of effective conditionality. The EU's democratic rules have not been able to be internalised through EU's persuasion or socialisation strategies. Turkey has been undergoing problems in the implementation of the formally adopted EU norms and values specifically in relation to the zero tolerance policy in the fight against torture and ill-treatment, freedom of expression, freedom of religion, women's rights, ILO standards including trade union rights, and minority rights.

Conclusion

On the eve of the European Council of December 2002, Turkish Prime Minister Recep Tayyip Erdoğan stated that 'Turkey anticipated getting a date from the European Union in December for the start of accession talks but even if the EU snubbed Turkey again, his government would rename the Copenhagen political criteria as *Ankara Criteria* and move on its reform drive' (Turkish Daily News 2004). This famous expression has been used many times by the prime minister, whenever Turkey faced restriction on its way towards EU membership. This expression led to the expectation that the Turkish government, seeing the membership process as an opportunity and a strong ground for the transformation of its domestic structure and democracy, would force itself to accelerate reforms regardless of whether the membership offered by the EU was credible or not. Indeed, in April 2007 the Turkish government on its own will, without any request by the European Commission, adopted a 400-page road map that sets out in detail the work and the timeline for completing Turkey's harmonisation process by 2013 (General Secretariat for the European Union 2007). The then Foreign Minister Abdullah Gül confirmed on the same date that reforms would be carried out regardless of the eventual entry to the bloc (*Euractiv* 2007).

However, all these expressions and steps, unfortunately, have not been able to make one argue that the role of a credible EU conditionality in Turkey's democratic transformation has decreased since after the opening of accession negotiations and until recently the performance of Turkey has dramatically weakened. During this period the only reforms which have contributed to Turkey's democratisation are some minor constitutional amendments in May 2007, launching by state television of a channel broadcasting exclusively in Kurdish on 1 January 2009, making amendments to anti-terrorism laws and therefore ending the prosecution of children under these laws solely for taking part in demonstrations on 25 July 2010 and the latest constitutional amendment package accepted by referendum on 12 September 2010.[24] It is obvious that the Turkish government could not realise what it intended. The purpose has not succeeded because of the conditions of uncertainty over eventual EU membership. Having a more democratic regime itself has not become a more important incentive than membership. This long-term and more

---

24 As Bertil E. Oder (Chapter 4 in this volume) rightly posits, it is highly disputable whether its provisions amount to a real improvement in the fields of human rights protection and democratisation in Turkey or, in other words, whether there is proper replacement of anti-democratic provisions with real liberal-democratic values and instruments of constitutionalism although 2010 constitutional amendments are welcomed and regarded as 'a step in the right direction' in 2010 Regular Report on Turkey's Progress. The package has been severely criticised on the grounds that it would shrink the independence of the judiciary due to the provisions on reorganisation of judiciary including the Constitutional Court and Highest Council of Judges and Prosecutors in Turkey. For more information about the controversial constitutional amendment package see the same chapter.

abstract benefit could not lead to a more favourable cost-benefit calculation for the Turkish policy-makers. In other words, domestic costs of compliance with the EU political conditions exceed the benefit, which is being a more democratic country.

It can also be concluded that the recorded changes before the opening of accession talks are not attributable to the democratisation *per se*. The policy changes are not a natural result of the democratisation process in Turkey. If they were so, then they would continue to take place even in the absence of a credible EU conditionality during the period after the opening of accession negotiations. The chapter argues that democratisation took place within the context of Turkey's Europeanisation process through a credible and strong conditionality which combined with the favourable domestic conditions that led to a significantly low number of veto players with significant net costs of compliance. The policy changes are, for the most part, attributable to the political pressure coming from the EU. By the same token, when this political pressure has weakened and membership perspective has lost its certainty and credibility, along with the high number of veto players with significant net costs of compliance, Turkey's Europeanisation through political conditionality has decelerated.

The Turkish government started a democratic initiative to expand the cultural rights of the country's Kurdish minority. The objective of the government was to find a solution to the Kurdish problem through democratic measures, efforts and compromise. There has been a severe resistance both on the part of the major opposition political parties and on the part of different circles of the Turkish public. This initiative has been harshly criticised particularly by the two main opposition parties since they doubt that this issue can easily lead to ethnic separation in the country at the end. In the framework of this initiative the government has taken steps such as starting Kurdish broadcasts in state television, allowing languages other than Turkish to be spoken in prisons and establishing a Living Languages in Turkey Institution in Mardin University, easing passage at checkpoints in south-eastern Anatolia and lastly adopting a new law ending the prosecution of children under anti-terrorism laws solely for taking part in demonstrations. However, some of these initial measures, like the last one, have faced important resistance and suffered delay and most of them have been found insufficient for overcoming flaws in Turkish democracy. This situation has been aggravated by the restarted armed attacks of PKK with important number of casualties that increased strong resentment among Turkish society and therefore damaged the support for more reform on the Kurdish issue.

Furthermore, after winning the referendum on constitutional changes in September 2010, Erdoğan agreed to make the new constitution the focus of the legislative term started following 2011 parliamentary elections. Indeed, the *new constitution* issue became the main centrepiece in Turkish politics shortly after the elections. It is obvious that it will be a difficult process to draft a new constitution that matches Turkey's ambitions in the twenty-first century particularly in terms of democracy and good governance and, therefore, needs both support of broad circles in the society and a consensus in the Turkish parliament. Accordingly, speaker of the Turkish Parliament, Cemil Çiçek, organised a conference on 19 September 2011 to discuss the issue with a number of professors studying constitutional and public law, and then an inter-party Constitutional Reconciliation Commission consisting of three nominees from all political parties represented in the Parliament was formed to draft a new constitution, which will replace the problematic 1982 Constitution.

It is obvious that the domestic costs of compliance with the EU for those parts of political criteria will be quite high for Turkey and the Turkish policy-makers need a sufficiently high benefit in order to tackle those high costs. This benefit is actually nothing but a credible eventual EU membership. In that context, the messages of the EU institutions, particularly of the European Council about how the rest of the accession process would advance have a vital importance. Considering the last developments around a new constitution the government needs a credible and strong EU conditionality more than ever before.

References

Açıkmeşe, S.A. 2010. Cycles of Europeanisation in Turkey: the domestic impact of EU political conditionality. *UNISCI Discussion Papers* [Online], 23, May. Available at: http://www.ucm.es/BUCM/revistas/cps/16962206/articulos/ UNIS1010230129A.PDF [accessed: 5 August 2011].

Aydın, M. and Açıkmeşe, S.A. 2007. Europeanisation through EU conditionality: understanding the new era in Turkish foreign policy. *Journal of Southern Europe and the Balkans*, 9(3), 263–74.

Aydın-Düzgit, S. and Keyman, E.F. 2004. European integration and the transformation of Turkish democracy. *Centre for European Policy Studies*, EU-Turkey Working Papers, 2, August.

Boulton, L. 2001. Turkey approves reforms to ease curbs on human rights. *Financial Times*, 24 September.

Börzel, T.A. 2002. Pace-setting, foot-dragging and fence-sitting: member state responses to Europeanisation. *Journal of Common Market Studies,* 40(2), 193–214.

Council of the European Union. 2005. *Negotiating Framework Document*, Article 4, Luxembourg, 3 October. [Online]. Available at: http://www.abgs.gov.tr/ index.php?p=123&l=2 [accessed: 17 January 2009].

Eralp, A. 2004. Turkey and the European Union, in *The Future of Turkish Foreign Policy*, edited by L.G. Martin and D. Keridis. Cambridge: MIT Press, 63–82.

Ethier, D. 2003. Is democracy promotion effective? Comparing conditionality and incentives. *Democratisation*, 10(1), 99–120.

Euractiv. 2007. Turkey to adopt reforms even if EU-entry blocked. 18 April. [Online]. Available at: http://www.euractiv.com/en/enlargement/turkey-adopt-reforms-eu-entry-blocked/ article-163243 [accessed 11 February 2009].

European Commission. 2004. *Regular Report on Turkey's Progress Towards Accession*, SEC(2004) 1201 {COM(2004) 656 final} [Online]. Available at: http://ec.europa.eu/comm/enlargement/-report2004/pdf/rr_tr_2004_en.pdf [accessed: 24 December 2008].

European Council. 2002. *Presidency Conclusions*, Paragraph 19, 12–13 December. [Online]. Available at: http://www.consilium.europa.eu/uedocs/cms_data/docs/pressdata/../73842.pdf [accessed: 18 May 2009].

European Council. 2004. *Presidency Conclusions*, Paragraph 18, 16–17 December. [Online]. Available at: http://www.consilium.europa.eu/ueDocs/cms_Data/docs/pressData/en/ec/83201.pdf [accessed: 29 April 2005].

General Secretariat for the European Union. 2007. *Türkiye'nin AB Müktesebatı'na Uyum Programı 2007–2013* (Turkey's Programme for Alignment with the *Acquis* 2007–2013), 17 April. [Online]. Available at: http://www.abgs.gov.tr/index.php?p=308&1=2 [accessed: 9 September 2009].

Grabbe, H. 2002. European Union conditionality and the *acquis communautaire*. *International Political Science Review*, 23(3), 249–68.

Keyman, E.F. and Öniş, Z. 2004. Helsinki, Copenhagen and beyond: Challenges to the new Europe and the Turkish state, in *Turkey and European Integration: Accession Prospects and Issues*, edited by M. Uğur and N. Canefe. London and New York: Routledge, 173–93.

Kirişçi, K. 2007. *The Limits of Conditionality and Europeanisation: Turkey's Dilemmas in Adopting the EU Acquis on Asylum*. Draft paper for the panel on Immigration, asylum and supranational governance: Implications of Europeanisation at the EUSA Tenth Biennial International Conference, Montreal, 17–19 May. [Online]. Available at: http://aei.pitt.edu/7936/01/kirisci-k-08g.pdf [accessed 9 June 2009].

Kubicek, P. 2005. The European Union and grassroots democratisation in Turkey. *Turkish Studies*, 6(3), 361–77.

Major, C. 2005. Europeanisation and foreign and security policy: undermining and rescuing the nation state? *Politics,* 25(3), 175–90.

Morlino, L. and Magen, A. 2009. Methods of influence, layers of impact, cycles of change: a framework analysis, in *International Actors, Democratisation and the Rule of Law. Anchoring Democracy?* edited by A. Magen and L. Morlino. London and New York: Routledge, 1–25.

Pridham, G. 1999. The European Union, democratic conditionality and transnational party linkages: the case of Eastern Europe, in *Democracy without Borders* edited by J. Grugel. London and New York: Routledge, 59–75.

Radaelli, C.M. 2000. Whither Europeanisation? Concept stretching and substantive change. *European Integration Online Papers (EIoP)* [Online], 4(8).

Available at: http://eiop.or.at/eiop/texte/2000-008a.htm [accessed 29 May 2008].

Schimmelfennig, F. 2004. Strategic calculation and international socialisation: membership incentives, party constellations and sustained compliance in Central and Eastern Europe. Revised draft for *International Organisations* special issue on 'International Institutions and Socialisation in Europe'.

[Online]. Available at: http://www.mzes.unimannheim.de/projekte/typo3/site/fileadmin/-research%20groups/1/teamBreader/Schimmelfennig_Strategic%20calculation%20and%20-international%20soc%26.pdf [accessed: 7 July 2011].

Schimmelfennig, F., Engert, S. and Knobel, H. 2002. *The Conditions of Conditionality*. Paper to the Workshop 4: *Enlargement and European Governance*, ECPR Joint Session of Workshops, Turin, 22–7 March. [Online]. Available at: http://www.essex.ac.uk/ECPR/events/jointsessions/paperarchive/-turin/ws4/Schimmelfennig.pdf [accessed: 16 June 2009].

Schimmelfennig, F., Engert, S. and Knobel, H. 2005. The impact of EU political conditionality, in *The Europeanisation of Central and Eastern Europe*, edited by F. Schimmelfening and U. Sedelmeier. Ithaca and New York: Cornell University Press, 29–50.

Schimmelfennig, F., and Sedelmeier, U. 2004. Governance by conditionality: EU rule transfer to the candidate countries of Central and Eastern Europe. *Journal of European Public Policy*, 11(4), 669–87.

Schimmelfennig, F., and Sedelmeier U. 2005a (eds). *The Europeanization of Central and Eastern Europe*. Ithaca and New York: Cornell University Press.

Schimmelfennig, F. and Sedelmeier, U. 2005b. Introduction: conceptualising the Europeanisation of Central and Eastern Europe, in *The Europeanisation of Central and Eastern Europe*, edited by F. Schimmelfennig and U. Sedelmeier. Ithaca and New York: Cornell University Press, 1–28.

Schimmelfennig, F. and Schwellnus, G. 2006. *Political Conditionality and Convergence: The EU's Impact on Democracy, Human Rights, and Minority Protection in Central and Eastern Countries*. Paper to the CEEISA Conference, Tartu, Estonia, 25-27 June. [Online]. Available at: http://www.eup.ethz.ch/people/schwellnus/papers/Schimmelfennig_Schwellnus.pdf [accessed: 17 May 2010].

Sedelmeier, U. 2011. Europeanisation in new member and candidate states. *Living Reviews in European Governance* [Online], 6(1). Available at: http://www.livingreviews.org/lreg-2011-1 [accessed: 2 June 2011].

Spendzharova, A.B. 2003. Bringing Europe in?: the impact of EU conditionality on Bulgarian and Romanian politics. *Southeast European Politics*, 4(2–3), 141–56.

Smith, K.E. 2003. The evolution and application of EU membership conditionality, in *The Enlargement of the European Union*, edited by M. Cremona. Oxford: Oxford University Press, 105–40.

Tocci, N. 2005. Europeanisation in Turkey: trigger or anchor for reform. *South European Society and Politics*, 10(1), 73–83.

Turkish Daily News. 2004. 1 June. [Online]. Available at: http://www.turkishdailynews.com.tr/-archives.php?id=36629 [accessed: 23 February 2006].

Ulusoy, K. 2008. EU-Turkey, 2004–2008: democratisation, civil-military relations, and the Cyprus issue. *Insight Turkey*, 10(4), 51–76.

Usul, A.R. 2011. *Democracy in Turkey: The Impact of EU Political Conditionality.*
    London and New York: Routledge.
Whitehead, L. 1996. *The International Dimensions of Democratisation: Europe
    and the Americas.* Oxford: Oxford University Press.

Chapter 4

Turkish Constitutional Transformation and the EU: Europeanisation towards Constitutionalism?

Bertil Emrah Oder

Introduction

After one year of living with a major constitutional amendment package accepted by referendum in 12 September 2010, the Turkish political elite has focused on a new constitutional debate during parliamentary elections of 2011. The 2010 constitutional amendment package was submitted to the Parliament by members of the ruling party, the Justice and Development Party (AKP), and it was adopted in the national referendum by 58 per cent of the votes casted in a higher voter turnout (73 per cent). In 2010 Progress Report of EU Commission, 2010 constitutional amendments are welcomed and regarded as 'a step in the right direction' (European Commission 2010: 8). Majority votes favouring constitutional amendment have been interpreted as a reflection of public confidence for social and economic policies of the AKP government that none of the governments after 1983 provided in such an effective and supportive manner. In parliamentary elections of June 2011, AKP as the ruling political party has not only increased its share of popular vote to 49.9 per cent, but it has also received 327 seats in the Parliament which are very close to qualified majority prescribed by constitutional amendment threshold, i.e. 330 seats. Some of the political parties, especially People's Republican Party (CHP) representing central left, and Peace and Democracy Party (BDP) known as the pro-Kurdish political movement claimed during election campaigns that democratic deficit as regards rights and freedoms, plurality as well as checks and balances are to be eliminated by constitutional reforms. They have even submitted specific vision documents on prospective constitutional amendments just before the elections. AKP did not make its own document public before elections even though it made references to the constitutional dynamics in its political declaration on elections. Shortly after elections in June, constitution issue, which is in fact one of the most popular and beloved discussion matters in Turkish political and legal discourse after 1960s, is revisited. On 19 September 2011, the speaker of the Turkish Parliament organised a conference with a representative amount of professors including constitutional lawyers and some experts in public law who demonstrated interest in constitutional issues. Finally, on 19 October 2011 an Inter-

Party Constitutional Reconciliation Committee was convened to deal with the constitutional progress. Taking into account recent developments partly portrayed above, the following observations aim at delineating patterns of constitutional transformation in Turkey after 1983 and question whether Turkey represents a model of Europeanisation in the sense of respecting values of constitutionalism 'in the right direction'.

1982 Constitution and Emergence of the EU as an External Factor

The European Economic Community (EEC) as an external factor emerged in the constitutional debate for the first time in the making process of the 1982 Constitution. The Constitutional Committee of Advisory Assembly submitted a constitutional draft including a rule of exception as regards sovereignty in case of membership in international organisations (Oder 2006). That rule led to an intensive discussion in the Advisory Assembly where some of the members described such an exception as a 'foreign hypothec' while others suggested that such a rule is not necessary and it paves the way for misunderstandings. It was criticised that an exception would amount to weakening of sovereignty where international agreements would not be subject to national will and parliamentary review. However, the speaker of the Constitutional Committee and some other members defended the position that such a rule is just 'a provision for future' by which Turkey's accession to the EU will have a constitutional basis. The speaker, Orhan Aldıkaçtı, asserted that proposed rule guarantees the binding force of international agreements which have organs with supranational powers (Aldıkaçtı 1982: 61). At the end, upon initiation of opposing motions the proposal was rejected after a formal voting. Such a proposal and debate in the Advisory Assembly demonstrates that the Turkish constitution-making elite has a constitutional imagination for a future with the EU (at that time EEC) even shortly after the 1980 military intervention and under control of military authority. EU membership became a matter of constitutional dispute at that time even though there was no hope for accession. This reveals that Turkey's accession to the EU is the embedded desire of Turkish political imagination on the grounds of the Ankara Agreement. The rejection of the proposal in the Advisory Assembly does not mean that Turkey's accession was not supported, but perceptions as regards weakening sovereignty of people or parliament overwhelmed.

Constitutional Developments after 1983 and EU Impact: Chronology, Methodology and Implementation Patterns

The 1982 Constitution was approved in a national referendum on 7 November 1982 and promulgated in the Official Journal on 9 November 1982. Approval of 1982 Constitution provided that the president of the military authority, i.e. National

Security Council, was also automatically elected as state president for a seven year term of office. Parliamentary elections took place approximately one year after the constitutional referendum on 6 November 1983 and the National Security Council exercised legislative and executive functions in this one year interim period. After parliamentary elections and establishment of a Turkish Parliamentary Presidency, which is prerequisite for operation of parliament under Turkish constitutional law, the National Security Council was dissolved. However, members of the National Security Council were appointed to Council of State Presidency that was provided as a temporary constitutional body accompanying the state president for six years, i.e. an exit-guarantee for the military body and a reflection of military tutelage in democratic transition.

In years 1983 through 1987, no constitutional amendment was observed even though critics as regards the 1982 Constitution were voiced in the public and academic debate. The first constitutional amendment was provided in 1987 and in 1987–2011 17 constitutional amendment packages were accepted. Those packages amended or abrogated the overwhelming majority of substantive constitutional provisions. Chronology, methodology and contents of those amendment packages will be touched upon below. Nevertheless, as an early remark one significant aspect as regards constitutionalisation and Europeanisation in Turkey should be emphasised. Not only the 1982 Constitution, but also sub-constitutional rules implementing the 1982 Constitution in forms of laws, decrees having the force of laws, regulations and by-laws were also adopted under military ruling by the Advisory Assembly, National Security Council and Council of Ministers, which was established and functioned under control of the military authority. Numbers of such implementing rules are estimated at approximately 800 (Tanör and Yüzbaşıoğlu 2011: 487).[1] Those rules were adopted between 12 September 1980 and 7 December 1983. Until 2001 a specific provision of the Constitution, namely transitional article 15 of the Constitution provided that such sub-constitutional norms enacted under military regime but in fact implementing constitutional rules in an effective and direct manner are immune from allegations of unconstitutionality before the courts (judicial immunity). Even though there was no constitutional obstacle or ban as regards amendment or abrogation of those sub-constitutional rules, parliamentarian majorities were not willing to make major changes to them. They were confined to minor attempts compared to the amount and wide content of such rules, and including the AKP majority in Parliament, the legislative elite did not make an in-depth analysis or discussion for the total elimination of authoritarian heritage of the 1980 intervention in Turkey. This can be explained by the fact that such sub-constitutional rules including almost all major laws as regards political and social sphere, such as Political Parties Act, National Education Act etc., were empowering ruling parties as well as politics of power instead of politics of deliberation. Despite a certain amount

---

1   Dissenting opinion of Güven Dinçer, Constitutional Court, E. 1990/32, K. 1990/25, K.t. 16 October 1990, AYMKD 26, 443.

of discontent reflected by the political elite, sub-constitutional rules established by military intervention have also mostly reflected right wing political discourse which was dominant in Turkish political paradigm and reality. One could have the impression that those rules and their underlying logic were implicitly accepted as an optimum balance under Turkish circumstances without any explicit consensus and deliberation on the point. Even laws known as EU harmonisation laws which were adopted after the 2001 constitutional amendments as a piecemeal approach to democratic and constitutional consolidation have provided only a partial revision in sub-constitutional laws and in their well-established patterns of application. In spite of the fact that judicial immunity was provided for sub-constitutional rules of military intervention until 2001, a plea of unconstitutionality against those was claimed before the Constitutional Court in many occasions on the ground of methods of interpretation and constitutional supremacy which is prescribed in the Constitution explicitly (Article 11 of the Constitution). Unfortunately, majority voting in the Constitutional Court construed the judicial immunity in a strict sense and refused to review the contended sub-constitutional rules until 2001.[2] After 2001 the constitutional amendment judicial immunity clause was removed, but still it is not possible to observe an effective progress in favour of democratic consolidation despite accumulation of legal amendments in specific fields. Without taking into consideration such implementing rules and patterns in Turkey, neither depth nor proper application of Europeanisation and constitutionalisation in Turkey could be genuinely elaborated. This early remark will be kept in mind in the following observations on constitutional amendments in Turkey.

Chronology of Constitutional Amendments and EU Impact

On 14 April 1987 Turkey made its EU application for full membership and Prime Minister Turgut Özal defined Turkey's accession process and its full membership as 'a long, narrow and steep path'. Shortly after Turkey's application to accede to the European Union, the first constitutional amendment was accepted by parliament in May 1987 and it was approved through referendum in September

---

2   See especially Constitutional Court, E. 1990/32, K. 1990/25, K.t. 16 October 1990, AYMKD 26, 429; E. 1993/4, K. 1995/1, K.t. 19 July 1995, AYMKD 33/2, 623–4; E. 1999/19, K. 1999/12, K.t. 3 May 1999, AYMKD 35/2, 435; E. 1999/21, K. 1999/17, K.t. 12 May 1999, AYMKD 35/2, 441. However, in 1991 the Highest Administrative Court uphold the view that decrees issued by Council of Ministers under military authority (12 September 1980–7 December 1983) are subject to judicial review. As a result of this case-law, Council of Ministers' decrees and other administrative acts issued under military regime could be judicially reviewed while laws and decrees having the force of law enacted under military authority were immune from judicial review. See the Highest Administrative Court, E. 1990/1, K. 1991/1, *Resmi Gazete* (Official Journal), 18 June 1991, no.: 20905: İnsan Hakları Merkezi Dergisi (Journal of the Human Rights Center, İHMD), May-September 1991, I (2–3), 43–6.

1987. In the very same year Turkey also recognised the right for lodging an individual application before the European Commission of Human Rights (Tebliğ 1991). Even though this recognition could be regarded as a step forward in respect of the Europeanisation of Turkey, it should be emphasised that Turkey added a declaration to its document of recognition which in fact attempts to minimise the jurisdiction and interpretation of the European Commission of Human Rights.[3] Turkey's approach to recognition was disputed in Turkish academic circles claiming that it is null and void from procedural and material perspectives since parliamentary procedures required by the Constitution are by-passed and Turkey's declaration prescribes reservations incompatible with the nature and effectiveness of the European Convention of Human Rights (Çelik 1988, Toluner 1988, Çavuşoğlu 1991). Particularly, Turkey's declaration that 'democratic society' in the Convention shall be interpreted as provided in the Preamble and article 13 of the Constitution was a matter of extensive discussion since such an approach contradicts the autonomous interpretation of the Convention which also identifies European values determining European public order. Therefore, Turkey's attempt was Europeanisation in a reversed sense that tried to make Europeanisation 'nationalised' and in turn ineffective. However, the European Commission of Human Rights rejected the application of Turkey's declaration in respect of the Convention by referring to 'the character of the Convention as a constitutional

---

3   On 28 January 1987 the Government of Turkey deposited the following declaration with the Secretary General of the Council of Europe pursuant to Article 25 of the Convention: 'The Government of Turkey, acting pursuant to Article 25(1) of the Convention for Protection of Human Rights and Fundamental Freedoms, hereby declares to accept the competence of the European Commission of Human Rights to receive petitions according to Article 25 of the Convention subject to the following: (i) the recognition of the right of petition extends only to allegations concerning acts and omissions of public authorities in Turkey performed within the boundaries of the territory to which the Constitution of the Republic of Turkey is applicable; (ii) the circumstances and conditions under which Turkey, by virtue of Article 15 of the Convention, derogates from her obligations under the Convention in special circumstances must be interpreted, for the purpose of the competence attributed to the Commission under this declaration, in the light of Articles 119 to 122 of the Turkish Constitution; (iii) the competence attributed to the Commission under this declaration shall not comprise matters regarding the legal status of military personnel and in particular, the system of discipline in the armed forces; (iv) *for the purpose of the competence attributed to the Commission under this declaration, the notion of 'a democratic society' in paragraphs 2 of Articles 8, 9, 10 and 11 of the Convention must be understood in conformity with the principles laid down in the Turkish Constitution and in particular its Preamble and its Article 13*; (v) for the purpose of the competence attributed to the Commission under the present declaration, Articles 33, 52, and 135 of the Constitution must be understood as being in conformity with Articles 10 and 11 of the Convention. This declaration extends to allegations made in respect of facts, including judgments which are based on such facts which have occurred subsequent to the date of deposit of the present declaration. This declaration is valid for three years from the date of deposit with the Secretary General of the Council of Europe' (emphasis added).

instrument of European public order in the field of human rights' (ECHR 1991). It also emphasised common values and common understanding in the collective enforcement system of the Convention as regards observance of human rights dedicated to 'establishing a common public order of the free democracies of Europe' (ECHR 1991: par. 20). In other words, the European Commission of Human Rights put up a barrier to Turkey's minimal and manipulated application of the understanding of European human rights.

The 1987 constitutional amendment initiated after the recognition of individual complaint before the European Commission of Human Rights and Turkey's application for full membership in the EU was of specific importance as regards the abolishment of political bans for the elite of political parties banned immediately after the military intervention in 1980. In a higher voter turnout of 95 per cent, 50.16 per cent of the votes casted were in favour of abolishment of political bans for former political elite. Without any doubt such a result enhanced democratisation in Turkey since it strengthened ideological pluralism by inviting previous actors and their agenda to the political game which would amount to a democratic normalisation and consolidation in conformity with expectations of external dynamics including the EU.

However, some hidden features of the 1987 amendment are to be questioned from the perspective of sincere consolidation efforts and European 'ways of doing things'. The 1987 amendment was not confined to the abolishment of political bans, but also redefined constitutional amendment procedure in the same package. Moreover, it prescribed conditionality of referendum in a sense of 'compulsory referendum' for abolishment of political bans even though the original constitutional amendment procedure did only include voluntary referenda which could be initiated at the discretion of the state president if the first draft of the amendment was sent back to the parliament and parliament insisted on the first draft. In other words, for incidental case of political bans an application of compulsory referendum was stipulated in the package. Besides such an incidental approach, appropriateness of referendum as an instrument for recognition of rights and freedoms that are universally protected and guaranteed in conformity with the UN and European human rights documents was highly questionable even though the result was positive by 50.16 per cent of the votes casted. Similar concerns were indirectly voiced before the Constitutional Court in 1987. The Constitutional Court refrained from dealing with the arguments as regards unconstitutionality of compulsory referendum for political bans and refused the case on the grounds of inadmissibility by making a reference to its jurisdiction being limited to formal review of constitutional amendments.[4] Since there was only 75.066 votes between 'yes' and 'no' votes (50.16 per cent 'yes' and 49.84 per cent 'no'), the majority of the ruling party in parliament preferred to take the advantage of early elections in November 1987 after the referendum in September 1987 and came into power again.

---

4   Constitutional Court, E. 1987/9, K. 1987/15, K.t. 18 June 1987, AYMKD 23, 285–6.

To sum up, constitutional and Europeanisation developments of 1987 do not demonstrate a coherent, sincere, deliberate and dedicated approach of democratic consolidation and harmonisation with the values of European public order as cited by the European Commission of Human Rights. Despite its failures and ambivalences, the 1987 approach is the first step towards constitutionalisation after 1983 surrounded by the European perspective of the government even in an insufficient sense. The 1987 approach also understands and discerns certain features, both deficits and dynamics of Turkish democratic consolidation as well as Europeanisation efforts in the long term.

Following the 1987 amendments, constitutional transformation has been carried out at intervals of one to four years through minor or major packages accepted in 1993, 1995, 1999 (two different amendment packages), 2001 (two different packages), 2002, 2004, 2005 (two different packages), 2006, 2007 (two different packages), 2008, 2010 and 2011. Significant aspects, methodology and dynamics of those amendments that are deemed to be relevant for assessment of Europeanisation in Turkey were related to enhancing political participation (1995); changing the restriction dynamic of fundamental rights and freedoms, hardening disclosure of political parties and domination of civilian authority in the National Security Council by restructuring its composition (2001); acceptance of state obligation as regards realisation of *de facto* equality between men and women and elimination of constitutional references to the death penalty (2004); election of state president by popular vote for a five-year term of office and reelection of state president for a five-year term of office (2007); abolishing headscarf ban at higher education institutions (2008); restructuring judiciary and Constitutional Court with minor changes in fundamental rights and freedoms (2010) (Oder 2002, Gönenç 2004 and 2010, Örücü 2008 and 2011).

Comparing Drives and EU Impact

Taking into account dynamics and political surroundings of the constitutional amendment history of Turkey after 1987, comparative analysis of constitutional amendment packages from perspective of EU impact necessitates putting specific emphasis on four different packages, namely 1995, 2001, 2004 and 2010 amendments.

For 1995 an amendment package which eliminated expressions of justification provided for 1980 military intervention and restrictions prescribed for political participation, associations and civic engagement in daily political life, the EU perspective – in terms of establishment of Customs Union between EU and Turkey – could have had an implicit progressive impact (Müftüler-Baç 2005: 19). The package was discussed first in Inter-Party Constitutional Reconciliation Committee as a political platform which is not regulated by Rules of Procedure of the Parliament. In general reasoning of the amendment proposal, the European impact in the sense of EU-Turkey association law or in other forms such as obligations arising from the Council of Europe or case-law of the European Court of Human

Rights is not observed. The general reasoning refers to a need for a new constitution to be made and based on consensus among different political and societal layers. However, in the report of the Parliamentary Constitutional Committee, which is a standing committee explicitly prescribed by the Rules of Procedure of Parliament, there are European references as regards discussions of proposed amendments. For example, in respect of defining the authority of judges as regards suspension of activities of associations, Article 11 of the European Convention of Human Rights was cited and in turn suspension grounds are extended to national security and public order in emergency cases besides 'to prevent the perpetration or the continuation of a crime or to effect apprehension' (Article 33 paragraph 5 of the Constitution and TBMM 1995: 24). Here, the Convention served interestingly as a ground for extension of legitimate restrictions. Similar approach of analogy is also implemented for imposition of restrictions on the rights of armed forces and security force officials and civil servants 'to the extent that the duties of civil servants so require'. Again, as regards rejection of collective bargaining agreements for public servants – but acceptance of collective bargaining meetings for them which shall result in a 'memorandum of consensus' to be submitted to the discretion of the Council of Ministers for transformation to an administrative or statutory rule – the Constitutional Committee refers to 'applications of EU member states' (TBMM 1995: 25–6). It is also striking that the Constitutional Committee approved improvements for the abolishment of doubtful misuse clauses and restrictions for the right to strike, but those are not accepted in the plenary session by the Parliament. For example, the abrogation of prohibition as regards political strike and lock-out was suggested by the 1995 Constitutional Committee, but it has been removed recently through the 2010 amendments. Even though the 1995 Constitutional Committee also proposed the removal of misuse clause on strikes and lock-outs 'detrimental to society and damaging national wealth', this clause is still observed in the Constitution (TBMM 1995: 28). In respect of judicial immunity of sub-constitutional rules enacted under military authority, the Committee also supported the removal of this clause and the extension of judicial review. However, the proposal was not accepted in the 1995 process and real progress in this field is provided in the 2001 amendments (TBMM 1995: 40).

Beginning from the 2001 amendments, the 'misfit' between the EU and Turkish constitutional order became defined by referring to the Copenhagen political criteria: 'the stability of institutions guaranteeing democracy, the rule of law, human rights and respect for and protection of minorities'. On 25 September 2001 the General Assembly of the Turkish Parliament agreed by an overwhelming majority to discuss a proposal for a constitutional amendment. The Inter-Party Constitutional Reconciliation Committee which had experience as in case of the 1995 amendments prepared the draft proposal. The committee was again a purely political structure which did not fall under the scope of the Constitution and the Rules of Procedure of the Parliament. The Inter-Party Constitutional Reconciliation Committee deliberated the constitutional amendment for approximately two years. The first draft was made public on 25 May 2001 and it was defined as 'most radical constitutional package' in the past 19 years (*Radikal* 2001a: 7). For the initiation of the constitutional amendment process in Parliament, 288 MPs and leaders of the coalition parties submitted the final draft to the parliament on 5 September 2001 (*Radikal* 2001b:5). Civic society supported the amendment by various declarations. The major associations of employers and trade unions made a joint declaration on 23 September 2001. They reflected that the package would secure 'the contemporary standards of the civilized world, peace and freedom, and social progress' (*Sabah* 2001). With the exception of a few critics of 'insufficiency' (*Cumhuriyet* 2001: 8), the Turkish daily newspapers applauded the package and emphasised the expectations of Europeanisation. They stressed that the package represented 'the first constitution with a civic character' that could bring Turkey into line with the values common to the member states of the European Union (EU) (*Radikal* 2001: 10, *Hürriyet* 2001: 1). All television channels emphasised the long-term impact of the amendment, which expounded a new constitutional concept of fundamental rights and freedoms, and set out the significant features of the proposal. To sum up, the 2001 constitutional package was approved in plenary session by the Parliament on 3 October 2001 in a climate of political consensus.

The 2001 constitutional amendments included 34 articles, of which 24 relate explicitly to the protection of fundamental rights. The package is the most comprehensive one introduced after 1983 as regards paradigm shift for protection of rights and freedoms in Turkey and rethinking particular guarantees. Through the 2001 process, European impact is explicitly cited in the general reasoning of a constitutional amendment proposal as a co-determinate of legal and political transformation in Turkey. The general reasoning of the proposal refers to the need for amendment on the grounds of pressing social needs and expectations, and of new political perspectives (TBMM 2001). On the other hand, it regards the amendment as 'indispensable' to meet the economic and political criteria for full membership in the EU. The general reasoning aims to meet the needs of society through an amendment of the Constitution which emphasises human rights and the rule of law as well as 'contemporary democratic standards and universal norms'. It accepts that the constitutional amendment is considered as an essential prerequisite for further new legislation that is also inalienable in order to comply with the obligations arising from accession partnership with the EU. Those political commitments cited in the general reasoning were also in conformity with the passages from the 2001 Turkish National Programme for the Adoption of the *Acquis Communautaire*. Both gave the impression that Turkey is resolved to meet the obligations arising from the accession process in a serious manner and is establishing a constitutional basis to review its sub-constitutional norms. This impression is proved by the fact that Turkey adopted nine sub-constitutional packages called the EU Harmonisation Laws after the 2001 amendments between the years of 2002–2009 for implementation of constitutional amendments in line with democratic consolidation and liberal values of European public order (Örücü 2004, Müftüler-Baç 2005).[5]

Again in 2004, European references can be extensively observed in general reasoning of the proposal and specific reasoning of articles proposed. Here, the 2003 National Programme as a road map for meeting requirements of Copenhagen criteria, 2003 Council Decision on Accession Partnership, EU Charter of Fundamental Rights, EU Draft Constitutional Treaty, obligations arising from *Acquis Communautaire* and the 2003 Progress Report of the EU Commission are expressly cited in either general reasoning or specific reasoning of articles (TBMM 2004). The 2004 amendment package represents the richest document in terms of European references and direct inclusiveness of many different types of acts enacted by EU despite the fact that it is a small-sized package of reforms including among others especially *de facto* application of gender equality, the abolishment of constitutional basis for death penalty – even though Turkey did not ratify Protocol no. 13 of European Convention of Human Rights at that time – and priority of international agreements on fundamental rights and freedoms in case of their conflicts with ordinary laws.

The 2008 package was a constitutional attempt for dealing with the headscarf problem at higher education institutions. Its general reasoning referred to 'non-existence of a problem of headscarf at higher education institutions in none of the countries adhered to Council of Europe' (TBMM 2008). The package was supported by the ruling party AKP and two opposition parties, namely Nationalist Movement Party and Democratic Society Party. Counter-arguments of the CHP were also based on European argument that case-law of the European Court of Human Rights confirmed the ban as regards headscarves in Turkish context – on the ground of rights' of the others, status of women and history of religious state in Turkey where majority belongs to Muslim identity (TBMM 2008:14 *et seq.*).[6] The package was annulled by the Constitutional Court referring to case-law of the European Court of Human Rights where the ban of headscarves in higher education is regarded as a legitimate restriction meeting pressing social needs of a democratic society in Turkish context.[7] Therefore, it was within the scope of margin of appreciation of Turkish authorities. Here, it is observed that Europeanisation gained a new momentum in political and judicial discourse since it is defended by different actors to consolidate or legitimise their positions.

Taking into account the political context and domestic discussions, 2010 constitutional amendments are not EU driven. From the perspective of Europeanisation, 2010 amendments do not amount to a top-down approach where the EU's demand or requirements of European integration is the initiating factor,

---

5   *It is to be reminded that certain norms of EU Harmonisation Laws were challenged before the Constitutional Court in 2002. The Court rejected the plea of unconstitutionality, see E. 2002/146, K. 2002/201, K.t. 27 December 2002, AYMKD 39/1, 323.*

6   See especially *Leyla Şahin v. Turkey*, No. 44774/98, 29 June 2004.

7   Constitutional Court, E. 2008/16, K. 2008/116, K.t. 5 June 2008.

but rather an EU argument and in that vein the addition of certain clauses for protection of rights and freedoms have been successfully displayed by the ruling AKP party to balance the package which has intensive provisions on reorganisation of judiciary including the Constitutional Court and the Highest Council of Judges and Prosecutors in Turkey. Whether this approach is instrumentalisation of the EU for a more delicate and hidden agenda such as the controlling of judiciary or a bottom-up approach of Europeanisation in terms of initiation where a candidate state integrates European values of constitutionalism and pushes them without any effort and demands of European actors, could be determined by elaborating implementation patterns of the 2010 amendments. This will be undertaken below under the sub-heading on implementation patterns.

Even though the EU impact for the 2010 amendments is not the decisive or initiating factor, examination of the 2010 package's reasoning has references to elements of Europeanisation. In contrast with the 2001 amendment package neither the EU nor Europeanisation is mentioned in the general reasoning of the 2010 amendment package. However, in specific reasoning clauses of certain articles references to Europe or the EU could be found out as constitutional benchmarks or political requirements to be met in the short-term (TBMM 2010). For example, as regards the establishment of an Ombudsman as a constitutional institution, an explicit – but not detailed – reference to applications of 'European states' – not specifically EU member states – in specific reasoning of the relevant article is cited. Here, specific reasoning emphasises also Turkey's National Programme for the Adoption of *Acquis Communautaire* which undertakes the establishment of an Ombudsman. Turkey's National Programme is the counter legal and political document of Accession Partnership which makes the obligations of Turkey arising from its candidate state status. National Programme is enacted by Council of Ministers in the form of a decree promulgated in the Official Journal, and it provides a road map for implementation of Turkey's obligations as prescribed in the Accession Partnership as short-term and mid-term obligations. As regards abrogation of the constitutional clause on loss of MP status in case of permanent dissolution of an affiliated political party, a similar approach can be observed. The relevant constitutional clause stated that the MP whose statements and acts are cited in a final judgment by the Constitutional Court as having caused the permanent dissolution of his party shall lose her/his seat in the Parliament on the date when the Constitutional Court's judgment in question and its justifications are published in the Official Journal. However, the specific reasoning regards such an isolating sanction as an infringement of principle of proportionality and core of the right, while it mentions the case-law of the European Court of Human Rights on Turkey without citing the relevant case of *Ilıcak v. Turkey* explicitly.[8] Similar references can be observed in specific reasoning explanations in articles on political parties which are later eliminated from the package ('European state

---

8   See *Ilıcak v. Turkey*, No. 15394/02, 5 April 2007; see also *Kavakçı v. Turkey*, No. 71907/01, 5 April 2007; *Sılay v. Turkey*, No. 8691/02, 5 April 2007.

practices'; 'case-law of European Court of Human Rights'; 'opinion of Venice Commission on prohibition of political parties in Turkey'; 'democratic standards common to Europe') (TBMM 2010: 10–12).[9] As regards restriction of military justice ('Accession Partnership', 'EU Commission Progress Reports', '2008 National Programme'),[10] recognition of individual complaints procedure before the Constitutional Court ('decreasing the number of Turkish applications before European Court of Human Rights'; 'European states' adoption of individual complaint and Recommendation 2004 (6) Council of Europe')[11] and restructuring the Constitutional Court ('applications of European states') European references could be indentified in the specific reasoning of articles.

However, the report of the Parliamentary Constitutional Committee demonstrates that opponents of specific provisions of the amendment package had also recourse to the European references. This overseen aspect is probably the most interesting feature of the controversy as regards the 2010 amendments since it reveals that different understandings of constitutional democracy, Europe or Europeanisation defended by different sides coexist in Turkey. The report of the Parliamentary Constitutional Committee demonstrates that opposing members criticise the package by emphasising democratic deficit and inadequate or improper application of European standards. The members refer mainly to weakness of deliberative democracy and civic participation in preparation of package, self-centric and biased approach of the AKP ruling party, ignorance of rules developed by the Venice Commission for dissolution of political parties, keeping military judges in the composition of the Constitutional Court, inappropriateness of submitting a whole package to the referendum, inadmissibility of recourse to referendum for liberties since they are universal values not to be tested by majority (TBMM 2010: 24–40, 52, 58, 63–4).[12] In assessing the rules of package on Constitutional Court, it can be observed that opposing members emphasised the role of checks and balances in a constitutional democracy. By referring to

---

9   See also *Opinion on the Constitutional and Legal Provisions Relevant to the Prohibition of Political Parties in Turkey*, Opinion No. 489/2008, European Commission for Democracy through Law, Venice 13–14 March 2009, Strasbourg.

10   See, for example, *2008/157/EC: Council Decision of 18 February 2008 on the principles, priorities and conditions contained in the Accession Partnership with the Republic of Turkey and repealing Decision 2006/35/EC, OJ L 51, 26 Februray 2008, 4–18:* [under short-term priorities of Accession Partnership]: – 'limit the jurisdiction of military courts to military duties of military personnel'.

11   See also Council of Europe, *Recommendation Rec (2004)6 of the Committee of Ministers (COM) to member states on the improvement of domestic remedies* (adopted by COM on 12 May 2004, at its 114th Session).

12   See especially dissenting opinions of Faruk Bal, Behiç Çelik and Nevzat Korkmaz (MPs of Nationalist Movement Party), Atilla Emek, Mehmet Ali Özpolat, Atilla Kart, Şahin Mengü, İsa Gök (MPs of People's Republican Party) and Hamit Geylani (MP of Peace and Democracy Party).

European experiences in respect of appointment of constitutional judges, they put emphasis on risks as regards the election of constitutional judges by the Parliament without the absolute necessity of a qualified majority. They have proposed the application of qualified majority principle in Parliament to provide consensus on prospective constitutional judges. In discussions on the Highest Council of Judges and Prosecutors, it is highly remarkable that opposing members cited EU reports referring to the dominant role of the Minister of Justice in the Council as well as her/his extensive investigation powers (European Commission 2010: 14, European Commission 2007: 10, European Commission 2006: 9). Views of opposing members stressed deep concerns as regards politicisation of justice through the continuing presence of the Minister of Justice in the Council and her/his extensive powers. They have also criticised the fact that the government relies on the EU for amendments on judiciary even though such amendments contradict with the expectations of the EU, and universal standards to be achieved for independence and impartiality of justice. Opinions of the Consultative Council of European Judges and Budapest Guidelines[13] were also reference norms of opposition in discussions as to whether judiciary clauses of amendment package would serve the impartiality and well-functioning of justice and 'they would impair the rule of law' by ignoring 'universal rules cited previously' (TBMM 2010: 26).

Comparing Methodologies and EU Impact

Comparing methodologies of constitutional amendments avails discerning similarities and differences between preparation phases of packages. It is remarkable that Turkish constitutional amendment politics followed different approaches. Those are to be summarised as follows:

1. Packages were put forward by a group of initiators representing the ruling party majority in the Parliament without taking notice of possible impact or size of amendment and without prior consultation or deliberation among political actors and/or societal groups, such as in 2004 ('death penalty, international agreements on fundamental rights etc.'), 2007 ('election of state president by popular vote') or 2010 ('restructuring judiciary and constitutionalisation of certain rights as fundamental rights').

2. Packages were initiated by a group of political actors from different political parties who have implicitly reached consensus, but not deliberated the amendments explicitly and extensively, such as in 2002 ('removal of

---

13   See, for example, *Opinion no 1 (2001) of the Consultative Council of European Judges (CCJE) for the attention of the Committee of Ministers of the Council of Europe on standards concerning the independence of the judiciary and the irremovability of judges*, 23 November 2001, Strasbourg; The Budapest Guidelines, [Online], Available at: http://www.coe.int/t/dghl/cooperation/ccpe/conferences/cpge/2005/CPGE_2005_05LignesDirectrices_en.pdf (accessed: 5 October 2011).

certain limits for exercising political right to be elected as MP') and 2008 ('headscarf').

3. Packages were extensively discussed and deliberated in an *ad hoc* body which is called the Inter-Party Constitutional Reconciliation Committee. The Committee is not a standing committee prescribed by Rules of Procedure of the Parliament. It is purely political and composed of members of political parties in the Parliament. They are represented on equal footing. Such committees are established in 1995 ('enhancing political participation'), 2001 ('changing dynamics of fundamental rights restrictions and strengthening civic society') and 2011 as regards ongoing constitutional process. The Parliamentary Constitutional Committee as a standing committee discussed the packages as soon as they were submitted to Parliament and some of the proposed articles of the Reconciliation Committee were rejected or modified according to formal voting applied in the Constitutional Committee. The Reconciliation Committee adopted a consensus approach as a working method principle. In delicate issues where there was no consensus in the Reconciliation Committee, it was apparent that the Constitutional Committee was also sensitive. In 1995 the Reconciliation Committee could not reach a consensus on features and formulations of the secular state currently cited in Article 24 final paragraph of the Constitution. The Reconciliation Committee did not put this matter in the package that was submitted to the Parliament. Even though this matter was discussed in the Constitutional Committee due to a motion, the Constitutional Committee acted in solidarity with the position adopted in the Reconciliation Committee and rejected the motion (TBMM 1995: 40).

The Inter-Party Constitutional Reconciliation Committee as prior consultation and deliberation body reflects inclusiveness and consensus democracy. Its operation became successful for better understanding and in-depth elaboration of constitutional matters in the long term. Follow-up of 1995 and 2001 amendments reveals also that those amendments, despite their deficits, proved to be more successful in terms of resolved implementation by ordinary laws. Here, it should be remembered that EU Harmonization Laws enacted between the years of 2002-2009 were indeed reflections of the 2001 amendments.

Remarks on Implementation Patterns and EU Impact

Here, implementation patterns of three different packages are insightful for assessing constitutional Europeanisation, namely 2001, 2004 and 2010 amendments.

The most significant legal and political aspect of 2001 amendment package relates to restructuring of general principles for the restriction of fundamental rights and freedoms (Oder 2002: 83–6, Gönenç 2004: 100). Before the amendment, article 13 of the Constitution was a general clause stating the grounds and principles for the restriction of all kinds of rights and freedoms. The general grounds were extensive and could be applied to all kinds of rights and freedoms: *'the indivisible integrity of the state with its territory and nation, national sovereignty, the Republic, national security, public order, general peace, the public interest, public morals and public health'*. Besides, the overwhelming majority of the specific provisions for the classic rights and freedoms prescribed 'specific grounds for restriction'. This constitutional design reflected a cumulative restriction approach and it has been accepted by constitutional case-law without taking into account specific characteristics of particular rights and freedoms.[14] Moreover, the specific provisions on rights and freedoms which did not prescribe 'specific restriction grounds' were to be interpreted in the light of the general restrictions. Accordingly, the freedom to claim rights and the right of petition, which do not prescribe specific restriction grounds, could be restricted with reference to general restriction grounds. By altering cumulative restriction approach (general and specific grounds of restriction) the 2001 constitutional amendments reformulated article 13 of the Constitution on restriction of fundamental rights and freedoms. The 2001 version of article 13 eliminated general restriction grounds and prescribed that the fundamental rights and freedoms shall be restricted only in accordance with the grounds contained in the specific provisions of the Constitution. The 2001 amendment also redefined limits of restriction by referring to the 'core of the rights' and freedoms which was also adopted by the Turkish Constitution of 1961. During the constitutional debates of the 1982 Constitution, the 'requirements of democratic order' were suggested instead of the core guarantee on the grounds that the former were sufficiently clear and easily justified the restriction. In contradiction with the intention of constitution-makers, the Constitutional Court interpreted the core guarantee as an element of the 'requirements of democratic order'. However, the Court assumed in certain cases that core guarantee was impaired only if the right or freedom was destroyed completely. After the 2001 constitutional amendment, infringement of core guarantee was interpreted in certain cases in an extensive manner, such as 'restriction of rights in great extent', 'hardening the exercise of rights in a serious manner', 'preventing the right to achieve its aim' and 'eliminating the effect of the right'.[15] Moreover, the 2001 amendments defined limits of restriction by referring to the 'letter and spirit of the Constitution', the 'requirements of democratic social order and the secular Republic' and the 'principle of proportionality'. Here, reference to proportionality and secular state are new limits of restrictions which should be used in favour of rights. Restructuring the general principles for the restriction of fundamental rights and freedoms (article 13 of the Constitution) reflects a political

---

14   The Constitutional Court stressed that not only specific grounds for the restriction of the freedom of statement, such as 'preventing crimes or punishing offenders', but also general grounds, such as 'public morals or the indivisible integrity of the state with its territory and nation', could justify the restriction of freedom of statement, see E. 1985/8, K. 1986/27, K.t. 26 November 1986, AYMKD 22, 381.

15   Constitutional Court, E. 2002/112, K. 2003/33, K.t. 10 April 2003, AYMKD 39/1, 493–4; E. 2006/121, K. 2009/90, K.t. 18 June 2009.

paradigm shift as regards human rights in Turkey. Progress in nine packages of EU Harmonisation Laws in 2002–2009 can be explained by such a paradigm shift incorporated in the Constitution.

As regards 2001 amendments and their judicial perception, disclosure case-law also submits examples of implementation patterns considering Europeanisation. In the 2001 amendments, instead of dissolution of political parties, which is a permanent and drastic measure, an alternative measure is provided. Accordingly, the Constitutional Court is empowered to deliver a decision depriving a party of public financing taking into consideration the nature of the unconstitutional conduct. This specific sanction was applied for the first time in 2008 for the ruling party AKP.[16] The judgment of the Constitutional Court in respect of the AKP party is interesting in assessing the effects of Europeanisation in Turkey. Europeanisation played two different roles in the AKP judgment (Oder 2009: 307). First, the Constitutional Court accepted that the AKP became a centre of anti-laic activities against the Constitution. However, the Court applied the deprivation of state aid as a sanction, but not disclosure. Here, deprivation which was adopted to comply with the case-law of the European Court of Human Rights prevented disclosure of a political party. Second, the Constitutional Court referred to the Europeanisation policy of the AKP which became visible in Harmonisation Laws as an argument for assessing the severity of unconstitutional conduct. The Court came to the conclusion that the Europeanisation policy of the AKP provides a legitimate ground for non-disclosure of the political party. The HAK-PAR judgment of the Constitutional Court is another example of implementation pattern reflecting the paradigm shift in 2001. In the HAK-PAR disclosure case, the Constitutional Court applied 'clear and present danger test' in favour of the political party.[17] According to the Court, statutes and programmes of political parties are to be deemed as a reflection of freedom of expression in cases where they do not establish a clear and present threat to democratic life.

In respect of the 2004 amendments, two major changes of the package are not implemented as sufficiently as expected: state obligation as regards realisation of *de facto* equality between men and women, and priority of international conventions in the field of fundamental rights and freedoms in case of conflicts with ordinary laws. Improvements as regards *de facto* gender equality are limited especially in the field of girls' education, prevention of domestic violence, honour crimes and forced marriage of girls (so-called 'child marriage or child bride' issue) as well as accelerating and facilitating measures for participation of women in public life. Even though *de facto* equality is to be implemented by further sub-constitutional norms and action plans besides adoption of new criminal and civil codes and there is no legal obstacle for their effective application, it is not possible to speak of gender mainstreaming in Turkey as a dedicated and coordinated public policy in line with EU gender equality policy. In the 2010 constitutional amendments,

---

16   Constitutional Court, E. 2008/1, K. 2008/2, K.t. 30 July 2008.

17   Constitutional Court, E. 2002/1, K. 2008/1, K.t. 29 January 2008.

the package included that 'measures providing *de facto* equality are not to be interpreted in contradiction with principle of equality' and it has been promoted as an improvement in terms of EU policies and expectations. However, such an interpretative clause could not be regarded as strictly necessary since according to the case-law of the Constitutional Court 'legitimate reason doctrine' and proportionality are appropriate grounds for deviations from equality in a formal sense (Oder 2010a: 207–38). Taking into account between the years of 2004–10 best practices of *de facto* gender equality are not carried out sufficiently in the field of affirmative action and there are not any judicial interpretations challenging *de facto* equality, introduction of such an interpretative clause in 2010 does not seem a real improvement.

It is also highly doubtful that prior application of international conventions in the field of fundamental rights and freedoms has major effects in case of conflicts with domestic laws. Careful examination of constitutional case-law demonstrates that such a provision has not provided an effective and meaningful use of international human rights law. In case of constitutional case-law it should be reminded that such a provision did not answer the question of conflicts between the constitutional norms and international human rights law. The Constitutional Court followed in its case-law three different approaches since 1963 on the role of international human rights instruments (Oder 2010b: 218–24): (1) Proper construction approach as an interpretative tool which assumes concordance between constitutional values and international human rights law. (2) Supremacy approach as a norm of conflict which assumes that international human rights law has supra-constitutional authority. (3) Exclusiveness approach ignoring international human rights law in constitutional interpretation.

Dominant method applied by the Court is proper construction method. However, it has two different implications: (1) Searching a real concordance between the Constitution and international human rights law in favour of the latter. (2) Interpreting international human rights law in the light of constitutional norms (limited or nationalised interpretation of international human rights law which is highly disputable as regards *telos* of relevant international laws). The 2004 amendment did not amount to a substantial change as regards second implication of proper construction method. In a recent case-law in 2011, the Constitutional Court reached in a majority ruling that the surname of a married woman need not be regulated as clearly pointed out by the European Court of Human Rights in Ünal *Tekeli v. Turkey.*[18] Accordingly, the majority ruling ignored the right of married women to use the surnames they had before marriage without the surname of their husbands.

As public debate, the discussions in the Constitutional Committee and in the Plenary Session of the Turkish Parliament clearly portray, and the numerical as well as the regulatory extent of the relevant articles demonstrate, reorganisation

---

18   Constitutional Court, E. 2009/85, K. 2011/49, K.t. 10 March 2011, Resmi Gazete Sy. (Official Journal) 28091, 21.10.2011; see also European Court of Human Rights, Ünal Tekeli v. Turkey, No. 29865/96, 16.11. 2004.

of the judiciary is the crucial element of the 2010 package (Varol 2011: 57). As regards implementation patterns and results of the 2010 amendments, it is absolutely necessary to shed light on some striking points. Following restructuring constitutional norms on Highest Council of Judges and Prosecutors through the 2010 amendments, specific laws on Court of Cassation and Highest Administrative Court paved the way for changing compositions of those supreme courts by appointments of Council which has also been reformed recently. As mentioned in an informative report prepared by the Association of Judges and Prosecutors (YARSAV) and partly discussed in the public sphere during elections of the Council and after reforming of the Court of Cassation and the Highest Administrative Court, two points are to be specifically emphasised among other critics (YARSAV 2011):

1. Elections of new members for the Highest Council of Judges and Prosecutors by first scale judges and prosecutors resulted in favour of a block voting of the list which is allegedly prepared and supported by the Ministry, and is also composed of former bureaucrats of the Ministry of Justice (Tahincioğlu and Karapınar 2011, Armutçu 2010, *Vatan* 2011). The right to be elected was in fact guaranteed for all first scale judges and prosecutors. However, it has been widely argued that the Ministry organised the preparation of a virtual list in a very delicate way and a well established sub-culture of Turkish judiciary based on patterns of obedience was overwhelming. The list was virtual since in High Council elections, every first scale judge and prosecutor has the right to cast as many votes as the number of full and substitute High Council members to be elected and majority voting illustrated –alleged pseudo – incidentally – a block list (the so-called Ministry list). This point cited by the YARSAV report has also been also criticised by the co-director of another association on judiciary, namely the Democratic Judiciary Association, which has regarded the constitutional amendments positively during the constitutional debates. The co-director of the Democratic Judiciary Association published a book claiming existence of a bargaining process between his association and the Ministry of Justice during the elections of the Highest Council of Judges and Prosecutors. He claimed that the Ministry offered the association two seats in its block voting list under the precondition that the association would not propose its own candidates. The co-director also claimed that during the allegedly relevant bargaining process one judge expressed his loyalty to the Ministry by saying he would even support a donkey as a candidate if the Ministry so proposed (Ertekin 2011). Here, one point is to be specifically noted. According to the first amendment text adopted by Parliament, first scale judges and prosecutors are expected 'to vote for only one candidate'. Upon the request of a group of MPs, the Constitutional Court reviewed the package and annulled this provision referring to

violation of rule of law as an irrevocable principle of the Constitution.[19] The Court stressed that such a limitation ('to vote for only one candidate') amounts to an unacceptable obstacle preventing reflection of voters' will to the end results of elections. It concluded that this should be regarded as a detrimental factor in respect of realisation of independent and impartial judiciary which is the basic element of rule of law. However, the Court's finding has led to the empowerment of majority tendencies in the voting and the representation of the minority is suppressed. The rumours and critics have ended up in an appeal to the Supreme Election Board claiming review of unfair elections and political influence exercised by the Ministry of Justice in the election process. The appeal referred to unconstitutionality of the so called 'Ministry list' application and candidate status of Ministry bureaucrats who are in administrative positions, but not judges and prosecutors in factual sense. The Board rejected the appeal unanimously by stating that there is no unconstitutionality and no sufficient evidence of fraud in the elections endangering fairness and democratic nature of elections.[20] Critics have also been intensified as regards new appointments, promotions and transfers to other judicial districts or positions. It has been claimed that merits and success of judges and prosecutors are ignored and the judiciary is politicised by the fact that those who are not in the line of government or who are supported by judges' and prosecutors' associations in the elections as candidates are not promoted, they are displaced or they become subjects of implicit discrimination or hidden practices of disregard. However, the 2011 Progress Report of the EU Commission focuses on positive aspects of the 2010 constitutional amendment in respect of the position of the Minister of Justice and the Undersecretary (European Commission 2011:17). It stresses that ministerial influence has in fact been reduced even though the Minister of Justice remains President of the High Council and the Undersecretary has an *ex officio* seat. The report refers to the increased number of members in the Council ('enlargement of the Council') and assumes that 'the Ministry now accounts for less than 10 per cent of the total membership'. The Report also takes into consideration that 'the Minister of Justice does not sit in any of the three chambers where work is conducted, nor does he participate in plenary meetings on disciplinary matters'. Nevertheless, the Minister has the veto power which could be

---

19　For judgment of the Constitutional Court see E. 2010/49, K. 2010/87, K.t. 7 July 2010.

20　See Supreme Election Board, Decision no. 985, K.t. 23 October 2010, Available at: http://www.ysk.gov.tr/ysk/docs/Kararlar/2010Pdf/2010-985.pdf [accessed: 10.10.2011]. For constitutionality of candidate status of Ministry bureaucrats see also Supreme Election Board, Decision no.: 879, K.t. 29 September 2010, cited in previous decision, but not publicised under the website of the Board.

exercised in the case of initiating disciplinary investigations against judges and prosecutors by the Council.

2. In the appointments of the Court of Cassation and the Highest Administrative Court after the 2010 amendments, gender equality which represents one of the core problems of Turkish judicial employment policy for many years is totally ignored. It has been emphasised that through new appointments numbers of female judges have decreased dramatically from 34–35 per cent to 2 per cent in supreme courts cited above (from 160 new judges in the Court of Cassation there are only five female judges and from 51 new judges in the Highest Administrative Court there is only one female judge) (YARSAV 2011). However, the 2011 Progress Report on Turkey does not take into consideration this development even though gender equality is one of the strongest European policies with extensive case-law of the European Court of Justice.

3. It is also disputable whether the bill of rights provisions in the 2010 amendments amount to a real improvement in the field of human rights protection in Turkey. Constitutional provisions on protection of personal data do not define specific limits of the right and refer directly to law ('simple restriction by law'/ *'einfacher Gesetzesvorbehalt'*) for regulation and limits. Right to information as a constitutional provision, which was provided and regulated in 2003 by the Law on Right to Information, does not provide totally new guarantees already safeguarded by relevant law. Removal of constitutional bans as regards political and solidarity strikes and lock-outs, general strikes and lock-outs, occupation of workplace and similar disobedience forms is not reflected to relevant law where cited activities are still subject to sanctions. Taking into account Article 54 paragraph 1 of the Constitution, a strike is still defined as a measure which would be applied only in case of conflict in collective bargaining process. This provision makes disputable whether other forms of strike are to be deemed legitimate under laws. The 2010 amendments provided a conflict resolution body (Supreme Arbitration Board) for collective agreement process of public servants. However, principles as regards its composition and working methods as well as other matters of collective bargaining are not clarified; those are delegated again to laws. Individual application to the Constitutional Court (so-called constitutional complaint procedure) was also adopted by the 2010 amendments against infringement of rights and freedoms – as provided by the European Convention of Human Rights – by public authorities in general. Nevertheless, implementing law ('Law on Establishment and Adjudication of Constitutional Court') limited its application in terms of addressees and acts decisively. Accordingly, legislative acts and general regulatory acts of administrative authorities are exempted from constitutional complaint, and legal personalities are subject to restrictions.

Failure of deliberative democracy and deficit of inclusiveness as major concerns in implementation of the 2010 constitutional amendments are also expressed in the 2011 Progress Report on Turkey. The Progress Report states that 'the adoption of legislation implementing the September 2010 constitutional amendments was not accompanied by broad and effective public consultation involving stakeholders in the country, despite government commitments to this' (European Commission 2011: 7).

As regards implementation deficits and ineffective or insufficient constitutionalism, the role of voters is also to be questioned. Prominent aspects of a constitutional state, such as freedom of expression and association, right to peaceful assemblies and demonstrations, or eradicating torture and ill-treatment, or control of police have not been among the most emphasised needs of the voters in Turkey (Kalaycıoğlu 2003: 14). Instead, patron-client type of political behaviours has been observed as a dominant feature of Turkish democracy perception. It has been asserted that 'the Turkish voters are most concerned about solving their immediate economic worries' and 'a mass of between 9 to 18,000 voters' visit the Turkish Parliament per day, 'mainly seeking jobs, or making job related demands, such as promotion, inter or intra-departmental transfers in national or local public sector companies, health care, etc.' (Kalaycıoğlu 2003: 13). Reflections of populist patronage are observed in political discourse during the referendum campaign on the 2010 amendments. The 2010 constitutional referendum became a popularity contest between ruling party and opposition where the content of amendments were not effectively and rationally discussed by political elite and civic society. EU or Europeanisation was not an integral part of referendum debates and speeches.

Remarks on Misfits between Turkey and the EU from the Perspective of Constitutionalism

Taking into consideration the findings elaborated above and using the concepts developed by *Börzel and Risse* on Europeanisation (2000), the following remarks on misfits between Turkey and the EU can be distinguished from perspective of constitutionalism:

- From perspective of constitutional law, insufficient adoption and implementation of Copenhagen political criteria determines the misfit between Turkey and the EU. However, in case of constitutional convergence certain factors harden or slow down Europeanisation as compared with the adoption of *Acquis Communautaire* where rules and procedures are normatively and in most cases clearly defined. Since the exact normative content, instruments and methods of application for fulfilment of Copenhagen political criteria are in fact provided in a manner where a candidate state's margin of appreciation overwhelms, it is indispensible that domestic political factors will determine realisation patterns of Europeanisation.

- As regards political culture and other informal institutions entailing collective understandings of appropriate behaviour, it should be underlined that Turkey is capable of adopting two different types of political approach. First, as observed especially in the 2001 constitutional amendments, Turkish political culture and informal institutions may follow basic patterns of consensus-oriented and cooperative political culture. Second, it is also possible as observed in the 2007 and 2010 amendments that Turkey also adopts confrontational, competitive and majoritarian approach as regards problem-solving. The fact that the 2001 amendments are more successful than any other constitutional attempt in terms of Europeanisation and constitutionalisation in Turkey can be explained by its consensus-oriented approach where political stakeholders shared the cost of change. The consensus-oriented approach also provided input legitimacy of the 2001 constitutional amendments which supported trust-building among different political positions to carry out democratic consolidation.

- The role of epistemic communities or effective presence of principled issue networks sharing values is still needed to be studied for assessing Europeanisation and constitutionalisation in Turkey. Social and constitutional learning process including a real claim to normative knowledge of constitutionalism and the EU as well as avoidance from failures of the past seems poor in Turkey.

- The case of Turkey necessitates making a distinction between 'input constitutional Europeanisation' and 'output constitutional Europeanisation'. Such a distinction would have two functions. First, it could provide a progressive approach for assessing levels of Europeanisation such as 'normative adaptation including adopting necessary legislation' and 'implementation including interpretation of legislation and its application patterns in practice'. Second, it would be an effective approach to distinguish the norms and practices which are pretentiously an EU adaptation even though they are put into effect to serve the aims contradicting with EU values and constitutionalism. Effects of EU adaptation can be assessed and followed rationally in short-term, mid-term and long-term by distinguishing input and output Europeanisation. 'Input-output' assessment gains specific importance for constitutional Europeanisation since the Copenhagen political criteria refers to principles of which application may vary according to the margin of appreciation of a candidate state deferring national institutional choices, state traditions and domestic understandings of political culture.

- Turkey has absorbed basic norms as well as formal and informal institutions of a constitutional state for a long period of time even though there are ruptures caused by political turbulences, instabilities or military interventions. Beginning from 1908 constitutional amendments of the first Ottoman Constitution (*Kanun-i Esasi*), values of liberal constitutionalism such as checks and balances, democratic elections, and rights and freedoms are discussed and internalised in different constitutional norms. The 1921 Constitution was a document of democratic constitutionalism since it referred to 'nation' and 'people' as owners of sovereignty. The 1924 Constitution was a reflection of political liberalism with its classical bill of rights, while the 1961 Constitution was a successful document of constitutionalism with extensive protection of rights and freedoms, instruments of checks and balances as well as judicial autonomy, even though it was made under the military authority of 1960. Even the very first version of the 1982 Constitution would not dare to eliminate the basic assumptions of constitutional state. Authoritative structure of the 1982 Constitution has been extensively eliminated by certain amendments provided gradually. In other words, Turkey has a long time of familiarity with shared values of European constitutionalism. This makes improvements as regards constitutionalism and constitutional Europeanisation easier and more difficult than previous candidate states. Such a paradox can be explained by the longstanding achievements and deficits of Turkey as regards constitutionalism. Differing from central and eastern European states, constitutionalisation and Europeanisation do not mean for Turkey a totally new challenge and excitement.

- Besides the long-term familiarity of Turkey with constitutionalism and European and international human rights mechanisms, it should be taken into account seriously that the main constitutional and political issue or dichotomy in Turkey is not only the tension between military tutelage and democratic institutions. It is to be considered that there is a high tension between majoritarian tendencies represented in a powerful manner by the Turkish right before and after military interventions, and counter-majoritarian tendencies supported by the Turkish central-left, partly progressive constitutional and administrative case-law, and ethnic and religious minorities in different forms. Even though the 1961 Constitution, which was adopted after the 1960 military intervention, internalised counter-majoritarian institutions such as the Constitutional Court and autonomous bodies and provided an effective protection of rights through a powerful bill of rights, constitutional developments after the 1971 and 1982 Constitutions followed arguments of Turkish right wing politicians. Those were based on following assumptions: majoritarian approach is to be adopted where judicial review is to be limited; parliament shall be operated easily and the executive – both Prime Minister and State President – shall be empowered. Military tutelage tried to balance the democratic institutions not by effective checks and balances of constitutionalism, but *de facto* authority of military and tutelage institutions, e.g. sub-constitutional rules immune from judicial review or the former National Security Board. Removal of military tutelage institutions does not amount to an 'all of a sudden constitutionalism' in Turkey. Enhancing effective judicial review, civic society, freedom of expression and association as well as ideological pluralism gains specific importance in Turkey's constitutional and political context for establishment of real constitutionalism.[21] However, the 2010 constitutional amendments and their implementation patterns are not directed to the enhancement of checks and balances and to real issues as regards a bill of rights in Turkey.

Conclusion

From the perspective of constitutional law and constitutional politics, EU conditionality means that constitutional Europeanisation is a prerequisite for the participation of Turkey in constitutional enterprise and pluralism of Europe which is based on *telos* of constitutionalism as 'limited government' at different levels, i.e. EU level (constitutionalism for EU institutions and constitutionalism beyond states) and member states' level (constitutionalism for member states and state-based notion of constitutionalism). Those levels of constitutionalism urge Turkey to realise both vertical and horizontal convergence with liberal and democratic values making the essence of real sense of constitutionalism. Vertical convergencewas in fact embedded in ex Article 6 paragraph 1 of the Treaty on European Union which explicitly refers to basic values of constitutionalism as foundations of the EU: 'the principles of liberty, democracy, respect for human rights and fundamental freedoms, and the rule of law, principles which are common to the Member States'. Article 2 of Treaty on European Union refers to the same approach: "The Union is founded on the values of respect for human dignity, freedom, democracy, equality, the rule of law and respect for human rights, including the rights of persons belonging to minorities. These values are common to the Member States in a society in which pluralism, non-discrimination, tolerance, justice, solidarity and equality between women and men prevail." Vertical convergence brings forth and facilitates horizontal convergence which amounts to convergence of constitutional values guaranteeing limited government through different norms and instruments on rule of law, checks and balances and fundamental rights and freedoms in the constitutions, constitutional conventions and constitutional politics of the Members States. Horizontal convergence does not refer to weakening the statehood or national identity embedded in the constitutions of member states and candidate states. Instead, it aims at enhancing the constitutional capacity in line

---

21   According to statistics of the Progressive Journalists Association there were 95 journalists imprisoned as of January 2012, available at: http://www.cgd.org.tr/index. php?Did=21 [accessed: 20 January 2012]. According to the 2011 July Report of the Turkish Association of Journalists, there were approximately 4500 investigations in February 2011 as regards crimes of affecting independent judiciary and secrecy of investigation, see Reports of Turkish Association of Journalists, available at:_http://www.tgc.org.tr/ basinraporlari.asp [accessed: 10 November 2011].

with constitutionalism, empowering the democratic and liberal statehood through constitutionalism, creating a constitutional space with entrenched constitutionalism and supporting pluralistic understanding of constitutionalism based on existence of many national constitutional identities with common values. Legal reflections of this approach can be found again in Article 4 and 6 of the Treaty on European Union. In respect of human rights, the EU refers to the European Convention of Human Rights and 'the constitutional traditions common to the member states' as general principles of EU law. The EU's respect for national identities also includes constitutional identities which are assumed and expected to include different norms and mechanisms in line with constitutionalism.

In the case of Turkey, the realisation of constitutionalism and Europeanisation does not follow a pattern of deliberate and planned action of political actors. While making process and *telos* of specific amendment packages are serving the aims of constitutional Europeanisation, others refer to Europeanisation for justification of political agendas which do not fully comply with values of constitutionalism or which bundle European friendly items with those representing the priorities, passions and ideologies of ruling majorities. Failure of deliberate and planned action of real sense constitutionalism is the main factor slowing down the democratic consolidation as well as Europeanisation in Turkey. It could of course be said that even the most controversial constitutional amendments eliminated anti-democratic or disputed provisions and provided improvement. However, absence of sincere motivation as regards constitutionalism and/or the fact that there is no proper replacement of eliminated provisions with real liberal-democratic values and instruments of constitutionalism are to be taken seriously. Therefore, it is advisable that Progress Reports do not make reference only to elimination of 'old rules' and importance of implementation of 'new rules', but they also focus on the question as to whether replacement, if any, satisfies the real needs of constitutionalism in an effective manner. They could also insist on consensus-oriented approach of law-making politics and consequences of possible implementation patterns which may weaken constitutionalism and Europeanisation. Since implementation patterns of constitutional norms are closely related with established political context and perceptions of the country, norms which sound liberal and democratic on paper may be ineffective, disregarded or applied in a manner contradicting basic values of constitutionalism according to deeply embedded illiberal and undemocratic patterns of political culture. That requires making a distinction between input and output constitutional Europeanisation as well as instrumentalisation and internalisation of constitutional Europeanisation.

References

Aldıkaçtı, O. 1982. *Danışma Meclisi Tutanak Dergisi* (Proceedings of Consultative Assembly), Vol. 8, B:129, 18 August, O: 3, 61.

Armutçu, O. 2010. HSYK'yı Adalet Bakanlığı Listesi Kazandı (Ministry of Justice's List became decisive for elections Highest Council of Judges and Prosecutors). *EurActiv* [Online, 18 October] Available at: http://www.euractiv. com.tr/politika-000110/article/hsyky-adalet-bakanl-listesi-kazand-012822 [accessed: 11 November 2011].

Börzel, T.A. and Risse, T. 2000. When Europe Hits Home: Europeanisation and Domestic Change. *European Integration online Papers (EIoP)* [Online], 4(15). Available at: http:/eiop.or.at/eiop/texte/2000-015a.htm [accessed: 29 November 2000].

Cumhuriyet. 2001. Selçuk: Yeni Bir Anayasa Şart. 24 September, 8.

Çavuşoğlu, N. 1991. Türkiye'nin İnsan Hakları Avrupa Komisyonu'na Kişisel Başvuru Hakkını Tanıma Bildirimine Koyduğu Hususlar Üzerine Bir Not (Annotation on Points in Turkey's Declaration as regards Recognition of Right to Individual Application before European Commission of Human Rights). İnsan Hakları Merkezi Dergisi *(Journal of the Human Rights Centre, İHMD),* 1(2–3), 21–9.

Çelik, E. 1988. Avrupa İnsan Hakları Komisyonu'na Bireysel Başvuru Hakkı ve Türkiye (Right to Individual Application before European Commission of Human Rights and Turkey), in *Bahri Savcı'ya Armağan*, Ankara: Mülkiyeliler Birliği Vakfı (MBV) Publications, 222–31.

Ertekin, O.G. 2011. *Yargı Meselesi Hallolundu: Yargıçların Eşekli Demokrasi İle İmtihanı (Judiciary Issue Has Been Dissolved: Testing Judges through Democracy with Donkeys).* Istanbul: Epos.

ECHR. 1991. *Chrysostomos, Papachrysostomou and Loizidou v. Turkey* (15299/89, 15300/89, 15318/89), 4 March.

European Commission. 2006. *Regular Report on Turkey's Progress Towards Accession.* SEC(2006) 1390. Brussels.

European Commission. 2007. *Regular Report on Turkey's Progress Towards Accession.* SEC(2007) 1436. Brussels.

European Commission. 2010. *Regular Report on Turkey's Progress Towards Accession.* SEC (2010) 1327. Brussels.

European Commission. 2011. *Regular Report on Turkey's Progress Towards Accession.* SEC (2011) 1201 final. Brussels.

Gönenç, L. 2004. The 2001 amendments to the 1982 Constitution of Turkey. *Ankara Law Review*, 1(1), 89–110.

Gönenç, L. 2010. *2010 Proposed Constitutional Amendments to the 1982 Constitution of Turkey.* TEPAV Evaluation Note, Ankara.

Kalaycıoğlu, E. 2003. *The Political Criteria: Fair or Strict Conditionality?* Paper to the Conference organised by St. Antony's College, University of Oxford: Turkey, the EU and the 2004 milestone: Is this time for real? Oxford, UK, 14–15 March 2003.

Müftüler-Baç, M. 2005. Turkey's political reforms: the impact of the European Union. *South European Society & Politics*, 10(1), 16–30.

Oder, B.E. 2010a. *Anayasa Yargısında Yorum Yöntemleri* (*Methods of Interpretation in Constitutional Adjudication*). Istanbul: Beta.

Oder, B.E. 2010b. Anayasa'da kadın sorunsalı: norm, içtihat ve hukuk politikası (*Women issue in the constitution: norm, case-law and legal policy*), in *Türkiye'de Toplumsal Cinsiyet Çalışmaları (Gender Studies in Turkey)*, edited by H. Durudoğan et al. Istanbul: Koç University Press, 207–38.

Oder, B.E. 2009. Turkey, in *The Militant Democracy Principle in Modern Democracies*, edited by M. Thiel. Burlington: Ashgate, 263–310.

Oder, B.E. 2006. Übertragung von Hoheitsrechten im Spannungsverhältnis zur nationalen Souveränität – Verfassungsrechtliche Vorgaben und verfassungspolitischer Änderungsbedarf (Transfer of Sovereignty in a Relation of Tension with National Sovereignty – Guidelines of Constitutional Law and Amendment as a Necessity of Constitutional Politics), in *Deutsch-Türkischer Forum für Staatsrechtslehre*. Berlin: LIT Verlag, 75–100.

Oder, B.E. 2002. Enhancing the human face of constitutional reality in Turkey through accession partnership with the EU, in *Turkey: the Road Ahead?* edited by B. Dunér. Stockholm: The Swedish Institute of International Affairs, 72–104.

Örücü, E. 2011. The Turkish Constitution Revamped Yet Again. *European Public Law*, Vol. 17(1), 11–23.

Örücü, E. 2008. Whither the Presidency of the Republic of Turkey?. *European Public Law*, 14(1), 35–53.

Örücü, E. 2004. Turkey: seven packages towards harmonisation with the European Union. *European Public Law*, 10(4), 603–22.

Radikal. 2001a. Son 19 yılın en köklü değişiklik paketi/Demokratik bir anayasa için (Most radical changes in the last 19 years/For a democratic constitution). 25 May, 7.

Radikal. 2001b. Anayasa için tam yol (Road ahead for the constitution). 6 September, 5.

Radikal. 2001c. Artık top Meclis'te (Now it is up to Parliament). 21 September, 10.

Sabah. 2001. Tarihi gün (Historical day). 24 September, 1.

Tahincioğlu, G. and Karapınar, T. 2010. Bakanlığın HSYK'sı (Highest Council of Judges and Prosecutors of the Ministry). *Milliyet* [Online, 18 October] Available at: http://www.milliyet.com.tr/-bakanligin-hsyk-si/siyaset/haberdetay/18.10.2010/1302929/default.htm [accessed: 11 November 2011].

Tanör, B. and Yüzbaşıoğlu, N. 2011. *1982 Anayasasına Göre Türk Anayasa Hukuku (Turkish Constitutional Law According to 1982 Constitution)*. 10th edition. Istanbul: Beta.

TBMM (Turkish Grand National Assembly). 1995. Doğru Yol Partisi Grup Başkanvekilleri Sakarya Milletvekili Nevzat Ercan, Bursa Milletvekili Turhan Tayan, Samsun Milletvekili İhsan Saraçlar, Anavatan Partisi Grup Başkanvekilleri Gümüşhane Milletvekili M. Oltan Sungurlu, Denizli Milletvekili Hasan Korkmazcan, Trabzon Milletvekili Eyüp Aşık, Sosyaldemokrat Halkçı Parti Grup Başkanı Ankara Milletvekili Seyfî Oktay,

İstanbul Milletvekili Ercan Karakaş, Batman Milletvekili Adnan Ekmen ve 292 Arkadaşının 7.11.1982 Tarihli ve 2709 Numaralı Türkiye Cumhuriyeti Anayasasının Başlangıç Metni ve Bazı Maddelerinin Değiştirilmesine Dair Kanun Teklifi, İzmir Milletvekili Cemal Tercan ve 153 Arkadaşının 2709 Sayılı Türkiye Cumhuriyeti Anayasasının 82 nci Maddesinin Değiştirilmesi Hakkında Kanun Teklifi, Zonguldak Milletvekili Güneş Müftüoğlu ve 170 Arkadaşının 2709 Sayılı Türkiye Cumhuriyeti Anayasasının 127 nci Maddesinin Değiştirilmesi ve Anayasaya Bir Geçici Madde Eklenmesine Dair Kanun Teklifi ve Anayasa Komisyonu Raporu (Constitutional Proposal and Report of the Constitutional Committee) (2/1007, 2/1110, 2/1312), [Online], Available at: http://www.tbmm.gov.tr/tutanaklar/TUTANAK/TBMM/d19/ c088/-tbmm19088123ss0861.pdf [accessed: 11 September 2011].

TBMM. 2001. Demokratik Sol Parti Genel Başkanı İstanbul Milletvekili Bülent Ecevit, Milliyetçi Hareket Partisi Genel Başkanı Osmaniye Milletvekili Devlet Bahçeli, Anavatan Partisi Genel Başkanı Rize Milletvekili Mesut Yılmaz ile 288 Milletvekilinin Türkiye Cumhuriyeti Anayasasının Bazı Maddelerinin Değiştirilmesi Hakkında Kanun Teklifi ve Anayasa Komisyonu Raporu (Constitutional Proposal and Report of the Constitutional Committee) (2/803), Dönem: 21, Yasama Yılı: 3, 25.9.2001, [Online], Available at: http://www. tbmmm.gov.tr/sirasayi/donem21/yil01/ss737m_[accessed: 15 October 2001].

TBMM. 2004. Adalet ve Kalkınma Partisi Grup Başkanvekilleri Ankara Milletvekilleri Salih Kapusuz, Haluk İpek, Bursa Milletvekili Faruk Çelik, Ordu Milletvekili Eyüp Fatsa ve Hatay Milletvekili Sadullah Ergin ve 193 Milletvekilinin; Türkiye Cumhuriyeti Anayasasının Bazı Maddelerinin Değiştirilmesi Hakkında Kanun Teklifi ve Anayasa Komisyonu Raporu (Constitutional Proposal and Report of the Constitutional Committee) (2/278), Dönem: 22, Yasama Yılı: 2,(S. Sayısı: 430), [Online], Available at: http://www.tbmm.gov.tr/tutanaklar/TUTANAK/TBMM/d22/c048/- tbmm22048083ss0430.pdf [accessed: 9 September 2009].

TBMM. 2008. İstanbul Milletvekili Recep Tayyip Erdoğan ve Osmaniye Milletvekili Devlet Bahçeli ile 346 Milletvekilinin; Türkiye Cumhuriyeti Anayasasının Bazı Maddelerinde Değişiklik Yapılmasına Dair Kanun Teklifi ve Anayasa Komisyonu Raporu (Constitutional Proposal and Report of the Constitutional Committee) (2/141), Dönem: 23 Yasama Yılı:2, (S. Sayısı: 101), [Online], Available at: http://www.tbmm.gov.tr/tutanaklar/TUTANAK/ TBMM/d23/c013/tbmm23013059-ss0101.pdf [accessed: 5 October 2008].

TBMM. 2010. TBMM (S. Sayısı: 497), Dönem: 23 Yasama Yılı: 4, Adalet ve Kalkınma Partisi Grup Başkanı İstanbul Milletvekili Recep Tayyip Erdoğan ve 264 Milletvekilinin; 7/11/1982 Tarihli ve 2709 Sayılı Türkiye Cumhuriyeti Anayasasının Bazı Maddelerinde Değişiklik Yapılması Hakkında Kanun Teklifi ve Anayasa Komisyonu Raporu (Constitutional Proposal and Report of the Constitutional Committee) (2/656).

Tebliğ. 1991. İnsan Hakları ve Ana Hürriyetleri Koruma Sözleşmesi'nin 25. Maddesi Uyarınca Türk Hükümetinin Beyanı (Communication 1991,

Declaration of Turkish Government pursuant to Article 25 of European Convention of Human Rights) Resmi Gazete (Official Journal), 19 January 1991, Sy.: 20760.

Toluner, S. 1988. Türkiye'nin Bireysel Başvuru Hakkını Tanıma Beyanının Milletlerarası Hukuk Açısından Değerlendirilmesi (Evaluation of Turkey's Declaration on Recognition of Right to Individual Application from Perspective of International Law). *Milletlerarası Hukuk ve Milletlerarası Özel Hukuk Bülteni (MHB),* 8(2) 237–49.

Varol, O.O. 2011. The Origins and Limits of Originalism: A Comparative Study. *Vanderbilt Journal of Transnational Law* [Online], 44, 1239–97. Available at: http://papers.ssrn.com/sol3/-papers.cfm?abstract_id=1912202 [accessed: 11 November 2011].

Vatan. 2010. İşte Bakanlığın HSYK Listesi (Here is Ministry's List for Highest Council of Judges and Prosecutors). [Online, 14 October]. Available at: http://haber.gazetevatan.com/iste-bakanligin-hsyk-listesi/334590/1/Haber [accessed: 11 November 2011].

YARSAV website. 2011. Türk *Yargısının Güncel Sorunlarına Dair Bilgilendirme (Information Letter as regards Current Problems of Turkish Judiciary).* Available at: http://www.yarsav.org.tr/-index.php?p=265 [accessed: 10 October 2011].

Chapter 5

Europeanisation of Civil Society in Turkey during the Accession Process to the European Union

Selcen Öner

Introduction

With the effects of globalisation and with the increasing diversification of societal needs, states cannot satisfy the expectations of all people. The importance of civil society has significantly increased in order to overcome new challenges of the twenty-first century. Civil society has an intermediary role between individual and state and it refers to collective actions of certain groups. Civil society is composed of various types of organisations such as Non-Governmental Organisations (NGOs), trade unions, business associations and social movements.

Civil society can play a crucial role in promoting democratisation. Western states and international organisations provide financial and moral support for development of civil society organisations (CSOs). CSOs can be defined as organisations, usually based on voluntary membership, that try to influence politics at global, supranational, national or local levels. They usually focus on issue-specific areas, such as human rights, environmental issues or the rights concerning gender, ethnicity and culture.

Turkey has had a strong state tradition. However, with the effects of globalisation and with the increasingly diversified societal needs, the Turkish state cannot cope with all the new challenges and it cannot satisfy all expectations of society which led to increasing importance of civil society in Turkey. The CSOs in Turkey increased a lot in quantitative terms ,while their capacity and influence started to improve in qualitative terms in the 1990s. Since then, the spectrum of CSOs has been gradually increasing, through the effect of global and domestic factors.

Regarding Turkey-EU relations, the CSOs have had a crucial role, especially in terms of being important actors in the democratisation process of the Turkish state. The EU perceives CSOs as crucial agents of domestic change in the candidate countries. Many Turkish CSOs, especially business associations such as the Turkish Industrialists' and Businessmen's Association (TÜSİAD) have been supporting Turkey's EU membership process and they have been pushing for legal and political reforms especially after official candidate status was given to Turkey at the Helsinki Summit in December 1999. The increasing interactions between Turkey and the EU since Turkey gained official candidate status have led to Europeanisation in various policy fields, with the EU having a crucial influence in the development of Turkish civil society and transforming the relationship between state and civil society in Turkey. Meanwhile the CSOs have a crucial role in Europeanisation process of Turkey.

In addition to its financial support, the EU has encouraged legislative reform in Turkey through the application of 'conditionality' principle.[1] In order to fulfil the Copenhagen criteria, legislative changes between 2001 and 2004, and the introduction of a new Law on Associations in 2004, have reduced or lifted several restrictions on civil society in Turkey. The Europeanisation of civil society in Turkey has allowed it to become influential in various policy fields.

This chapter will focus on the EU's influence on the process of transforming Turkish civil society in legal and practical terms. It first reviews the historical background of relations between the state and civil society in Turkey. Secondly, it evaluates the changes in the legal framework of civil society in Turkey through the application of 'conditionality' principle by the EU and by using 'external incentives model'[2] and it analyses the transformative power of the EU on the practices of civil society in Turkey by using the 'social learning model'.[3] It analyses how the behaviour of Turkish CSOs has been transformed by Europeanisation since the Helsinki Summit in 1999, how much they cooperate with their counterparts in the member states of the EU, and to what extent they prefer using EU financial sources. This chapter draws on 11 face to face in-depth interviews, conducted between 2009 and 2011 with representatives of various CSOs in Turkey. Qualitative analysis has been made. Finally, the chapter discusses the ongoing challenges during the Europeanisation process of civil society in Turkey and what can be done in order to cope with these challenges.

Historical Background: The Increasing Role of Civil Society in Turkey

The most important obstacle to the development of civil society in Turkey has been Turkey's state-centric political culture (Weber 2006: 85). The relative

---

1   The EU uses the principle of 'conditionality' during its enlargement process. It asks its candidate countries to fulfil certain criteria in order to accept them as a member of the EU.

2   This is one of the Europeanization models which were developed by Schimmelfenig and Sedelmeier (2005) in order to evaluate Europeanization of Central and Eastern European countries. This model is based on "logic of consequences". According to this model Europeanization is driven by the EU through rewards and sanctions.

3   This model is based on the 'logic of appropriateness'. A candidate country can adopt the rules, values and norms of the EU, if it regards the EU norms and demands for rule adoption as appropriate in terms of collective identity, norms and values. For further detail see Schimmelfennig and Sedelmeier, 2005.

weakness of civil society in Turkey can be explained by its strong state tradition and centralised government structure (Ergun 2010: 509). With the introduction of the 1924 Constitution, freedom of association was formally recognised, but the state had the ability to limit it for the sake of alleged public interest. Thus, the number of CSOs remained low. Although the 1961 Constitution provided the legal framework for the rise of a civil society in Turkey, the military coups in 1971 and 1980 led to constitutional amendments that limited basic freedoms. Civil society was usually perceived as a threat to the general good (Grigoriadis 2009: 45).

The 1982 Constitution did not envisage a pluralistic democracy; thus, it did not provide favourable conditions for activities of CSOs. For example, Article 33 prohibited associations from engaging in political activities, pursuing political aims, or taking joint action with labour unions or foundations. Relations with international associations were forbidden, and associations could not use languages other than Turkish in their official contacts. The justifications for banning an association were loosely described, thereby maximising the opportunities for state intervention. The first amendment to Article 33 was made in 1995, as part of a reform programme to overcome objections by the European Parliament (EP) to the Customs Union agreement between Turkey and the EU. This allowed CSOs to engage in political activities and collaboration with political parties and other associations (Grigoriadis 2009: 56–7).

Civil society grew after the 1980 military *coup d'etat*, by specialising on issue-based activities as the only possible way to express discontent about social conditions and government policies, although successive governments have not considered civil society actors as important stakeholders in Turkey's social and political transformation (Ergun 2010: 509–10). In particular, human rights organisations, which usually criticise the state, have had a rather problematic relationship with it. On the other hand, business associations have been tolerated and even supported by state officials, and associations providing social services, have been supported too (Weber 2006: 86). Economic liberalisation in Turkey, and the shift from import substitution to an export-oriented economy in the 1980s, have also been influential in the development of civil society in Turkey (Grigoriadis 2009: 47).

Until the 1990s, civil society in Turkey satisfied basic social needs, and was mostly based on voluntarism, with weak organisational structures and small memberships (Ergun 2010: 510). As Keyman and İçduygu (2003: 226) argue, a combination of globalisation, increased interaction with international counterparts, and the crisis of Turkey's strong state tradition led to important quantitative increases and qualitative improvements in CSOs in Turkey during the 1990s. The United Nations Conference on Human Settlements (Habitat II), held in 1996 in Istanbul, was an important turning point for the position of civil society in Turkey. It brought many international CSOs to Turkey and provided several opportunities for cooperation between local and international CSOs, both to share experiences and allow local CSOs to find new sources of financial aid (Grigoriadis 2009: 47). Habitat II paved the way for Turkey's participation in the global movement of civil society, while awareness of CSOs increased in terms of their role in providing social justice and sustainable development (Bikmen and Meydanoglu 2006: 6).

The Turkish state's slow response to the 1999 earthquake in the Marmara region was another important turning point for civil society in Turkey because it showed that CSOs are necessary for the rapid and effective solution of many problems of Turkish society (Keyman and İçduygu 2003: 227). For example, the Search and Rescue Association (Arama Kurtarma Derneği-AKUT) was one of the most successful CSOs, whose quick response to the 1999 earthquake increased both people's respect and understanding of the importance of civil society in Turkey. The increasingly prestigious image and visibility of CSOs in the eyes of the Turkish public increased their self-confidence (Grigoriadis 2009: 54), so that they began to play an increasing role in representing various social problems and transmitting society's demands for democratisation and the necessity for effective governance to the country's political actors (Keyman and İçduygu 2003: 221).

Local CSOs have become increasingly willing to interact and cooperate with international actors to benefit from their experience and get funds to realise their goals through projects. The EU has been the most important external actor supporting the strengthening of civil society in Turkey. The civil society actors have become increasingly involved in social and political transformation, particularly Turkey's democratisation process. They have been increasingly internationalised through increased interaction with the international community. Human rights organisations and women's organisations are examples of CSOs that are playing an important role in improving and protecting civil rights in Turkey (Ergun 2010: 509–11). Overall then, in the first decade of the twenty-first century, civil society in Turkey has become more visible and active, and is having a growing influence on public opinion and government policies.

The Transformative Power of the EU: The Europeanisation of Civil Society in Turkey

Europeanisation process does not only take place in the EU's member states, but can also take place in candidate countries like Turkey, through the principle of 'conditionality'. In order to get rewards of the EU, especially in order to be a member of the EU, the candidate countries have to fulfil certain criteria. According to Radaelli (2003: 41) Europeanisation can occur through 'vertical' and 'horizontal' ways. In 'vertical Europeanisation', rules and policies are defined at the EU level, then they have to be adopted by the domestic level. On the other hand, in 'horizontal Europeanisation', there is no pressure on domestic level by the EU, rather the impact of the EU on domestic level is through market mechanisms or through socialisation.

As Börzel (2002: 193) argues, Europeanisation has 'bottom-up' and 'top-down' dimensions. 'Bottom-up' Europeanisation which is also defined as 'uploading' refers to the incentives of member states to influence policies at

European level. 'Top-down' Europeanisation which is also called 'downloading' refers to the impact of the EU on domestic level. Europeanisation has various aspects such as 'political Europeanisation', 'policy Europeanisation' and 'societal Europeanisation'. Political Europeanisation focuses on the influence of the EU on domestic actors, policy Europeanisation deals with Europeanisation of public policies and societal Europeanisation refers to Europeanisation of identities. Identities of domestic actors may change through social learning (Diez, Agnantopoulos and Kaliber 2005: 5). Through socialisation process 'beliefs, norms and values are diffused and institutionalised' (Radaelli and Pasquier 2007: 43). Europeanisation leads to socialisation through increasing interactions between domestic actors and the EU. The EU transfers its values and norms to the CSOs. These norms and values are internalised by CSOs in order to be part of the European community. Thus, the identities of CSOs have been influenced from the Europeanisation process in the long term.

The 'social learning model' can be traced back to constructivism and the 'logic of appropriateness', which suggests that actors choose to do what is most appropriate and legitimate. In this model, a state adopts the EU rules if it thinks that they are appropriate. Social learning can emerge in two ways. The EU may persuade the government of the appropriateness of its rules, or societal groups and organisations may lobby the government to adopt new rules. The likelihood of compliance increases if EU norms resonate and have legitimacy locally, and if the state itself identifies with the EU (Schimmelfennig and Sedelmeier 2005: 6–18).

Europeanisation of Legal Framework of Civil Society in Turkey

The civil society in Turkey has been influenced by Europeanisation, especially since the Helsinki Summit in December 1999, as has the legal framework that civil society operates within. For the EU, civil society has a central role in terms of consolidating democracy in a candidate country like Turkey. Accordingly, through a 'social learning mechanism', EU norms are spread and internalised through interactions between CSOs in Turkey and those in the EU member states. The EU has supported this process through establishing direct exchanges between civil society actors in Turkey and the EU (İçduygu 2007: 182). The EU has influenced civil society in Turkey both in vertical and horizontal ways (Göksel and Güneş 2005). In legal terms Europeanisation process of civil society in Turkey is through a vertical way, meanwhile CSOs in Turkey have been under horizontal Europeanisation process through participating in EU projects and increasing interactions with their counterparts.

After the Helsinki Summit, the Commission published an Accession Partnership Document that outlined the short and medium-term reforms Turkey had to undertake to fulfil the Copenhagen criteria and to adopt the EU *acquis*. It called for Turkey to strengthen its legal guarantees of the rights to freedom of association and peaceful assembly, and encouraged the development of civil society. The European Commission's regular progress reports on Turkey have emphasised the insufficient protection of freedom of association as one of Turkey's main deficiencies.

The EU has had a transformative effect on Turkey particularly in terms of the legal framework within which civil society acts. In addition to the changes made to Article 33 of the Turkish Constitution, further amendments were made in 2001 when general rules and restrictions on the right to establish associations were reduced. With the second reform package in March 2002, Articles 7, 11 and 12, which restricted relations with international associations, were amended, grounds for banning an association were limited, and the freedom to establish and join associations was extended. However, through the reforms of the Civil Code in 2002, the state maintained its control over relations between CSOs and international organisations. With the introduction of the third reform package of August 2002, the limitations on civil servants' right to establish associations and the possibility of a ban on association activities for civil defence purposes were lifted. With the fourth reform package in January 2003, associations were allowed to use any language in their non-official correspondence and restrictions on making announcements or distributing publications were made more flexible with the obligation to send copies of these documents to the relevant authorities before distribution being removed. In July 2003, with the introduction of the seventh reform package, restrictions on the establishment of associations by people convicted of certain crimes, or by former members of a political party or an association closed down by a court decision were amended. In addition, higher education students were allowed to establish associations related to art, culture and science, not just education (Grigoriadis 2009: 58–9).

In August 2003, the Department of Associations was established in the Ministry of Interior to take over various functions from the Directorate General of Security, and responsibility for inspecting associations was transferred from local police headquarters to an entity attached to the local governor's office in provinces or to junior state officials in districts. During this period, Turkey also signed and/or ratified several European and international human rights conventions, including the International Covenants on Civil and Political Rights and on Economic, Social and Cultural Rights and the International Convention on the Elimination of All Forms of Racial Discrimination. The supremacy of European and international conventions over domestic law was accepted through an amendment to the Constitution (Weber 2006: 89–90).

With the introduction of the new Law on Associations, limitations on the establishment of associations on the basis of religion, ethnicity, region or any other minority status were lifted. In addition, previous requirements to seek permission to join foreign bodies, to open branches abroad or hold meetings with foreigners, and to inform local government officials of general assembly meetings were lifted. The new law also lifted all restrictions on student associations, and the establishment of temporary and informal networks or platforms for all CSOs was allowed. Governors were now required to issue warnings before taking legal action against associations, and security forces were no longer allowed to enter an association without a court order. Associations were allowed to conduct joint projects and receive financial support from public institutions and other associations and they no longer needed to get permission to receive funds from abroad. Finally, associations acting outside the scope of their statutes could be fined, but no longer dissolved (Grigoriadis 2009: 59–60). These changes within the legal framework of civil society in Turkey can be explained mainly on the basis of 'external incentives model'.

As a result of these legal changes, as Çiğdem Nas (2011), deputy of the general secretary of the Economic Development Foundation (İKV) argues, the environment in which the CSOs act has become more independent in legal terms and their fields of activities have extended. Thus, the relations between the state and CSOs have changed, which has increased the self-confidence of CSOs and their influence in Turkey.

Europeanisation of Civil Society in Turkey through Social Learning: 'Civil Society Dialogue'

As well as supporting civil society friendly legislative reform through 'conditionality', and encouraging the development of CSOs, the EU has also provided them with crucial financial support. In fact, this support started before official candidate status was given to Turkey in 1999, as Turkey has been a member of the Euro-Mediterranean Partnership since its introduction in 1995 and received financial aid from the EU through the MEDA I programme between 1995 and 1999, from which the CSOs benefited. After 1999 the EU provided more financial opportunities for civil society in Turkey. However, the amount of financial aid by the EU to civil society in Turkey is still not substantial; moreover, inexperienced and financially weak CSOs have problems with contract administration. Those which have used the EU funds used them for the expansion of their activities, through capacity building programmes, and to improve their organisational and operational capability (Grigoriadis 2009: 55).

CSOs in Turkey used to be based on voluntary participation and funded by modest membership fees and donations. Europeanisation has made them increasingly professionalised, issue-oriented and project-focused, which has provided them with extra funds for their activities (Ergun 2010: 519–20). The EU's grant programmes have influenced the CSOs' agendas, leading them to develop more focused proposals (Grigoriadis 2009: 55). In the calls for proposals, the EU clearly defines its expectations from the CSOs. In order to obtain a grant, they have to focus on certain issues. Thus, the EU has influenced the agendas and priorities of CSOs. Nas (2011) argues that, through EU projects, the CSOs' priority fields are being influenced by the EU and making EU projects or participating in them as partners have led to emergence of 'epistemic communities', composed of increasing numbers of multilingual EU specialists, with the necessary expertise in EU grant applications and project management. Through preparing and implementing common projects these experts can exchange know-how and experiences with their counterparts in the member states of the EU. Such interactions are also internationalising Turkish CSOs and they led to Europeanisation process of civil society in Turkey through 'social learning' mechanism.

Thus, one important effect of the EU's imposition of financial and other requirements on Turkish CSOs has been to create 'social learning' opportunities. It means that the CSOs have been learning 'European' ways of conducting civil society activities. Through EU funding, they have been able to build or develop their capacities, diversify their activities, become more active and visible, and acquire better skills to engage in issue-based work (Ergun 2010: 513–16).

The EU's involvement in Turkish civil society has gone through several stages. In 2005 the EU Commission adopted a Communication that established objectives and priorities for the development of a 'civil society dialogue' between the EU and the candidate countries (Ministry for EU Affairs 2009). The Commission recognises that a dialogue for improving mutual knowledge and encouraging a debate on perceptions regarding society and political issues on both sides is necessary, especially in the case of Turkey. The dialogue will increase bilateral exchanges, thereby contributing to the increased participation of civil society in political, cultural and economic development of the candidate countries (Communication 2005: 3–4). Nas (2011) argues that 'civil society dialogue' between Turkey and the EU plays a crucial role in terms of spreading EU values, especially in the fields of human rights, women's rights and environmental issues. Thus, 'civil society dialogue' has significantly contributed to Europeanisation process of civil society in Turkey through 'social learning' mechanism.

Of all CSOs, business associations in Turkey have been influenced the most by the Europeanisation process, and have been the most active and influential pressure groups supporting Turkey's EU membership process, with TÜSİAD and İKV being the pioneers since the 1990s. TÜSİAD, in particular, has been very influential in pushing for democratisation and reform process in Turkey. Its role has been significant, both in the process before official candidacy status was given to Turkey in 1999, and during the reform process in the post-Helsinki era. Europeanisation is important for TÜSİAD because it entails economic and political modernisation, and represents a further step towards the goal of achieving stability and progress in line with Western standards (Bayer and Öniş 2010: 182–7). In the post-Helsinki period, they have been joined by the Union of Turkish Chambers and Stock Exchanges (TOBB), a semi-official business association, whose membership is obligatory for all registered business entities in Turkey. They have not only pushed for further political Europeanisation, but have also acted as agents of societal Europeanisation through their membership in European business networks, such as BUSINESSEUROPE, and through their lobbying activities in Brussels (Yankaya 2009: 4). TÜSİAD, İKV, the Confederation of Turkish Tradesmen and Craftsmen (TESK), the Confederation of Progressive Trade Unions of Turkey (DİSK) and

Women Entrepreneurs Association of Turkey (KAGİDER) have all established representative offices in Brussels (Kubicek 2005: 368).

One of the business organisations which has been influenced by the Europeanisation process particularly in the post-Helsinki period is Independent Industrialists' and Businessmen's Association (MÜSİAD), founded in 1990, which is a voluntary business association with an Islamist orientation, whose membership is made up primarily of representatives of small and medium-sized firms (Yankaya 2009: 6). In the early and mid-1990s, MÜSİAD was dominated by anti-West and anti-EU rhetoric. However, it increasingly adopted a pro-EU stance (Öniş and Türem 2008: 309), and the degree of MÜSİAD members' integration into European business spaces is an indicator of their increasing economic Europeanisation. It has been influenced by the Europeanisation process of Turkey which led to questioning of previously accepted patterns of doing business and trying to adapt to European business norms. MÜSİAD plays a key role in the socialisation of its members, and the creation of international business networks, through the visits that it organises to various EU member states, and through its offices in several EU countries. It also acts as an agent for the Europeanisation of the Turkish Small and Medium-Sized Enterprises (SME) sector in terms of organisation, by supporting the establishment of EU-defined SME structures in Turkey, which facilitates the lending by EU institutions and international banks that is crucial for the development of the Turkish SME sector. MÜSİAD provides information services to its members about the status of the EU accession process, new EU regulations and EU funds for CSOs. It encourages them to integrate with the EU business world and to be open to the European market. In addition, since 1999, the MÜSİAD firms have increasingly tried to win the CE mark.[4] MÜSİAD itself has been a member of the European Confederation of Associations of SMEs since 2003, and it has been in favour of further Europeanisation of the Turkish economy. Overall, as a result of socialisation in European business spaces, European business norms and principles are being internalised for economic success and good economic governance. Nevertheless, as Yankaya (2009: 2–11) notes, MÜSİAD does not give explicit and unequivocal support to Turkey's political integration with the EU.

As already mentioned, the EU's influence on Turkish civil society has been realised through increased interaction between local and European organisations, common projects, funding provided by the EU for various civil society activities and the establishment of networks (Ergun 2010: 507). Through Europeanisation, the roles, priorities and objectives of Turkish civil society have been transformed. The level of trust in the ability of CSOs to contribute to political and social change and democratic consolidation process of Turkey has increased, as has the public's interest in the activities of the CSOs. There is less scepticism towards civil society in Turkey (Grigoriadis 2009: 63). In particular, as Nas (2011) argues, the human rights, women's and environmental movements have been positively influenced by

---

4   It proves that their products comply with EU health and safety standards.

internalisation of EU values, and the transnational activities of civil society have increased. For example, Ayla Sevand (2010), who is vice President of KAGİDER, states that KAGİDER's office in Brussels has organised meetings with officials of the Commission and Members of the EP, and that they have a project on 'women ambassadors', through which they try to increase communication between Turkish women and women in the member states. They focus particularly on Germany, France and Austria, because their public opinion is more sceptical towards Turkey's membership to the EU. KAGİDER organised visits to these countries and took successful Turkish women, and organised seminars on topics like women in work life and the position of women in religion.

Overall then, there is clear evidence that the EU has been influential in transforming state-civil society relations in Turkey. The legal changes established a much more democratic framework for CSO activities and CSOs are increasingly acknowledged and taken more seriously, especially with the EU's encouragement to establish a dialogue between the state and civil society (Ergun 2010: 517–19). However, there are still problems in terms of the implementation of new laws, further legal reform is still needed in order to support development of civil society in Turkey and further interactions and cooperation with CSOs in the member states is necessary in order to go on Europeanisation process of civil society in Turkey.

Challenges during the Europeanisation Process of Civil Society in Turkey

After the start of the negotiations with the EU on 3 October 2005, the level of interest of Turkish CSOs to the accession process of Turkey has decreased. The loss of enthusiasm of Turkish government about the EU membership, ambiguous signals from some of the EU political elites and proactive multi-dimensional approach in Turkish foreign policy led them to focus on projects in order to survive or search for other alternatives in different parts of the world.

The CSOs still experience some problems in preparing EU projects, and there is a lack of human resources in this field (Göksel and Güneş 2005: 67). There is not enough specialisation in different EU policy fields and the level of cooperation among CSOs is still insufficient in Turkey. Actually the level of cooperation between Turkish CSOs was higher before the start of the EU accession negotiations on 3 October 2005 in order to push the Turkish government for reforms and they made important lobbying activities in Brussels to push the EU to start accession negotiations. As Ural Aküzüm (2009), Chairman of the Arı Movement confirms, 'before getting the date for accession negotiations a serious network was established'. Arda Batu (2009), a member of the administrative board of the Arı Movement, states that 'there is a low level of cooperation among CSOs in Turkey'.

After the start of negotiations with the EU, the CSOs started to focus on projects in order to get funds from the EU and they usually try to find partners from the member states of the EU. Bahar Özsu (2010), from the EU Information Centre at

İstanbul Chamber of Commerce (İTO), admits that there is not close cooperation among CSOs, even between the chambers of commerce and chambers of industry in Turkey. Another practical challenge that she notes was the lengthy and difficult procedure for CSO representatives to get visas to participate in EU projects. This decreases the momentum of interactions between CSOs in Turkey and those in the member states. For example, she recalls that 'for a project which will last for 3 years, they gave me a visa for 10 days, although I asked for a multiple entrance visa' (Özsu, 2010). Regarding cooperation between CSOs in Turkey, Alper Akyüz (2009), who was working at AEGEE, but currently working at Bilgi University as the head of the programme on NGO Education and Research, complains that 'there is a perception of civil society as a zero-sum game; rather civil society is a field which becomes more effective by sharing'. Concerning interactions between Turkish CSOs and their partners abroad, Akyüz (2009) states that 'it has become more flexible with the change in the Law on Associations, but there are still state interference sometimes'. Serdar Yeşilyurt (2011), who is Director of Representation Office to the EU of Confederation of Businessmen and Industrialists of Turkey (TUSKON) argues that 'we have been cooperating usually with European partners, rather than Turkish ones'. He adds that 'we cooperate with TÜSİAD one or two times, we cooperated more with TOBB for projects'. Şükrü Güner (2009), Secretary General of Turkey Europe Foundation (TAV), states that 'the level of cooperation is not enough, there are only temporary meetings'. He adds that sometimes meetings are held with İKV and TOBB, but there is not frequent sharing of information among the CSOs in Turkey. He complains that there is still scepticism towards CSOs; they are not taken into consideration enough by the government. He emphasises that the government has to support CSOs materially and morally, which is crucial for their survival and effectiveness.

On the other hand, Sevand (2010) from KAGİDER points out that her organisation has been cooperating with TUSİAD, and has common projects with the Foundation for Educating Mother and Child (AÇEV). In terms of contacts with the CSOs in the EU member states, she mentions that they have been in contact with the women's organisations, particularly the Women's Forum. Özge Genç (2009), responsible for the Programme on Democratisation at the Turkish Economic and Social Studies Foundation (TESEV), argues that 'connections between the CSOs are better compared to five, ten years ago. Cooperation is easier through e-groups and blogs.'

Currently, it appears that the state regards supporting the development of civil society as a necessity for consolidation of democracy in Turkey, rather than 'homework' of Turkey in order to fulfil Copenhagen criteria. The Turkish government's decision to invite several CSOs to consult about the negotiation process was a big step forward in terms of accepting civil society as a legitimate and important actor in the reform process. However, CSO representatives are usually dissatisfied with the outcomes of those meetings, because they think that their views are merely listened to, but do not seem to have a crucial influence on governmental decisions (Grigoriadis 2009: 63–4). Thus, they are not satisfied just to be consulted by the government.

In order to increase the CSO involvement in the negotiation process, the level of specialisation of the CSOs is critical. Since the end of 2009, there has been a stronger intention about consulting CSOs in Turkey during the development process of the 'Communication Strategy'[5] by the Secretariat General for EU Affairs which was transformed into EU Ministry since 2011. Sabiha Şenyücel (2009), responsible for the Programme on Foreign Policy at TESEV, states that 'to communicate with the negotiation team depends on the efforts of the CSOs'. She adds that if they cannot reach the negotiation team directly, they may reach them through the media. Genç (2009), who is responsible for the Programme on Democratisation at TESEV, argues that:

> There is not a tradition of giving information to the CSOs especially among the bureaucrats. When there are meetings they are usually technical, the bureaucrats usually do not participate in the debates and they do not usually reply to the questions in detail … The relationship between bureaucracy and civil society has to develop much more.

Yeşilyurt (2011) from TUSKON puts forward that 'Turkish civil society does not know how to express their position in any given situation. They do not know how to express their demands, they do not know how to use media.' Aküzüm (2009), from the ARI Movement, is critical that 'around 1000 people are gathered, but just a few of them have a chance to make a speech at the information and consulting meetings for the CSOs'. Akyüz (2009) argues that 'the CSOs which are invited only have a chance to express their opinions in a very short time; in that period they cannot explain their thoughts well'. Güner (2009) from TAV asserts that 'there has to be a permanent consultation mechanism to the CSOs; we participate in the meetings between the government, public authorities and the CSOs like a guest'.

About the 'Communication Strategy' of Turkey, Sevand (2010) from KAGİDER states that they gave their opinions about the strategy, but she adds that they were expecting to be consulted more during the negotiations with the EU. As Nas (2011) argues, during the negotiation process, mere consultation is not enough for the CSOs anymore. They have become more professional and result-oriented. Moreover, they have become aware of their rights and they are more assertive. Thus, they are starting to expect a more institutionalised consultation mechanism during the negotiations with the EU.

---

5   The 'Communication Strategy' has been prepared by the Secretary General of EU Affairs in 2009 in order to enhance communication between Turkey and the EU. Its goal is to overcome prejudices and stereotypes about Turkey and scepticism towards Turkey's membership of the EU and to inform the Turkish public about the EU. This strategy has been implemented by the EU Ministry since its establishment in 2011.

Currently, one of the main problems of Turkish civil society is institutionalisation. As Nas (2011) argues, 'there is too much diversity within the civil society of Turkey; some of the CSOs are highly institutionalized and they are administered more professionally, some of them not'. There is a need to transform their organisational structures from an individual-based mentality to a more institutionalised one, with resources being found in a sustainable way. There are only a limited number of bottom-up civil society movements. Yeşilyurt (2011) from TUSKON admits that CSOs in Turkey have a problem of institutionalisation. Nas (2011) comments that the CSOs have become more project-oriented due to the effect of the Europeanisation of civil society in Turkey. This sometimes leads to the criticism that the influence of the EU has alienated local CSOs from their grassroots base, so that they focus on projects, rather than local activities, which distances CSOs from voluntary work (Ergun 2010: 515–16).

According to Nas (2011), another major challenge for Turkish CSOs is the sustainability of their goals and projects. In order to be sustainable, a CSO has to have connections with a business organisation or a community. It is difficult for CSOs to be totally independent, because they have to be closer to the actors which provide financial resources. Compared to NGOs, business organisations are more advantageous in financial terms. NGOs have started to focus more on projects in order to be sustainable. Bahar Özsu and Cansu Denef Oktay (2010), from the EU Information Centre at İTO, state that the questions they get usually focus on EU funds, how to apply for EU projects and the credits of the European Investment Bank. Oktay (2010) emphasises that more resources should be transferred to civil society in order to strengthen it, while Akyüz (2009) complains that many CSOs first think of Euros when they think about the EU, such that even some CSOs are established only to benefit from EU funds. As Güner (2009) from TAV puts it, 'in order to be much more active, we have to be strong in economic terms, which depends on the projects'. Thus, financial sustainability is one of the main challenges of civil society in Turkey. Because of decrease in the momentum of Turkey-EU relations and financial problems, the Association of Turkey-EU Relations (TurkAB) had to be closed in 2009.

The Progress Reports which have been prepared by the EU Commission mentions the progress of civil society in Turkey while criticising its deficiencies in legal and practical terms. The European Commission's 2009 Progress Report on Turkey accepted that the legal framework on associations is now broadly in line with EU standards. However, it still required further progress in terms of implementation. It added that there is a growing awareness within public institutions and by the public about the crucial role played by CSOs, although the legal framework for the collection of donations and tax exemptions for CSOs needs to be strengthened to improve their financial sustainability (2009: 20–21).

The Progress Report of 2010 reported on the State Minister for EU Affairs and Chief Negotiator's frequent meetings with civil society stakeholders to promote their participation in the accession process (2010: 9). In the field of human rights institutions, the report noted that the draft law on the establishment of the Turkish Independent Human Rights Institution had been submitted to Parliament in February 2010, and opinions from the CSOs were discussed by the relevant parliamentary sub-committee. The report emphasised the importance of conducting this process in close consultation with the CSOs. It criticised the lack of resources, independence and impact of human rights institutions. More positively, it noted a continuation in 'raising awareness in public institutions and in the public at large about the role played by CSOs' but warned that 'CSOs continue to face disproportionate administrative checks and fines. Moreover, the bureaucratic requirements for fund-raising, obtaining public benefit status and lack of simplified rules for small or medium-sized associations prevent a more enabling environment for associations. More restrictive legislation applies to foreign associations' (2010: 17–22).

It noted that the 'launching of closure cases against the Lesbian, Gay, Bisexual, Transgender and Transvestite Association (LGBTT) restrains the full exercise of freedom of association' (2010: 22). Continued limitations on trade unions rights were criticised on the grounds that they are not in line with EU standards and ILO conventions. Finally, although the report found that 'the constitutional amendments broaden trade union rights in the public service', it added that 'the constitutional package did not introduce the right to strike for civil servants' (2010: 29–30).

The Progress Report of 2011 reported that legislation in freedom of association is broadly in line with EU standards and the inclusion of CSOs in policy processes has advanced. Particularly it was mentioned that since the appointment of the new Minister of Family and Social Policies, the communication with women organisations has increased. However, women organisations face financial difficulties like other NGOs (2011: 28–33). It was argued that disproportionate controls and restrictive interpretation of the law remain. Funding rules for CSOs remain restrictive. Moreover, they are still facing closure cases and disproportionate administrative checks and fines. It criticises that 'membership in associations continues to require a Turkish residency permit and foreign CSOs are subject to specific regulations' (2011: 28). Legislative and bureaucratic obstacles still persist which negatively affect financial sustainability of CSOs, such as those related with collection of domestic and international aid, obtaining public benefit status for associations and tax exemptions for foundations. In addition to these, the lack of simplified rules causes difficulties for small or medium-sized associations. More restrictive legislation towards foreign associations was criticised in the last progress report. In order to allow opening of a representation in different countries, the Ministry of the Interior has to consult the Ministry of Foreign Affairs. It was mentioned that some foreign CSOs were rejected or have not received any reply from the Ministry of Interior without being informed about the specific reasons behind that decision (2011: 28).

Although civil society in Turkey has benefited a lot from the EU, there has been a decrease in the level of interest of civil society about the EU. Nas (2011) argues that, because the EU has its own internal problems like the debt crisis in Greece, the EU's attractiveness has decreased in Turkey including its civil society.

She claims that for business organisations, there are extra burdens because of adopting the EU *acquis*. For this reason, sometimes they may prefer the *status quo*, which already includes the customs union with the EU. Nas puts forward that civil society in Turkey has started to look from a more global perspective, rather than a European one. New connections and links emerged with various regions, , which may compensate for the EU to a certain extent. In accordance with increasingly multi-dimensional approach in Turkish foreign policy, there has been increasing trade and various connections with the neighbouring regions, and with various regions of the world, which has decreased the primacy and indispensability of the EU for business organisations. She claims that, if relations between Turkey and the EU deteriorate, or even break off or if Turkish democracy is threatened by authoritarian tendencies, then civil society may come to the fore again. Yeşilyurt (2011) from TUSKON argues that 'there is not a tendency to act together in Brussels'. He claims that the civil society can be more influential on Turkey-EU relations, if political governance will establish a suitable atmosphere. He adds that 'it is easier to act together with other Turkish CSOs in Africa or in any other region rather than Europe, because each organisation has its own contacts already in Europe'. Nas (2011) claims that the role played by the EU in terms of transforming civil society in Turkey has now started to be played by Turkey's civil society in the Middle East and Africa. Thus, it can be argued that civil society in Turkey which has been under Europeanisation process, may influence spreading the European values to the neighbouring regions, including Middle East and Africa through interacting with civil societies in those regions.

The Civil Society Index (CSI) project, conducted by the Third Sector Foundation of Turkey (TÜSEV), is the first internationally comparative study of civil society's structure, values, environment and impact in Turkey, based on data collected between 2004 and 2005. It found that civil society in Turkey still has only limited strength, but that it has been undergoing an era of transformation. The low level of participation, inadequate skills and resources of the CSOs and undeveloped linkages among CSOs are the main deficiencies. The environment within which civil society operates has improved due to the reforms introduced in order to fulfil the Copenhagen criteria, providing a better legal framework for CSOs and expanded civic rights and liberties. However, there are still deficiencies regarding adherence to the rule of law, centralised state administration, and undeveloped linkages between the state and civil society and between the private sector and civil society. In terms of values, there has been an increase in the strength of civil society in promoting gender equality and environmental sustainability (2006: 5).

The CSI study also shows that CSOs in Turkey are shifting from being informal, loose groups to more organised institutions. Although the number of the CSOs has increased, it is still low, when we take into consideration the size of the population of Turkey. There are only 108 associations and six foundations per 100,000 citizens. While strong and capable CSOs are emerging, there is still a necessity to promote further citizen involvement. Because of the lack of resources and organisational management skills, the CSOs' ability to recruit professional staff is limited, which limits their skills and capacity. There has been a rise in the number of CSO networks and platforms, especially in environmental movement, women's movement and human rights organisations. There has been an increase in the number of meetings and conferences organised with international CSOs especially under EU-related initiatives, which encourage collaboration. In terms of relations between the government and civil society, there are still some instances of excessive government interference and control. In terms of funding, as civil society expands in terms of size and scope of its activities, there is an increasing need for financial resources. Particularly the EU is becoming a crucial source of funds for CSOs, although new strategies have to be found to broaden the base of donors and to increase the flow of resources to CSOs. The study notes that, although CSOs have a crucial role in promoting democracy, they have deficiencies in the fields of internal democracy, good governance, transparency and accountability (2006: 7–10).

As Table 5.1 shows, the CSOs in Turkey think that the EU and the pre-accession process have had a generally positive impact on the development of civil society in Turkey, especially in terms of transforming the legal framework and promoting certain values. However, they criticised the EU's detailed and tough funding procedures for the projects, also its bureaucracy and lack of transparency. The EU's most positive and significant effects were through the reforms of laws related to civil society and the increasing ability of CSOs to promote democratic values. The EU's least significant but positive effects were related to promoting the capacity for collective action and increasing dialogue between the state and CSOs. The results of the CSI survey show that civil society in Turkey is at a 'critical turning point in its role as an agent of positive social change' (2006: 11).

Referring to the CSI project, İçduygu (2007: 190–92) argues that the respondents, who are from CSOs that are in a better condition in terms of their resources and central locations, perceive that the EU process had a positive impact on the transformation of civil society in Turkey. He puts forward that respondents from the centres perceive the impact of the EU process on the civil society in Turkey positively, compared to respondents from the peripheries. He argues that civil society in Turkey believes that the EU's impact has been limited, while the impact of the EU on value dimension of the civil society in Turkey is more visible. He claims that the EU process is transforming the values of Turkish CSOs in two ways: Firstly, if they work on value-related issues, the process enables EU recognition and the possibility to obtain resources from the EU; secondly, the process usually challenges them to redefine their perceptions about these values.

The second CSI study which took place in 2010 shows that civil society in Turkey is going on its transition process with more weaknesses than strengths. It pointed out that the acceleration of civil society's transition has decreased. It claims that it may build on its strengths to increase its role and influence in social and political life of Turkey or it may enter a period of stagnation (İçduygu, Meydanoglu and Sert 2011: 18). In the last CSI study it was found that civic engagement is still very narrow in Turkey, where different regions and social groups can participate in civil society at varying degrees. Thus, CSOs should

Table 5.1   CSOs' view on impact of the EU on civil society in Turkey

%	No Impact	Limited Negative	Limited Positive	Somewhat Positive
Legal frameworks	0	9.4	7.1	46.5
Dialogue with state	3.1	0.8	33.9	38.6
Financial capacity	6.6	2.5	29.5	33.6
Promoting democratic values	1.6	1.6	14.2	48.8
Promoting capacity for collective action	3.2	2.4	42.1	32.5

Source: Civil Society Index 2006: 11

develop innovative mechanisms to increase citizen participation. CSOs still have insufficient level of institutionalisation, they have problematic governance structures and insufficient resources. They should develop written policies and share them publicly to promote transparency and increase the level of participation of public to civil society activities. Foundations and associations in Turkey usually work on social solidarity and social services, while there are still a limited number of organisations which work on rights and related policies. The EU process continues to be perceived mostly positively especially in terms of establishing more democratic legal framework, improvement of financial capacity and encouraging societal movements. Compared to the previous study, the last report stated that government-civil society relations are in a worse position (2011: 143–5).

Conclusion

Since Turkey was given an official candidate status by the EU, several linkages and networks have been established between civil society actors in Turkey and the EU, which have been the driving forces of Europeanisation in Turkey, particularly the Europeanisation of Turkish civil society. The EU's institutions and programmes have transformed the activities of civil society through their engagement with CSOs in Turkey (İçduygu 2007: 191–4). This influence has included supporting financing of their activities, the identification of areas where reform is necessary and monitoring improvements during the pre-accession process. Through its annual progress reports, the Commission in particular has pressured the government to carry out further reforms and draft the new Law on Associations. The resulting quantitative and qualitative development of Turkish civil society has increased its strength and influence so that civil society has started to be seen as an asset, rather than a threat by the state (Grigoriadis 2009: 64).

   The main transformative power of the EU on civil society in Turkey can be observed in changes in the legal framework of civil society through the principle of 'conditionality'. EU funds have influenced civil society through supporting certain types of CSOs and influencing their agendas and priorities.

The interactions with the EU have promoted a socialisation process for CSOs which led to increasing level of cooperation between CSOs in Turkey and those in the member states of the EU. However, the level of cooperation among CSOs in Turkey is still low. In order to increase interactions between members of CSOs in Turkey and those in EU member states, the former have to become more informed about EU funding and project management. In addition, EU visa requirements for Turkish CSO representatives have to be made at least easier and more flexible.

The civil society can contribute to accession process of Turkey to the EU and it is one of the main agents of Europeanisation process in Turkey. Before the start of the accession negotiations in 2005, CSOs were much more active in terms of pushing the government for reforms, and lobbying in Brussels for Turkey's membership. With the stagnation in Turkey-EU relations there is a decreasing enthusiasm to the process among CSOs. The CSOs' level of interest in the accession process has decreased for several reasons. The most important one was the blocking of 18 chapters because of the Cyprus issue and France, whose former President was against full membership of Turkey. Unclear and inconsistent signals from the EU have also led to increasing scepticism towards Turkey's membership, which has negatively influenced the momentum of the Europeanisation process in Turkey. Thus, there is a high level of pessimism in Turkish society including CSOs about the membership prospect of Turkey to the EU. Consequently, many CSOs prefer to focus on EU projects to remain financially sustainable, rather than focusing on lobbying activities in Brussels and in other member states of the EU or pushing the Turkish government for further reforms.

Overall, Europeanisation process has transformed the legal framework of civil society in Turkey; however, there are still many deficiencies in the implementation of the law. Currently, the influence of civil society in Turkey still cannot match the influence of civil society in EU member states (İçduygu 2007: 193). The last CSI study put forward that the acceleration of transformation of civil society in Turkey has decreased (2011: 145).

During negotiations with the EU, the participation of CSOs should be encouraged more by the government, and a regular institutionalized consultation mechanism must be established. The 'Communication Strategy', which was pioneered by the Secretariat General for EU Affairs of Turkey, should be developed more and CSOs should be more active in the implementation of this strategy. Through increasing interactions with their counterparts in the member states of the EU, 'social learning' of civil society in Turkey should go on in order to overcome challenges to reaccelerate the transition process of civil society in Turkey. If Europeanisation of Turkey including its civil society will go on and the values of the EU will be internalised particularly through its civil society, Turkey may play a crucial role in its neighbouring regions, including the Middle East and Africa, by spreading the values of the EU through increasing interactions between CSOs in Turkey and civil society in those regions.

References

Bayer, R. and Öniş, Z. 2010. Turkish big business in the age of democratic consolidation: The nature and limits of its influence. *South European Society and Politics*, 15(2), 181–201.

Bikmen, F. and Meydanoglu, Z. 2006. *Civil Society in Turkey: An Era of Transition – CIVICUS Civil Society Index Report for Turkey*. Istanbul: TÜSEV Publications.

Börzel, T. 2002. Pace-setting, foot-dragging and fence-sitting: member state responses to Europeanisation. *Journal of Common Market Studies*, 40(2),193–214.

Ministry for EU Affairs (Republic of Turkey). 2009. *Civil Society Dialogue I*. [Online]. Available at: http://www.abgs.gov.tr/index.php?p=5966&l=2 [accessed: 7 May 2010].

Communication from the Commission to the Council, the European Parliament, the European Economic and Social Committee and the Committee of the Regions: Civil Society Dialogue between the EU and Candidate Countries. 29 June 2005. Brussels.

Diez, T., Agnantopoulos, A. and Kaliber, A. 2005. File: Turkey, Europeanisation and civil society. *South European Society and Politics*, 10(1), 1–15.

Ergun, A. 2010. Civil society in Turkey and local dimensions of Europeanisation. *European Integration*, 32(5), 507–22.

European Commission. 2009. *Regular Report on Turkey's Progress Towards Accession*. [Online]. Available at: http://ec.europa/enlargement/pdf/keydocuments/2009/tr_rapport_2009_en.pdf [accessed: 29 November 2009].

European Commission. 2010. *Regular Report on Turkey's Progress Towards Accession*. [Online]. Available at: http://ec.europa.eu/enlargement/pdf/key_documents/2010/package/tr_rapport_2010_-en.pdf [accessed: 5 December 2011].

European Commission. 2011. *Regular Report on Turkey's Progress Towards Accession*. [Online]. Available at: http://ec.europa.eu/enlargement/pdf/key_documents/2011/package/tr_rapport_2011_-en.pdf [accessed: 8 November 2011].

Göksel, D.N. and Güneş, R.B. 2005. The role of NGOs in the European integration process: the Turkish experience. *South European Society and Politics*, 10(1), 57–72.

Grigoriadis, I.N. 2009. *Trials of Europeanisation: Turkish Political Culture and the EU*, New York: Palgrave Macmillan Pub.

İçduygu, A. 2007. The anatomy of civil society in Turkey: toward a transformation, in *Remaking Turkey: Globalization, Alternative Modernities and Democracy*, edited by E.F. Keyman. Lanham: Lexington, 179–197.

İçduygu, A., Meydanoglu, Z. and Sert, D. 2011. *Civil Society in Turkey: At a Turning Point – CIVICUS Civil Society Index Project Analytical Country Report for Turkey II*. Istanbul: TÜSEV Publications.

Keyman, E.F. and İçduygu, A. 2003. Globalization, civil society and citizenship in Turkey: actors, boundaries and discourses. *Citizenship Studies*, 7(2), 219–34.

Kubicek, P. 2005. The European Union and grassroots democratization in Turkey. *Turkish Studies*, 6(3), 361–77.

Öniş, Z. and Türem, U. 2008. Business, globalization and democracy: a comparative analysis of Turkish business associations, in *The Politics of Modern Turkey: Critical Issues in Modern Politics, Vol.II: Political Institutions and Processes*, edited by A. Çarkoğlu and W. Hale. New York: Routledge, 303–27.

Radaelli, C.M. 2003. The Europeanisation of public policy, in *The Politics of Europeanisation*, edited by K. Featherstone and C.M. Radaelli. Oxford: Oxford University, 27–57.

Radaelli, C.M. and Pasquier, R. 2007. Conceptual issues, in *Europeanisation: New Research Agendas*, edited by P. Graziano and M.P. Vink. Basingstoke: Palgrave Macmillan, 35–45.

Schimmelfennig, F. and Sedelmeier, U. 2005 (eds). *The Europeanisation of Central and Eastern Europe*. London: Cornell Unv.

Weber, W. 2006. Relations between the state and civil society in Turkey: Does the EU make a difference?, in *Turkey and the EU: Internal Dynamics and External Challenges*, edited by J.S. Joseph. New York: Palgrave Macmillan, 83–95.

Yankaya, D. 2009. The Europeanisation of MÜSİAD: Political opportunism, economic Europeanisation, islamic euroscepticism. *European Journal of Turkish Studies*, 9, 2–18.

Interviews

Aküzüm, Ural, Arı Movement, 1 October 2009 at 18.30.

Akyüz, Ali Alper. Bilgi University, 15 July 2009 at 16.00.

Batu, Arda. Arı Movement, 1 October 2009 at 18.00.

Genç, Özge. TESEV, 13 July 2009 at 16.00.

Güner, Şükrü. TAV, 16 July 2009, at 16.00.

Nas, Çiğdem. İKV, 17 March 2011, at 16.30.

Oktay, Cansu Denef, European Information Centre (İTO), 2 June 2010 at 15.30.

Özsu, Bahar, European Information Centre (İTO), 2 June 2010 at 15.30.

Sevand, Ayla, KAGİDER, 3 June 2010, at 12.00.

Şenyücel, Sabiha. TESEV, 13 July 2009, at16.00.

Yeşilyurt, Serdar, TUSKON, 11 July 2011, at 15.00.

Chapter 6

From EU Conditionality to Domestic Choice for Change: Exploring Europeanisation of Minority Rights in Turkey

Gözde Yılmaz

Introduction

The Helsinki Summit in 1999 represents a turning point for EU-Turkey relations. Turkey gained status as a formal candidate country for the EU providing a strong incentive to introduce democratic reforms for the ultimate reward of membership. Since 2002, the country has launched a number of reforms in minority rights. Many controversial issues, such as denial of the existence of the Kurds, or the lack of property rights granted to non-Muslim minorities in the country, have made progress. Even though the reforms in minority rights may represent a tremendous step for the Europeanisation process of Turkey, the trend in minority-related policy change is neither progressive nor smooth.

Starting the analysis from an empirical puzzle, which is the variance in minority-related policy change in Turkey between 1999 and 2010, the chapter aims to answer how the change in the minority-related policies in Turkey can be explained and under which conditions minority rights measures have been adopted and constrained. By focusing on this specific question, I analyse minority-related policy change in three time periods with a preparation phase of 1999 and 2001: progressing formal rule adoption with very limited implementation between 2002 and 2004; slow down in formal rule adoption with limited implementation between 2005 and 2007; and revival of formal rule adoption with progressing implementation between 2008 and 2010.

The chapter argues that none of the theoretical frameworks of external Europeanisation is capable of explaining the minority-related change in Turkey covering the whole time period between 1999 and 2010. Yet, providing a partial explanation to the process, EU conditionality and domestic choice for change conceptualised by the external incentives and lesson-drawing models need further scholarly attention. The present analysis proves that there is a sequential operation of the two models, enabling the continuum of change from 1999 to 2010.

Theorising External Europeanisation? Mechanisms of Domestic Change

It is important to note that the literature on Europeanisation of candidate countries focused dominantly on top-down adjustment or adaptation pressures from the EU, and eastern enlargement and CEECs (Sedelmeier 2011: 5). This trend posed limitations to the research area. First of all, the general focus of the impact of EU conditionality on accession countries beginning with Eastern enlargement has limited the scope of analysis in the literature. Research in the context of EU conditionality and eastern enlargement, on the one hand, broadened the scope of analysis in the Europeanisation literature by focusing enlargement process, on the other hand, limited the scope by relying mainly on top-down approaches.

Most research in the literature placed heavy emphasis on EU conditionality and domestic mediating factors (domestic adjustment costs, veto players or domestic opposition) (Kelley 2004, Schimmelfennig and Sedelmeier 2005, Pridham 2005). As Pasquier and Radaelli (2007: 40) ascertain, there are two classic problems in the Europeanisation literature: '(i) prejudging the impact of the EU on domestic politics and policy; (ii) assuming that if some domestic changes look similar to those proposed by Brussels, this must be an instance of Europeanisation'.

In spite of the heavy reliance on EU conditionality, the literature on Europeanisation of accession countries also provides different perspectives to the process. One of them is the lesson-drawing model relying on domestic choice of the candidates for change. The lesson-drawing model usually neglected in the literature is based on the idea that domestic policy dissatisfaction with the *status quo* leads policy-makers to learn policies and rules from abroad (Schimmelfennig and Sedelmeier 2005: 21, Rose 1991: 11). Policy dissatisfaction may arise through a number of factors such as a policy failure, change in the environment, or electoral competition (Rose 1993: 60–61). The EU, in this model, is not the primary factor behind policy changes. Rather, policy change is domestically driven and voluntary, thereby a domestic choice.

Domestic change is a consequence of the attempt to solve domestic policy problems in the model (Schimmelfennig and Sedelmeier 2005: 22). According to the model, change is more likely as the perception that domestic rules are working satisfactorily decreases and dissatisfaction with domestic rules increases (Rose 1993, Schimmelfennig and Sedelmeier 2005). The model starts from a specific policy failure leading to domestic dissatisfaction with the *status quo* of policy makers, which is the stimulus for policy makers to search for new policies to transfer from elsewhere (Rose 1991: 11).

To sum up, while scholars focus more on the impact of the EU, there is a tendency to neglect the possibility of domestic choice. As Börzel and Risse (2009: 8) stress, the lesson-drawing model is the least-researched area in the literature. Moreover, as Schimmelfennig and Sedelmeier (2005: 21) discuss, particular cases in the CEECs accession process 'lie at the borderline between domestic choice and EU-induced rule adoption'. Though, the case of Turkey provides the opportunity to perceive different forms of motivations for change. Considering the limitations in the literature, the present research provides a different perspective by focusing on Turkey as a case study and including a bottom-up approach to the analysis.

The EU and Minority Rights: Common, Double or Any Standards?

International standards for minority rights were mostly shaped in the 1990s. However, there is still no consensus on the definition of minorities, as neither the United Nations (UN), nor the Council of Europe (CoE), or the Organisation of Security and Cooperation in Europe (OSCE) as the active organisations for the protection of minorities and also the EU clarified it within their documents. Even though the definition of minorities still remains a controversial issue, the definition of Francesco Capotorti (1979) has been widely recognised but not officially accepted by the international community, including the EU.

In the 1990s, the EU started to put heavy emphasis on minority rights through the accession process of CEECs due to the potential threat of minority discontent to stability and democracy throughout Europe in the post-Cold War era (Ram 2003: 28, Kurban 2008: 272). However, the Union has developed neither a minority standard within the internal *acquis* nor a European standard for all member states (Schwellnus 2005: 56, Nas 1998, Toggenburg 2000). Despite the principle of non-discrimination, which is a part of *acquis communautaire* for the adoption by candidate countries, being a highly developed standard, minority rights remain a vague issue within the Union (Schwellnus 2005: 51). Double standards in minority rights have become a highly debated issue due to the EU's differential treatment of the issue concerning member and candidate states (Schwellnus 2001: 3). While neglecting the member states' treatment to its minorities, the EU has been paying increasing attention to minority protection in candidate countries. The principles of respect for minorities and protection of minorities have become a part of the EU enlargement policy since the 1993 Copenhagen Summit by the explicit reference to minority protection in the Copenhagen Criteria (Sasse 2008: 846).

Recently in 2009, the adoption of the Treaty on the European Union is a vital development in minority rights within the EU. The Lisbon Treaty refers to the 'minorities' explicitly for the first time as an EU primary law. Nevertheless, the Treaty does not provide a definition of the term 'minority', which in return, leaves the issue open. However, the Lisbon Treaty is a very important step for the Union confirming rights of persons belonging to minorities as a value on which the Union is founded; therefore, not any more limited to a condition for accession to the EU.

In the accession process, the EU expects three main conditions to be fulfilled in minority rights by candidate states; membership to the CoE and adoption of the CoE Framework Convention for the Protection of National Minorities, adoption of the Council Directive 2000/43, comprising of the principle of non-discrimination, and adoption of measures, specified for each country in the individual country reports and Accession Partnerships (Ram 2003: 34–5, Rechel 2008: 174).

Yet, application of EU conditionality in minority rights is problematic. The problems in the EU's approach of minority rights, such as the lack of a common standard in the area, limit the positive minority-related policy change in candidate states. The accession process of CEECs demonstrates the limited impact of the minority rights, especially considering the implementation problems of these countries (Brosig 2010, Rechel 2008, Sasse 2008). Nevertheless, the CEECs achieved minimum levels of legislation on minority protection and most of them even adopted minority-related measures more than any previous accession candidates and also member states (Johnson 2006: 51).

To summarise, minority protection has not developed as an EU rule and it remains a highly contested issue due to its nature, remaining within the sovereignty of the member countries. Moreover, EU conditionality in minority rights varies across candidate countries depending on the degree of their minority problem. The problems in the EU's approach to minority rights, such as the lack of common standards on minority rights or the existence of double standards for member and candidate states, limit the positive minority-related policy change in candidate states. The accession process of CEECs demonstrates the limited impact of the EU (Brosig 2010: 400, Rechel 2008, Sasse 2005, Ram 2003).

Minority Rights in Turkey: Policy Change in Progress

The concept of minority in the country is derived from the 1923 Lausanne Peace Treaty, which is still in force today and cited by many as the official policy in regard to minority rights. The Treaty defines minorities in Turkey as non-Muslims limited to only Armenians, Greeks, and Jews (Nas 1998). The rights of these minorities are under the protection of the international arena (i.e. the League of Nations at the time the treaty was signed). Therefore, Turkey has rejected the international definition of the minority concept on the basis of racial, linguistic, or religious differences (Oran 2004: 64). As a result, Turkey, from the very emergence of the Republic, has denied the existence of Muslim minorities such as Kurds and Alevis and their rights to preserve their differences (Grigoriadis 2008: 31).

The discriminatory character of the Ottoman *Millet System* has been preserved in Turkey with a denial of the existence of Muslim minorities and a restricted definition of non-Muslim minorities to Armenians, Greeks and Jews. As a result, minority rights in Turkey, prior to the launch of the reforms in the area, were a restricted policy area, both rhetorically and practically. Both the official and societal stance over minorities were shaped by the denial of minorities and the perception of them as 'threats' to the integrity of the state, as tools of foreign interference to the internal policies of the state and as second class citizens (Grigoriadis 2008: 31, Oran 2004: 64). Furthermore, until the early 2000s Turkey did not have any legal document except the Lausanne Treaty. Moreover, in the 1982 Constitution no article dealing with minority rights was present (Minority Rights Group International Report on Turkey 2007: 10). In addition, the Lausanne

Treaty, as the only official document for minority protection, has not been fully implemented (Oran 2009). In contrast, some articles of the 1982 Constitution were used to restrict minority rights. Reforms of these restricted policies concerning minority rights began to change at the turn of the twenty-first century.

Having a progressing trend, Turkey's legal adoption and implementation of minority rights will be demonstrated via analysing two forms of rule adoption in three time periods, 2002 and 2004, 2005 and 2007, 2008 and 2010. Beginning in February 2002, the coalition government of the Nationalist Movement Party (MHP), True Path Party (DSP) and Motherland Party (ANAP) started to launch reforms for the legal harmonisation of Turkish laws with EU laws, though not focused on minority issues. After the 2002 elections, the Justice and Development Party (AKP) government continued enthusiastically the reforms in a number of policy areas, including minority rights. Eight reform packages passed the parliament between 2002 and 2004. The reform packages included both amendments of some rules restricting minority rights and the adoption of new measures to improve minority protection.

Legal adoption in this period touched several areas in minority rights ranging from removing bans on broadcasting in other languages than Turkish used in the daily life of citizens to the property rights of the non-Muslim foundations (Yılmaz 2011). The government also granted minorities some legal protection by ratifying international agreements: the 1965 UN Convention on the Elimination of All Forms of Racial Discrimination in 2002, and both the International Covenant on Civil and Political Rights and the International Covenant on Economic, Social and Cultural Rights in 2003 (Secretariat General for EU Affairs of Turkey 2007: 19). The legal reforms in this period, therefore, represent a break from the previous policies providing a momentum for positive change in minority protection.

Between 2005 and 2007, legal adoption slowed down significantly in the area. Even though there were some legal changes, such as the new Law on Foundations, or the adoption of the ninth harmonisation package, legal adoption was inconclusive in this period when compared to the period between 2002 and 2004 (Yılmaz 2011).

The year 2008 represents the revival of legal adoption in minority rights. The government launched a number of legal reforms including the adoption of new foundations law, a law on de-mining the Turkish-Syrian border, minority circular – declaring the right of non-Muslim minorities to exercise their cultural rights, which are part of their identities – and, the Kurdish initiative to solve the Kurdish problem (European Commission 2009, Freedom House 2010, Yılmaz 2011, Turkish Official Gazette 2010).

Even though Ankara has adopted and amended a number of legal rules since 2002 in regard to minority protection, legal adoption is not complete. For instance, Turkey has not signed the CoE Framework Convention for the protection of National minorities nor eliminated the restrictive interpretation of the Lausanne treaty, which were consistently demanded by the EU (European Commission 2009:

28). What we have seen in the case of Turkey is the selective legal approximation of the minority-related rules demanded by the EU.

Implementation of minority rights, which is indicated by the practical implementation of the rules adopted in the previous years, has surprisingly shown a progressing trend. Between 2002 and 2004, the implementation of minority-related rules was very limited. Despite remaining limited, implementation of minority protection rules in this early phase still took place. The implementation ranged from property rights of non-Muslim foundations to broadcasting and teaching in languages other than Turkish (Yılmaz 2011: 17–18, Hammarberg 2009: 4).

Between 2005 and 2007, the implementation process continued to progress despite a slowdown in legal adoption of EU rules. Nevertheless, progress in implementation did not halt as a whole and implementation of earlier legal reforms was systematically promoted (Freedom House 2007: 2). For instance, broadcasting in languages other than Turkish, including Kurdish, moved on further in 2007, despite severe restrictions (Freedom House 2009: 3, UN Committee on the Elimination of Racial Discrimination 2008: 27). Consequently, the period represents a limited degree of implementation.

Since 2008, many restrictions on the implementation of many minority-related rules have been removed and the process has intensified (Yılmaz 2011). Several rules adopted in the previous periods have begun to be implemented properly such as broadcasting in other languages or the Foundations Law. A considerably tolerant environment has been reached in the period, in part due to the debates launched by the government on several issues, which were not touched in the past such as the Armenian issue and Kurdish issue. This period is one of intensifying implementation, although still limited.

To conclude, both legal adoption and implementation process of minority rights in Turkey varied across time (see Table 6.1). Earlier studies on the accession of CEECs revealed that legal reforms were principally dutiful in the pre-accession period (Falkner, Oliver and Holzleithner 2008: 2). However, the research also stresses that implementation in these countries was problematic (Falkner, Oliver and Holzleithner 2008: 2). This suggests a need to explore the factors led to progressing implementation in the case of Turkey.

Table 6.1   Rule adoption and implementation in minority rights

Form of Rule Adoption Year	Formal Rule Adoption	Implementation
2002–2004	Progress	Very limited
2005–2007	Slow down	Limited
2008–2010	Revival	Progressing

How to Explain Europeanisation of Minority Rights in Turkey?

In this section, the chapter analyses scope conditions of three external Europeanisation mechanisms in order to explain the differentiated outcome of Turkish minority policy by dividing the process into three time periods, which were determined on the basis of variation in policy change: progress with very limited implementation between 2002 and 2004; slow down with limited implementation between 2005 and 2007; and revival with progressing implementation between 2008 and 2010.

EU Conditionality Fading Away?

Analysing the impact of EU conditionality, I use an external incentives model provided by the external Europeanisation literature (Schimmelfennig and Sedelmeier 2005). According to the model, the likelihood of domestic change increases: with the determinacy of rules set as conditions for rewards (determinacy hypothesis); with the size and speed of rewards (rewards hypotheses); with the credibility of conditional threats and rewards (credibility hypothesis) (Schimmelfennig and Sedelmeier 2005, Kelley 2004). On the other hand, domestic change is less likely with the number of veto players incurring net adoption costs (opportunity costs, welfare, and power losses) from compliance (adoption cost hypothesis) (Börzel and Risse 2000, 2003, Kelley 2004, Schimmelfennig and Sedelmeier 2005). Though the empirical analyses in a wide range of research in the area prove that credibility of EU conditionality and the size of adoption costs are the key factors in regard to domestic change in accession countries (Schimmelfennig and Sedelmeier 2005, Magen and Morlino 2009, Kelley 2004). Therefore, this chapter takes into consideration the most relevant conditions for domestic change.

Credibility of EU Conditionality

The credibility of EU conditionality, operating through a carrots and sticks policy, depends on EU's ability to provide new opportunities and constraints for domestic actors (Kelley 2004, Magen and Morlino 2009, Schimmelfennig and Sedelmeier 2005). It is widely recognised that the credibility of EU conditionality has been the most important factor that influence efficacy of EU conditionality in the enlargement process.

The credibility of EU conditionality stemmed from the linkage of political criteria, which was outlined in the 1993 Copenhagen Summit, to the EU membership. The consistency of references to political criteria and the instances of referring to non-political criteria for accession by the EU institutions and member states constitute the primary determinants of the credibility of EU conditionality. Exploring the linkage of membership to political and non-political criteria in Turkey's accession process, the analysis reveals that the credibility of EU conditionality for Turkey gradually became weaker by 2004 due to the increasing references by EU institutions to non-political criteria for Turkey's accession to the Union.

Between 1999 and 2004, both the Commission and the Council clearly stated that the membership conditions, which include the same criteria for all candidate countries, for Turkey depended solely on the political criteria (European Commission 2002: 5–8, European Council 2002: 3, European Commission 2003: 15). These remarks delivered a certain signal that Turkey was on the track towards accession negotiations when the country fulfilled the Copenhagen criteria.

Since 2004, the credibility of EU conditionality was weakened due to the sharp decrease in references to the political criteria and increase to the non-political criteria for membership of Turkey, including EU's absorption capacity, open-ended nature of accession negotiations with Turkey, the peaceful settlement of border disputes and good neighbourly relations, Cyprus problem, and even the population of Turkey (European Commission 2004a, European Council 2004, European Commission 2004b, European Commission 2004c).

The 2005 debate flourished among member states questioning the decision of launching accession negotiations with Turkey had also an extensive negative impact on the process. The settlement of the Cyprus problem as another non-political criterion for Turkey to meet has become the focal point of Turkey's accession negotiations since 2006 (European Council 2006: 22, European Commission 2006: 24). The EU through its official statements has urged Turkey to find a peaceful settlement for the Cyprus problem and after the Republic of Cyprus (RoC) membership to the Union to recognise the divided island as one represented by the Greek side. While the first demand needs to be considered as a non-political criterion outside of Copenhagen criteria, the latter is a valid and legitimate demand of the Union on the basis that 'the recognition and equal treatment of all member states is a fundamental rule of the EU' (Schimmelfennig 2008: 927). The recent period from 2008 to 2010 proved even lower levels of credibility due to peaceful settlement of disputes, specifically for the Cyprus issue, and public support for the enlargement (European Commission 2009b: 21, European Commission 2010: 13–22, European Council 2010: 3–4). Moreover, the issue of Turkey's recognition of RoC has become a serious obstacle for Turkey's possible membership to the Union (European Commission 2008a, 2009a, 2010, European Council 2008, European Commission 2008b, 2009b).

In return, the translation of decreasing credibility of EU conditionality to the domestic arena has become evident by 2006. The privileged partnership debate caused a high drop in public support for EU membership in Turkey from 74 per cent in 2002 to 50 per cent since 2006 (Öniş 2009: 25). The debate strengthened the anti-European coalition in Turkey via the failure of the Cyprus settlement and the demand of the EU and refusal of Turkey to open Turkish ports to the RoC (Aybet 2006: 532–3).

As a result, the credibility of EU conditionality in the accession process of Turkey has been weakened starting with 2004, which, in return, has limited EU's impact in minority rights in Turkey and also has harmed EU's image in the international arena. While RoC was accepted as a member state without solving its problem with the Northern Turkish part of the island, Turkey has been forced to recognise RoC as a member state and its accession negotiations has been interrupted due to the issue. Such an act by the EU has weakened its image as a value and norm exporter to wider Europe. In return, the EU, for the first time in its enlargement history, has been perceived as an unreliable partner.

Veto Players and Adoption Costs

Domestic factors in the external incentives model are conceptualised under an undifferentiated veto players and adoption costs factor (Sedelmeier 2011: 30). The underspecification of the domestic factor in the model leads to *ad hoc* operationalisation and different conceptualisations of adoption costs (Sedelmeier 2011: 30). Moreover, the number of veto players cannot be expected as being fluid over a short period of time. Therefore, rather than conceptualising veto players on the grounds of their number, this chapter draws from the power and impact of the veto players incurring adoption costs, the relevant costs to minority rights.

By 2002, Kemalist elites concentrated on key state institutions (the CHP in the parliament, the president, officials in the Turkish Armed Forces (TAF), and judicial elites) acted as the main veto players in Turkey (Çınar 2011: 13). Kemalism as the state ideology of Turkey has been challenged by the whole reform process and especially by minority reforms. The Kemalist ideology has two important characteristics: secularism, which endures strict separation of religion and state and the unitary nature of the State reflecting a single Turkish identity (Posch 2007: 10). As Ulusoy (2007: 477) points out, the reforms challenge 'the whole political project upon which the Republic was established in 1923'. Therefore, Kemalist elites acting as veto players incurred a high degree of adoption costs, particularly in regard to minority rights. First of all, the reforms in minority rights broke many taboos in the first principle of Kemalism, the unitary nature of the State, such as the long denial of existence of Muslim minorities – mainly Kurds. Moreover, the Kurdistan Workers' Party (PKK) constituted the main reference point in dealing with minorities by the veto players perceiving minority reforms endangering the unitary of state. Second, the secular character of Turkey was even more problematic for veto players due to the Islamist roots of the ruling party, the AKP. Through time, the reaction by the veto players increased to the AKP policies on the basis of danger created by the Islamic roots of the party against the secular state.

Since the AKP formed a majority in the time period under consideration, the impact of the CHP (Republican People's Party) as the main opposition party remained limited (Kumbaracıbaşı 2009: 76). Therefore, the main veto players emerged as the President, the TAF and the Constitutional Court, representing the judicial veto players (Kumbaracıbaşı 2009: 76, Çınar 2011: 13). The president with veto powers, the TAF perceived as the guardian of Kemalist ideals with popular support from the wider public to that end, and the Constitutional Court with the power of jurisdiction as final decisions over constitutionality of laws, governmental decrees and rules for parliamentary procedures had all immense powers to veto the reform process including minority rights (Kumbaracıbaşı 2009: 62–70). It is important to note that these actors were active in different time periods, such as the military between 2005 and 2007 and the increasing role of the Constitutional Court by 2007.

To begin with, between 2002 and 2004 the consensus among domestic actors was strong and the adoption costs for minority reforms were lower than any periods. First, domestic actors in Turkey reached a consensus in this period to launch reforms comprising minority protection measures (Aydın-Düzgit and Çarkoğlu 2006: 73). Among veto players, the TAF and the CHP were supportive of the reform process in this period, which was mainly characterised as the measures taken for EU accession process (Aydın-Düzgit and Çarkoğlu 2006: 71). Especially the TAF defined the EU membership as a national goal and approached the process supportively (Turkmen 2008: 153). Second, the arrest of Abdullah Öcalan, the leader of the PKK, in 1999 and the ceasefire of the PKK significantly decreased the adoption costs (Bahcheli and Noel 2011: 108). These developments enabled the government to launch minority reforms, in this period, due to the decreasing public anger and attitude to treat minority issues as giving concessions to the PKK (Öniş 2003: 14). As a result, domestic adoption costs triggering the reaction of veto players in regard to minority rights were at a low degree between 2002 and 2004 (Saatçioğlu 2010: 10, Aydın-Düzgit and Keyman 2007: 75).

After 2005, a number of events stirred the nationalist sentiments in Turkey. Patton (2007: 345) portrays it as reactionary nationalism caused by the demands of the EU about sensitive issues such as the Cyprus problem, cultural rights to the minorities (especially Kurds are the subject of the reaction), and the Armenian issue. With the privileged partnership debate, the reactions from domestic actors against any European demand boomed dramatically in this period. Rather than the number of veto players, which remained constant, both the power and impact of the veto players are high in this period. Moreover, the end of the ceasefire in 2004 and the revival of PKK terrorism had particular importance in this context, which fuelled the nationalist sentiments further in Turkey (Aydın-Düzgit and Çarkoğlu 2006: 61–4, Bahcheli and Noel 2011: 108). As Patton (2007: 346) emphasises, nationalists put pressure on the government by asserting 'the EU-induced reform laws have weakened the Turkish state, made it impossible to effectively fight terrorism and encouraged Kurdish separatism'.

Additionally, the period after 2005 witnessed a series of political crises between the pro-reformist government of the AKP and veto players primarily Kemalist opposition led by the CHP, the TAF, the president, Ahmet Necdet Sezer, and the Constitutional Court. This group became active in vetoing the reforms through the direct veto of the president and the indirect submission of cases to the Constitutional Court.

The contention between the Kemalists and the AKP became intensified in 2007 with the presidential elections and the power of the president to be raised by the AKP (Kumbaracıbaşı 2009: 59, Toktaş and Kurt 2010: 394). The conflict between them surfaced even before the announcement of candidates for presidency. First, the military announced their concerns on the presidential elections with a press conference on 12 April 2007 by the Chief of Staff, Yaşar Büyükanıt stressing the importance of secularism and the ideals of the Republic to which the future President should be bound by heart (NTVMSNBC 2007). The next day, the president, Sezer, made a speech stating, 'internal and external forces had joined together in their shared interest in questioning the basic values of the secular republic' (Polat 2009: 9). These statements led to a series of nationwide protest against the government to demonstrate support to secularism (Polat 2009: 9).

The sharp reaction of Kemalists against the election of Gül as the President was reflected in 2007 by a post of e-memorandum by the TAF on 27 April 2007 criticising the AKP policies and raising attention to secularism and unitary of state (Polat 2009: 9, Posch 2007: 23). Most importantly, the memorandum raised the issue of PKK and stressed the ethnic definition of the nation on the basis of Kemalist ideals: '... anybody who is against the motto of "Happy is who calls himself/herself a Turk" is and will be the enemy of the Republic of Turkey' (Turkish Armed Forces Press Release 2007). The e-memorandum reveals the reaction of the TAF against minority reforms that challenge the definition of national identity and unitary of state. As a consequence, the impact of veto players was significantly high in the period between 2005 and 2007.

By 2008, the polarisation of actors in the domestic arena continued to dominate the political scene in the country. The headscarf issue as a part of the constitutional amendments proposed by the AKP in early 2008 fuelled the contention between the AKP and the CHP, military, and the Constitutional Court (Gençkaya and Özbudun 2009: 107). The headscarf issue was accompanied by the closure case against the AKP on the basis of being a centre for anti-secular activities in 2008. The Court, at the end, decided against the closure of the party, yet, ruled to deprive the AKP from treasury aid on the grounds that the party was becoming a centre for anti-secular activities (Somer 2011: 30). As could be seen in these two cases, the Constitutional Court became a focal point for veto players in the period between 2008 and 2010 against both the AKP and its reforms.

The adoption costs due to the continuum of PKK's deadly attacks also increased in this time period (Baçık and Coşkun 2011: 251). Even though the government attempted to launch peace talks with the PKK in 2009, the organisation has recently escalated its attacks to military targets. As a result, both the power and impact of the veto players and adoption costs remained at a high degree between 2008 and 2010.

To sum up, veto players and adoption costs for change had a significant impact on the political reforms in Turkey. Though the weight of different players on the process varied over time (e.g. the increasing impact of the Constitutional Court and the decreasing impact of the military forces), it could be argued that veto players constrained minority-related policy change. However, the continuum of the reforms in the area by 2008, despite the growing impact of veto players, ruled out the veto players and adoption costs factor in the analysis. Yet, both the credibility of EU conditionality and veto players and adoption costs prove explanatory power to explain the progress in rule adoption with very limited implementation between 2002 and 2004 and slow down with limited implementation between 2005 and 2007. While the high credibility of EU conditionality and consensus among domestic actors for reform provided a trigger for acceleration of reforms between 2002 and 2004, the weakened credibility by 2005 and the increasing contention between the government and veto players led to the slowdown of the process between 2005 and 2007. Yet, the revival with progressing implementation cannot be explained by the model, in which theoretically complete stagnation of the process is expected. In this context, the lesson-drawing model provides a nuanced explanation to the recent process of change in minority rights.

A Recent Upsurge in Policy Dissatisfaction

Policy change, especially minority-related, is naturally influenced by the domestic settings. Although policy change is often bound to the impact of EU conditionality and interventions by the domestic opposition as a drawback to policy change, the domestic context facilitates policy change in some cases rather than constraining it; as it is in the case of minority-related policy change in Turkey (Engert, Knobel and Schimmelfennig 2003, Kelley 2004, Schimmelfennig and Sedelmeier 2005). In Turkey, minority-related policy change has been facilitated through policy dissatisfaction of the single party government of the AKP, by 2002 with an increasing trend by 2008, reflecting a pro-minority position- positive commitment to minority protection.

Policy dissatisfaction of the Turkish government with the previous minority policies between 2002 and 2010 were driven by a number of factors. Yet, political values of the government, the existence of failure in minority rights and also identification of the failure by the government are among the most important factors stimulating policy dissatisfaction, which drives governments to adopt new policies in order to solve problems in the area. A three-step process is evident in this context: first, diagnosing the failure in minority rights; second, the rise of policy dissatisfaction; and last, taking action against failure.

The existence of failure in a policy area is the main condition for reformist governments to search alternative policies in order to replace the previous problematic ones. Policy failure implies that there are discontinuities and dislocations in a given policy such as an inability of minority protection measures (Rose 1993: 60). If policy-makers ignore or heed these problems in a specific area, they may face loss of support or even loss of public office due to the public discontent of the policies (Rose 1991: 12). This results in increasing policy dissatisfaction that works via the threat of sanctions pushing policy-makers to take action against the problematic issues.

Change in Political Values: From Anti-minority Governments to a Pro-minority Government

As the AKP came to power as a reformist party, its political values in general and in regard to minority issues was radically different than the previous parties. By the establishment of the party, the AKP has defined itself as a political reformist emphasising the necessity of democratic governance in Turkey and pledges to be a change agent for bringing democracy to the country through embracing universal values to guarantee individual rights (AKP Election Manifesto 2002: 2).

In this context, the political stance of the party towards minority rights, originated from its main political values primarily aiming to consolidate a democratic system in the country, constitutes the most important determinant in their minority policy. First of all, the AKP has a more pluralistic notion of democracy than majoritarian (Özbudun 2006: 548). In this context, the party considers diversity as a cultural richness that reinforces solidarity in the country rather than a source of gap within the society (Özbudun 2006: 547). Second, the AKP adopts a political stance that refrains any sort of nationalist ideology (Özbudun 2006: 549, Taşkın 2008: 62). The leader of the party, Erdoğan, continuously emphasises that the AKP is against religious, ethnic, and regional nationalism (AKP Party Speech 2003, AKP Party Speech 2006a, AKP Party Speech 2008, AKP Party Speech 2009a). Third, the party adopts a minority approach on the basis of individual rights based on the principle of non-discrimination. The AKP, therefore, promoted an inclusive approach for all citizens, comprising minorities and relying on equality, unity, solidarity and fraternity of the nation. In this context, the party embraces an all-inclusive identity of *Türkiyelilik* (being from Turkey) on the basis of a territorial-historical notion of identity (Taşkın 2008: 62).

To conclude, in contrast to previous restrictive state policy on minority rights, the AKP represents a movement in favour of change in the official minority policy (Aras and Toktaş 2009: 705). Previously, the governments in the country were cautious about both minorities, who were perceived as a threat to the country and tools of foreign interference, and minority rights. The AKP has become one of the most important main change agents in the country, especially in minority rights, with its reformist political values and democratic ideals.

Failure Leads to Dissatisfaction with Minority Rights: AKP's Solution-oriented Approach

> Are there problems of ethnic elements in this country? Yes. All, the Turks, Kurds, Lazs, Circassians, Georgians, Abkhasians, Romas, have their problems in their own way … The Sunnis have problems. The Alevis have problems. Other religious groups have their own problems … the Christians and Musevis also have problems more or less … Are there problems of minorities in this country? Yes. (AKP Party Speech 2010)

Since the AKP government has begun to rule Turkey in 2002, though accelerating in the last years by 2008, the leadership of the party has signalled their dissatisfaction with minority policy in many speeches and adopted a pro-minority political stance. In response to the problems in the area, the party aims to appease its dissatisfaction in the area via a solution-oriented approach. To illustrate this, three issues will be explored: the adoption of inclusive supra-identity against the prior exclusive national identity; the adoption of new foundations law against the problems of non-Muslim foundations; and the Kurdish initiative against the Kurdish problem.

Firstly, the AKP increasingly focused on the tension and polarisation within the society, especially among minority groups and nationalist forces (e.g. AKP Party Speech 2002, AKP Party Speech 2003). In order to prevent further escalation of tension and polarisation among different groups within the society, the AKP adopted an approach eliminating the exclusive definitions of national identity stirring further tension among different groups. In contrast to previous official definition of restrictive 'Muslim Turk' identity, the AKP brought an inclusive definition of national identity on the basis of citizenship, which stems from the comprehensive definition of identity based on *Türkiyelilik*. Erdoğan states in many instances that: '… citizenship of the Republic of Turkey is the supra-identity for all of us' (AKP Party Speech 2005, AKP Party Speech 2008, AKP Party Speech 2009b).

Most importantly, adopting an inclusive approach for national identity, the AKP targeted specifically minorities. A number of speeches by the party reveal the attempt of the party to unite different minority groups in the country under the umbrella of *Türkiyelilik*:

> We are together and one in this country as Turkish, Kurdish, Laz, Circassian, Georgian, Abkhaz, Bosnian. No ethnic element should and can struggle for superiority over others (AKP Party Speech 2008).

> Did not we say that we are together and one in this country with Turkish, Kurdish, Laz, Circassian, Yuruk, Pomak, Roman and we do not accept discrimination (AKP Party Speech 2009a).

Second, the party recognised the limitations in the foundations law directly related to the problems of the non-Muslim minority foundations (AKP Party Speech 2006b). In response to this, the problems in property rights of non-Muslim foundations were, at first, eased in 2003 via an amendment to Article 1 of the Law on Foundations, including the extension of the application period for community foundations to register real estate holdings to 18 months (Turkish Official Gazette 2003). The government continued to amend the law concerning foundations until 2008, which provided further property rights to religious foundations. Finally in 2008, a new Foundations Law was adopted by the Turkish Parliament (Hammarberg 2009: 11). The law provided non-Muslim foundations to be represented in the Foundations' Council and provided for further property rights to these foundations (Hammarberg 2009: 11). Moreover, the implementation of the Law on Foundations, adopted in 2008, proceeded smoothly (European Commission 2009: 21).

Third, in 2006 and later in 2009, Erdoğan recognised the existence of the Kurdish people and the existence of a Kurdish problem, which was officially denied by the state institutions previously (AKP Party Speech 2006c, Hürriyet 2009). Moreover, the government started both a parliamentary and public discussion in order to solve the Kurdish problem (Freedom House 2010). The discussion initiated public and political awareness for making peace with the PKK via the democratisation of Turkey and granting of further rights to Kurdish people, while also encompassing other minorities (Freedom House 2010).

The Kurdish initiative, launched by the AKP government in 2009, represents a vital development in the Kurdish problem by departing from the previous official policy of Turkey in regard to the Kurdish issue. The Kurdish initiative, with a view to extending cultural and linguistic rights to the Kurdish minority, which was also perceived as a major problem in the EU accession talks, was an important step for further progress in the protection of minorities (Freedom House 2010: 4). However, the fate of the initiative has remained in doubt due to the ban of the pro-Kurdish DTP (Democratic Community Party) and the protests, against the initiative, following it (Freedom House 2010: 4).

It is important to note that dissatisfaction works through sanctions, in which there may be the risk of losing support and popularity or losing office for policy-makers (Rose 1993: 61). Therefore, the AKP has been under constant pressure to keep its popularity in the elections.

Several factors contributed to the strategic calculations of the AKP for elections, which necessitate keeping the party's voter base intact and attracting further votes via targeting reformist groups, including minorities in the country. The 2007 elections demonstrated that the party's reformist approach including minority rights yielded results via the reward of increase in party's votes, being 47 per cent share of the total votes. The AKP seemed to persuade the Kurds with its problem-solving approach via clearly stating the existence of the Kurdish problem; differing from the previous official denial of the problem; and providing an approach to solve the problem through the improvement of democracy and human and minority rights (Polat 2009: 1). As a result, the election fever of the party exerted immense pressure on the AKP to keep both its reformist base of votes and attract minority votes via providing solutions to the problems of these groups.

Concluding Remarks

Since 2002, Turkey has adopted and amended a number of legal rules in regard to minority protection with intensive implementation in recent years. The positive change in the area is significant in both the daily life of the citizens of Turkey, and in legal and behavioural adoption. The country has attained a high degree of change in minority protection between 2002 and 2004, which has been pursued since 2008.

Even though the recent legal reforms launched by the government are few, the implementation of the rules adopted in previous years has intensified since 2008.

Yet, empirical data demonstrates the limited capability of the models provided by the literature to explain the whole process between 2002 and 2010 with its ups and downs. However, the chapter explored that EU conditionality which is conceptualised by the external incentives model and domestic choice for change which is conceptualised by the lesson-drawing model has a sequential impact to the process. Triggering a solid ground for reforms by providing rewards and constraints to the domestic actors, EU conditionality drove change in the area between 2002 and 2004. Yet, the decrease in the credibility of EU conditionality and increase in the relative power and impact of veto players incurred adoption costs lead to a slowdown in the reform process between 2005 and 2007. This time period, thereby, can be conceptualised as a transition phase from the impact of EU conditionality to domestic choice for minority-related change in the country. The recent time period between 2008 and 2010 witnessed an upsurge of policy dissatisfaction of the government with minority rights. The rise of the degree of policy dissatisfaction could be bound to the loss of credibility in Turkey's accession process and the government's ideological base relying on both pro-reformist and pro-minority approach. Moreover, a number of interviews conducted by the author confirm that the political fate of the AKP, coming to power via its reformist approach, depends on the continuum of the party's reformist agenda. In order not to be sanctioned by the domestic voter, the AKP devoted itself to preserve its pro-reformist agenda.

Even though the momentum in Turkey's accession process has been lost, the endogenous factor of policy dissatisfaction strengthened its position to drive change. Therefore, Ankara continued minority reforms via domestic motivation for change. The analysis confirms that the AKP government, as Prime Minister Erdoğan often states, '… label (s) the criteria (Copenhagen) as Ankara criteria and carry(s) on the path (of reforms)' (AKP Party Speech 2006c)

As a result, the case of Turkey demonstrates minority-related policy change as a result of sequential impact of EU conditionality and government's policy dissatisfaction with previous minority policies acting as a pioneer for change. Yet, the perfect situation for effective policy change necessitates both positive impact of EU conditionality and pro-minority policy preferences of the government led by policy dissatisfaction. Without one another, policy change remains both limited and selective.

References

AKP Election Manifesto. 2002. [Online]. Available at: http://www.akparti.org.tr/ tbmm/belge.asp [accessed: 30 April 2011].
AKP Party Programme. 2001. [Online]. Available at: http://eng.akparti.org.tr/ english/-partyprogramme.html [accessed: 27 April 2011].

AKP Party Speech. 2003. 2 December.
AKP Party Speech. 2005. 22 November.
AKP Party Speech. 2006a. 14 March
AKP Party Speech. 2006b. 21 March.
AKP Party Speech. 2006c. 26 September.
AKP Party Speech. 2008. 11 November.
AKP Party Speech. 2009a. 20 October.
AKP Party Speech. 2009b. 13 October.
AKP Party Speech. 2010. 22 June.
Aras, B. and Toktaş, Ş. 2009. The EU and minority rights in Turkey. *Political Science Quarterly,* 124(4), 697–720.
Aybet, G. 2006. Turkey and the EU after the first year of negotiations: reconciling internal and external policy challenges. *Security Dialogue,* 37(4), 529–49.
Aydın-Düzgit, S. 2007. *Seeking Kant in the EU's Relations with Turkey.* Istanbul: TESEV Publications.
Aydın-Düzgit, S and Çarkoğlu, A. 2006. EU Conditionality and Democratic Rule of Law in Turkey. Development and the Rule of Law Working Paper. Centre on Democracy. Stanford University.
Aydın-Düzgit, S. and Keyman, F.E. 2007. Europeanisation, democratisation and human rights in Turkey, in *Turkey and the European Union Prospects for a Difficult Encounter,* edited by E. LaGro and K.E. Jorgensen. Basingstoke: Palgrave Macmillan. 69–89.
Baçık G. and Coşkun B.B. 2011. The PKK problem: explaining Turkey's failure to develop a political solution. *Studies in Conflict and Terrorism,* 34, 248–65.
Bahcheli T. and Noel S. 2011. The Justice and Development Party and the Kurdish question, in *Nationalisms and Politics in Turkey Political Islam, Kemalism and the Kurdish Issue,* edited by M. Casier and J. Jongerden. Abingdon, Oxon: Routledge, 101–20.
Börzel, T.A. and Risse, T. 2003. Conceptualising the domestic impact of Europe, in *The Politics of Europeanisation,* edited by K. Featherstone and C.M. Radaelli, Oxford: Oxford University Press, 57–80.
Börzel, T.A. and Risse, T. 2000. When Europe hits home: Europeanisation and domestic change. *European Integration Online Papers (EIoP),* 4(15).
Brosig, M. 2010. The challenge of implementing minority rights in Central Eastern Europe. *Journal of European Integration,* 32(4), 393–411.
Capotorti, F. 1979. Study on the Rights of Persons Belonging to Ethnic, Religious and Linguistic Minorities. United Nations. E/CN4/Sub2/384/Rev1.
Consolidated Versions of the Treaty on European Union. 2010. *Official Journal of the European Union,* 53. Luxembourg.
Çınar, M. 2011. Turkey's present ancient regime and the Justice and Development Party, in *Nationalisms and Politics in Turkey Political Islam, Kemalism and the Kurdish Issue,* edited by M. Casier and J. Jongerden. Abingdon, Oxon: Routledge, 13–27.

Duyulmuş, C.U. 2008. *Europeanization of Minority Rights in Turkey 1999–2007*: Proceedings of the 7th Biennial Conference of the European Community Studies Association-Canada (ECSA-C): The Maturing European Union, Edmonton, Alberta, 25–27 September 2008.

European Commission. 2002. *Regular Report on Turkey's Progress Towards Accession.* SEC (2002) 1412. Brussels.

European Commission. 2003. *Regular Report on Turkey's Progress Towards Accession.* SEC (2003) 1426. Brussels.

European Commission. 2004a. *Regular Report on Turkey's Progress Towards Accession.* SEC (2004) 1201. Brussels.

European Commission. 2004b. *Issues Arising from Turkey's Membership Perspective.* SEC (2004) 1202. Brussels.

European Commission. 2004c. *Communication from the Commission to the Council and the European Parliament Recommendation of the European Commission on Turkey's progress towards accession.* COM (2004) 656. Brussels.

European Commission. 2006. *Regular Report on Turkey's Progress Towards Accession.* SEC (2006) 1390. Brussels.

European Commission. 2008a. *Regular Report on Turkey's Progress Towards Accession.* SEC (2008) 2699. Brussels.

European Commission. 2008b. Enlargement Strategy Paper. COM (2008) 674 Final. Brussels.

European Commission. 2009a. *Regular Report on Turkey's Progress Towards Accession.* SEC (2009) 1334. Brussels.

European Commission. 2009b. Enlargement Strategy Paper. COM (2009) 533. Brussels.

European Commission. 2010. Enlargement Strategy Paper. COM (2010) 660. Brussels.

European Council. 1993. Copenhagen European Council. 21–22 June. Presidency Conclusions. SN 180/93. Copenhagen.

European Council. 2002. Brussels European Council. 24–25 October. Presidency Conclusions. Brussels.

European Council. 2004. Brussels European Council. 25–26 March. Presidency Conclusions. 9048/04. Brussels.

European Council. 2006. Brussels European Council. 11 December. Press Releases. 16289/06. Brussels.

European Council. 2008. *Council Decision of 13 February 2008 on the principles, priorities and conditions contained in the Accession Partnership with the Republic of Turkey and repealing Decision 2006/35/EC.* Brussels.

European Council. 2010. Brussels European Council. 16–17 December. Presidency Conclusions. Brussels.

Falkner, G., Oliver T. and Holzleithner. E. 2008. *Compliance in the Enlarged European Union. Living Rights or Dead Letters?* Hampshire/Burlington: Ashgate Publishing.

Freedom House. 2007. *Countries at the Crossroads. Country Report – Turkey*. [Online]. Available at: http://www.freedomhouse.org/template. cfm?page=140HYPERLINK "http://www.freedomhouse.org/template.cfm?p age=140&edition=8&ccrpage=37&ccrcountry=173"&HYPERLINK "http:// www.freedomhouse.org/template.cfm?page=140&edition=8&ccrpage=37 &ccrcountry=173"edition=8HYPERLINK "http://www.freedomhouse.org/ template.cfm?page=140&edition=8&ccrpage=37&ccrcountry=173"&HYP ERLINK "http://www.freedomhouse.org/template.cfm?page=140&edition =8&ccrpage=37&ccrcountry=173"ccrpage=37HYPERLINK "http://www. freedomhouse.org/template.cfm?page=140&edition=8&ccrpage=37&ccrcoun try=173"&HYPERLINK "http://www.freedomhouse.org/template.cfm?page= 140&edition=8&ccrpage=37&ccrcountry=173"ccrcountry=173 [accessed: 10 August 2010].

Freedom House. 2009. *Freedom in the World – Turkey*. [Online]. Available at: http://www.freedomhouse.org/template.cfm?page=22HYPERLINK "http:// www.freedomhouse.org/template.cfm?page=22&year=2009&country=7722" &HYPERLINK "http://www.freedomhouse.org/template.cfm?page=22&year =2009&country=7722"year=2009HYPERLINK "http://www.freedomhouse. org/template.cfm?page=22&year=2009&country=7722"&HYPERLINK "http://www.freedomhouse.org/template.cfm?page=22&year=2009&country =7722"country=7722 [accessed: 10 August 2010].

Freedom House. 2010. *Freedom in the World – Turkey*. [Online]. Available at: http://www.freedomhouse.org/template.cfm?page=363HYPERLINK "http:// www.freedomhouse.org/template.cfm?page=363&year=2010&country= 7937"&HYPERLINK "http://www.freedomhouse.org/template.cfm?page =363&year=2010&country=7937"year=2010HYPERLINK "http://www. freedomhouse.org/template.cfm?page=363&year=2010&country=7937"&H YPERLINK "http://www.freedomhouse.org/template.cfm?page=363&year=2 010&country=7937"country=7937 [accessed: 10 August 2010].

Gençkaya, Ö.F. and Özbudun, E. 2009. *Democratisation and the Politics of Constitution-Making in Turkey*. Budapest: Central European University Press.

Grigoriadis, I. 2008. On the Europeanisation of minority rights protection: comparing the cases of Greece and Turkey. *Mediterranean Politics*, 13(1), 23–41.

Hammarberg, T. 2009. Review Report on Human Rights of Minorities. Council of Europe. CommDH (2009) 30.

Hürriyet. 2009. *Kürt açılımını başlattık* [Online, 23 July] Available at: http://www. hurriyet.com.tr/gundem/12129354.aHYPERLINK "http://www.hurriyet.com. tr/gundem/12129354.asp"sp [accessed: 23 July 2009].

Johnson, C. 2006. Use and abuse of minority rights: assessing past and future EU policies towards accession countries of Central, Eastern and South-Eastern Europe. *The International Journal on Minority and Group Rights*, 13(1), 27–51.

Kelley, J. 2004. *Ethnic Politics in Europe: The Power of Norms and Incentives*. Princeton, NJ: Princeton University Press.

Kumbaracıbaşı, A.C. 2009. *Turkish Politics and the Rise of the AKP*. Abingdon, Oxon: Routledge.

Kurban, D. 2008. Avrupa Birliği'nin anayasal duzeninde azınlık hakları: açılımlar, fırsatlar ve olasılıklar, in *Türkiye'de Çogunluk ve Azınlık Politikaları: AB Sürecinde Yurttaşlık Tartısmaları*, edited by A. Kaya and T. Tarhanlı. Istanbul: TESEV, 269–86.

Leiber, S. 2007. Transposition of EU social policy in Poland: are there different 'worlds of compliance' in East and West? *Journal of European Social Policy*, 17(4), 349–60.

Magen, A. and Morlino, L. 2009 (eds). *International Actors, Democratisation and the Rule of Law. Anchoring Democracy?* London and New York: Routledge.

Minority Rights Group International Report. 2007. *A Quest for Equality: Minorities in Turkey.*

Nas, Ç. 1998. The approach of the EP to the issue of ethnic minorities and minority rights in Turkey within the context of the European minority rights sub-Regime. *Jean Monnet Working Paper*. 18(98). Department of Political Studies, University of Catania.

NTVMSNBC. 2007. Org. Buyukanit'in Konusmasinin Tam Metni (The full text of General Buyukanit's Speech). 13 April. [Online]. Available at: http://arsiv.ntvmsnbc.com/news/405466.asp [accessed: 20 October 2011].

Oran, B. 2004. *Türkiye'de Azınlıklar Kavramlar, Teori, Lozan, İç Mevzuat, İçtihat, Uygulama*. İstanbul: Iletisim.

Oran, B. 2009. *Western Impact and Turkey*. Seminar Series in Harvard Kennedy School of Government. [Online]. Available at: http://baskinoran.com/konferanslar.php [accessed 13 September 2010].

Öniş, Z. 2003. Domestic politics, international norms and challenges to the state: Turkey-EU relations in the post-Helsinki era, in *Turkey and the European Union Domestic Politics, Economic Integration and International Dynamics*, edited by A. Çarkoğlu and B. Rubin. London, Portland: Frank Cass, 9–34.

Öniş, Z. 2009. *The New Wave of Foreign Policy Activism in Turkey Drifting Away from Europeanisation?* Danish Institute for International Studies. Report 5, Copenhagen.

Özbudun, E. 2006. From political Islam to conservative democracy: the case of the Justice and Development Party in Turkey. *South European Society and Politics*, 11(3–4), 543–57.

Patton, M. 2007. AKP reform fatigue in Turkey: what has happened to the EU process? *Mediterranean Politics*, 12(3), 339–58.

Posch, W. 2007. Crisis in Turkey: just another bump on the road to Europe? *Institute for Security Studies Occasional Paper*, 67.

Polat, R.K. 2009. The 2007 parliamentary elections in Turkey: between securitisation and desecuritisation. *Parliamentary Affairs*, 62(1), 129–48.

Pridham, G. 2005. *Designing Democracy: EU Enlargement and Regime Change in Post-Communist Europe*. Basingstoke, New York: Palgrave Macmillan.

Ram, M. 2003. Democratisation through European integration: The case of minority rights in the Czech Republic and Romania. *Studies in Comparative International Development*, 38(2), 28–56.

Rechel, B. 2008. What has limited the EU's impact on minority rights in accession countries? *East European Politics and Societies*, 22(1), 171–91.

Rose, R. 1991. What is lesson-drawing? *Journal of Public Policy*, 11(1), 3–33.

Rose, R. 1993. *Lesson-drawing in Public Policy: a Guide to Learning across Time and Space*. New Jersey: Chatham House Publishers.

Saatçioğlu, B. 2009. How closely does the European Union's membership conditionality reflect the Copenhagen Criteria? Insights from Turkey. *Turkish Studies*, 10(4), 559–76.

Saatçioğlu, B. 2010. Unpacking the compliance puzzle: the case of Turkey's AKP under EU conditionality. *KFG Working Paper Series*, 14, Freie Universität Berlin.

Sasse, G. 2005. EU conditionality and minority rights: translating the Copenhagen criteria into policy. *EUI Working Paper RSCAS*, 16.

Sasse, G. 2008. The politics of EU conditionality: the norm of minority protection during and beyond EU accession. *Journal of European Public Policy*, 15(6), 842–60.

Schimmelfennig, F. 2008. EU Political accession conditionality after the 2004 enlargement: consistency and effectiveness. *Journal of European Public Policy*, 156, 918–37.

Schimmelfennig, F., Engert, S. and Knobel, H. 2003. Costs, commitment and compliance: the impact of EU democratic conditionality on Latvia, Slovakia and Turkey. *Journal of Common Market Studies*, 41(3), 495–518.

Schimmelfennig, F. and Sedelmeier, U. 2005 (eds). *The Europeanisation of Central and Eastern Europe*. Ithaca, London.

Schwellnus, G. 2001. Much ado about nothing? Minority Protection and the EU Charter of Fundamental Rights, *Constitutionalism Web-Papers*, ConWEB, 5. [Online]. Available at: http://www.qub.ac.uk/schools/SchoolofPoliticsInternationalStudiesandPhilosophy/HYPERLINK "http://www.qub.ac.uk/schools/SchoolofPoliticsInternationalStudiesandPhilosophy/FileStore/ConWEBFiles/Filetoupload,38355,en.pdf"FileStore/ConWEBFiles/Filetoupload,38355,en.pdf [accessed: 23 December 2010].

Schwellnus, G. 2005. The adoption of non-discrimination and minority protection rules in Romania, Hungary and Poland, in *The Europeanisation of Central and Eastern Europe,* edited by F. Schimmelfennig and U. Sedelmeier. Ithaca and London: Cornell University Press, 51–70.

Secretariat General for EU Affairs of Turkey. 2007. *Political Reforms in Turkey*. Ankara.

Sedelmeier, U. 2011. Europeanisation in new member and candidate states. *Living Reviews in European Governance* [Online], 6(1).

Available at: http://www.livingreviews.org/lreg-2011-1 [accessed February 2011].

Somer, M. 2011. Democratisation, clashing narratives, and 'twin tolerations' between islamic-conservative and pro-secular actors, in *Nationalisms and Politics in Turkey Political Islam, Kemalism and the Kurdish Issue*, edited by M. Casier and J. Jongerden. Abingdon, Oxon: Routledge, 28–47.

Taşkın, Y. 2008. AKP's move to 'conquer' the centre-right: its prospects and possible impacts on the democratisation process. *Turkish Studies*, 9(1), 53–72.

Tocci, N. 2008. The EU and conflict resolution in Turkey and Georgia: hindering EU potential through the political management of contractual relations. *Journal of Common Market Studies*, 46(4), 875–97.

Toktaş, S. and Kurt, Ü. 2010. The Turkish military's autonomy, JDP rule and the EU reform process in the 2000s: an assessment of the Turkish version of Democratic Control of Armed Forces (DECAF). *Turkish Studies*, 11(3), 387–403.

Toggenburg, G. 2000. A rough orientation through a delicate relationship: the European Union's endeavours for (its) minorities, *European Integration Online Papers (EIoP)*, 4(16).

Turkish Armed Forces Press Release. 2007. Turkish General Staff. 27 April. Ankara.

Türkmen, F. 2008. The European Union and democratisation in Turkey: the role of the elites. *Human Rights Quarterly*, 30(1), 146–63.

UN Committee on the Elimination of Racial Discrimination. 2008. *Reports Submitted by States parties under the Article 9 of the Convention. Third periodic reports of States parties due in 2007. Turkey.* 12 November. CERD/C/TUR/3.

Ulusoy, K. 2007. Turkey's reform effort reconsidered, 1987–2004. *Democratisation*, 14(3), 472–90.

Yılmaz, G. 2009. Towards an interactive approach for external Europeanization: minority-related policy change in Turkey, in *Proceedings of the KFG The Transformative Power of Europe Conference*. Berlin: Freie Universität Berlin.

Yılmaz, G. 2011. Is there a puzzle? Compliance with minority rights in Turkey. *KFG Working Paper Series*, 23.

Chapter 7

Contribution to the Europeanisation Process: Demands for Democracy of Second Wave Feminism in Turkey

Sevgi Uçan Çubukçu

Introduction

This chapter aims to analyse the developments of women's struggle for gender equality in Turkey after the 1990s in the framework of Europeanisation process. In this respect, the Europeanisation process in the case of Turkey manifests an important experience at the intersection of feminism and democratisation initiatives and civil society. Europeanising has become the impetus of many steps to provide gender equality in Turkey as it has also become in EU member states. EU policies have benefited from the issues of identifying gender roles and providing equality between men and women in legal adaptation process and implementation since the beginning of the 1990s during the economic, political, and social transformation process. On a national basis, the women's movement in Turkey has utilised the EU membership as an international dynamic in its struggle to eliminate discriminatory regulations and practices against women. In this way, although the discrimination on gender still continues in many areas, there has been important progress through a variety of legal changes (such as changes in Turkish Civil and Penal Codes) on the issues of equality in business life, active attendance in politics, revealing and preventing violence against women, etc. EU membership, which developed at the same time as the demands of democratisation, has an important impact on the transformations materialised in the 1990s and 2000s in Turkey. Women's non-governmental organisations, scholars and activists progressed their demands in parallel with cohesion to EU legislation practices. In this framework, as Bache and Marshall argued (Bache and Marshall 2004: 4),

> Much of the literature on Europeanisation surveyed above draws heavily on historical institutionalism. However, as Olsen (2002) argued, Europeanisation is not limited to changes in political – administrative structures and policy content, but 'European values and policy paradigms are also to some (varying) degree internalized at the domestic level, shaping discourses and identities.' Olsen's arguments point to a shift within discourses on Europeanisation toward

frameworks accommodating broader definitions of institutions, taken from sociological (or constructivist) institutionalism.

In this context, it will not be an exaggeration to say that the stress made by the EU on equality of opportunity, and providing gender equality in every aspect has functioned as a leverage both for spreading the consciousness and awareness of man-women equality and for women activists, women's organisations, researchers speaking out their demands for equality and democracy. Especially, 'Gender Mainstreaming' approach has made a very important impact on the process of creating equal opportunities in employment, for example Reports on Equality Between Women and Men which have been on the agenda since 1982 and The Community Framework Strategy for Gender Equality 2001–2005, and creating institutions dealing with providing man-woman equality, materialising and implementing the necessary changes on gender discrimination on a legal basis.

The feminist movement during the last decade played a key role in Turkey's democratisation process and in integration with the European Union. At the beginning of the 1980s, women in Turkey were rebelling against and contested the problems that they had been compelled to experience due to their sex; they protested against these problems by arranging conferences and campaigns and attending demonstrations and mass meetings arranged without formal permission. In those years, the independent women's movement[1] presented an example of 'civil disobedience' – which ultimately led to important results – against and despite the anti-democratic, oppressive and authoritarian political order of the period. Today, a quarter of a century later, the socio-political environment takes as its primary target the policies of compliance with European Union laws. In this environment, women are organising: they intervene with the state and the law; they criticise and dissect scientific methods and subjects through the means of women's studies; they struggle against violence; they form a network of civil support on both the national and the international level; and, overall, the women's movement exposes the fact that 'complete democracy' is possible only on the condition that 'women's human rights' are established. In almost every achievement that will lead to a change in the secondary status of women in Turkey, the independent women's movement has, in fact, a great role. Essentially, it is the role that they have played in this concern that this article aims to express. Along with this, and despite the changes that have occurred, it can be seen that legislation is not sufficient by itself, and that there will be intense struggles and conflicts – such as have already occurred – in the process of application. This is because there is a political determination and a

---

1   In this article, the *'independent women's movement'* and *'feminism'* are used with the same meaning. Although there are indeed some individuals and groups within this movement which do not call themselves 'feminists', a categorical definition – in line with the common demands of the women's movement – is here preferred. Though such concepts are in danger of blurring today, feminism is an abstraction needed always as an ideology expressing women's *'awareness of being a social group'*.

social structure, which leaves such legislation – which is itself not bereft of sexism – insufficient in practice. It is certain that we are in a period of struggle as far as deploying references to the process of EU membership so as to eliminate and impede an ossified cultural structure, codes and interest groups, and to have such legislation put into practice. In this context, a correspondence between the reforms of human rights and democracy that should be made in the legal and practical areas, and the agenda of the women's movement, is seen to emerge by itself. However, this intersection does not mean a reproduction of the sexist viewpoint that supports the idea that there is no effect of the women's struggle of a quarter of a century on the process of democratisation in Turkey, rather than supporting the legal, political and social attainments that women got through struggling against their oppressive state. This is because it is known that the denial or underrating of their struggle against the sexist system nourishes the invisibility of women in history. Therefore, the influence of the efforts and struggle of the independent women's movement – which are characterised by future-oriented legal and social reforms at many levels – on the process of modernisation and democratisation in Turkey should be registered. With these reforms, we mean the changes and regulations achieved in many areas, such as the issuance of the new *Civil Law*, the amendment in the *Criminal Law*, the struggle against violence against women, the increase in women's studies at universities, the guaranteeing of equality between men and women by amendment to the *Constitution*, attempts at establishing mechanisms which may verify equality, the Law on the *Protection of Family*, the elimination of '*honour murders*', anti-hierarchical and anti-authoritarian organisation operations and models, and local, national and international networks of solidarity.[2]

This need is necessary not only for the continuity of the historical and social visibility of women, but it is also urgent for a freedom-advocating 'ideal of democratic society' purified of sexist discrimination. To come closer to this ideal will be possible only with the acceptance of a mentality of 'appearing' as an individual by escaping from the historical legacy presented by the processes of modernisation and democratisation, which tend to 'represent' women as nothing more than a means to an end. Bearing this in mind, the following chapter aims to show that women are a determining dynamic for transformation, which is required by the project of 'Democratic Turkey' in the process of Europeanisation.

This chapter will be focused on exploring the relationship between the second wave feminism and democracy in the concept of the Europeanisation process in Turkey. It begins by briefly reconstructing debates on the relationship between human and citizenship rights, gender and democracy; and then it will e given a brief overview of the changes in the meaning of key concepts, such as 'Westernisation',

---

2   There are different arguments on this issue; One of them is that the Europeanisation process has created many opportunities for democratisation of civil society and state in Turkey. For instance the development of a gender sensitive approach in the European Union has opened a new opportunity frame for the Turkish women's NGOs. See, (Işık 2007: 53–66).

'Europeanisation' and 'Modernisation'; and finally it will be the struggles of gender equality in the framework of a contribution to the democratisation process in Turkey.

Rethinking Gender and Democracy

Relationship between feminism including gender equality and democracy developing through social justice, equality and freedom themes dates back to ancient Greece. Ancient Greek democracy is known as excluding another social group with slaves: Women. Democracy takes over the acceptance of a patriarchal system which does not see women as individual and social subjects and what makes them the secondary gender for a long time. Although women gain significant achievements in getting to be an individual and social subject, the overwhelming nature of unequal gender roles of patriarchal mentality is not eliminated.

From the seventeenth century, feminism gained visibility as a political ideology as women were demanding equal rights in Europe. The democratisation since the sixteenth century gained momentum and became widespread and in the nineteenth century, another social group, 'working classes' were demanding equal rights. In this context, the concepts of feminism and democracy, and the resulting discourse in the development of the partnership is worth noting as are the basic references of equality, freedom and solidarity. Essentially, the partnership beyond the basic references in the historical equivalent of an analogy is falling. Eighteenth- and nineteenth-century ideological paradigm and the liberal definition of democracy, freedoms and rights was set on the basis of the 'individual' in experience of liberal democratic states in Europe.

Identification of freedoms and rights which are defined on the basis of 'the group' became possible in the 20th century (Pateman 2004: 129). This is why development of the historical phenomenon of the working class as a subject is the emergence of social and political, individual rights and liberties which the discourse of democracy, the concept of limited scope and content of social rights and freedoms recognised and expanded into the frame receipt. Thus, an understanding of freedom is used in a negative content, political and social rights based on the axis of the whole of society could be a positive transition to freedom (Berlin 1969).

An important social and political actor in the development of democracy in Europe, as well as the working class, women were also loaded in a similar function. Equality, liberty and the principles of solidarity became a reference in this ideological climate. Women were demanding equality for themselves, and the concept of 'sisterhood' entered into relations of solidarity. Women, people with the promise of legitimacy in a democratic political order winning rights of citizenship such as an equal right to vote, property acquisition, the right to work, education and health care rights and so on.

Twentieth-century social justice, equal rights, equal sharing, egalitarian principles, such as the right to work became the hegemonic discourse of the democratisation movement. In this context, the perspective of the participation of men and women having equal opportunities in public life are among the demands of the First Wave of Feminism. On the other hand, the perspective of equality in the public sphere, and the assertion that citizens are equal before the law and have equal opportunities in the public sphere in which the roles and responsibilities of men and women does not prescribe a gender-specific role, did not lead to real equality (Phillips 1997: 33). Second Wave Feminism, with the slogans *'private is political'* or *'equal pay for equal work'* problematised the shortcomings of first-wave feminism and pushed the boundaries of democracy (Phillips 1995: 126). In Continental Europe, the struggle for equality between the sexes – emphasising the duality of private and public space produced by the unequal gender division of labour, received critical scrutiny. Women increasingly began to enjoy their rights such as law, education, right to vote and so on in the public sphere.

From the Concept of 'Westernisation' to the Process of 'Europeanisation'

In the context of Turkish political thought, 'Westernisation' is a concept with a variety of different aspects. Westernisation – which has different political, social and cultural ramifications – exhibits differences in the basic underlying principle of Turkish modernisation. When discussing 'the history of Turkish modernisation', we must view Westernisation as a concept with a dynamic function. Once thought of as a 'neutral' concept, Westernisation has since then attained more 'political' connotations. In fact, it has been employed in the Turkish modernisation debate as the main reference point in the processes of 'mental' and 'institutional' formation as well as in that of 'identity' formation. In the Ottoman period, Westernisation was used to indicate 'technology transfer' and thus, it was conceived of as having a 'neutral' content. The idea of 'Westernisation' as merely a technical process can be seen to commonly prevail in the Republican period as well. However, against this conception, some pro-modernisation thinkers have claimed that modernisation should not be conceived of as a process limited to technological aspects, but should also include the idea of wider cultural and social change (Berkes 1975).

Westernisation manifests itself as the representation of many Western institutions and mental patterns, and even as the representation of the patterns of daily life, all of which was introduced during the process of modernisation. Thus, a study of Westernisation, conducted independently of the process of modernisation, would inevitably prove insufficient. Westernisation included such notions as 'liberation' and 'progress' both in the so-called Tanzimat period (1839–76), during the Ottoman era and in the early years of the Turkish Republic. In this paradigm, the transformation of the political system by modernisation was considered essential. This concept's attainment of more cultural and institutional content and its subsequent transfer to a more ideological plane constitute the breaking points explaining this process. Westernisation, which was a 'civilisation project' in its initial stages, became more conservative by gradually accruing more cultural and ideological content.[3] However, cultural preferences constitute the main point of differentiation in these fractured meanings which have emerged in the course of this concept's development. Generally speaking, these various attitudes – which are commonly situated in the positivist worldview that is the fundamental element of Turkish political modernisation and of the mentality underlying it – separate in terms of the differing degrees of emphasis each attitude places on the traditional structure.

Up to this point in the chapter, the historical references of the different perceptions of the concept of Westernisation have been examined. As observed, the historicity of this concept played an important role in the process of the Turkish-Ottoman society's foundation of its nation-state and its process of identity-formation. It is evident that the paradigm of Westernisation continues to affect Turkish society in this century as much as it did in the early days of the previous century. In the perspective of the new perceptions and models of democracy as being a global fact as well as a formative process emergent in the period after nation states and modernity, Westernisation has again become a part of current debate. With the transformation to the 'new right' after 1980, relations with Europe – which have become a part of the current agenda in terms of Turkey's integration into the world economic system – have thus attained a more concrete content. Turkey's submission of an application for membership to the EU has meant much more than this particular concrete undertaking in Turkey (Samur 2008: 383). In this manner, it has been revealed that 'Europeanisation', which had previously been conceived of solely on the technical and economic plane, is actually also a cultural fact. Previously developed in political areas such as law, democracy, democratisation and human rights, this process has revealed the cultural dimensions of Europeanisation or Westernisation (Olsen and Trenz 2010: 6). This process has been enforced by certain external dynamics, such as the Copenhagen Criteria, which have prompted Turkey to reflect on its own identity and social structure.

The Discourse of Democracy: Beyond Equality

Since the beginning of the twentieth century, the demand by women to have the rights of suffrage and electability – which the status of citizenship that came about with the model of the nation state allowed – as well as basic human rights like education, health care, etc., is still an ongoing struggle, even in the most developed

---

3   Another aspect of Westernisation, in the opinion of H.B. Kahraman, is the fact that, while it was merely a 'metaphor' in its initial stages, by gradually attaining a more concrete content it has become the means of modernisation for Turkey's political, social and cultural structure. Therefore, even though modernisation emerged with its own distinct features, Turkish modernisation was realised only with the accompanying phenomenon of Westernisation (Kahraman 2001: 9–10).

democratic societies of the EU. The central theme of first-wave feminism, which emerged at the end of the nineteenth and the beginning of the twentieth century, is composed precisely of these rights that the nation state offers to its citizens. On the other hand, it is known that in the relatively developed democratic societies of the EU, these rights have been or are being presented to women only later, and in phases. Within this framework, first-wave feminism is defined as 'egalitarian feminism' because of its demand for women to be 'equal citizens' with men.[4] First-wave feminism is followed by second-wave feminism, which struggles against all the established rules of the sexist system in order to enable women to use all their acquired rights in social, cultural, political and economic lives, and which emerged with the discourse of 'freedom'. In the common discourse of the universal women's movement, the struggle for democracy – which develops on the grounds that women may benefit from human rights just the same as men – has followed a similar course in the Turkish sphere. This development is not limited to authoritarian political regimes, such as those in the Middle East, but is in fact an ongoing one in many European countries, which have democratic political regimes.

Along with the advantages and disadvantages that citizenship rights presented to women through the tradition of state control,[5] the universal women's movement – despite certain local and national differences within – comes together on the axis of the struggle for 'freedom and equality'. Therefore, the ontological character of the Turkish women's movement of the 1980s falls into the second-wave feminist paradigm. At the same time, the Turkish women's movement's unique process of democratisation emerged as the first democratic reflex of the political system in the period following the 1980 *coup d'état* (Arat 1992: 94). This is because the women's movement is not only a social opposition exposing the problems specific to women, but also because it brought a holistic criticism to the ossified relationships and mechanisms present in all social areas of culture, politics, sociology, economy, etc. This approach, by interrogating social integrity in all its

---

4   The Ottoman-Turkish Women published many journals, such as *Hanımlara Mahsus Gazete* (Journal of Women), *Kadınlar Dünyası* (Women's World), *İnci (Pearl)*, *Genç Kadın* (Young Women) etc. and organised many conferences and activities in the early period of First-Wave Feminism in Turkey. These activities are defined as the 'Ottoman Women's Movement'. See (Çakır 1994).

5   For a discussion of the argument that legislation incorporated from above, by the state – as in the case of women in Turkey obtaining the right of suffrage and representation as well as civil rights – leads to the emergence of 'pro-state feminism' in societies with an authoritarian tradition, and that this attitude might entail a danger of overshadowing the struggle of the women's movement and its civil character, see (Tekeli 1990: 20). Also, for a discussion about how Turkey – which has been the only Middle Eastern country in which women's rights was dealt with openly and broadly at an early date – has a significant place among the Western democratic nations as well, and another discussion on how all countries have a 'common essence' in overseeing women's sexuality despite their cultural differences, see (Kandiyoti 1997: 65).

dimensions, contains the formation of a new 'democratic society project' within itself. In this sense, second-wave feminism in Turkey – as in all other societies – has a perspective in which the themes of 'holisticism' and 'multi-fragmentation', of 'differentiation' and 'similarity', emerge. This rupture experienced in Turkish politics exposes how the numerous facts that constitute the chronology of the women's movement actually form an influence greater than their own reality.

The Unfinished Struggle: Violence against Women

The post-1980 women's movement is seen to have emerged on the basis of reaction to violence against women, particularly domestic violence. In this period – during which the gap between private and public space widened – feminist women expressed the fact that the most important means used to oppress and control women socially was domestic violence. The women's movement which supported the idea that 'the private is political' arranged its first mass demonstration in Istanbul in 1987, protesting the social legitimisation of the beating of women. As a part of 'the Anti-Beating Campaign', which started immediately following this demonstration, women, using slogans such as 'Scream! Let Everybody Hear', carried out another campaign – called 'purple needle' – against sexual harassment, in 1989. Keeping the subjects of virginity checks and rape on the agenda, they protested the differentiation of 'chaste-unchaste women' and managed to get Article 438 cancelled on the grounds that it was in violation of the principle of equality. Previously, according to article 438, there would be a decrease in punishment if rape victims were prostitutes. Besides making a detailed description of violence – including violence in all its physical, sexual, psychological, economic, and emotional aspects – the independent women's movement created a change in the perception of the cultural structure and an awareness of it and created alternative spaces for the solution of this problem. The first examples of such actions are the *Mor Çatı Kadın Sığınağı Vakfı* (The Purple Roof Women's Shelter Foundation) and the *Ankara Kadın Dayanışma Vakfı* (The Ankara Women's Solidarity Foundation), which were founded in 1990 by activist women.

The struggle carried out by the women's movement against violence resulted in the formation of their own independent institutions and also the displacement of the state's position in regards to violence. Along with this acceleration – forced by the United Nations 1995 Beijing Declaration, the Social Services and Children's Protection Institute (SHÇEK) issued the regulation concerning women's guesthouses and women's consultation centres, and shelters in all regions were provided with legal status.[6] This development, along with the issuance of the Protection of the Family Act number 4320, created a significant breakthrough in the perception of 'violence', which has since been employed as the legitimate mechanism of the patriarchal structure of the state and of society (Istanbul Bar Association 2003). Violence, it is shown, stems from unequal power relations within the society, and shelters and consultation centres are required in order for women – who have been socially impoverished – to be protected from violence and to be empowered. The planned legislative amendment – which makes the opening of women's shelters a compulsory duty for the state – has been put into effect.

The Declaration on the Elimination of Violence against Women adopted by the United Nations General Assembly in 1993 describes violence against women as 'any act ... that results in ... physical, sexual or psychological harm or suffering to women, ... whether occurring in public or in private life'. All the types of violence mentioned in this declaration are known to exist domestically in Turkey. It is not so coincidental that the women's movement caused violence to be defined and designated, and acted with 'solidarity' on this problem during its last 25 years of history. 'Violence against women', which is the most important mechanism of the sexist system on both the historical and global planes, continues in all societies in different forms, varying only according to cultural, historical and economic differences, but regardless of whether or not a tradition of democracy is present. For instance, mechanisms such as 'prohibition of abortion' in societies whose majority is Catholic, 'female circumcision' in many places in Africa, 'honour' murders in Turkey, 'the tradition of sati' in India, 'stoning' in Nigeria, etc., are the local or cultural manifestations of the violence that women experience globally.

Considering the density, diversity and prevalence of 'violence against women', it is known that there are still many violations of women's human rights, at even the most primitive levels, in Turkey, although some progress has been made. Struggle against violence has the character of changing the unequal sexist structure of society, as well as being an effort to earn women's basic human rights. In this manner, stopping violence against women requires regulations and amendments that would enable women to have an equal chance of individual improvement and empowerment, as well as equal access to public life. In this regard, all the varieties of demand for the elimination of violence against women that the independent women's movement in Turkey can advocate also carry content that helps democratic mechanisms in the country to work.

---

6   General Assemblies on Women's Shelters – organised since 1998 by feminists in cooperation with independent women's organisations, Social Services and the centres of the Children's Protection Institute, which have become greater in number during last decade – have become platforms for sharing experiences and information and making new policies concerning violence against women at the national level.

The Changes of the Legislative Framework: Towards Gender Mainstreaming

In 1979, the United Nations General Assembly adopted the 'Convention on the Elimination of All Forms of Discrimination against Women' (CEDAW), which Turkey ratified in 1985.[7] According to this convention, Turkey committed itself to making legal regulations to eliminate sexist discrimination, abolishing discriminatory criminal codes, and making arrangements to encourage women's access to political and economic space. In the following quarter of a century, women from Turkey exhibited a strong civil determination to reflect the CEDAW onto domestic law, and to have it put into practice. Women – who are well aware of the liabilities that the CEDAW, one of the most important reference texts in the international community, holds governments responsible for – followed up their rights as mentioned in the CEDAW and formed an important social pressure group on the political regime via campaigns, mass demonstrations, the formation of societies, etc. (Berktay 2003: 51–5).

This struggle – which has been carried out with a democratic consciousness unequalled even in most of those societies whose culture of democracy is older and more internalised, like some EU countries – is an example of a significant 'civil disobedience' active in making all kinds of legal, political and institutional regulations with the aim of eliminating violations of women's rights (Galligan et al. 2007: 117–20). Even if these activist women were aware that legal and institutional regulations were not sufficient to change society and form a new culture, they were also aware of the 'dissuasive power' that these regulations exert in eliminating the discriminations that women experience in all spheres. Turkey, by signing the CEDAW, committed itself to the elimination of all sorts of practices and rules which supported discrimination against women, and accepted this convention as a meta-national norm (Uçan-Çubukçu 2004a: 61–2; Kıvılcım-Forsman 2004: 156–7).

Another important aspect of second-wave feminism in Turkey, and one which has emerged within the last decade, is the change that it has brought about both in the state apparatus and on the legal plane, which are all in line with international developments. Many such changes can be enumerated: as for instance, the Turkish Republic Prime Ministry Directorate General on the Status and Problems of Women (KSSGM) – which was founded in 1990 – is an institution that plays an important role in making equality among the sexes a state policy and in the usage of this rhetoric. National reports prepared by the Turkish Republic Prime Ministry Directorate General On The Status And The Problems Of Women (KSSGM) are not only documents presenting the data concerning the social, political and economic status of women within the country, but are also important references as regards what should or is to be done in order to make improvements concerning women's

---

7   Also, the UN has given the right for application to injured parties in cases of violation of the convention by its CEDAW Optional Protocol.

status, as well as what the state promises to do in this concern. In general, such studies done in cooperation with women either directly or indirectly connected to the women's movement allow women to get into the sphere of public policy and give them important experience in terms of gender mainstreaming (Terzi 2004: 125).

With an amendment passed in 1997 on the Law on Surnames, women earned the right to use their own family names along with their husbands. However, the real breakthrough in women's citizenship rights was brought about by the amendment passed on Civil Code. With the new Civil Code – which came into effect on 1 January 2003 – the principle of equality between women and men in domestic life was established. With this law, the principle of the head of the family was abolished, certain changes guaranteeing the equal rights and duties of the spouses came into effect, and women were given the right to have a say in decisions concerning their children and other domestic affairs. Along with these changes, the law ensures the equal sharing between the spouses of those assets which have been acquired within the period of matrimony, as well as legally ensuring the elimination of all sexist discrimination from the social and cultural structure. Therefore, as Kıvılcım-Forsman analysed (2004: 163):

> In this process, a series of critical legal reforms were introduced with the harmonization packages to comply with targets set in the National Programme in order to fulfil the Copenhagen political criteria and harmonise with the Union Acquis. A part of these are about changing provisions in the Turkish legislation that discriminate against women, about achievement of equality between women and men and realization of women's human rights. The women's movement has been actively involved in this process of legislative changes, played a part during the preparatory stage of the reform packages and lobbied through media and directly in the Parliament for the approval of alternative texts made up through its joint efforts. In this regard, the candidacy process has enhanced the communication of the women's movement with national political authorities, their participation in preliminary legislative processes and opportunities of putting pressure on decision-making mechanisms.

It is not wrong to define this achievement as a product of the hegemony set up by the women's movement in the state and in civil society by way of using democratic methods such as 'lobbying', 'making suggestions', and 'supervising the process'. However, the decision that the Civil Code will be effective only for the period and cases occurring after its issuance date means that an important part of society lies beyond its scope (Burchill 2003: 11). Therefore, this reform – which was put into action so as to eliminate inequalities resulting from gender in the private and public spheres – is still insufficient according to the standards of the European Commission's reports.

The new Civil Code, which is the most significant achievement of the last 25 years of the women's movement in Turkey, would lead to very important influences in the realisation of democracy and of women's human rights in Turkey, and it is a development which will bring about the foundation on which gender roles and stereotypes may be changed. With this change, a woman is now recognised as an 'individual'. In this process, the European Union institutions have monitored and evaluated the detailed legal forms to achieve gender equality and their realisation is a crucial force for reforms amending decades-old provisions that discriminate against women. In Kıvılcım-Forsman's words (2004: 163),

> Recommendations made by institutions of the Union as a result of this monitoring and evaluation activity largely parallel to the agenda and demands of the women's movement in Turkey and the fact that the undertakings of the Turkish governments have been tied to measurable criteria with regard to time and realization is a stepping stone for activities carried out by the women's movement on the national level.

Another important development is in the amendments, forced by the women's movement to be taken into consideration for implementation in the *Turkish Criminal Code*, which is now a draft in Parliament. These amendments include: the right to have an abortion within 20 weeks of pregnancy for those women pregnant due to rape; the elimination of 'the instigation deduction' in the article concerning 'honour' murders; the increase of maternal leave to a total period of four months; and punishment for domestic rape as well as sexual harassment in the workplace. These regulations will prevent the law from those sexist cultural elements allowing it to define women in terms of men and oppress them accordingly. The most important change is to consider 'sexual crimes' as 'crimes against society' rather than simply 'crimes against individuals'. Thus, the female body and sexual identity is now legally perceived within the frame of an individual's rights and freedoms, rather than within the criteria of ethics and honour set up by social customs and usages (TCL women's workshop 2003).[8]

In 2004, although 'affirmative action' has not been used, article 10 of the Constitution was amended so as to create a justification for the legal and *de facto* regulations that will ensure equality between men and women.[9] Decisions delivered by the European Convention on Human Rights and the European Court of Human Rights carry a legally binding character for the elimination of discrimination based on sex. Furthermore, with the Treaty of Amsterdam – adopted in 1997 – the EU took the principal decision that equality between men and women must be established in all political areas, laws, programmes and activities. This new principle, promoting regulations beyond positive discrimination in establishing equality between men

---

8   For a detailed discussion of the opportunities that this change will lead to, see (Berktay 2003: 53–4).

9   For a discussion of sexist content in the political and intellectual environment, arguing for positive discrimination – which is a principle and value guaranteeing the legislative and actual regulations that will eliminate the unequal status allotted to women, see (Uçan :18–20) and (Berktay 2004: 168).

and women, is known as 'Incorporating Equal Opportunities for Women and Men into all Community Policies and Activities' (Gender Mainstreaming). This principle requires incorporating equal opportunities and practices at all levels for women. Moreover, this principle does not only work on such levels – like equality of opportunity, institutional equality or legal equality –but it also aims to change established cultural stereotypes, behavioural patterns and roles based on gender.

Developments leading to the feminisation of societies and politics – as well as those leading to the democratisation of societies in both the international community and Turkey, the European Women Lobby (EWL),[10] and the solidarity and cooperation of women's non-governmental organisations on both the national and international level – all these are a consequence of the struggle and efforts of women's initiatives; As Börzel argues in Chapter 1, 'At the domestic level, domestic actors pressure their national executives to pursue policies at the European level that are favourable to their interests'; these domestic changes could be defined as an experiment of Europeanisation process at the national level in Turkey.

The Discourse of Differentiation and Dialogue: 'Pluralisation'

After establishing its ideological build up and becoming widespread as a political movement, the post-1980 feminist movement experienced a period in which differing feminist perceptions emerged. These differences emerged in the ideological references used to explain the cause of the women's problem. Even during this period, in which different forms of activity and organisation and different theoretical explanations became evident, women continued to keep intact the traditions of 'acting together' and of 'solidarity'. In the 1920s and 1930s, the 'egalitarian feminism' demanding equality between men and women in education, legislation and politics prevailed in Turkey. In the period until the 1960s, there was stagnation on both the national and international levels due to the fact that women had been given their civil, social and political rights (Tekeli 1988). Despite the socialist women's political awareness, the woman's problem did not become a primary subject in the 1960s and 1970s due to the hypothesis and assumption that it would be solved by a holistic transformation of the society.

In the 1980s, women, who brought the women's problem to the centre of political agenda, begun to experience a differentiation in their ideas and viewpoints although they continued to work in cooperation and solidarity. While egalitarian feminists differed in that they defended Kemalist ideology, radical feminists located themselves within the context of a critical outlook on the sexist character

---

10   The European Women's Lobby is an organisation which aims to incorporate equality between women and men in Europe, establishing in 1990 a connection on the EU level between women's organisations and policy-making mechanisms. EWL is also the most comprehensive and influential among the networks of women's organisations. See Economic Development Foundation 2003.

of this ideology (Abadan-Unat 1988: 331–6). According to the radical feminists, egalitarian feminism demanded women enter the public sphere only in order for them to have equal rights with men. However, radical feminists themselves demanded more than 'equal rights'; they wanted to interrogate and change the political, cultural and legal heritage from within which these rights were given. In this manner, it was accepted that they had a viewpoint that included and then exceeded the demands of egalitarian feminism. *Socialist feminists*, on the other hand, located themselves in a way from which they questioned the 'reductionist' political heritage that considers the women's problem as a part of the social transformation, as well as the 'total' perspective that aims at such a transformation (Berktay 1990: 293–5). In these years, though it was not yet as strong as these other approaches in terms of theoretical and political power, '*Islamist feminism*' emerged within the Islamic ideology, supporting the thesis that women were victims of sexist discrimination due to their choice of clothing (i.e., the headscarf), as they cannot enter the public sphere because of this choice. However, the weakness of this approach as compared to the others is that the Islamist feminists had no critical approach towards the sexist structure of the ideology and communal relations within which they were located. The critique of the Islamist paradigm on the grounds of gender from within, which was very discrete at the beginning became more systematic later. While Islamist women's magazines such as *Mektup* (*Letter*) or *Kadın ve Aile* (*Woman and Family*) had no critique of the Islamic rules in the 1980s, it can be seen that Islamist groups of women such as *Başkent Kadın Platformu* (Başkent (Capital City) Women's Platform) and *Gökkuşağı Kadın Platformu* (Rainbow Women's Platform) have begun to question the sexist structure of Islam both theoretically and politically in recent years (Eraslan 2002: 255). During the last decade, 'Kurdish feminism', which women developed out of their local cultural identities, has been added to the different approaches and practices reflected in the perception and organisation of the women's problem in Turkey. Kurdish women have published some Kurdish women's magazines such as *Roza* and *Jujin* in which they put forth the fact that they have been subjected to a different and multi-layered structure of oppression, forced onto them both by the state and their own patriarchal tradition, due to their cultural identity. 'Local feminisms', 'project feminism' and 'young feminism' can be added to the previously existent feminist frameworks: the 'traditional feminism' of the 1980s, which had a pro-state approach; the oppositional framework of 'radical feminism' and 'socialist feminism'; and also 'Islamic feminism' and 'Kurdish feminism', which both can be considered as 'the other feminisms' (Abadan-Unat 1988: 331–6; Berktay 1990: 293–5; Eraslan 2002: 255). As can be seen from this panorama, 'awareness' and 'critical outlook' – that is, the 'female consciousness', which the process of modernisation in Turkey procured for women – emerged out of the paradox of every woman's questioning and support of their own cultural, class and political belonging. Political differentiations played an enriching role in the improvement of the female viewpoint and sensibility that made it possible to reveal all dimensions of the sexist system.

It can be seen that the real division in feminism emerges through the problem of the objectification of women rather than due to these different approaches. For instance, pro-state feminism takes woman as the object of the modern, Kurdish feminism takes woman as the object of racist discrimination or nationalism, and Islamist feminism considers woman as the object of the traditional. In opposition to these, there are also approaches that consider woman as a 'subject', without the instrumentalisation of her being prevalent in all other 'kinds' of feminism, and these approaches are actually more prevalent. Thus, these different perceptions of feminism as questioning of patriarchal relations in its differing manifestations led to a 'rupture' in the statement that 'there is a common women's problem'.

This differentiation and internalisation within the feminist discourse makes it possible to study the sexist content of the social culture and political mechanisms in Turkey from the standpoint of language, religion, class, etc., with a comprehensive theoretical and political richness. Although emergent differences led to the separation of feminist women into groups according to their differing ideological and cultural belonging, these women still cooperated in their political activities, and thus these differences do not thus far exhibit a character inhibitory of their solidarity. Therefore, it can be said that feminist groups having their own publications with which to convey their own words, and carrying on their own activities and debates, improve the handling of the women's problem in Turkey and the scope of the efforts used to handle it. In other words, feminism in Turkey gets transformed – by means of different senses of belonging such as class, ethnicity, language and religion – from its 'total' and 'monolithic' content into a 'pluralist' and more 'comprehensive' content. What is more, the presence of differing feminist approaches and groups of women creates a female consciousness revealing of the fact that there are many likewise differing forms of oppression and relations of inequality. This is exactly the content that reveals the dimension of the discourse of democracy and human rights – which excludes women – and also its definition of 'the absent citizen'.

Changes in Structural Level: Institutionalisation

While feminist protest first arose around singular and specific problems like sexual harassment, beating, etc., it in fact has also considered these problems as parts of a systematic whole. The 'cross politics' style, carried out upon different belongings or different states of womanhood, has become possible with a unity and women's solidarity that prevent fragmentation, despite their differences. This characteristic, which could previously be seen *ad hoc* in demonstrations organised about specific problems, has become manifest within the last decade through the formation of autonomous structures so as to actualise a concrete function. In this manner, change has occurred – as in the case of the street movement or 1980s protest feminism – as well as the process of being included in public policies, which occurred as a result of becoming widespread and institutionalised. With this evolution, women from within the women's movement began to form a number of societies so as to carry out cultural, vocational or charitable activities to increase solidarity among women. For instance, many autonomous structures have been established in order to create a network of communication and flow of information among structures such as *Kadının İnsan Hakları Vakfı* (the Women's Human Rights Foundation); institutions such as *Mor Çatı* (the Purple Roof) and *Kadın Eserleri Kütüphanesi* (the Library for Women's Works), which can be considered important sites for the feminism from which they emerged; centres and societies such as *Ka-der Kadın Adayları Destekleme ve Eğitme Derneği*, i.e., the Society for Support and Training for Female Candidates) and *Kadın Hakları Merkezi* (the Women's Rights Centre) within the İstanbul Bar, which directly intervene with the political and legal status of women; and women's organisations such as *Uçan Süpürge* (Flying Broom), by way of development projects concerning women (Uçan-Çubukçu 2004b).[11]

Another consequence of second-wave feminist criticism in Turkey is that women's studies is itself turning into not only an academic discipline but also a critique of the questions, methods, and means of study of all other disciplines. Where previously there was almost no scientific research done from a female viewpoint, today there are an increasingly large number of graduate programmes or undergraduate courses and scientific papers on women's studies. For instance, many universities have opened centres for women's studies and these centres have begun the education process. Thus, as such an important break was seen in the rules and methods of the normally unchanging sensibility of positive science, it has become possible to realise new projects and new scientific research with the aim of making women and the female viewpoint visible in history, science and culture.

Today, many disciplines within the field of both the social and the positive sciences carry out many detailed scientific studies on sexist discrimination experienced within the field itself. Ever since the Action Plan enacted in 1999, the EU has been determined to provide financial support to research aiming at the elimination of inequality between men and women in the scientific fields, and has taken this as a primary area of action by way of various policies and mechanisms.

It is not wrong to say that women's organisations are the most influential agents in creating a new society and a new culture both on the national level by producing important reference texts in the processes of societal transformation, such as amendments in Civil or Criminal Law, and also on the international level by attending directly to networks such as the European Women's Lobby – founded in 1990 – or by cooperating directly with the women's organisations

---

11 There is quite a large number of societies attempting to eliminate social conditions that lead to considering women second-class citizens, such as Çağdaş Yaşamı Destekleme Derneği (the *Society for Supporting Contemporary Life*), *Kadın Haklarını Araştırma ve Geliştirme Derneği* (the *Society for Researching and Improving Women's Rights*), *Emekçi Kadınlar Derneği* (the *Labouring Women's Society*), *Kadın İşgücünü Geliştirme Derneği* (the *Society for the Development of the Female Labour Force*), etc. These organisations work within the women's movement, organising around women's problems and solidarity culture.

of other countries. The developments mentioned above are both second-wave feminism and, as a whole, women's concrete achievements towards their target of 'achieving *de facto* rather than merely *de jure* equality'. Moreover, these demands were declared prior to the approach of 'gender mainstreaming', accepted and are today attempting to be realised in the EU. Europeanisation impacts on the rights of women in Turkey by both accelerating the process of reform and providing an external support mechanism by allying with local women's organisations.

Conclusion

This chapter aimed to define the development of second wave feminism in the context of Europeanisation process in Turkey. Europeanisation is a two way process; it refers to a 'bottom-up' and a 'top-down' dimension. There is a link between the two dimensions of Europeanisation; in other words, the concept of Europeanisation that can be explained as an effect of the European Union's aims and ideals (such as democracy, civil rights, gender equalities etc.) on the national level is also an interaction process. The argument of gender equality that lies in the heart of democracy is tried to be analysed in the case of Turkey. In this framework, it is argued that the women's movement has played the key role, as the most important pressure group, on the democratisation process of Turkey in the last decade; That is why: 'Women's organisations have a special role to play in converting the EU enlargement from being a goal in itself or an economically-driven process into an instrument for justice, gender equality, improved policies and a better standard of living for all' (Berktay 2004:172). The demands of women's struggle in Turkey overlap with the European perspective of gender equality. And is aided and supported by the change engendered by the Europeanisation process after 1999.

The history of second-wave feminism in Turkey must be considered by taking into account not only the announced problems, criticisms and solutions, but also the radical demands and suggestions found within the discourse, as the 'data' and 'provisions' for 'what kind of a society' is dreamed of. In the discourse of first-wave feminism, women's demand to 'be citizens' emerged as 'participation' on the levels of education, economics, politics and state affairs; however, second-wave feminism – in a content that exceeded the demand for 'participation' – criticises the institutions, mechanisms and functioning of society more radically, as being the fields that established and maintained the sexist system. The situation thus focuses on '*how* the participation will be' rather than on merely 'equal participation' for instance, new questions – such as 'what kind of politics?' and 'what kind of gender roles?' – emerge from such a critique. As a consequence, the independent women's movement, which made the definition of 'equal citizen' for women accepted by way of making the 'women's problem' visible to a certain extent at the beginning of the twentieth century, has evolved with concrete demands towards an actual 'solution' for the problem by producing the concept of 'gender' over a period of 50 years.

Consequently, in order to eliminate all kinds of inequalities that historically have reduced women to the status of second-class citizens throughout the world, the women's movement has become an important pressure group within the last quarter of a century. During this period, women's demands and achievements came about as a result of a dialogic style dependent on bargaining in the relations between state and civil society. This involves a fundamentally different perception towards the discourse and functioning of politics – such as having a non-hierarchical structure and an anti-centralist, democratic and conciliatory element within the group – as well as a sensibility favouring the self-improvement and self-realisation of the women. The most important merit and object of this discourse is the fact that it encompasses relations consisting of a fairer, horizontal and collective division of labour, as well as a societal project organised around such principles. Women, along with their demand for the extension of the public sphere and the transformation of society's sexist structure, have had an important influence in accelerating this process of social transformation by focusing on the private sphere – an area which the state feigned ignorance of – working within the bounds of a variety of legal, economic and political regulations.

In the last two decades, the feminist (or independent women's) movement in Turkey – which acted as a coalition of different ideologies and cultures – has constituted an important social power in the process of creating a democratic society. The women of Turkey are among the leading social agents establishing the new society of the new century with, on the one hand, their sensitivity towards differentiation on the level of micro cultures, and on the other hand, their closeness to international documents and dynamics. The independent women's movement, which is an ontological resistance against the state's attitude of restriction of the individual's rights and freedoms, thus constitutes an influential civil power in establishing the tradition of democracy in Turkey. Therefore, the most important conclusion emerging from this chapter is that the women civil society organisations were the essential civil actors for putting gender mainstreaming into practice in the process of Europeanisation and so, it can be said that Europeanisation in the area of gender equality and women's rights should be defined as a 'bottom-up' process in Turkey.

References

Abadan Unat, N. 1988. Söylemden Protestoya: Türkiye'de Kadın Hareketlerinin Dönüşümü (From Discourse to Protest: The Transformation of Women's Movements in Turkey) in *75 Yılda Kadınlar ve Erkekler* (*75 Years of Women and Men*), Istanbul: History Foundation Publications.

Arat, Y. 1992. 1980'ler Türkiye'sinde Kadın Hareketi: Liberal Kemalizm'in Radikal Uzantısı (The Women's Movement in 1980s Turkey: The Radical Extension of Liberal Kemalism), in N. Arat (ed.) *Türkiye'de Kadın Olgusu* (*The Phenomenon of Woman in Turkey*), Istanbul: Say Publications.

Bache, I. and Marshall, A. 2004. Europeanisation and Domestic Change: A Governance Approach to Institutional Adaptation in Britain, *Queen's Papers on Europeanisation*, (5).

Berkes, N. 1975. *Türk Düşününde Batı Sorunu* (The Question of the West in Turkish Thought), Istanbul: Bilgi Publishers.

Berktay, F. 1990. Türkiye Solu'nun Kadına Bakışı: Değişen Bir Şey Var Mı? (The Turkish Left's Attitude towards Woman: Has There Been Any Change?), in Ş. Tekeli (ed.). *Kadın Bakış Açısından 1980'ler Türkiye'sinde Kadınlar* (*Women of 1980s Turkey from a Female Perspective*), Istanbul: İletişim Publishing.

Berktay, F. 2003. *Tarihin Cinsiyeti* (Gender of History), Istanbul: Metis Publishing.

Berktay, F. 2004. Afterword, in F. Berktay (ed.). *The Position of Women in Turkey and in the European Union: Achievements, Problems, Prospects.* Istanbul: KA-DER Press.

Berlin, I. 1969. 'Two Concepts of Liberty', in *Four Essays on Liberty*, Oxford: Oxford University Press.

Burchill, R. 2003. International Law of Democracy and the Constitutional Future of the EU: Contributions and Expectations, *Queen's Papers on Europeanisation*, (3).

Çakır, S. 1994. *Osmanlı Kadın Hareketi (The Ottoman Women's Movement)*, Istanbul: Metis Publishing.

Economic Development Foundation, 2003. *Avrupa Birliği'nde Kadın Hakları ve Türkiye* (Women's Rights in the EU and Turkey), Istanbul: Economic Development Foundation Publications.

Eraslan, S. 2002. Uğultular ... Silüetler ... (Buzzings ... Silhouettes ...) in A. Bora and A. Günal (eds). *1990'larda Türkiye'de Feminizm* (*Feminism in Turkey in the 1990s*), Istanbul: İletişim Publishing.

Galligan, Y., Lavero, S., Calloni, M. 2007. *Gender Politics and Democracy in Post-socialist Europe*, Leverkusen, Opladen: Barbara Budrich Publishers.

Istanbul Bar Association, 2003. *Ailenin Korunmasına Dair Kanun ve Yeni Medeni Kanuna İlişkin Uygulama Sorunları* (Problems of Practice for the Law on the Protection of the Family and the New Civil Law), Istanbul: Istanbul Bar Publications.

Işık, N. 2007. Gender Mainstreaming and Politics, in *The Debate on Gender Mainstreaming in Turkey*, Istanbul: Heinrich Böll Foundation.

Kahraman, H.B. 2001. Avrupa: Türk Modernleşmesinin Xanadu'su: Türk Modernleşmesi Kurucu İradesinde Yeni Bir Bakış Denemesi (Europe: The Xanadu of Turkish Modernisation: A New Perspective on the Founding Will of Turkish Modernisation), *Doğu-Batı* (East–West), 14(1).

Kandiyoti, D. 1997. *Cariyeler, Bacılar, Yurttaşlar: Kimlikler ve Toplumsal Dönüşümler* (Concubines, Sisters, Citizens: Identities and Social Transformations), Istanbul: Metis Publishing.

Kıvılcım Forsman, Z. 2004. Women's Rights as a Precondition of Turkey's European Union Membership, in F. Berktay (ed.), *The Position of Women in Turkey and in the European Union. Achievements, Problems, Prospects*, Istanbul: KA-DER Press.

Olsen, E.D.H. and Trenz, H.J. 2010. Deliberative Polling: A cure to the democratic deficit of the EU, *ARENA Working Paper,* (online), (13), Available at http:// www.arena.uio.no [accessed: 30.01.2012].

Pateman, C. 2004. Kardeşler Arası Toplumsal Sözleşme (Social Contract between Brothers), in J. Keane (ed.). *Sivil Toplum ve Devlet, Avrupa'da Yeni Yaklaşımlar* (Civil Society and the State, New Approaches in Europe), Ankara: Yedi Kıta Publishing.

Phillips, A. 1995. *Demokrasinin Cinsiyeti* (Gender of Democracy), Istanbul: Metis Publishing.

Phillips, A. 1997. Sexual Equality and Socialism, *Dissent*, (44).

Samur, H. 2008. Değişen ve Popülerleşen Bir Kavram Olarak Avrupalılaşma, ÇÜ. Sosyal Bilimler Enstitüsü Dergisi (Ç.Ü. Journal of the Social Sciences Institute) 17, (2).

Tekeli, Ş. 1988. Birinci ve İkinci Dalga Feminist Hareketlerin Karşılaştırmalı İncelemesi Üzerine Bir Deneme (An Essay on A Comparative Study of the First- and Second-Wave Feminisms), in *75 Yılda Kadınlar ve Erkekler (75 Years of Women and Men)*, Istanbul: History Foundation Publications.

Tekeli, Ş. 1990. 1980'ler Türkiye'sinde Kadınlar' (Women of 1980s Turkey), in Ş. Tekeli (ed.), *Kadın Bakış Açısından 1980'ler Türkiye'sinde Kadınlar (Women of 1980s Turkey from a Female Perspective)*, Istanbul: İletişim Publishing.

Terzi, Ö. 2004. Gender Equality Policies in the European Union, in F. Berktay (ed.). *The Position of Women in Turkey and in the European Union. Achievements, Problems, Prospects*, Istanbul: KA-DER Press.

Uçan Çubukçu, S. 2004a. Post-1980 Women's Movement in Turkey: A Challenge to Patriarchy, in F. Berktay (ed.). *The Position of Women in Turkey and in the European Union. Achievements, Problems, Prospects*, Ed. Fatmagül Berktay, Istanbul: KA-DER Press.

Uçan Çubukçu, S. 2004b. Contribution to Substantial Democracy: Non-Governmental Women's Organisations in Turkey, *The Position of Women in Turkey and in the European Union. Achievements, Problems, Prospects*, in F. Berktay (ed.), Istanbul: KA-DER Press.

Chapter 8

Social Policy in the EU and Turkey: the Limits of Europeanisation

Dimitris Tsarouhas

Introduction

Social policy has received little attention during the course of Turkey's accession negotiations, and most of the debate regarding Turkey's EU future has concentrated on political and security-related aspects instead. Yet it would be wrong to dismiss social policy as an unimportant policy area of little significance to Turkey's EU aspirations.

Social policy matters at the EU level, not only because of the effects of the economic crisis on peoples' incomes and jobs, but also because the EU level has by now replaced the national one as the most effective platform on which to design and implement social policy (Teague 2000). Furthermore, Turkey is a rapidly growing economy whose expected transition from a middle- to high-income country poses a new set of challenges regarding its socio-economic cohesion and the avoidance of gross inequities harmful to the realisation of the country's potential (Tsarouhas 2010). Social policy is in that sense of growing significance for Turkey, and its evolution will affect the country's socio-economic model for decades to come. Whether a more prosperous Turkey will remain a deeply unequal Turkey, with all the consequences that such inequality besets upon the educational, social and economic development of the country, is a vitally important policy question.

In what follows, I begin with a brief exposé on the Europeanisation literature and subsequently discuss the concept with reference to candidate countries. The next section links the theoretical discussion to EU social policy and briefly looks at the evolution of the latter, as well as the extent to which social policy is subject to an Europeanisation trend for EU states. In the next part Turkish social policy is discussed in more length by use of two yardsticks: the hypothesised Europeanisation effect on candidate countries' policies, and the effect of 'soft' policy harmonisation, i.e. cognitive Europeanisation, on social policy structures at the national level of social policy-making, design and implementation. The conclusion summarises the main findings.

The chapter's main argument points to a weak Europeanisation effect on Turkish social policy reform. At best, 'Europe' is used as a legitimisation device for policies conceived and designed at the national level and with domestic political priorities in mind. Although the end result is an approximation of some of Turkey's social policy structures to those prevalent in some EU states, this tends to be more the result of the policy design chosen and less of policy transfer mechanisms at work. Accounting for the limited effect of Europeanisation is the weak development of EU social policy, the demonstrated weaknesses of the soft coordination approach in introducing substantial policy change (as exemplified in the unsatisfactory progress Turkey has made towards signing up to the Joint Inclusion Memorandum) and the related neglect of social policy as a major item in pre-accession negotiations. In that sense the Turkish record on social policy reveals interesting similarities with the pre-accession record of Central and Eastern European countries (CEECs) and their policy trajectory prior to EU accession.

Before proceeding, some definitional clarifications are in order. European social policy can denote social policy arrangements in EU (European Union) member states, or refer to initiatives taken and policies formulated at the EU level by member states in cooperation with other institutions. In this chapter I adopt the second definition when referring to European social policy. Moreover, Turkey has a 'Social Policies' Ministry, yet this is part of a bigger Ministry that includes 'family policies' (*aile politikasi*). The Ministry does not deal with social policy conventionally defined, as this is the primary responsibility of the Ministry for Labour and Social Security (MLSS), focusing instead on issues such as domestic violence, assisting people with special needs and so on.

Europeanisation

Origins and Usage

Since Europeanisation is used with increasing frequency in the academic literature (Mair 2004), albeit in an often loose manner, it is important to start with some basic analytical distinctions.

Europeanisation is distinct from European integration. While the former acknowledges the two-way process of interaction between the EU and national level, the latter is about member state adjustment to obligations stemming from Brussels-made commitments. Moreover, one should distinguish between Europeanisation and harmonisation, the latter being the effect of EU rules and policies across a range of state activities and affecting both institutions and policies (Page 2003). It is more useful to ask whether Europeanisation brings about policy convergence or divergence, considering that it is by now empirically shown that Europeanisation does not impact all states and/or policy actors in the same way across the Union, and it rarely brings about harmonisation in policy outcomes (Radaelli and Pasquier 2008: 39).

Europeanisation was first used in the 1990s (Ladrech 1994), and has grown ever since to encompass not only member states but also candidates and even potential candidate countries. It first came into being as a result of the inadequacy of classic European integration theories to analyse, explain and account for the impact of the EU on member states (Bache and Jordan 2006: 18). One of the best definitions of Europeanisation is provided by Radaelli (2000: 4), who sees Europeanisation as

> Processes of a) construction, b) diffusion and c) institutionalization of formal and informal rules, procedures, policy paradigms, styles 'ways of doing things' and shared beliefs and norms which are first defined and consolidated in the making of EU decisions and then incorporated in the logic of domestic discourse, identities, political structures and public policies.

The richness of the above definition captures the formal and informal character that Europeanisation entails, and allows one to go beyond purely mechanistic readings of Europeanisation as transposition or rule conformity and see it as a complex process of socialisation into new ways of acting.

What – and How – Europeanisation?

The traditional approach to Europeanisation looked at its 'top-down' effects, the extent that is to which EU pressures have led to changes in domestic policy structures – or indeed have failed to do so. The 'goodness of fit' explanation was then used to explain the resulting empirical data, arguing that both the EU-member state match but also institutional and structural features of the polity ought to be considered when assessing the resulting fit or misfit (Börzel and Risse 2003). This approach allowed for the introduction of the new institutionalist literature on the Europeanisation debate by offering the opportunity to use sociological or rationally grounded institutionalist approaches to measure the effect of Europeanisation on national policy settings.

The alternative, 'bottom-up' approach uses the EU level as intermediate; it starts and finishes with the domestic level, as it tracks the EU effect on domestic politics and policies, including political actors (Vink and Graziano 2008: 9). Seeking to answer the question of the *real* (rather than assumed) EU effect on domestic policies, the bottom-up approach is well-placed to employ methodologically sound approaches, such as process-tracing, to come up with the right explanandum in case of policy change.

A key challenge in the Europeanisation literature, as the discussion above implies, is to identify its mechanisms, that is, the ways in which it has a clearly discernible and measurable impact on policies and politics. Knill (2001) offers three: institutional compliance, changing domestic opportunity structures and framing beliefs and expectations.

Institutional compliance refers to explicit European policies that prescribe a specific institutional model that has to be introduced. This offers member states limited discretion on how to implement change, and can therefore be seen as representing 'hard' Europeanisation. Changing domestic opportunity structures describes instances where European policies alter the distribution of power and resources between domestic actors and as a result allow for institutional change to occur. The final mechanism, framing domestic beliefs and expectations, suggests that the EU aspires to restructuring the cognitive input of actors by driving them towards a new mental understanding of change that will, in turn, be the result of their socialisation process. This last mechanism stands in contrast to the first as it is based on 'soft law' mechanisms of domestic change, and can be linked to the policy framing debate (Radaelli and Schmidt 2004) on the use of policy language justifying particular policy choices as more appropriate than others. It has also been termed cognitive Europeanisation (Guillén and Alvarez 2004).

Europeanisation and Candidate Countries

Schimmelfenning and Sedelmeier (2005) have discussed Europeanisation in candidate countries, nicely linking two debates relevant to the discussion of Europeanisation mechanisms introduced above. First, the pressure exerted by Brussels on aspiring member states to assume the formal/legal *acquis communautaire* and implement it in their national legal and administrative structures (hard mechanism); second, the pressure by the EU on candidate countries to internalise its set of normative codes of conduct and 'appropriate' policy behaviour, a much less formal yet not necessarily less powerful form of pressure (soft mechanism) (Bache and Jordan 2006: 32, see also Bulmer and Radaelli 2004: 2).

Two different parts of the enlargement literature have looked, first, at the process of conditionality and rule adoption by member states and, second, the way that Europeanisation affects state structures and policies. A third strand (Schimmelfennig and Sedelmeier 2008: 89) has examined the ways in which the process of accession has affected individual policy areas, such as transport, the environment or social policy.

The extent to which rules have been adopted and patterns of policy-making have changed is subject to multiple factors, but a general rule of thumb has emerged with time and is particularly applicable to Turkey. First, EU rule adoption by candidates is heavily (and positively) correlated to the credibility of the commitment made by the Union to (eventually) accept the candidate. Second, with respect to individual policy areas, a pattern emerges whereby it is the significance that the Union places on that particular policy area, rather than veto players or domestic costs associated with policy change, that account for the degree of compliance with EU rules. Finally, Europeanisation understood as domestic change motivated by the influence exerted by the EU resulting from its 'carrot-and-stick' capability offered by accession conditionality is much more likely to occur for candidates compared to countries the EU is merely associated with (see Heritier 2005).

Domestic policy change should be seen as the result of an interactive process. On the one hand international institutions and actors press for policy change through direct or indirect means based on their policy leverage; at the same time governments operate within the constraints of their political environment, administrative capacities and ideological orientation (Guillén and Pallier 2003).

Furthermore, it is important to differentiate between the types and extent of influence that the EU process can have on candidate countries' policies. The EU can be a *model* in the sense of transposing into national law and custom EU practices; it can be a *template*, in terms of offering a way of doing things without necessarily mimicking EU practices; and it can also be a *legitimising device*, offering legitimacy to policy-makers' choices and priorities and allowing them to make discursive use of 'Europe' so as to promote their preferred policy choices (on this issue see Vink and Graziano 2008).

The experience of previous candidate countries on social policy varies. Guillén and Alvarez (2004) suggest that Spain, a catching-up country in the 1980s whose social policy structures were weakly developed, first expanded and then rationalised its welfare state under EU influence. More important than copying into Spanish law the EU social policy *acquis*, Spanish policy-makers were affected by the Union in that the latter offered a template of reform and a means to concentrate on the kind of society desired in the future (Guillén and Alvarez 2004).

Both Spain and Portugal have been influenced by EU membership in terms of making a qualitative as well as quantitative (social protection expenditure) leap forward in their welfare arrangements. Geographical proximity was combined with domestic pressures for change to enhance social protection. Attaining 'European levels' of social protection has been essential in driving reform forward, as has been the EU template in constructing a universal healthcare service, especially in the case of Portugal (Guillén et al. 2001).

Yet the CEE experience suggests that the EU factor can play out differently too. Frege (2002) suggests that the EU has played a secondary role to the international financial institutions in social policy restructuring in Hungary, and has been happy to go along with 'American-style liberalisation' of social policy. In contrast to Southern Europe, where social policy expansion was encouraged by the EU, retrenchment and 'Americanisation' rather than Europeanisation occurred in CEE. This does not have to be the case in Turkey (Manning 2007: 498), but is closely connected to the nature and salience of social policy in the EU.

EU Social Policy

European social policy is underpinned by an oxymoron: on the one hand, the idea that social policy at Community level should be strengthened, and that the common challenges faced by EU states battling high levels of social exclusion and poverty necessitate a form of Europeanised response, is very popular (Begg and Berghman 2002: 180). The economic crisis and its socially disruptive consequences reinforce the need for more concerted action on the social policy front at supranational level.

On the other hand, however, there is strong resistance among many member states to the idea of a Europeanised social policy and the uploading of policy competences to the Union, as these national-level competences have been negotiated over a long time, are associated with the nation state and its obligation to serve citizens' welfare, and have thus acquired a nearly untouchable status. Moreover, EU social policy has always had a meaning different from the one attributed to it at national level. Rather than centred on income redistribution, services provision and social protection, EU social policy has traditionally meant labour market regulation, anti-discrimination legislation and regions-based income support. In recent years, social policy has gone beyond labour market regulation and anti-discrimination rules to embrace a more comprehensive understanding of social policy. EU action is nowadays a mix of legislation, regulation and policy coordination.

The latter has been increasingly adopted in an attempt to address problems common to member states without removing the latter's competences. This process has with time led to new debates as to whether some sort of latent or 'creeping' Europeanisation may be on the cards, especially since 'soft' methods of policy coordination, primarily the Open Method of Coordination (OMC), were adopted in policy areas such as pensions, healthcare and social exclusion. According to an optimistic reading, this enhanced the scope of EU activism in social policy beyond the labour market and emerged in parallel to the Union's adoption of a citizenship-based perspective in its understanding of social policy (Threlfall 2007).

Until the 1980s and with the exception of the Social Action Programme (Daly 2007: 2), social policy received little attention within the Community. At a time when welfare capitalism was on the ascendancy across Europe, the notion of a European social policy framework was of secondary importance to the construction of a common market. After all, the belief that market excesses should be corrected at the national level was part of a national settlement and cross-party consensus on the role of the state in economic policy. For the founders of the Union, social policy thus remained a national concern (Tsoukalis 1993: 151). This was despite the fact that the Rome Treaty had in places explicitly addressed social policy issues, going as far as envisaging social systems' harmonisation at some point in the future. However, the social policy *acquis* was largely confined to employment regulation and anti-discrimination laws, implemented with varying degrees of success in the member states.

Commission President (1985–95) Jacques Delors played a decisive role in giving a push to Europe's Social Dimension. Delors made use of the new opportunities offered by the Single European Act, and especially Article 118a that foresaw the possibility of majority voting on health and safety issues, thus bypassing national vetoes. This increased the *acquis* on health and safety issues over time and broadened the scope of employee protection. In addition, Delors sought to give a powerful say to the social partners on employment regulation and social issues by initiating the European Social Dialogue (Hantrais 1995). Today, agreements reached between the two sides go some way towards offering a solid regulatory layer over employment conditions and include agreements (which in some cases have become Directives following TEU provisions) on parental leave, part-time work, flexi-work, tele-work, stress at work and violence at work. Other achievements during that era are the 1989 Fundamental Social Rights of Workers (that excluded the UK) and the Social Protocol annexed to the Maastricht Treaty. Both documents marked progress in the social policy field (O'Connor 2005: 347), yet their minimalist and strictly voluntary character narrowed the room for manoeuvre available to the pro-social policy coalition. The definition of social policy remained circumscribed and the headline goal of EMU overshadowed 'Social Europe'.

At the beginning of the 1990s, the EU was still busy seeking to establish new legislative norms in the field of social policy and promote institution-building in order to respond to popular pressure for a stronger social dimension (Tsarouhas 2007: 33). Although some member states wished to see social policy emerge as an autonomous actor in EU policy-making, it was quite clear that a move beyond employment policy was not seen as particularly necessary. One pertinent example is the refusal by the Council to adopt the 4th Poverty Programme, which was premised on a serious funding increase compared to the previous one (Larsen and Taylor-Gooby 2004: 185). During that time, the realisation that institution-building was becoming more difficult led to the adoption of a policy coordination approach. The concept of social exclusion was introduced as persistently high unemployment rates marginalised large parts of the population and an attempt to introduce a more holistic approach to social issues began.

The 1997 Amsterdam Treaty was a step forward in that it made social exclusion policies subject to QMV voting. Three years later, the Nice European Council set particular objectives for the Union in combating both poverty and social exclusion and set out to do so by mobilising all relevant actors, facilitating employment participation, assisting the most vulnerable and preventing the risk of exclusion (Daly 2006: 466). This constituted a major development, to the extent that poverty now became an integral part of Union policy, at least in rhetorical terms, in contrast to the limited and under-funded anti-poverty programmes of the past. What is more, social policy was explicitly recognised as a productive factor as well as an instrument to tackle inequalities and social exclusion (Larsen and Taylor-Gooby 2004: 188).

More significant yet was the incorporation of social exclusion in the EU's flagship Lisbon Agenda in the year 2000. 'Lisbon I' was premised on the assumption of a virtuous circle guiding the relationship between jobs, growth and (preventing) social exclusion. Using clearly defined objectives and based on common guidelines, the EU made a leap forward in its perspective. It ceased conceiving social policy in labour market terms only and broadened its scope insofar as it spelled out a comprehensive approach marrying employment opportunities with 'rights, resources, goods, services, helping the most vulnerable [and] preventing social exclusion' (Daly 2007: 5). This was a social rights approach that conferred a new dynamic to social policy. To implement the new approach, the EU relied on the Open Method of Coordination (OMC), a system previously tried out in economic and employment policy.

In the year 2000 it was decided that poverty and social exclusion policies would be subject to the OMC, a 'soft law' approach to social policy based on numerical and qualitative targets debated and agreed upon by member states and with the Commission playing a coordinative and regulatory role. Essentially this stands for fixing EU Guidelines and setting implementation timetables; translating these into policy initiatives based on national peculiarities and institutional traditions; setting benchmarks to assess best practice and follow these up by use of periodic monitoring, evaluation and peer review. The goal would be to facilitate policy learning (Zeitlin and Pochet 2005) by incentivising countries to imitate best practice followed elsewhere without evoking the stick of legal sanctions in case of failure to do so.

Eighteen indicators to measure progress and reduce social exclusion were first agreed upon at the 2001 Laeken Summit, and elaborate definitions of poverty were developed. Action Plans were formulated by member states but the process appeared to be running out of steam following the midterm review of the Lisbon Strategy and the publication of the 2004 Kok Report. Its unflattering conclusions on EU progress towards meeting the Lisbon objectives (High Level Group 2004) led to a fundamental change in approach. Social exclusion was merged with the pensions and healthcare OMCs (both had been initiated in 2004) and the term itself was replaced with 'active social inclusion', making the previously loosened link with labour market activation stronger yet again. In addition, efficiency has become a dominant theme of the new policy approach replacing the previous emphasis on prevention as the best way to tackle social exclusion (Daly 2007: 7). The EU response to the economic crisis suggests that social policy is unlikely to become a more salient policy area in the near future, despite the fact that the June 2010 EU Council meeting agreed a headline goal of lifting 20 million Europeans out of poverty by 2020 (European Commission 2011b).

Soft law in general and the OMC in particular are reliant upon cognitive Europeanisation understood as 'the shaping and reshaping of the perception of and attitudes towards social problems and the way to tackle them' (Guillén and Alvarez 2004: 286). In addition to the implementation of the *acquis* and its transposition into national law, this is an alternative way to judge the effect of the EU on member states and candidate countries' policies. It relies less on hard evidence and more on discursive changes related to the design and conceptualisation as much as the actual legislative changes introduced by states. In the field of the 'Social OMC', candidate countries are expected to sign on to the 'Joint Memorandum on Social Protection and Social Inclusion'. Following that, their progress in aligning their social policy practices with the EU equivalent is monitored through conferences and implementation reports. Turkey has yet to complete the process of signing up to the Joint Inclusion Memorandum.

Social Policy in Turkey

An Overview

To analyse the extent to which EU candidacy and its alleged Europeanisation effect has influenced Turkish social policy, I begin with a brief overview of its main characteristics.

First, the Turkish state devotes a low percentage of public expenditure to social protection. Organisation for Economic Cooperation and Development (OECD) figures point to an increase in such expenditure from 7.6 per cent in 1990 to approximately 11 per cent in 2009 (Tsarouhas and Bölükbaşı 2007, OECD 2009). This remains substantially below the OECD-27 average of 22.4 per cent. Connected to low expenditure is the fact that social policy in Turkey essentially amounts to a combined system of health and pension coverage, as well as state-provided education. The combined nature of health and social security is important for expenditure too. Health expenditure per capita in different regions in Turkey is linked to the coverage of social security schemes. As the social security coverage ratio increases, so does health expenditure per capita (Yilmaz and Emil 2010: 58). According to the Turkish Statistical Agency's data, 13 per cent of the population receive a regular pension, 2 per cent unemployment benefit and 3 per cent are in receipt of child benefit (see Aybars and Tsarouhas 2010: 757).

Low expenditure is combined with real and persistent risks of social exclusion and poverty. The percentage of people at risk of poverty after social transfers stands at 26.5 per cent, the highest among all EU states and candidate countries (Eurostat 2010). Although Turkey is a dynamic and vibrant economy with high growth potential, its socio-economic status suggests the need for major improvements. The latest UNDP Human Development Index, a comparative measure of life expectancy, life standards, education and literacy ranks Turkey 83rd among 169 nations. The country is now in the 'High Human Development' category – but only just, as the next level (medium human development) begins with countries ranked 86 and below. The worst performing EU state, Bulgaria, occupies the 58th spot, EU candidates Croatia and Macedonia rank 51st and 71st respectively. More importantly, perhaps, in medium- and low-income countries, the correlation between economic growth and improvements in health and education is weak (UNDP 2010: 4).

Social policy in Turkey has traditionally been very fragmented. The initial steps towards the establishment of social security took place in the 1940s and sought to provide coverage for workers and employees. In a country with a large agricultural sector and rural population, this left a large share of the population uncovered. Most Turkish citizens were residing outside urban centres and were thus left out of all social security schemes (Boratav and Özuğurlu 2006). Over time, steps have been made to integrate different forms of coverage.

Access to services varies greatly and the primary determinant of access has traditionally been employment status. In that sense, the Turkish system is similar to the Bismarckian, employment-based and status-determining system, whereby civil servants enjoy conditions of access and benefit types of higher quality compared to white-collar workers in the private sector, blue-collar employees and agricultural labourers. Yet as will be discussed later, recent reforms aim at improving some forms of welfare access for the most vulnerable, easing on gross inequities and unifying service provision.

Additionally, Turkey has traditionally lacked a societal constituency pressing for a 'social state', despite the fact that such a proclamation was written into the country's constitutional charter in 1961. This, combined with a statist tradition dating from the Ottoman era and a strongly centralised state that has not decentralised health or education decisions to the municipal level means that social policy is a top-down affair with little input from other actors. On the other hand, recent years have witnessed a growing trend towards private medical and pension insurance. Turkey's economic dynamism combined with a strongly liberal political economy framework has driven a large part of the population to private providers for such coverage (Adar 2007: 168).

A final point by way of introducing the Turkish social policy landscape is the significance of informal mechanisms of welfare transfer that often replace absent state-run services or institutions. The family is a central unit of social care as well as income support and sits in tandem with clientelistic practices aiming to bypass an occasionally stifling bureaucracy (Buğra and Keyder 2006).

Social Policy Reform in Turkey

In recent years, the Turkish social policy landscape has undergone rapid transformation. Accounting for this transformation goes through tracing the process of change, centring on the two policy areas that constitute the essence of Turkish social protection: pensions and healthcare.

Social Security

Starting from the 1980s, Turkey's political economy had acquired a strong pro-market, liberal bias that viewed social security as a heavy burden on state finances and the main culprit for repeated fiscal crises (Tsarouhas and Bölükbaşı 2007: 15). Meanwhile, the system was heavily imbalanced, as the ratio of pensioners to active contributors was rapidly deteriorating, and the system's corporatist character was increasingly detached from the reality of the Turkish labour market dominated by informality and low female employment rates (Buğra and Keyder 2006, Aybars and Tsarouhas 2010). In addition, populist politics during the 1980s and 1990s led to an effective abolishment of the minimum retirement age.

Although worthwhile reform proposals were made by a host of institutions, it was the World Bank's package of recommendations that eventually led to reform in 1999. The package included both short-term measures to make social security viable and long-term changes to transform the administrative and organisational structures of social security (Aybars and Tsarouhas 2010: 753). The 1999 reform first increased the retirement age for both sexes, increased the minimum contribution period and raised the premium ceilings (OECD 2006).

Further and more drastic reforms have been implemented in recent years, in line with World Bank recommendations and backed by strong IMF support. A package of laws that cleared legal hurdles by 2008 has established a new administrative structure whereby the Social Security Institution (*Sosyal Güvenlik Kurumu*, SGK) is now the umbrella institution covering the funds for private sector employees (*Sosyal Sigorta Kurumu*, SSK), civil servants (*Emekli Sandiği*, EK) and the self-employed (*Bağ-Kur*). A single pension system has thus been created. Secondly, the state now assumes the responsibility of making contributions to the social security system to ensure its future viability, a first in Turkey, and unifies all social security institutions under the Ministry for Labour and Social Security. Third, further changes in the eligibility criteria, minimum contribution and retirement age have been set. They include a long transition period, yet the end point is a drastic rise in retirement age, reaching 65 years for men and women by 2048 and rising to 68 years by 2075 (Aybars and Tsarouhas 2010). Fourth, and as will be discussed in more detail below, the changes also entail an attempt towards universal healthcare provision.

Criticism has been raised against the reforms, the most significant of which relates to 'the marketisation of services and encouragement for the private sector to collaborate in a public-private mix of service provision' (Yakut-Çakar 2007: 124). This is likely to deepen inequalities, the argument goes, in a country where inequality is already very high (Boratav and Özuğurlu 2006). Moreover, it has been argued that the reforms do little to address the underlying problem of informal employment and these employees' entry to the formal economy. Still, the reforms make social security more viable in the long run and increase efficiency in what used to be a loosely coordinated system.

The international financial institutions have been active in the reform process through reports, press releases and public statements pushing for change and seeking to build consensus around the blueprints of their own proposals. The recent changes have been very much in line with their preferences, and their ability to influence this debate came in the wake of a long-term structural adjustment programme signed with Turkey in the wake of the latter's 2001 financial crisis. To use only one example, when the changes on social security structures were announced in 2006 the IMF announced its willingness to release a large loan to Turkey (Adar 2007: 167). Moreover, the World Bank's Country Partnership Strategy with Turkey 2008–11 declared the implementation of the social security reform a 'key priority' (World Bank 2008: 11), and announced support for the implementation of the Health Transformation programme (see section below) through 'analysis, advice and financing' (World Bank 2008: ii).

Health Care

Healthcare constitutes the second major item of the Turkish welfare state. The country spends approximately 6 per cent of its GDP on healthcare, with more than 70 per cent stemming from public sources (Ministry of Health 2009). Though its mortality, morbidity and life expectancy rates have all improved drastically over the last decade, Turkey still compares badly on these data with EU-27 countries. What is more, a lack of physicians, nurses and primary care units makes changes in the healthcare system all the more important.

Healthcare reform had been on the cards for decades. Yet political instability stemming from successive short-lived coalition governments combined with periodic economic crises had led to reform neglect of a fragmented healthcare system that only covered about two-thirds of the population. For the rest, who are particularly poor and socially vulnerable, a Green Card scheme was created in 1992. Beneficiaries are decided by district heads (*muhtar*) and the main criterion is an income of less than one-third of the minimum wage. The system did not achieve its main objective of leading to universal coverage (World Bank 2005).

In 2003 a law was passed to discontinue fragmentation in healthcare provision (divided as it was between the Health Ministry, university hospitals, military hospitals and the private sector) and create a more equitable system of healthcare delivery. Successive laws have been enacted ever since to fulfil this framework objective. Since 2005 Green Card holders are entitled to outpatient care and SSK insures have access to all public hospitals and pharmacies. Since 2006, the pharmaceuticals' list extends to all insurers under the various funds, including Green Card holders.

Since 2007, benefits across the health insurance systems have been harmonised for people insured under all major funds, ceasing the practice of privileged access for civil servants and their dependants, and restricted access to the rest (*Resmi Gazete* 2008). The new General Health Law is universal and covers all residents of Turkey. It foresees automatic coverage for all people under the age of 18. According to the new system, the state contributes to social insurance (as do employers and employees), while tax revenues are used to cover the healthcare needs of those who are not insured. Other provisions of the law encourage private health insurance by allowing private providers to make user charges between 30–70 per cent more than SGK (Yıldırım and Yıldırım 2011: 190), and introduce a referral system so as to encourage the (underdeveloped) primary healthcare services through family practitioners.

The new package of health laws is potentially driving the healthcare sector towards universalism. In deciding to opt for obligatory coverage for all under the age of 18, Turkey is following on the steps of other South European states who have introduced universalism in the recent past (Aybars and Tsarouhas 2010). Combined with the fact that Turkey suffers from high child poverty rates, this change is potentially transformative of healthcare delivery and services in the country, particularly as healthcare expenditure as a percentage of GDP continues to grow, reaching 5.6 per cent in 2010 (European Commission 2011c).

Turkish Reforms and the Role of the EU

How extensive has the EU role been then in the conceptualisation and implementation of these far-reaching reforms? To answer one ought to consider the earlier discussion on different degrees of leverage that the EU maintains, as well as the fact that no candidate country is under direct pressure to conform to a particular social security or healthcare system as there is only a limited *acquis* on these policy areas. It is thus significant to look for the EU factor by means of cognitive Europeanisation and the extent to which Turkish policy-makers have used EU devices, standards, data and policy frameworks to argue their case for reform.

Findings suggest that government ministers and parliamentarians have evoked EU comparisons and periodically sought to legitimise reforms by creating linkages between the social security situation in the EU and Turkey. In the process, some use of EU standards and member states' practices becomes evident. Parliamentary minutes from the relevant debate in 2006 reveal how the then Labour Minister argued the case for reform by comparing social security expenditure in Turkey and 'European countries' (Turkish Parliament 2006a). The government party's spokesperson on that law argued that the reform was an attempt to bring Turkish standards into line with those prevalent in the EU (Turkish Parliament 2006b). Later, the Labour Minister explicitly asserted that the new law was part of Turkey's alignment with the EU *acquis*, as well as the government's economic programme (Çelik cited in Duyulmuş 2009: 21).

Furthermore, EU norms and standards were not purely an act of rhetorical legitimisation. There was some attempt at lesson-drawing where EU requirements acted as a template for changes in the Turkish system. In 2008 Parliament discussed the revised version of the social security law following some annulments introduced by the Constitutional Court the year before. One of them pertained to principles on pay increase for actual periods of service for certain occupations (Duyulmuş 2009). The Labour Minister drew attention to a study that was later presented by an assigned official. The study, conducted by the General Directorate for Insurance, examined EU regulations on pay increase for different occupations groups and suggested a Turkish regulation in line with those standards (Turkish Parliament 2008).

Duyulmuş (2009) has argued that the use of EU norms, standards and practices as legitimising practices for reform by policy-makers was frequently used in 2005 and 2006. Ever since, however, a steady decline in such usage is observable, and the social security reform issue becomes framed more and more in terms of domestic considerations and needs. Importantly, the lessening of references to the EU and its member states coincides with the cooling of EU-Turkey relations and the growing perception in Turkey of insurmountable obstacles on the way towards full membership.

The fact that the accession process is technically going on, and that the social policy and employment chapter can be opened once opening benchmarks have been met, means that a certain dynamic is still evident. To illustrate, the number of EU experts in the MLSS has gone up from 25 in 2006 to 60 in 2010 (MLSS 2011). This is in line with higher budgetary allocations on the part of the EU to Turkey as part of the Instrument for Pre-accession Assistance (IPA) launched in 2007. Moreover, it is noteworthy that since 2009 the MLSS Activity reports include as part of the Ministry's core aims and objectives the alignment with EU standards and practices in the field of employment protection, social exclusion and social dialogue. The list of aims and objectives did not include such references in the years 2006 until 2008, the period when EU-Turkey relations were less troublesome.

Despite such progress, opening the social policy and employment chapter has not been possible, as Turkish standards still fall short of the *acquis* and corresponding ILO Conventions. The constitutional amendments approved by a referendum in 2010 marked an important step forward. Restrictions on civil servants' right to collective bargaining and collective agreements were lifted, the ban on membership in more than one trade union was abolished and the right to have more than one agreement covering the workplace was granted. However, the strike ban on civil servants remained in place. Moreover, the labour rights granted by these changes have yet to be enacted, as the social partners continue to disagree on a new threshold for collective bargaining and the right to organise at workplace level (European Commission 2011c: 78).

With regard to the emphasis paid by Turkish policy-makers on efficiency and budgetary savings in both healthcare and social security this sits well with the EU's policy on welfare state modernisation. This is evident in terms of its positive evaluation of the social security reform in terms of fiscal savings (Verbeken 2007). It can also be explained by the fact that the EU's adopted reform angle, emphasising cuts over expansion and efficiency over distributional effects, is in accordance with the Turkish government's approach to social welfare.

When it comes to healthcare, the legislation that Turkey ought to transpose relates to substance abuse, mental health, blood tissues and cells as well as a general financing framework (chapter 28). Progress on that field has been steady (European Commission 2007), and negotiations opened in December 2007. The 2009 progress report released by the Ministry for Health included the Ministry's objectives for the 2009–13 period, in which carrying out the 'European Union harmonization/accession process' was included as part of its strategic aims and objectives (Ministry of Health 2009: 118). Yet this comprehensive document on the Health Transformation Programme makes scant reference to the EU accession process and opts for references/benchmarks by use of World Health Organisation standards instead.

Conclusion

Assessing the effect of Europeanisation on Turkey is a difficult task due to the country's uncertain EU trajectory and the continued turbulence on its way towards full membership. The credibility of EU commitment to this particular enlargement round is in doubt, unlike that of the recent CEE enlargement, and Turkish progress towards meeting the political criteria for membership has been unsatisfactory.

In the area of social policy things become still more complicated for two main reasons. Firstly, unlike the *acquis* on labour law, social dialogue and employment protection, the *acquis* on social protection is very limited and so the direct EU leverage over Turkey and the rest of the candidate countries is rather minimal. EU social policy, reinvigorated for a brief period in the early 2000s, remains low on the Union's policy priorities and plays a marginal role in pre-accession negotiations. While Turkey is part of the IPA and has been receiving an increasing amount of EU funds in recent years, the amounts committed to social policy through the 4th IPA Component (Human Resources Development) remain insignificant compared to regional policy or institution-building. To illustrate, in the 2009–11 period and out of a total budget of €2.2 billion, the Human Resources Development component of IPA amounts to €196 million with only 20 per cent falling under 'social inclusion' (European Commission 2009). When it comes to the policy coordination element, candidate countries become actively part of the 'Social OMC' following the completion of their 'Memorandum on Social Protection and Social Inclusion'. Turkey has yet to finalise this process and therefore EU leverage over the country's social policies is very low.

Secondly, Turkey's starting point on social policy issues, from a qualitative and quantitative point of view, differs greatly from the EU-15 pattern and resembles the situation in CEE states prior to accession. That means that lesson-drawing from the EU-15 becomes more complicated and this is important due to Turkey's inclination to be compared with EU-15 states rather than with its closer neighbours in CEE.

With regard to the empirical data discussed above, Turkey, unlike many of its EU counterparts, has undertaken bold reforms in the areas of social security and healthcare. In the process of doing so and certainly in the early years of implementation (approximately between 2003 and 2006), there is a weak yet discernible impact of 'cognitive Europeanisation' acting as a legitimising device. Policy-makers tried to argue the case for reform on grounds of their own, efficiency-oriented policy priorities but sought to frame reform in terms of convergence with European norms and standards. Over time this becomes weaker although the MLSS has recently adopted EU terminology on social exclusion.

In terms of the *direction* of social policy reform, the ongoing attempt to universalise healthcare coverage in Turkey has a lot in common with similar experiences in countries like Portugal. Both Portugal and Spain had used EU membership as a cognitive guide to reform their welfare structures towards greater equity in healthcare and an increase in social expenditure. The Turkish Health Transformation plan and increased social expenditure point to a very interesting similarity. It should be stressed, however, that the Turkish reform plans also entail a bigger role for the private sector in service provision, increased use of user charges to access public healthcare and performance-related pay. All of these sit well with the Turkish government's political orientation and point to the high salience of domestic factors in shaping welfare reform.

Finally, the data of the Turkish case also point to some similarities with the welfare reform pattern followed by CEE states in the 1990s, in particular with regard to the highly influential role of the international financial institutions. The World Bank and the IMF have been key actors in shaping the contours of social security and healthcare reform in Turkey through finance, project initiation, implementation, expert advice and support. Their role has been more direct and more visible than that of the EU. Turkey's long-established cooperation with both of those institutions, the 2001 crisis and the congruence in reform outlook between the international financial institutions and successive Turkish governments are the key factors accounting for their ability to influence Turkish social policy over a number of years.

References

Adar, S. 2007. Turkey: reform in social security. *Journal of European Social Policy*, 17(2), 167–8.

Aybars, A.I. and Tsarouhas, D. 2010. Straddling two continents: social policy and welfare politics in Turkey. *Social Policy & Administration*, 44(6), 746–63.

Bache, I. and Jordan, A. 2006. Europeanisation and domestic change, in *The Europeanisation of British Politics*, edited by I. Bache and A. Jordan. London: Palgrave, 17–33.

Begg, I. and Berghman, J. 2002. Introduction: EU social (exclusion) policy revisited? *Journal of European Social Policy*, 12(3), 179–94.

Boratav, K. and Özuğurlu, M. 2006. Social policies and distributional dynamics in Turkey, 1923–2002, in *Social Policy in the Middle East*, edited by M. Karshenas and V.M. Moghadam. Basingstoke: Palgrave Macmillan, 156–89.

Börzel, T. and Risse, T. 2003. Conceptualizing the domestic impact of Europe, in *The Politics of Europeanisation*, edited by K. Featherstone and C. Radaelli. Oxford: Oxford University Press, 57–80.

Buğra, A. and Keyder, Ç. 2006. The Turkish welfare regime in transformation. *Journal of European Social Policy*, 16(3), 211–28.

Bulmer, S. and Radaelli, C. 2004. The Europeanisation of public policy, in *Member-States and the European Union*, edited by C. Lequesne and S. Bulmer. Oxford: Oxford University Press, 338–59.

Daly, M. 2006. EU social policy after Lisbon. *Journal of Common Market Studies*, 44(3), 461–81.

Daly, M. 2007. Whither EU social policy? An account and assessment of developments in the Lisbon Social Inclusion Process. *Journal of Social Policy*, 37(1), 1–19.

Duyulmuş, C.U. 2009. *Social security reform in Turkey: different usages of Europe in shaping the national welfare reform*. Paper to the RC 19 Conference, 20–22 August. [Online]. Available at: http://www.cccg.umontreal.ca/RC19/PDF/Duyulmus-C_Rc192009.pdf [accessed: 2 August 2011].

European Commission. 2007. *Screening Report: Turkey. Chapter 28 – Consumer and Health Protection*. [Online]. Available at: http://ec.europa.eu/enlargement/pdf/turkey/screening_reports/-screening_report_28_tr_internet_en.pdf [accessed: 9 August 2011].

European Commission. 2009. *Commission Decision on a Multi-annual Indicative Planning Document (MIPD) 2009–2011 for Turkey*,(2009) 5041.

European Commission. 2011. *Europe 2020: An Agenda for New Skills and Jobs.* Luxembourg: Publications Office of the European Union.

European Commission. 2011b. *The Measurement of Extreme Poverty in the European Union.* Brussels: DG for Employment, Social Affairs and Inclusion.

European Commission. 2011c. *Regular Report on Turkey's Progress Towards Accession.* SEC (2011) 1201. Brussels.

Eurostat. 2010. Persons at risk of poverty after social transfers. [Online] Available at: http://epp.eurostat.ec.europa.eu/tgm/table.do?tab=table&init=1&plugin=1 &language=en&pcode=t2020_52 [accessed: 15 June 2011].

Frege, C. (2002). Understanding Union effectiveness in Central Eastern Europe: Hungary and Slovenia. *European Journal of Industrial Relations*, 8(1): 53–76.

Guillén, A. and Alvarez, S. 2004. The EU's impact on the Spanish welfare state: the role of cognitive Europeanisation. *Journal of European Social Policy*, 14(3), 285–99.

Guillen A., Alvarez, S. and Silva, P.A. 2001. *Redesigning the Spanish and Portuguese Welfare States: the Impact of Accession into the European Union.* Centre for European Studies Working Paper, No. 65.

Hantrais, L. 1995. *Social Policy in the European Union.* New York: St. Martin's Press.

Héritier, A. (2005). Europeanization Research East and West: a Comparative Assessment, in *The Europeanization of Central and Eastern Europe*, edited by F. Schimmelfennig and U. Sedelmeier. Ithaca: Cornell University Press, 199–209.

High Level Group. 2004. *Facing the Challenge: the Lisbon Strategy for Jobs and Growth.* Luxembourg: Office for Publications of the European Communities.

Knill, C. 2001. *The Europeanisation of National Administrations.* Cambridge: Cambridge University Press.

Ladrech, R. 1994. Europeanisation of domestic politics and institutions: the case of France. *Journal of Common Market Studies*, 32(1), 69–88.

Larsen, T.P. and Taylor-Gooby, P. 2004. New risks at the EU level: a spillover from open market policies, in *New Risks, New Welfare: The transformation of the European Welfare State*, edited by P. Taylor-Gooby. Oxford: Oxford University Press, 181–208.

Manning, N. 2007. Turkey, the EU and social policy. *Social Policy and Society*, 6(4), 491–501.

Mair, P. 2004. The Europeanisation dimension. *Journal of European Public Policy*, 11(2), 337–48.

Ministry of Health. 2009. *Health Transformation Programme in Turkey: Progress Report.* MoH Publication No. 749. [Online]. Available at: http://www.saglik. gov.tr/EN/dosya/2-1217/h/-htp2009jan.pdf [accessed: 10 August 2011].

MLSS (Ministry of Labour and Social Security). 2011. *2010 Faaliyet Raporu* (2010 Activity Report). [Online]. Available at: http://www.calisma.gov.tr/csgbPortal/ ShowProperty/WLP%20Repository/tkb/-dosyalar/faaliyetraporu2010 [accessed: 15 August 2011].

O'Connor, J.S. 2005. Policy coordination, social indicators and the social-policy agenda in the European Union. *Journal of European Social Policy*, 15(4), 345–61.

OECD. 2006. *Economic Survey: Turkey*. Paris: OECD.

OECD. 2009. *Society at a Glance: Social Indicators*. Paris: OECD.

Page, E.C. 2003. Europeanisation and the persistence of administrative systems, in *Governing Europe*, edited by J. Howard and A. Menon. Oxford: Oxford University Press, 162–76.

Radaelli, C. 2000. Whither Europeanisation? Concept stretching and substantive change. *European Integration Online Papers (EIoP)* [Online], 4(8). Available at: http://papers.ssrn.com/sol3/-papers.cfm?abstract_id=302761 [accessed: 15 July 2011].

Radaelli, C. 2003. The Europeanisation of public policy, in *The Politics of Europeanisation*, edited by K. Featherstone and C. Radaelli. Oxford: Oxford University Press, 27–56.

Radaelli, C. and Schmidt, V. 2004. Policy change and discourse in Europe: conceptual and methodological issues. *West European Politics*, 27(2), 183–210.

Radaelli, C. and Pasquier, R. 2008. Conceptual issues, in *Europeanisation: New Research Agendas*, edited by P. Graziano and M.P. Vink. New York: Palgrave, 35–45.

Resmi Gazete (Official Gazette). 2008. *Sosyal Sigortalar ve Genel Sağlık Sigortasi Kanunu Bazı Kanun Hükmünde Kararnamelerde Değişiklik Yapılmasina Dair Kanun* (Decree Law Regarding Changes Introduced to the Social Security and General Health Insurance Law). No: 5754, Sayı: 25798, 8 May, Ankara.

Schimmelfennig, F. and Sedelmeier, U. 2005 (eds). *The Europeanisation of Central and Eastern Europe*. Ithaca: Cornell University Press.

Schimmelfenning F. and Sedelmeier, U. 2008. Candidate countries and conditionality, in *Europeanisation: New Research Agendas*, edited by P. Graziano and M.P. Vink. Houndmills: Palgrave Macmillan, 88–101.

Teague, P. 2000. EU social policy: institutional design matters. *Queen's Papers on Europeanisation*, 1.

Threlfall, M. 2007. The social dimension of the European Union. *Global Social Policy*, 7(3), 271–93.

Tsarouhas, D. 2007. European integration and social policy: from institution-building to policy coordination, in *Bridging the Real Divide: Social and Regional Policy in Turkey's Accession Process*, edited by D. Tsarouhas, E. Ertugal and A.I. Aybars. Ankara: METU Press, 17–43.

Tsarouhas, D. and Bölükbaşı, T. 2007. Exogenous pressures and social policy: Greece and Turkey in comparative perspective. *EUI Working Paper*, RSCAS 2007/38.

Tsarouhas, D. 2010. How is the 'European BRIC' faring? Social policy, the labour market and industrial relations in Turkey. *South East Europe Review*, 13(3), 313–25.

Tsoukalis, L. 1993. *The New European Economy: The Politics and Economics of Integration*. Oxford: Oxford University Press.

Turkish Parliament. 2006a. 88. *Birleşim Tutanaklari* (Minutes of the 88th Parliamentary Session). 22. Dönem (22nd legislative period) Cilt: 116 (Issue: 116), 13 April.

Turkish Parliament. 2006b. 89. *Birleşim Tutanaklari* (Minutes of the 89th Parliamentary Session). 22. Dönem (22nd legislative period) Cilt: 116 (Issue: 116), 18 April.

Turkish Parliament. 2008. *Butce ve Plan Komisyonu Tutanaklari* (Minutes of the Budget and Planning Commission). [Online]. Available at: http://www.tbmm. gov.tr/komisyon/planbutce/ssgss/-04_03_2008.htm [accessed: 26 July 2011].

UNDP. 2010. *The Real Wealth of Nations: Pathways to Human Development*. New York: United Nations Development Programme.

Verbeken, D. 2007. The pension reform challenge in Turkey. *ECFIN Country Focus*, 4(3), 1–6.

Vink, M.P. and Graziano, P. 2008. Challenges of a new research agenda, in *Europeanisation: new research agendas*, edited by P. Graziano and M.P. Vink. New York: Palgrave Macmillan, 3–20.

World Bank. (2005). *World Development Indicators 2005*. Washington DC: World Bank.

World Bank. 2008. *Country Partnership Strategy with Turkey, 2008–2011*. Report No. 42026-TR. [Online]. Available at: http://www.worldbank.org.tr/WBSITE/ EXTERNAL/COUNTRIES/-ECAEXT/TURKEYEXTN/0,contentMDK:216 78953~pagePK:141137~piPK:141127~theSitePK:361712,00.html [accessed: 11 August 2011].

Yakut-Çakar, B. (2007). Turkey, in *Social Policy and International Interventions in South East Europe*, edited by B. Deacon and P. Stubbs. Cheltenham: Edward Elgar, 103–29.

Yıldırım, H.H. and Yıldırım, T. 2011. Healthcare financing reform in Turkey: context and salient features. *Journal of European Social Policy*, 21(2), 178–93.

Yılmaz, H. and Emil, F. (2010). *Social Expenditure at Different Levels of Government: Turkey*, Ankara. [Online]. Available at: http://siteresources.worldbank. org/INTTURKEY/Overview/-22827911/socialexpendituresinTurkey.pdf [accessed: 20 October 2011].

Zeitlin, J. and Pochet, P. 2005 (eds). *The Open Method of Coordination in Action: The European Employment and Social Inclusion Strategies*. Brussels: P.I.E. – Peter Lang.

Chapter 9

Europeanisation of Turkish Environmental Policy with Special Reference to Sustainability Discourse

Rana İzci

Introduction

Special circumstances of Turkey define Turkey's commitments and position within various multilateral environmental regimes to which Turkey is a party. Special circumstances of Turkey basically acknowledge that Turkey has not completed its development yet, and thus its responsibilities arising from the multinational environmental agreements should be described accordingly.[1] However, as a member of the Organisation for Economic Cooperation Development (OECD) and a candidate country for EU membership, Turkey faces many difficulties to establish this position at international level. Moreover, ambiguities over Turkey's candidacy further complicate the situation. Thus, opening of the chapter on the environment in the EU-Turkey accession talks heated up the debates on the EU membership and the state of the environment in Turkey.

Environmental policy is one of those areas in which 'the EU received the competence to legislate on' late when compared to many other areas of policy-making (Börzel 2007: 227). Yet, environmental policy is also regarded as one of the 'most developed areas of EU policy-making' (Börzel 2007: 227). Furthermore, experiences of both the Southern Europe and the Central and Eastern Europe (CEE)

---

1 In the climate change negotiations, special circumstances of Turkey are officially recognized at the seventh meeting of the Conference of the Parties in 2001 and Turkey became the 189th party to the UNFCCC on 24 May 2004. Special circumstances refers to the fact that Turkey has the lowest per capita GDP in all OECD members and thus commitments arising from the international conventions should be arranged according to the common but differentiated responsibilities without harming its economic growth and development. On 5 February 2009 the Turkish Grand National Assembly approved a law to join the Kyoto Protocol and Turkey became a party to the Kyoto Protocol on 26 August 2009. Turkey has no commitment for quantified emission reduction or limitation since it was not listed in Annex B of the Kyoto Protocol (Ministry of Environment and Urbanisation 2011).

accessions clearly demonstrate that environment matters for the EU enlargement.[2] The environment was initially one of the main drives of the revolutions in the CEECs (Carmin and Van Dever 2005, Von Homeyer 2005). Nevertheless, their economic and social considerations triumphed over environmental concerns particularly during the economic restructuring and the EU accession process. Therefore, many argued that CEE enlargement would end the progressive environmental policy in the EU while others argued that enlargement would bring advantages both for the EU and the accession countries. On the one hand, financial burden and administrative challenges arising from complying with the EU environmental *acquis* created several tensions in the CEE countries (CEEC). On the other hand, the question how the accession would affect the existing policy areas and achievements set off further intense discussions about the enlargement itself

Turkey's candidacy is often compared to those of CEE and Southern European countries. Although there are similarities in all these cases, Turkey's situation differs both in general terms and environmental policy. Briefly, Turkey is also subject to the same EU conditionality as the CEE countries. Nevertheless, the Turkish case is not identical with those countries. Although Turkey has to make political reforms and adjust its market conditions with those of the EU, it is neither a country with transition to market economy nor democracy.

Environmental concerns have steadily been included in the agenda of Turkey-EU relations since 1995. However, Turkey has a relatively well developed environmental policy and administration compared to those countries and has been party to various international environmental regimes since 1970s. Therefore, in terms of environmental policy the Turkish case is also different from the Southern European countries' situation even though modernisation and economic development are initially shared motives for the EU accession both for Turkey and the Southern European countries.

This chapter assumes that the approximation of EU environmental *acquis* and international developments challenge the notions of sustainability and development in Turkey. It thus questions whether – and to what extent – any change has occurred in the existing development-environment link in Turkey due to the EU conditionality both at the declaratory level and in practice. It also asserts that EU conditionality might be a useful tool to analyse the changes in Turkey's environmental policy at international level.

This chapter will primarily focus on the changes in policy principles and the policy content with special reference to sustainable development. It will also attempt to understand how and to what extent Europeanisation of Turkish environmental policy can affect Turkey's international commitments.

---

2   Accessions of Austria, Finland and Sweden also triggered the debates on higher environmental protection standards within the EU from a different perspective. The EU had to review its health and environmental standards since these issues were very sensitive issues in these three states. For further information see European Commission 1998a.

Thus, this chapter first sets the background to the emergence of the environment as an issue area in Turkey-EU relations and then looks at the evolution of the sustainable development as a policy principle and the prevailing sustainability discourse in Turkey. Evolution of environmental policy in Turkey clearly indicates that environmental considerations have always been assessed with reference to development targets. This, in turn, reveals the conflicting notions of sustainability and asserts that the notion of sustainability is built upon the weak interpretation of sustainable development which prioritises policy coordination and changes in consumption patterns over green planning.

Development plans have a binding character and shape all policies and investments in Turkey. They also frame the environmental discourses at the state level. Therefore, development plans will be examined to understand how environmental considerations take place and sustainable development is formulated at the declaratory level. Along with Development plans, official documents such as the Environmental Law, and Accession Partnership Documents and related documents will also be examined to explore the evolution of sustainable development in Turkey and the EU impact.

Subsequently, this chapter tries to understand the impact of EU-Turkey relations on Turkish environmental policy with special emphasis on the sustainable development as well as Turkey's position to international environmental regimes. Since participation is one of the core ideas of the sustainable development discourse, civil society participation in environmental policy-making will also be briefly explored with a view to analyse whether the accession negotiations can induce any change with regard to the policy-making process in Turkey.

Europeanisation of Environmental Policy in a Candidate Country: Theoretical Context

Accession partnership documents prepared for the CEEC clearly displayed the increased EU membership conditions and the EU impact on domestic policies (Grabbe 1999). Consequently, Europeanisation literature has soon became analytically relevant to search for the EU influence and pressure on applicant countries' domestic politics.

Europeanisation is still regarded as a contested concept despite its increasing popularity as a research agenda (Vink and Graziano 2007: 3–4). Therefore it is even more difficult to define and analyse the concept of Europeanisation in candidate countries. Moreover, diffusion of EU policies and norms to the countries with membership perspective has further intensified the conceptual and methodological debates on the Europeanisation research (Schimmelfennig and Sedelmeier 2007: 89).

Nevertheless, two main approaches seem to dominate Europeanisation research in candidate countries, namely, rationalist institutionalism and constructive or sociological institutionalism. In short, rational institutionalism approach – in candidate countries – focuses on the credibility of EU conditionality and offers a model – external incentives model – based on the logic of consequences to analyse Europeanisation (Sedelmeier 2011). In this model, it is assumed that (credibility of the) promise of rewards by the EU and the cost-benefit calculation of actors are the main factors that might explain Europeanisation in candidate countries. Sociological or constructive institutionalism, on the other hand, mainly focuses on the normative dimension of the EU demands (Sedelmeier 2011). Social learning model deriving from logic of appropriateness thus goes beyond the cost-benefit analysis of the rewards and emphasises the recognition of the EU demands and rules as legitimate and appropriate in candidate countries (Sedelmeier 2011).

Among all, the external incentives model is often regarded as the most appropriate mechanism of Europeanisation in candidate countries. This argument is also valid for Turkey and explains well the extent and direction of Europeanisation of Turkish environmental policy in most cases. Given the high cost of compliance with the environmental *acquis*[3] *and* development targets and priorities of Turkey, discussions over Turkey's membership within the EU clearly damage the credibility of EU conditionality in Turkey paving the way for implementation and enforcement problems. Sometimes, it might also cause delays in transposition of certain parts of EU environmental *acquis*. Limited progress is therefore the most pronounced outcome of Europeanisation. However, there are certain cases where this model can not entirely explain the domestic change in Turkish environmental policy. At this point, this chapter seeks explanatory factors which might facilitate domestic change in Turkish environmental policy and tries to understand the extent of EU-induced impact in this change. Analysis of the emergence of national climate change policies in Turkey serves as a good example in search of these factors.

Nonetheless, this chapter presumes that almost all actors in Turkish environmental policy regard the EU as an opportunity structure which enables them to achieve their own goals. This perception can be traced for instance in the government's energy investments, attempts of the private sector to take part in the European Carbon Market and also environmental organisations' involvement in EU projects.

An Environmental Agenda for Turkey-EU Relations

EU-Turkey relations have started to influence Turkish environmental policy particularly by the establishment of the Customs Union in 1995. The environment-trade link which was one of the central themes of the global environmental politics also dominated the environmental concerns in EU-Turkey relations. Thus, various reports and research were conducted particularly on the environmental

---

3   According to the estimations of the Ministry of Environment, the cost of complete compliance with EU environmental *acquis* requires an investment of approximately 60 billion Euros. For further information see Ministry of Environment and Forestry 2006.

standards, on trade, environment and competitiveness link and environmental policy-making. Soon after the 1999 Helsinki Summit, the impact of the EU on Turkish environmental policy became more visible. The 1998 Progress report clearly indicated the big misfit between Turkish and EU environmental legislation with regard to standards, measurement methods and monitoring requirements which in turn creates high adaptational pressure on Turkey to change (European Commission 1998b). However, alignment with the environmental *acquis* remained limited since 2005 despite the progress achieved in a number of fields and Turkey's European Environment Agency membership in 2003.

Developments have gained pace with the accession negotiations in 2005. Several projects on the state of the environment in Turkey, on environmental legislation and the cost of complying with the EU environmental *acquis* were accomplished and important documents such as EU integrated environmental approximation strategy were prepared. Screening process was completed in 2006 and, the environment chapter of accession negotiations was opened on 21 December 2009.

Opening of the accession talks both stirs up debates about the EU impact on domestic policy making in Turkey and brings Turkey's development concerns into the limelight once again. Environmental policies have been developing since the 1970s in Turkey and the institutional structure at the ministerial level began to evolve in the 1990s. However, there are still problems for integration of environmental considerations into development plans. Development has always been a thorny issue in Turkish politics and is associated with modernisation and rapid economic growth for Turkey. Although sustainable development is recognised as a policy principle, sustainable growth seems to dominate the development agenda. At this point, the low credibility of EU conditionality and high costs of alignment with EU environmental *acquis* are creating create further difficulties for solving the development versus environment dilemma in Turkey.

Plainly, external dimension of the EU policies and the fifth enlargement expanded the scope of the question about the transformative power of the EU. In order to analyse the EU impact on the candidate countries, Europeanisation literature was called upon by increasing research on different areas of domestic politics particularly since the year 2000. Although Europeanisation literature includes several controversies regarding conceptual and methodological debates as a research agenda, pre-accession conditionality and post accession developments in CEEC countries increase the popularity of Europeanisation research both in new member and candidate countries. Most Europeanisation research in Turkey also depends on the policy and/or institutional fit/arguments while the some others look at how the EU matters in Turkish politics. Contemporary studies on Turkish environmental politics include the *European dimension* of change in Turkish politics to a greater extent.

Emergence of Sustainable Development in Turkey's Development Agenda

There is no doubt that heydays of the environmentalism have significant impact on the development of Turkish environmental policy. International developments have certainly affected and continued to affect Turkish environmental policy. Thus membership to regional and international organisations and participation in environmental regimes challenged both environmental politics and legislation (Algan and Mengi 2005).

Environmental considerations also started taking place in the development plans in the 1970s to respond to those international developments.[4] For instance, the 1972 United Nations Conference on Human Environment had profound effects on environmental policy in Turkey which could be traced in the Third Five Year Development Plan (1973–77). It was the first development plan which included a specific part on environmental concerns (Algan and Mengi 2005, State Planning Organisation 1973). Nevertheless, this plan also proclaimed that environmental policy considerations should not impair development of the country (State Planning Organisation 1973).

Institutionalisation of environmental policy started with the establishment of the Committee for Coordination of environmental problems as the first independent environmental body in Turkey in 1974.[5] In the fourth development plan (1979–83) however a more comprehensive view on the environment was visible (State Planning Organisation 1979). Not only was the scope of the environmental policy enriched but also preventive action was pronounced for the first time. Direct national regulations on the protection of the environment also started in the 1980s and the Environmental law came into effect in 1983.

Attempts to integrate the idea of sustainable development into policy-making particularly sped up after the 1992 UNCED in Rio (Talu 2006). With the Sixth Five Year Development Plan (1990–94) sustainable development understanding was integrated into fundamental objectives and policies of a development plan for the first time (State Planning Organisation 1989). Subsequently, the Seventh Five Year Development Plan (1996–2000) asked for the preparation of a National Environmental Action Plan (NEAP) to achieve a comprehensive strategy to put the environmental concerns at the heart of socio-economic decision-making.

---

4   So far nine development plans have been produced by the State Planning Organization (*Devlet Planlama Teşkilatı*) in Turkey. Since its establishment in 1961, the State Planning Organization defined the priorities and shaped socio-economic development of Turkey. The State Planning Organisation was renamed as the Ministry of Development in June 2011.

5   In terms of institutional structure, the Ministry of Environment was established in 1991. In 1993 two ministries, the Ministry of Forestry and the Environment were incorporated. In June 2011, this institutional structure also changed; two new ministries were formed: Ministry of Environment and Urbanisation and Ministry of Forestry and Hydraulic Works.

In the NEAP, it was clearly stated that there was not much internalisation of environmental concerns into economic and social decisions despite positive legal and institutional developments (State Planning Organisation 1998).

Specific targets and timetables were set to achieve four broad objectives; improvement of living standards, increasing environmental awareness and consciousness, improvement of environmental governance and achievement of sustainable economic, social and ecological development. Nevertheless, the NEAP never became a legally binding text. The NEAP was also criticised by the EU for not having enough interest in the adoption of the environmental *acquis* (European Commission 1999).

Sustainable Development in Rhetoric and Practice: The Impact of EU-Turkey Relations on Environmental Discourses and Policy Principles

From early 1980s to mid 1990s, three developments had significant impact on Turkish environmental policy, namely, creation of the World Commission on Environment and Development in 1983 (and its report in 1987), the United Nations Conference on Environment and Development in 1992 and establishment of the Customs Union between the EU and Turkey in 1995. The Fifth (1985–89) and Sixth Development (1990–94) plans thus reflect the main storylines of environmental discourses of those years (Talu 2006, Algan and Mengi 2005). For instance, while in the Fifth Development Plan, the concept of intergenerational equity was underlined, in the Sixth Development Plan sustainable development took place as the basic principle for the management of the natural resources (State Planning Organisation 1984, 1989, Algan and Mengi 2005: 97).

The Customs Union, on the other hand, raised strong reservations about the direct link between competitiveness and environmental protection. Even before the Customs Union came into effect, various studies conducted on the impact of the Customs Union on Turkish industry. Environmental standards were often regarded as non-tariff barriers which might weaken the competitiveness of Turkish industry. Some action plans were prepared to increase the competitiveness of Turkish industry. For instance, The Report of the Turkish Industry and Business Association (TÜSİAD) on the Non-tariff Technical Barriers to Environmental Protection represents well the increasing concerns for international competitiveness (TÜSİAD 1998). The period that the Seventh Development Plan covered (1996–2000), therefore, was very important for the evolution of Turkish environmental policy. The emphasis on the international commitments became apparent (State Planning Organisation 1996). In this plan, sustainable development was accepted as the basic principle; nevertheless environmental challenges were still regarded as management problems (Algan and Mengi 2005: 97). Before the Helsinki Summit, the 1999 Progress report underlined the need for long-term prospect for complying with the EU environmental *acquis* and pointed out that no progress achieved in certain areas such as water, nature protection, chemicals and industrial pollution control and risk management and that there was limited progress on medical waste control and air quality and noise control (European Commission 1999).

From 1999 to 2001: Sustainable Development and the EU Conditionality

Subsequent to the EU Helsinki Summit (1999) where Turkey was recognised as a candidate country on an equal footing with other candidate countries, the EU prepared the first Accession Partnership Document (AP) for Turkey in 2001. This document contained short and medium term priorities and objectives to be achieved fulfilling the Copenhagen criteria and complying with the *acquis communautaire*.[6] The AP set short and medium term environmental principles indicating the need to develop administrative capacity for transposing, implementing and enforcing EU environmental *acquis*.

Among those priorities set out in the first AP, emphasis on a principle significantly took the centre stage; 'Integration of sustainable development principle into the definition and implementation of all other sectoral policies' was listed as a medium-term priority (Council of the European Union 2001: 21). The Sixth Development Plan clearly indicated the necessity of integration of environmental concerns into all areas of economic activity. Implementation of this principle however proved to be difficult. Therefore, the EU conditionality within this framework denoted an urgent necessity to meet the sustainability targets in Turkey putting pressure on the policy content and implementation of the certain principles. In 2001 the National Program (NP) for the adoption of the EU *acquis* was prepared by Turkey and environmental priorities were also set (Turkish National Action Programme 2001).[7] However, this programme did not include the sustainable development as part of complying with the environmental policies but rather referred to the goals for achieving sustainable rural and agricultural policies (Algan and Mengi 2005). Nevertheless being a member of the European Environmental Agency in 2003, and, the establishment of an office in Ankara by the Regional Environmental Centre for Central and Eastern Europe (REC), in 2004, ushered new practices for Turkey.[8] While the former provided progress on environmental management systems, the latter brought a new dynamic among the environmental stakeholders and made the scientific information more understandable for the lay people.[9]

---

6   This document was revised in 2003, 2005, 2008.

7   National Programme for the adoption of the *acquis* was also renewed in 2003 and 2008.

8   Regional Environmental Centre is an international organisation founded in 1990 by the European Commission, Hungary and the United States. The REC is legally based on a charter signed by the governments of 30 countries and the European Commission, and on an international agreement with the government of Hungary. For more information see http://www.rec.org/about.php?section=mission.

9   REC Turkey was also designated by the Ministry of Environment and Forestry as the national focal point for UNFCCC Article 6 – Education, Training and Public Awareness.

All in all, complying with the EU environmental *acquis* also requires Turkey to be a party to various international environmental regimes which in turn revives the old heated debates on global responsibilities and national development plans in Turkey. International developments on global climate change, therefore, marked a watershed with regard to Turkish environmental policy. For a long time Turkey remained reluctant to become a party both to the United Nations Conference on Climate Change (UNFCCC) and the Kyoto Protocol since Turkey was placed together with developed countries in both Annexes of the UNFCCC despite its objections not to be listed in both Annexes of the UNFCCC. This situation plainly exacerbated Turkey's concerns on its development targets and international commitments. Once the UNFCCC regime was established, Turkey started to face further difficulties. Together with many other *developed* parties, the EU also rejected the Turkish proposal to be deleted from these Annexes due to Turkey's EU candidacy.

Nonetheless, in order to demonstrate Turkey's good faith in international climate regime and decisiveness in EU candidacy, a Specialised Commission on Climate Change was established by the State Planning Organisation in 1999 and it published a report on climate change in 2000 in preparation for the Eighth Development Plan (2001–2005) of Turkey (Türkeş 2002). The Eighth Five Year Development (2001–2005) plan and the Long-Term Strategy (2001–23) also came into force in the same year. The Eighth Development Plan is particularly important for two reasons though it is very much criticised for not stating the sustainable development among the fundamental goals and policies. Firstly, the need and necessity for complying with the EU *acquis communautaire* was strongly underlined in the fundamental objectives, principles and policies section of the Eighth Development Plan (State Planning Organisation 2000). Secondly, the Eighth National Development Plan created the conditions for Turkey's accession to the UNFCCC despite the delays in its ratification.[10]

From 2001 Onwards: Timing and Economic Gains

The turning point for Turkey's climate policy was the recognition of its unique position within the UNFCCC at the seventh meeting of the Conference of the Parties in 2001 (Depledge 2009: 281). After a long struggle, Turkey achieved its aim of being deleted from the Annex II of UNFCCC and became a party to the UNFCCC on 24 May 2004.[11] Turkey's hesitation to be a party to the international climate regime mainly stemmed from the challenges concerning its development targets which, however cannot be confined only to Turkey. China, India and many other fast growing economies have also faced such difficulties and raised similar concerns.

---

10   The Inter-ministerial Coordination Board on Climate Change was also established in 2001 and its structure was revised in 2004.

11   The Turkish Grand National Assembly established a Research Commission on causes and effects of climate change in 2007. The First National Communication of Turkey on Climate Change was prepared in January 2007.

Nonetheless, Turkey-EU relations and Turkey's candidate state status have further complicated the situation for Turkey. In its 2003 NP, it was stated that being party to the Kyoto Protocol could be considered depending on the present conditions in Turkey (Turkish National Action Programme 2003). Present conditions imply a wide range of conditions from the pace and direction of EU-Turkey relations to the developments with regard to the climate change negotiations at the international level. Thus, there were three major arguments on whether Turkey should sign the Kyoto Protocol and if so when to sign. According to the anti-Kyoto stance in Turkey, Turkey had the lowest per capita greenhouse gas emissions among the OECD countries and signing the Kyoto Protocol would hamper its economic development so Turkey should never sign it.

Some others, however, argued that Turkey should sign the Protocol only after becoming an EU member state. Otherwise it would create a big financial burden for Turkey. The last group, however, argued that Turkey should sign the Protocol as soon as possible since being a party to the Protocol would provide an important opportunity to shape Turkey's position in the post-2012 climate regime. They also argued that the cost of complying with the EU environmental *acquis* and the cost of necessary arrangements arising from being a party to the Kyoto Protocol should be considered together, supporting each other (Hürriyet Daily News 2009). They also think that being party to the Protocol would help Turkey to negotiate its position in better terms for the post-2012 period (TÜSİAD 2009). The supporters of the second and the third argument had one assumption in common; Turkey could benefit from the carbon market and related mechanisms to support its investments for socio-economic development. There were, however, other groups such as Global Action Group (*Küresel Eylem Grubu*) who thought that Turkey should sign the Kyoto Protocol but not for economic gains that might arise from a being party to the climate regime but for sustainability, equity and justice concerns.

UNFCCC and the Kyoto Protocol are not the only international environmental regimes that the EU conditionality forces Turkey to participate in. Aarhus Convention[12] and Espoo Convention,[13] for instance, are two other examples of international environmental regimes to which Turkey is not a party but the EU conditionality challenges Turkey to change its position.

The 2003 NP clearly affirmed that Turkey would be a party to those Conventions only after Turkey's accession to the EU (Turkish National Action Programme 2003). Turkey's reservations on the grounds of sovereignty and security prevent her from participating in these Conventions – particularly in terms of transboundary water management (Ministry of Foreign Affairs 2011). Moreover, contrary to the Kyoto Protocol, there is no economic benefit to be gained in becoming party to

---

12   Aarhus Convention on Access to Information, Public Participation in Decision Making and Access to Justice in Environmental Matters entered into force on 30 October 2001.

13   Espoo Convention on Environmental Impact Assessment in a Transboundary Context entered into force on 10 September 1997.

those Conventions but rather there is fear that economic losses can occur due to long stakeholder consultation processes arising from those Conventions. It should be remembered that Turkey signed the UNFCCC and the Kyoto Protocol only after its unique position was accepted and it became clear that Turkey would not get any emission reduction targets within the current regime. Therefore, one could argue that despite EU conditionality, there is a limited EU induced change on the participation of Turkey in the international environmental regimes to which the EU is a party.

Timing (UNFCCC decision on Turkey in 2004 and accession negotiations in 2005) however, seems to be an important factor facilitating the change in Turkey's position with regard to the climate change regime. Possible economic gains that might arise from mitigation and adaptation policies, both under the current regime and in the post-2012 period are other actors facilitating the change in the climate change policy of Turkey. On the other hand, national security concerns impede the internationalisation of the issues covered by Aarhus and Espoo Conventions which in turn, causes inertia as a response to EU conditionality.

On 5 February 2009 the Turkish Grand National Assembly approved a law to join the Kyoto Protocol. Soon after, Turkey became a party to the Kyoto Protocol on 26 August 2009. Accordingly, the National Climate Change Strategy Document was prepared in 2009 and came into effect in 2010. In June 2011, the final draft of Turkey's National Climate Change Action Plan was released. The Plan was completed in August 2011. However, it was also criticised particularly for not having clear mitigation targets. Moreover, serious controversy still exists whether and how much signing of both the UNFCCC and the Kyoto Protocol have so far contributed to achieving and enhancing sustainability targets in Turkey.

2006 marks another turning point both in the evolution of Turkish environmental policy and the EU impact on Turkish environmental legislation. In 2006 the Environment Law[14] was renewed and the EU Integrated Environmental Approximation Strategy was published. Sustainable development was recognised as the aim of the environmental policy in the renewed environmental law and was stated as one of the fundamental principles of the environmental approximation strategy.

However, the use of sustainable environment and sustainable development within the same sentence in the renewed Environmental Law created some doubts about the perception of the concept at the state level. Moreover, exclusion of mining, oil and geothermal activities from Environmental Impact Assessment in the Environmental Law also raised serious concerns over the nature protection and sustainability in general. Mining activities around national parks and in areas with high ecological sensitivity have already caused both local and nationwide concerns and protests in the civil society.[15] The 2011 Progress Report also

---

14   Law Number: 5491 Ratification date: 24 June 2006.

15   A number of protests took place in different parts of Turkey against mining activities in mountainous areas, areas close to national parks and human settlements. For instance, since 2007, increasing number of environmental platforms organised protests against gold

criticized the insufficient implementation of procedures for public consultation in energy investments (European Commission 2011).

The Ninth Development Plan, contrary to the previous ones, covers a seven-year period, and is prepared as the main document contributing to the EU membership taking into consideration the financial year of the EU (2007–13). Turkey's Programme for Alignment with the *acquis* (2007–13) was also announced for the same period listing and scheduling the legislative process for harmonisation with the full membership perspective. In the Ninth Development Plan, a more comprehensive analysis of the development policies took centre stage rather than a sectoral approach on which the previous development plans were based (State Planning Organisation 2006). Increasing the competitiveness and employment, strengthening the human development and social solidarity, regional development, increasing the quality and efficiency of the public sector services constitute the main development axes of the Ninth Development Plan.

At first glance, examination of cross-cutting themes of economic problems and social challenges presents a convenient approach for the implementation of sustainable development. Nevertheless, environmental protection together with the development of urban infrastructure took place under the competitiveness axis of this plan. The Ninth Development Plan, Special Expertise Commission on the Environment therefore raised criticisms against dealing with the environment heavily in terms of urban infrastructure and efficient and rational use of natural resources for increasing the competitiveness of the country (State Planning Organisation 2007). In the Ninth Plan, it seems that environment is mainly regarded as an asset for sustainable economic growth and competitiveness. In sum, the Ninth Development Plan gives a special importance for the EU membership and follows the lines of the Lisbon strategy highlighting the competitiveness themes and good governance.

Nevertheless, it represents the characteristics of a weak sustainable development strategy for the country going not far beyond end-pipe technological solutions, market-led policy instruments, limited civil society participation and institutional reform (Baker 2006). It seems that the Turkish environmental policy has still been conducted in terms of the environment regime rather than the sustainability regime (Von Homeyer 2005).[16] On the other hand, the Ninth Development Plan established the legal ground for the preparation of National Climate Action Plan

---

mining activities in *Kaz Dağlari* (Mount Ida) which is a well known mountainous area in the North Aegean with its rich ecosystems.

16   Von Homeyer (2005) defines three environmental regimes to analyse EU environmental governance, namely; the internal market regime, the environmental regime and the sustainability regime. 'Environmental product standards' constitute the basis of the internal regime while the environmental regimes rest upon the production processes and standards (Von Homeyer 2005: 57-60). The sustainability regime, on the other hand, rests on the principle of 'decoupling economic growth from environmental degradation and resource consumption' (Von Homeyer 2005: 60).

for mitigation policies and measures in line with its special circumstances and would carry out its commitment under the UNFCCC.

Ecological concerns and Societal Mobilisation: Business Interest and Civil Society Participation in Policy-Making

As the state of the environment indicates, ecological systems suffer largely from the economic growth in Turkey. According to the 2010 Environmental Performance Index, Turkey has a low performance for maintaining ecosystem vitality which in turn would challenge its adaptive capacity to respond various environmental challenges but particularly climate change (Yale Centre 2011). Turkey has a poor record in protecting the biodiversity, ranking 140th in biodiversity and habitat conservation and also in its general environmental performance – ranking 77th among 163 countries – according to the 2010 Environmental Performance Index (Yale Centre 2011). Turkey's poor record in nature protection was also underlined in the 2011 Progress Report even stating a danger for the position of wetlands under the Convention of Wetland of Special Importance.

Turkey is one of the fast growing economies and the 'seventeenth largest economy' in the world (International Energy Agency 2010: 13). This economic growth, however, brings various challenges for the environment particularly in terms of energy investments and nature protection. Turkey's greenhouse gas emissions per capita are well below the OECD countries and the EU average (Organisation for Economic Cooperation Development. 2008). However, Turkey has the highest greenhouse gas emissions increase between the years 1990 and 2007 (United Nations 2009). The total GHG level increases are mainly due to energy generation, energy consumption and industrial processes (Ministry of Environment and Urbanisation 2011). Energy-related carbon emissions have also been growing since 1990 at a rate faster than economic growth in the country (Kaygusuz 2004). Moreover, as Turkey's energy supply heavily depends on imported fossil fuels, Turkey is likely to face big challenges with regard to its energy needs.

On the other hand, the share of renewable energy sources in energy production in Turkey has also increased between 1990 and 2004 (Toklu et al. 2010). Hydropower is the most important kind of renewable energy supplies, which is followed by wind energy as a growing energy resource. However, these investments are challenged by certain factors, such as where to locate the renewable energy power plants, or the private sector participation in the construction and operation of new power plants. For instance, on 2 April 2011, a recent environmental movement, *the great march of Anatolia* (*Anadoluyu vermeyoz*), began in the Black Sea Region to protest against these sorts of investment, particularly new hydropower projects that might damage nature (Drynet 2011, Aktar 2011).

These protests illustrate increasing concerns for sustainability and equity in Turkish civil society. Serious concerns are also being raised about those energy investments since water shortages and changes in the wind force due to climate change might affect the effectiveness of renewable energy investments in the future. However, a small but growing number of private companies show their interest in renewable energy investments and puts pressure on the government to revise existing regulations. The private sector's interest in renewable energy sectors mainly derives from two reasons. The first one is the Turkish government's renewable energy plans to meet a growing demand for energy, to reduce dependence on imported energy sources and to decrease the cost of climate change mitigation measures.[17] The second one is the fact that Turkey is one of the most successful emerging voluntary markets for carbon trade. Although Turkey can only make voluntary carbon projects in accordance with the Gold Standard, there is an increasing willingness to run such projects through investments in wind energy and small hydropower plants (Feiler et al. 2009). What is clear is that both government and private sector interest in renewable energy sources often clash with civil society demands on protection of ecosystems and rural livelihoods.

In line with international developments and the course of EU-Turkey relations, a growing number of business organisations also admitted that environmental protection could offer new incentives for investments and employment. The idea of profiting from environmental protection has been a motto for many sectors in Turkey as in the case of waste management and generating renewable energy. Environmental Protection and Packaging Waste Recovery and Recycling Trust (ÇEVKO) established by 14 leading industrial companies in 1991 presents one of the best examples in this field.

Financial mechanisms to support sustainable business practices have also been developed to a large extent in Turkey. The Development Bank for Turkey, for instance, provides financial support for environmental projects. Several leading companies have also established a number of associations and platforms such as the Turkish Business Council for Sustainable Development[18] to show their interest in promoting sustainable development in Turkey. EU Business Awards for the Environment is also open to Turkish companies since 2005. Globalisation and Turkey-EU relations are regarded as the main motives behind these attempts of reconciling development and environmental protection. Through such attempts, Turkish Business World also seeks more opportunities at the international level to raise their specific interests while protecting the environment

Specific platforms are also established jointly by the private sector and other stakeholders on different themes. To illustrate, *iklim platformu* (the climate platform) was initiated by TÜSİAD and REC Turkey. However, EU climate change policies (mitigation and adaptation) and targets alarmed some industries and public opinion with regard to economic growth. Moreover, ambiguities surrounding Turkey's EU membership and controversies on the EU environmental policy

---

17   Law on Utilisation of renewable resources for the purpose of generating electrical energy (Law no. 5346) was enacted in April 2005. The law amending the law on utilisation of renewable sources (Law no. 6094) was ratified in December 2010.

18   The Council is a member of World Business Council for Sustainable Development.

along with recent economic and financial crises in the world have challenged the environmental priorities in Turkey. Even the recently acclaimed development and environment understanding seemed to be distressed to some extent (Seufert et al. 2011). Moreover, state-centred environmental foreign policy and semi-corporatist state tradition and policy-making which is sensitive to industrial interests often hinder sustainability concerns and climate change policies in Turkey (Mazlum 2009). Then again, mounting interest of non-governmental organizations (NGOs) on environmental issues and environmental protests all over the country challenge such traditions in Turkey.

Generally Turkish environmental movements are analysed into two different periods; before and after the 1980s. Before the 1980s environmental awareness and movements in Turkey mainly dealt with health and sanitation issues along with preservation and conservations activities (Adem 2005). Apparently, the 1970s brought activism in the environmental politics and the number of non-governmental organisations increased. The 1980s however marked a turning point both for the organisation structure and professionalisation of the environmental movements. HABITAT II in Istanbul can be considered as another watershed in environmental politics particularly for the internationalisation of the environmental movement. This new trend also brought project-based working of the environmental NGOs (Adem 2005: 80).

Accession negotiations also fostered project-based working and provided some new opportunities for the environmental NGOs in Turkey to enhance their capacities. Instrument for Pre-accession Assistance (IPA) and EU programmes facilitate the participation of Environmental NGOs into the policy processes and the implementation of the environmental *acquis* in Turkey. Civil society dialogue is another instrument from which environmental NGOs can benefit. Some environmental NGOs and business interest groups also try to exploit further opportunities to raise their concerns at the EU level. For instance, Buğday Association for Supporting Ecological Living[19] and Turkish Foundation for Combating Soil Erosion, for Reforestation and the Protection of Natural Habitats[20] (TEMA) are members of the European Environmental Bureau which has close contacts with EU institutions and try to influence European environmental policy process.

REC Turkey also runs grant programmes for environmental NGOs and initiates certain platforms and seminars to increase the stakeholder participation. Even though there are still strong complaints about the efficient participation in the environmental policy-making, stakeholder meetings gradually offer more opportunities to enhance participation of Environmental NGOs in those processes. Nevertheless, some Environmental NGOs and platforms still have difficulties in benefitting from these programmes and funds since they do not have enough

---

19   Buğday Association was founded in 2002 with the aim of sustaining traditional agricultural production and encouraging life styles in harmony with nature.

20   TEMA was founded in 1992 with the aim of protection of ecosystems, increasing environmental awareness and supporting environmental friendly national policies.

resources. They cannot even apply for the EU funds and programmes due to lack of financial and administrative resources. To illustrate, co-financing is a great problem particularly for local NGOs as well as for environmental initiatives and platforms in applying for the EU funds and programmes. Therefore the rise of nationwide environmental movements cannot be explained by the EU impact since environmental platforms often constitute the core of these movements and related protests. Moreover, there are also other challenges that prevent the Environmental NGOs from taking an active part in the formulation and implementation of the environmental policies such as existing modes of governance in the country.

> Citizens and environmental groups in Southern European countries, where hierarchical and adversarial regulatory styles still dominate, could have benefited most from the new opportunities provided by EU environmental policies. But they have been the least likely to exploit them since they lack the necessary resources to pressure their governance into compliance (Börzel 2007: 232).

Environmental NGOs and citizens in Turkey experience similar difficulties. Access to information is sometimes limited and the degree (and the likelihood) of participation might vary according to the position of the government on certain issues due to high economic growth expectations, national security concerns and coordination problems among different branches of the environmental bureaucracy. Turkey's status as a candidate country gradually challenges these dynamics and procedures. Two conclusions can be drawn from Turkish experience:

1. NGOs can now participate in different processes in which they thought they could never take part in formerly.
2. Governments now more frequently ask the opinion of the NGOs on different issues.[21]
3. Briefly, EU candidacy has improved access to information for the NGOs and increased the opportunities to participate in the policy-making processes. Moreover, both NGOs and the government enhanced their capacities to act together. Nevertheless participation and consultation seem rather limited and at some cases are pretended; just for procedural requirements.[22]

Concluding Remarks

The interaction between the EU and its member states always leads to vigorous debates about the transformative power of the EU. Enlargement and external dimension of EU policies extend these debates beyond the EU borders. What is more, Europeanisation studies have recently amplified the discussions on the

---

21 Personal interview with an expert at TEMA (9 June 2011) İstanbul.
22 Personal interview with an expert at TEMA (9 June 2011) İstanbul.

power of the EU to change domestic structures and policies of the candidate states. Increasing interest in Europeanisation studies in the candidate countries can, therefore, be regarded as an attempt to reconsider their relationship with the EU in different areas. On the other hand, this interest can also be explained as a need for the deeper interrogation of main dynamics of the change(s) in social, economic and political structures of those countries.

Since the 1960s, dramatic ups and downs in Turkey-EU relations also affected the academic interest in European studies. Broadly speaking, European studies have a more comprehensive scope compared to those prior to the 1999 Helsinki Summit where Turkey was recognised as a candidate country on an equal footing with other candidate countries. For instance, Pre-Helsinki European studies in Turkey mainly focused on six policy areas whereas the number and the scope of those studies dramatically increased after 1999 (İzci et al. 2010: 104–7). Environmental policy is one of those policy areas on which the impact of the EU has been widely studied since 1999 compared to many other policy areas in Turkey. The opening of the environment chapter in the accession negotiations, however, draws more attention to Turkish environmental policy.

Despite its popularity as a research agenda, definition of Europeanisation entails several ambiguities. Thus, conceptual and methodological difficulties engender serious questions about the research design and the case selection. Having regarded as a contested concept, Europeanisation even increases the controversies about the European studies literature. These controversies further complicate the Europeanisation studies in the candidate countries. Nonetheless, Europeanisation poses a new or refreshed look to analyse the politics and policy both in Member and candidate countries. All in all, change matters in all these debates.

It is no doubt that the world itself is in a constant change. The legacy of the post cold war motto *change is the only constant thing* that still seems to reign in every aspect of the life. Nevertheless, not all changes are so desirable. The environmental change is, among others, one of the biggest challenges that the world has to face and one of the least desired changes, forcing people to change themselves and the existing structures in turn. This change clearly brings the long established unsustainable relationship between environment and development to light.

Although it is also regarded as a contested concept, sustainable development calls for a global response eroding the dividing line between the national and international politics. Both international developments and growing environmental consciousness in Turkey also challenge the long established unsustainable development patterns in Turkey. Nevertheless, special circumstances of Turkey still dominate the environmental agenda in Turkey. This situation, in turn, causes difficulties for Turkish society organising its 'economic relationship with nature' and rethinking 'collective identities' (Eder and Kausis 2001: 393–4). On the one hand, the growing protests (particularly concerning the energy investments) underline environmental concerns in Turkey; on the other hand, environmental measures (arising from international commitments and the EU candidacy status) might sometimes be regarded as obstacles to the socio-economic development of Turkey.

Since the establishment of the Customs Union, the EU has a growing impact on Turkish environmental policy from product standards to policy styles challenging the long-established discourses and practices as well as accelerating the change(s) that has already taken place due to globalisation and grass roots mobilisation. Moreover, Turkey-EU relations force Turkey to change its development patterns and environmental governance more directly than many international environmental regimes to which Turkey is a party. However, this change also seems limited. Although sustainable development has already been integrated into national development plans, implementation of sustainable development is still regarded as being very costly. At this point low credibility of EU rewards cannot contribute to the implementation of sustainable development practices in Turkey.

Turkey-EU relations also influence the internationalisation of Turkish environmental policy. EU conditionality forces Turkey to become a party to various international environmental regimes. Security concerns and economic gains, however, play crucial roles both in the internationalisation and Europeanisation of Turkish environmental policy. When security concerns are low and the possibility of economic gains are high (both in global and EU markets), even if there are problems with the internationalisation of the policy field as in the case of climate change, domestic change is likely to occur regardless of the credibility of EU conditionality. High security concerns and low expectations of economic gains as in the case of the Aarhus and Espoo Conventions, however, complicate the internationalisation of the issue and lead to a serious resistance to EU conditionality. At this point, credibility of EU conditionality – a clear membership perspective – plays a crucial role.

Through different channels, the EU tries to reach civil society and there is a considerable EU impact on the civil society participation in Turkey. However, regardless of the improved and increased opportunities for interaction with stakeholders, participation in environmental policy-making still seems problematic in Turkey. It also seems that there is little EU impact on environmental movements in Turkey.

Overall, Turkish environmental policy has had an external dimension since the 1970s and has been gradually subject to EU-induced change particularly since 1995. Therefore internationalisation of Turkish environmental policy can be regarded as a facilitating factor in terms of Europeanisation. However internationalisation often depends on various other factors due to the *special circumstances* of Turkey. Moreover, EU demands are regarded as unclear even after Turkey officially gained candidacy status and accession negotiations started. Therefore EU-induced change in internationalisation of Turkish environmental policy is also very limited.

To conclude, controversies over Turkey's prospective membership within EU members result in the low credibility of membership perspective which in turn complicates the full compliance with EU environmental *acquis*. Therefore, domestic change due to EU conditionality still remains limited. Nevertheless, a thorough analysis of Europeanisation of environmental policy in Turkey unquestionably requires a deeper investigation of the factors that complicate any EU-induced change in the Turkish environmental movement and detailed examination of veto players in each sector of environmental policy.

References

Adem, Ç. 2005. Non-state actors and environmentalism, in *Environmentalism in Turkey: Between Democracy and Development?* edited by F. Adaman, and M. Arsel. Aldershot: Ashgate, 71–86.

Aktar, C. 2011. March of Anatolia against the plunder of nature, culture, cities. *Hürriyet Daily News* [Online, 29 April]. Available at http://www.hurriyetdailynews.com/n.php?n=the-great-march-of-anatolia-against-the-plunder-of-nature-culture-and-cities-2011-04-29 [accessed: 18 July 2011].

Algan, N. and Mengi, A. 2005. Turkey's sustainable development policies in the EU accession process. *European Environmental Law Review*, April, 95–7.

Baker, S. 2006. *Sustainable Development*. Oxon: Routledge.

Börzel T.A. 2007. Environmental policy, in *Europeanisation: New Research Agendas*, edited by P. Graziano and M.P. Vink. Houndmills: Palgrave Macmillan, 226–38.

Carmin J. and Van Dever, S.D. 2005. Assessing conventional wisdom: environmental challenges and opportunities beyond eastern accession, in *EU Enlargement and the Environment*, edited by J. Carmin and S.D. Van Dever. London: Routledge, 315–33.

Council of the European Union. 2001. Council Decision of 8 March 2001 on the principles, priorities, intermediate objectives and conditions contained in the Accession Partnership with the Republic of Turkey. *Official Journal of the European Communities*. (2001/235/EC). L 85/13. [Online]. Available at: http://www.abgs.gov.tr/files/AB_Iliskileri/Tur_En_Realitons/Apd/Turkey_APD_2001.pdf [accessed: 27 September 2011].

Depledge, J. 2009. The road less travelled: difficulties in moving between annexes in the climate change regime. *Climate Policy* 9(2009), 273–87.

Drynet. 2011. Büyük Anadolu yürüyüşü başladı. No. 8, May 2011, 4.

Eder, K. and Kousis, M. 2001. Is there a Mediterranean syndrome, in *Environmental Politics in Southern Europe, Actor, Institutions and Discourses in a Europeanizing Society*, edited by K. Eder and M. Kousis. Dordrecht: Kluwer Academic Publ., 393–406.

European Commission. 1998a. *Communication from the Commission to the Council and the European Parliament. The Review Clause – Environmental and Health Standards Four Years after the Accession of Austria, Finland and Sweden to the European Union*. COM(1998) 745 final. Brussels, 11 December.

European Commission. 1998b. *Regular Report from the Commission on Turkey's Progress Towards Accession*. [Online]. Available at: http://ec.europa.eu/enlargement/archives/pdf/key_documents/1998/-turkey_en.pdf [accessed: 11 July 2011].

European Commission. 1999. *Regular Report from the Commission on Turkey's Progress Towards Accession.* [Online]. Available at: http://ec.europa.eu/enlargement/archives/pdf/key_documents/1999/-turkey_en.pdf [accessed: 11 July 2011].

European Commission. 2010. *Communication from the Commission to the European Parliament, the Council, the European Economic and Social Committee and the Committee of the Regions. 2020 by 2020 Europe's Climate Change Opportunity.* COM(2008) 30 final. Brussels, 23 January. [Online]. Available at: http://eur-lex.europa.eu/LexUriServ/LexUriServ.do?uri=COM:2008:0030:FIN:EN:PDF [accessed: 20 June 2011].

European Commission. 2011. *Regular Report from the Commission on Turkey's Progress Towards Accession.* [Online]. Available at: http://ec.europa.eu/enlargement/pdf/key_documents/2011/package/-tr_rapport_2011_en.pdf [accessed: 14 July 2011].

Feiler, J., Zsuzsanna I., Khovanskaya M. and Stoycheva D. 2009. *Shaping the Post 2012 Climate Regime: Implications for Central and Eastern Europe and Turkey.* REC Publications. [Online]. Available at: http://documents.rec.org/topic-areas/post2012climate.pdf [accessed: 27 September 2011].

Grabbe, H. 1999. A partnership for accession? The implications of EU conditionality for the central and east European applicants. *Robert Schuman Centre Working Paper 12/99.* San Domenico di Fiesole (FI): European University Institute. [Online]. Available at: http://www.esiweb.org/-enlargement/wp-content/uploads/2010/01/grabbe_conditionality_99.pdf [accessed: 27 September 2011].

Hürriyet Daily News. 2009. Climate policy inseparable from EU perspective. [Online, 24 December] Available at: http://www.hurriyetdailynews.com/default.aspx?pageid=438&n=climate-policy-inseparable-from-eu-perspective-2009-11-24 [accessed: 27 September 2011].

International Energy Agency. 2010. *Energy Policy of IEA Countries. Turkey 2009 Report.* [Online]. Available at: http://www.iea.org/textbase/nppdf/free/2009/turkey2009.pdf [accessed: 14 July 2011].

İzci, R., İnce Z., Zengin S. and Tüzen, Z. 2010. The impact of Turkey-EU relations on academic research agendas in Turkey: new research areas in European studies, in *Changing Europe and Turkey: Current Debates,* edited by Ç. Nas and R. İzci, İstanbul: Marmara University European Union Institute, 93–114.

Kaygusuz, K. 2004. Climate change mitigation in Turkey. *Energy Sources,* 26(2004), 564–5.

Mazlum, S.C. 2009. Turkish foreign policy on global atmospheric commons: climate change and ozone depletion, in *Climate Change and Foreign Policy: Case Studies from East to West,* edited by P. Harris. London: Routledge, 68–84.

Ministry of Environment and Forestry 2006. *EU Integrated Approximation Strategy (2007–2023).* Ankara: Ministry of Environment and Forestry.

Ministry of Environment and Urbanisation. 2011. *National Climate Change Action Plan 2011–2023.* Ankara: Ministry of Environment and Urbanisation.

Ministry of Foreign Affairs. 2011. Avrupa Birliği ile Su Konusu [European Union and Water Issue] [Online] Available at: http://www.mfa.gov.tr/avrupa-birligi-ile-su-konusu-.tr.mfa [accessed: 27 December 2011].

Organisation for Economic Cooperation Development. 2008. *Environmental Performance Reviews: Turkey 2008.* Paris: OECD. doi: 10.1787/9789264049161-en.

Regional Environmental Centre. Mission Statement [Online] Available at: http://www.rec.org/-about.php?section=mission [accessed: 14 July 2011].

Schimmelfennig F. and Sedelmeier, U. 2007. Candidate countries and conditionality, in *Europeanisation: New Research Agendas*, edited by P. Graziano and M.P. Vink. Houndmills: Palgrave Macmillan, 88–101.

Sedelmeier, U. 2011. Europeanisation in new member and candidate states. *Living Reviews in European Governance* vol.6 2011. no.1 [Online]. Available at: http://www.astrid-online.it/Riforma-de/Studi-e-ri/SEDELMEIER_lreg-2011-1.pdf [accessed: 12 December 2011].

Seufert, G., Subidey T. and Cesar C. 2011. *SGI Sustainable Governance Indicators 2011. Turkey Report.* SG1 2011/2. Germany: Bertelsmann Stiftung. [Online]. Available at: http://www.sgi-network.org/pdf/SGI11_Turkey.pdf [accessed: 18 July 2011].

State Planning Organisation. 1973. Üçüncü Beş Yıllık Kalkınma Planı *(1973-1977)* [The Third Five Year Development Plan (1973–1977)]. Ankara. [Online]. Available at: http://ekutup.dpt.gov.tr/-plan/plan3.pdf [accessed: 14 July 2011].

State Planning Organisation. 1979. *Dördüncü Beş Yıllık Kalkınma Planı (1979–1983)* [The Fourth Five Year Development Plan (1979–1983)]. DPT 1664. Ankara. [Online]. Available at: www.dpt.gov.tr/DocObjects/Download/1973/plan4.pdf/ [accessed: 27 September 2011].

State Planning Organisation. 1984. *Beşinci Beş Yıllık Kalkınma Planı (1985-1989)* [The Fifth Five Year Development Plan (1985–1989)]. DPT 1974. Ankara. [Online]. Available at: http://ekutup.dpt.gov.tr/plan/plan5.pdf [accessed: 27 September 2011].

State Planning Organisation. 1989. *Altıncı Beş Yıllık Kalkınma Planı (1990–1994)* [The Sixth Five Year Development Plan (1990–1994)]. DPT 2174. Ankara. [Online]. Available at: www.dpt.gov.tr/-DocObjects/Download/1971/plan6.pdf- [accessed: 14 July 2011].

State Planning Organisation. 1996. *Yedinci Beş Yıllık Kalkınma Planı (1996–2000)* [The Seventh Five Year Development Plan (1996–2000)]. Ankara. [Online]. Available at: http://www.dpt.gov.tr/-DocObjects/View/13742/plan7.pdf [accessed: 27 September 2011].

State Planning Organisation. 1998. *Ulusal Çevre Stratejisi ve Eylem Planı* [National Enviromental Action Plan]. Ankara. [Online]. Available at: http://ekutup.dpt.gov.tr/cevre/eylempla/ucep.html [accessed: 11 July 2011].

State Planning Organisation. 2000. *Sekizinci Beş Yıllık Kalkınma Planı (2001–2005)* [The Eighth Five Year Development Plan (2001–2005)]. Ankara.

[Online]. Available at: http://www.dpt.gov.tr/-DocObjects/View/13743/plan8. pdf [accessed: 27 September 2011].

State Planning Organisation. 2006. *The Ninth Development Plan 2007–2013: Competitiveness, Employment, Human Development, Regional Development, Effectiveness in Public Services.* Ankara. [Online]. Available at: http://ekutup. dpt.gov.tr/plan/ix/9developmentplan.pdf [accessed: 14 July 2011].

State Planning Organisation. 2007. *Dokuzuncu Kalkınma Planı (2007-2013)* Çevre Özel İhtisas Komisyonu Raporu [The Ninth Development Plan (2007–2013) Report of the Environment Special Expertise Commission]. 2737-OİK: 688. Ankara. [Online]. Available at: www.dpt.gov.tr/-DocObjects/Download/3192/ oik688.pdf [accessed: 14 July 2011].

Talu, N. 2006. *Avrupa Birliği Uyum Sürecinde Türkiye'de Çevre Politikaları* [Environmental Policies in Turkey in the EU Harmonisation Process]. Ankara: TMMOB Çevre Mühendisleri Odası.

Toklu, E., Güney M.S., Işık, M., Çomaklı Ö. and Kaygusuz, K. 2010. Energy production, consumption, policies and recent developments in Turkey. *Renewable and Sustainable Energy Reviews*, 14, 1172–86.

Turkish National Action Programme for the Adoption of the *Acquis*. 2001. [Online]. Available at: http://ec.europa.eu/enlargement/pdf/turkey/npaa_full_ en.pdf [accessed: 13 October 2011].

Turkish National Action Programme for the Adoption of the *Acquis*. 2003. The Environment. [Online]. Available at: http://www.abgs.gov.tr/index. php?p=196&l=2 [accessed: 13 October 2011].

Türkeş, M. 2002. *Türkiye Dünya Sürdürülebilir Kalkınma Zirvesi Ulusal Hazırlıkları, İklim Değişikliği ve Sürdürülebilir Kalkınma Ulusal Raporu* [National Preparations for Sustainable Development Summit, National Report on Climate Change and Sustainable Development]. Ankara: TTGV. Available at: http://www.ttgv.org.tr/content/docs/iklim-degisikligi-ve-surdurulebilir-kalkinma.pdf [accessed: 13 October 2011].

TÜSİAD. 1998. *Dış Ticarette Çevre Koruma Kaynaklı Tarife Dışı Teknik Engeller ve Türk Sanayi için Eylem Planı* [Environmental Non-Tariff Technical Barriers to Trade and Action Plan for Turkish Industry]. 98–233. Istanbul. Available at: http://www.tusiad.org.tr/__rsc/shared/file/cevre.pdf [accessed: 21 September 2011].

TÜSİAD. 2009. *Being party to the Kyoto Protocol will strengthen Turkey's hand.* Press Release [Online, 5 February]. Available at: http://www.tusiad.us/ specific_page.cfm?CONTENT_ID=840 [accessed: 17 October 2011].

United Nations. 2009. *National Greenhouse Gas Inventory Data for the Period 1990–2007.* FCCC/SBI/2009/12. [Online, 21 October]. Available at: http:// unfccc.int/resource/docs/2009/sbi/eng/-12.pdf [accessed: 29 July 2011].

Vink M.P. and P. Graziano. 2007. Challenges of a new research agenda, in *Europeanisation: New Research Agendas*, edited by P. Graziano and M.P. Vink. Houndmills: Palgrave Macmillan, 3–20.

Von Homeyer, I. 2005. Differential effects of enlargement on EU environmental governance, in *EU Enlargement and the Environment*, edited by J. Carmin and S.D. Van Deveer. London: Routledge, 52–76.

Yale Centre for Environmental Law and Policy. 2011. *Environmental Performance Index 2010*. [Online]. Available at: http://epi.yale.edu/file_columns/0000/0157/epi2010_report.pdf [accessed: 23 July 2011].

Chapter 10

Europeanisation of Turkish Foreign Policy after more than Ten Years of EU Candidacy

Özlem Terzi

Introduction

This chapter analyses the process of Europeanisation in Turkey with respect to the foreign policy field in more than 10 years of EU candidacy. A comprehensive look at the conduct of Turkish foreign policy since 1999 shows that there have been major changes of policy, even though most of these changes have not resulted in a solution of the most basic problems of Turkish foreign policy. Besides, it is possible to see a major adaptation in the ways of thinking behind the actual policy pursuit that are reflected in the foreign policy rhetoric. These changes reflect a successful learning process for Turkish policy-makers that the EU candidacy has provided. On the other hand, with the stalling of the process of Turkey's EU accession – whose fault falls on both sides – some of these policy changes have caused concerns as to whether Turkey is undergoing a 'shift of axis'. Especially the performance of Turkish foreign policy after 2008 shows that Turkey has adopted more of an independent foreign policy to promote its influence in the Middle East after the Israeli attack on Gaza in December 2008. Although the EU influence on the foreign policy of the AKP government is much easier to see in its first term in office (2002–2007), the government has lost its interest in EU membership in its second term in office (2007–11). The EU influence becomes almost untraceable in its third term after the summer of 2011. Despite the fact that the influence of the EU has diminished in time, the AKP government had started to speak foreign policy in a new and more European manner as soon as it won its first elections in 2002 and maintained that language despite all the setbacks in its EU accession prospect even though the target of foreign policy can be argued to have changed in time.

This chapter argues that the EU candidacy has definitely changed the way Turkey pursues its foreign policy. This process of change was triggered and supported by the EU. The reason for most of the failures in the completion of the process lies in the fact that the EU accession prospect for Turkey has diminished. On the other hand, it is possible to see that despite all concerns about a shift of axis, Turkish foreign policy continues to be conducted in a European manner that was well learned. However, its longevity or sincerity can be questioned in time. The chapter firstly summarises how the overall process of Europeanisation has influenced the actors involved in the making of foreign policy through a theoretical perspective. Then it presents some examples in the pursuit of Turkish foreign policy that represent a major change in policy content due to EU candidacy. These would be cases like the Cyprus problem, Turkey's relations with Armenia and Greece. The chapter then focuses on Turkey's relations with the Middle Eastern countries that have also intensified in the last 10 years with the exception of deteriorating relations with Israel. Lastly, the chapter analyses some of the most recent incidents that have contributed to the 'shift of axis' debates, i.e. Turkish stance on *Mavi Marmara*, the nuclear capabilities of Iran, and the 'Arab Spring' and discusses whether the Europeanisation process still explains the changes in Turkish foreign policy as the second decade of the twenty-first century, the 2010s, begins.

Transformation of Actors during the Europeanisation Process of Foreign Policy

Tracing the roots of Europeanisation in Turkish foreign policy presents a good example for a case study on the different theories that explain how the process of Europeanisation works. The process of Europeanisation of foreign policy in Turkey rests on the change brought about by the 'logic of appropriateness' argument, according to which actors are guided by a collective understanding of what constitutes proper, socially accepted behaviour in a given structure. Adoption of these new 'appropriate behaviours' by Turkey is brought about by a re-definition of 'national interests' and also of what constitutes a 'rational choice'. As Börzel and Risse (2003) mention, collective understandings (in the EU) influence the ways in which actors define their goals and what they perceive as 'rational' action. 'To act appropriately' is defined by James March and Johan P. Olsen (2004) as to proceed according to the institutionalised practices of a collectivity, based on mutual, and often tacit, understandings of what is true, reasonable, natural, right and good, and involves a learning process. From this perspective, Europeanisation is understood as the emergence of new rules, norms, practices, and structures of meaning to which member states are exposed and which they have to incorporate into their domestic practices and structures (Börzel and Risse 2003). In an edited volume by Brian Hocking and David Spence (2005), member state officials stated in interviews that being a part of European diplomacy requires compliance to a common framework for appropriate behaviour. This article argues that the basic changes in Turkish foreign policy between 1999–2008 are a result of Turkey's desire to display an 'appropriate behaviour', which has evolved in time to a seeming internalisation of the values to be upheld in foreign policy like peace, stability and good neighbourly relations finding their place under Davutoğlu's 'zero-problem with neighbours' policy.

Several studies have applied the concept of Europeanisation to national foreign policies of EU member states (Manners and Whitman 2000, Tonra 2001, Tonra and Christiansen 2004). Ian Manners and Richard Whitman (2000) ask what the impact of the evolving European environment is on the foreign policies of EU states. They take into consideration the way in which EU member states adapt their foreign policy through membership of the EU, as well as towards the EU itself, and towards the other member states of the EU. It can be supposed that the sharing of information and common practices in the EU leads to socialisation and the new habit of working together transforms the common perceptions of policy-makers (Manners and Whitman 2000). As Adrian Hyde-Price (2004) reminds us, perceptions are vital in the policy-making process. Perceptions shape the boundaries of rational decision-making. One could also ask whether a re-definition of self or of national interest is taking place within this socialisation process. As Lisbeth Aggestam (2004) explains; identity and foreign policy interests may be redefined as a consequence of current transformations, be they internal or external to the state. She reminds us of the Deutschian perspective that says different social communicative processes between actors may affect and shape their identities and interests. High levels of interaction between states can encourage the development of a growing 'we feeling' and a common 'role identity'. She argues that identities may be reconstructed through cooperative and positive interaction with other actors. It is thus arguable that the process of candidacy shapes Turkey's identity and the role model.

Henrik Larsen (2005) explains that Europeanisation transforms the domestic structures of the nation states and the meanings attached to them, which when applied to foreign policy, does not only entail an approximation of procedures or general national rhetoric about European belonging, but also an approximation with respect to policy substance with the Union. Studying on this subject, Ben Tonra (2001) draws attention to the process of socialisation, in which officials acquire a habit of thinking in terms of consensus building. He also states that the creation of European Foreign and Security Policy has limited the extent to which national foreign policies react independently. Consensus and consultation have become important features of the domestic foreign policy process. Moreover, member states have gained greater effectiveness through the collective voice and common action. As a result of a 10-year candidacy it is possible that Turkey has developed a reflex of consultation with the EU countries when responding to international developments. Despite all populist exclamations on foreign policy topics by the AKP leaders, the high numbers of Common Foreign and Security Policy (CFSP) alignments by Turkey shows that Turkey and the EU continue to work together on world affairs.

These findings indicate a process whereby new habits become practices, which shape the participants and may lead to a re-orientation of their beliefs and behaviour. As Jakob C. Ohrgard (2004) mentions, implicit in the processes of socialisation and upgrading of common interests is the idea that eventually the participants might come to conceive their interests differently than as a direct result of their participation in the enterprise. For the Turkish case, it is possible to see that Turkey defines its interests differently in Cyprus now. It is also the case for Turkish policy towards the Middle East and the desire to bring about a region of peace and cooperation among Turkey's Southern neighbours. However, in this case, it is possible to see the traces of both a new 'European' understanding and a reflection of the AKP's Islamist background. Another question Manners and Whitman (2000) ask is whether participation in CFSP and external relations of the Union provides a constriction or an opportunity on foreign policy choices and actions. The case studies done on the impact of EU membership on member countries' foreign policy practitioners have revealed that some countries have acquired new areas of interest in their foreign policies. Their relations with third countries have also gained an additional level as an EU member country-third country relationship after their accession to the Union. Their foreign policies are increasingly shaped by discussions within the EU and if they can gain the support of other members, their national foreign policies become more effective as EU policies. The member states also acquire a feeling of common destiny as a result of coordination and flow of information among them. Additionally, the discussion of foreign policy subjects within the Union had a limiting effect on the populist acclamation by governments toward their domestic environments (Hocking and Spence 2005). Another important result of research on the transformation of foreign policy of member states due to EU membership is that member states may behave in different ways than their traditional national policy rhetoric on certain issues (Ekengren and Sundelius 2005, Miles 2005). Thus the EU framework rationalises foreign policy decisions by making them less susceptible to populist acclamations and turning them into responses shared by a collectivity. This aspect of Turkish foreign policy is questioned after 2009 as the government pays more attention to gaining public support at home and in the streets of the Middle East than among other European policy-makers. Moreover, the notions of national sensitivities and special relationships persist (Manners and Whitman 2000) among EU member states and they still do for Turkey.

The process of Europeanisation of foreign policy functions a little differently in a candidate country. The EU negotiators could make demands, which were unattractive to the candidates, but which the Central and Eastern European negotiators accepted because the overall attraction of joining the Union outweighed the disadvantages of parts of the deal (Grabbe 2006: 2). Whether this rationale also applies to Turkish policy-makers is a question whose answer is a major determinant of the Turkey's EU willingness, since many political parties state that Turkey does not or should not feel obliged to accede to the EU and also that Turkey would not step backward on issues of national concern in return for the prospect of EU membership.

A question for Turkey would then be whether any foreign policy change would/could be attributed to the EU. Such an example of this case would be the impetus provided to the AKP government by the prospect of starting accession negotiations to change the long-lasting 'state-policy' toward the Cyprus problem. No government in Turkey would dare to change the decades-long policy on Cyprus without the EU carrot at the end. Another reason for the change of policy by the government was the new aim in foreign policy to solve long-standing disputes with neighbouring countries, a motto developed by Ahmet Davutoğlu, a professor of International Relations, who was chief advisor to Prime Minister Tayyip Erdoğan and later became foreign minister in 2009. On the other hand, no foreign policy change in Turkey would be publicly attributed to the EU cause, since other parties would then claim a 'selling out of the national cause' for the sake of joining the EU.

So, the 'external incentives model' that explains candidate country compliance makes sense only up to a limit in the case of Turkey. The 'social learning model' based on the logic of appropriateness is much more relevant to explain changes in Turkish foreign policy in a more comprehensive perspective. In this model, actors are motivated by internalised identities, values and norms. It is expected that a state adopts EU rules only if it is persuaded of the appropriateness of those rules. The likelihood of compliance increases with the identification of the target government with the Western or European international community (Schimmelfennig 2004). It is possible to see an example of such a move by Turkey when Abdullah Gül as the then foreign minister attended a meeting of the Organisation of Islamic Countries (OIC) in 2005 and advised the promotion of democracy among Muslim countries.

The theoretical result of this section would be to present the following questions for the Turkish case: Firstly, are the Turkish foreign policy-makers undergoing a process of changing their self-perception and envisaging the position of Turkey in the world as that of a future EU member, rather than that of a regional power on the verge of Southeast Europe and the Middle East? The process of EU candidacy should be expected to bring about a new self-perception in the candidacy as that of a future EU member. However the long, painful and actually fruitless process of EU candidacy has diminished the hopes for an EU prospect in Turkish public opinion as well as among the decision-makers. Lately, Turkish policy-makers have spoken of Turkey as a regional power rather than a prospective EU country. Even if there was a new self-perception of Turkey as a European country between 1999–2004, it is hardly damaged after the publication of the 2005 Negotiating Framework Document stating the scenario that Turkey may not become a member even if it successfully concludes the negotiations, and the ensuing decision in 2006 on the practical suspension of negotiations (General Affairs Council 2006).[1]

Secondly, do Turkish policy-makers believe in the appropriateness of EU rules and aims with respect to foreign policy? Even the most controversial decisions of Turkish foreign policy-makers on enhancement of relations with Syria and the rest of the Arab countries were justified as widening the region of economic integration and peaceful relations with neighbouring regions. Turkey was trying to enjoy the same rights as Europeans do with its Middle Eastern neighbours by establishing

---

1 General Affairs Council Meeeting of 11 December 2006 stated that 'As concerns Turkey, the Council decided in particular to suspend negotiations on eight chapters relevant to Turkey's restrictions with regard to the Republic of Cyprus, and will not close the other chapters until Turkey fulfils its commitments under the additional protocol to the EU-Turkey association agreement, which extended the EU-Turkey customs union to the ten member states, including Cyprus, that joined the EU in May 2004.'

the FTAs, passing through the visa-free travel arrangements, and eroding the image of its neighbours as zones of instability for Turkey. When resisting against sanctions on Iran Turkey was saying that channels of communication should be kept open with the neighbour country and that Turkey would rather play the role of a credible mediator rather than become party to the conflict. Turkey has been speaking the European language so well as to become irritating at times. But for sure this is a language well learned by now, even though it may not be used to serve the same interests as defined by the EU countries.

Is there a change in the composition of policy-makers to resemble those in the EU member states? This is actually the most solid case of the Europeanisation of Turkish foreign policy. The actors involved in the making of decisions resemble every much their European counterparts now. The influence of the military has been deeply curbed and the government has become much more outspoken on its foreign policy preferences. There is an active involvement of the civil society organisations in the foreign policy realm – which was previously reserved for the civilian and military bureaucracy – through reports, conferences and lobbying.

Europeanisation of Turkish Foreign Policy in Practice

The significance of the prospect for European Union membership in Turkish foreign policy today can only be compared to the significance of NATO membership of Turkey during the Cold War. After the Cold War, and especially in the post-9/11 circumstances of the international arena, Turkey's EU membership is a marker of its identity and belonging, just like NATO membership was during the Cold War years. The aim of EU membership was always seen by Turkish policy-makers as a part of the grander aim of belonging in the West. After the Cold War, Turkey has felt a certain need to remind its Western belonging to European countries as the former 'East' Europeans lined up for membership to the EU ahead of Turkey. After 9/11, Turkey also asserted that its membership in the EU was a matter of building security both for Turkey and the West in general and as a signal of the inclusive nature of the European ideal.

The dual nature of Turkey's identity as belonging both in the East and West was not only a slogan of the AKP leadership but also the motto of the foreign policy pursued by Ismail Cem, who was the foreign minister from the Democratic Left Party in the coalition government between 1997 and 2002. The AKP government has been comparatively much more proactive than previous governments in pursuing ambitious foreign policy goals, ranging from the search for a solution in the Cyprus problem to the framing of a new relationship with Armenia, although it has failed so far on both accounts. Another change has been in the increasing self-confidence of the government with respect to setting prestigious goals for foreign policy. The attainment of a temporary seat at the UN Security Council has clearly been a foreign policy success of the AKP government, since it was previously believed that without a solution of Turkey's problematic foreign relations, such a support for Turkey at the UN was unachievable. After the experiences of 2009–10 at the UN Security Council, the government announced a new candidacy for 2015–16. The appointment of a Turkish citizen as the Secretary-General of the Organisation of Islamic Conference (OIC) was one of the first declared foreign policy goals of the AKP and was prone to raise questions as to the change of preferences of the new government regarding foreign policy. However, this influence was balanced by the position of Mevlut Çavuşoğlu as the Chairman of the Council of Europe's Parliamentary Assembly.

Turkey's foreign policy towards neighbouring countries has evolved to become more 'soft-power' based and cooperation-oriented, instead of a focus on the long-prevailing perceptions of threat. It is certain that Turkey has adopted the EU rhetoric of 'good-neighbourly relations' and the aim of 'developing an area of peace and stability'. The eventual policy outcomes – support for a comprehensive resolution of the Cyprus problem even after the Annan Plan referenda, seeking of a rapprochement with Armenia, aiming at resolution of disputes in the Aegean with Greece, and a dialogue-oriented policy towards Iran, Iraq and Syria – display the results of a change in behaviour of Turkey in the 'appropriate' direction, hinting at a certain learning process and successful norm internalisation, although a little belatedly, in the post-Cold War era.

The immediate launch of the talks on the Aegean with Greece showed that it was easier to initiate appropriate behaviour on some topics more than others. Turkey faced no internal discussion as to the need for the resolution of disputes in the Aegean. Rapprochement with Greece after the 1999 earthquakes was real and there was increasing optimism as to the future of relations between Greece and Turkey.

The AKP government had in its party programme and its election manifesto the aims of acceding to the EU and the solution of the Cyprus problem (AK Parti 2001, 2002). The AKP did not support the 'no-resolution is a solution' policy of the previous Turkish governments. AKP leaders were somehow able to see that the traditional policy on Cyprus, which had by then become a 'state policy' rather than a 'government policy', was actually becoming detrimental to Turkey's interests, since it played into the perception that Turkey did not desire an internationally recognised resolution to the problem on the island. In order to reverse this position that Turkey found itself in, any Turkish government that aimed at eventual accession to the Union had to come to terms with the traditional policy on Cyprus and change it in a way that would both secure the rights of the Turkish Cypriots and help Turkey out of the impasse of securing its interests in Cyprus without endangering its EU membership prospect. The only rational outcome would mean facilitating the unification of the island under conditions favourable to all parties of the dispute, while at the same time strengthening the EU accession prospect for Turkey.

The adoption of a whole new policy on Cyprus by the AKP showed that it was easier for a new government to start anew on certain contested issues. The AKP government was quick to accomplish this policy change and influence the Turkish Cypriot leadership for a change of position on talks. It would be false to claim that it was easy for the AKP government to change the decades-long 'state' policy on

Cyprus. There was strong opposition from the military in this respect, but as the pressure on Turkey mounted for a united Cyprus to accede to the Union instead of the single accession of the Greek Cypriot part, the military also preferred to keep quiet on its reluctance. It is possible to see in this instance the re-definition of the 'national interest'. However, the change of policy rests on a certain calculation of the costs and benefits of alternative policy options, rather than upholding a certain preference for the unification of the island. However, the consequent policy shift in Turkey on the Cyprus issue is not to be taken for good. It can be reversed in time, if the policy change does not produce the results it is expected to, which is to facilitate Turkey's accession process to the EU.

Another major foreign policy issue that the AKP government tried to tackle was the improvement of relations with Armenia, the opening of the closed border and the establishment of diplomatic relations. The government saw that Turkey actually had a lot to gain by changing its policy towards Armenia which was not proving adequate to force the Armenians on the withdrawal from Azerbaijani territories, but instead was impoverishing both Eastern Anatolia and Armenia. Trade in Eastern Anatolia could flourish if the border was opened and help in further stabilisation of the region. However, as soon as the protocols with Armenia were signed, the nationalist circles succeeded in turning the debate into one about selling out Azerbaijan for the sake of international approval. The protocols did not envisage a certain shift of policy for Turkey to deal with the issue of increased international recognition of the 'Armenian genocide', but it established a basis for future dialogue between Turks and Armenians. Despite the domestic and international support the AKP government received for the signing of the protocols, it was not in a position to bring the protocols for ratification to the Parliament since the AKP leaders linked the issue to a preliminary improvement in the talks between Azerbaijan and Armenia on the Nagorno-Karabagh dispute. The government failed to uphold its own cause and fell hostage to the policies of Azerbaijan for the future of its relationship with a neighbour country. Whatever the reasons of the failure, they point to a certain miscalculation of the government of its strengths and weaknesses. Turkey's shift of policy on Armenia oscillates between a more 'appropriate' position in European eyes and that of a reflection of the realist understanding of international politics. The signing of the protocols marked the major shift of policy preference in favour of opening up the diplomatic channels to Armenia. It was a certain step to meet the demands of the EU institutions for the opening of the border between Turkey and Armenia, and to avoid the US pressure for the recognition of the 'Armenian genocide'. But as soon as these steps were made public, there was a nationalist backlash from the opposition parties that proved to be rather influential on the government. The government hesitated between performing the expected 'appropriate behaviour' by going to the Parliament for ratification of the protocols, and returning to the nationalist rhetoric against Armenia linking the improvement of relations to displaying solidarity with Azerbaijan due to kinship and also interests in gas and oil supplies.

The parliamentary decision in March 2003 for Turkey not to cooperate with the US on its intervention in Iraq had seemed like the ultimate convergence of Turkish foreign policy with that of France and Germany and was hailed as being more European than that of the Eastern European countries which were keen on supporting the US, and were at the same time just on the brink of acceding to the Union. However, it should be kept in mind that the outcome of the parliamentary vote was not the primary intention of the Turkish government and that the government's proposal had actually lost the parliamentary vote. The outcome was mainly the result of the doubts and insecurities of the public opinion that could soundly reflect itself on the parliament's decision.

Turkey's preference for a diplomatic solution to the crisis on Iran's nuclear capabilities is also to be seen in this respect, which is the unwillingness of the public to see war being waged on another neighbouring country. It is also crucial to note that whatever the perils of Iran's nuclear capabilities, none of the parties in the parliament mention it as a matter of concern or insecurity for Turkey. Surprisingly, the Turkey that perceived a fundamental threat from the Islamist regime in Iran in 1990s, does not perceive the same danger from the increased weapon capabilities of this regime. One possible point of view can be to see it as a major policy choice of AKP. However, all parties in Parliament seem to converge on the non-desirability of an international intervention in Iran on top of the experience of Iraq.

When compared with the 1990s, Turkey in the first decade of 2000 has become much more solution-oriented in its foreign policy disputes and aimed at building a zone of peace and stability in its neighbouring regions. Turkey's candidacy to the EU, as well as the improvement of domestic security after 1999, has led her to pursue a more peaceful foreign policy toward its immediate southern neighbours Syria and Iraq. Changes in Turkey's policy toward Syria and Iraq were influenced by the democratisation and de-securitisation processes regarding issues of political Islam and Kurdish separatism. The de-securitisation of these two major issues in Turkish domestic politics has also resulted in the de-securitisation of Turkey's relations with its neighbours to the south and east (Aras and Karakaya Polat 2008). However, can all this change be attributed to the EU candidacy? It would be fair to claim that the triggering force of change was EU candidacy that gained ground even before Turkey was declared as a candidate country. The change in foreign policy started with Ismail Cem as the foreign minister in 1997, who initiated dialogue with Syria in the course of the ousting of the Kurdistan Workers' Party (PKK) leader Abdullah Öcalan from the country in 1998 and built a strong personal friendship with the Greek Foreign Minister George Papandreou. This change was supported and sustained with the ensuing candidate status of Turkey to the EU.

Declaration of Turkey as a candidate country in the new enlargement wave of the EU was important to assert the continuation of Turkey's belonging in the West after the Cold War. However, the coalition government under Ecevit between 1999 and 2002 that succeeded in achieving the candidate status for Turkey experienced quite a lot of difficulty to meet the Copenhagen criteria, which was actually the new definition of what the 'West' or 'Europe' signified after the Cold War. In the post-Cold War era, the West did not only mean democracy but rather liberal democracy. Despite the fact that Turkey was considered a democracy during the Cold War years, whether it was liberal was the big question that the 'West' or 'Europe' faced while making up its mind about Turkish accession.

Thus, the EU accession process is one of political liberalisation for Turkey, and resulted in discussions on whether Turkey really wanted to become a member of the EU and whether the government actually had a sustainable will to go through the required reform processes in this path. The acceptance of Turkey's Western identity in the West is linked with Turkey's incorporation of the values of liberal democracy like human rights and rule of law as well as the promotion of peace and stability. Putting aside the religious definition of the West on terms of Judeo-Christianity, it is of utmost importance in determining Turkey's identity that Turkey shares in these values. The former Commissioner for Enlargement Olli Rehn has stated in his congratulatory message on Turkey's election for a temporary seat at the UN Security Council that it would be a big gain for Europe if Turkey promoted the values that the EU supported in the international arena (Milliyet 2008). Whether it is possible to evaluate Turkey's term in the UN Security Council as such will be discussed further below.

An Alternative Explanation for Turkey's Good Neighbourly Relations: Neo-Ottomanism and the Inheritance of the National View Movement

It is possible to discern two different political streams among AKP constituents. The founding members of the party descended from the National View *(Milli Görüş)* Movement, but parted from that Movement in order to establish a new party that would be able to stay in government through making its peace with the Republic and its major accomplishments. The National View Movement attributes great importance to foreign policy. Turkey's membership in OIC became stronger in coalitions in which Erbakan participated. His initiation of D-8, the league of developing countries that are also Islamic is worth mentioning in this respect. The National View Movement became vocal with respect to the Balkans only reactively and did not initiate substantial policies or strategies toward the region. It mainly focused on providing aid to Muslim communities. The Movement envisages Turkey as a big brother to the Islamic nations in the Balkans and envisages them as potential members of the OIC. In their perception of Balkans, it is not the Turkish-ness but Islam that is important and the determining factor in their priorities (Bakır 2007).

The founders of AKP seceded from the Virtue party,[2] the latest party of the National View of Erbakan tradition, which was strongly anti-European and thus

---

2   The Virtue Party was the fourth party of the national view movement, established after the closure of the Welfare Party by the constitutional court. For further information on the history of the AKP see Uzgel (2009).

anti-EU. The reformists in the National View Movement were able to defy the anti-western tradition in their previous party. Signalling the importance of 'neo-Ottomanism' in its foreign policy orientation and the National View heritage, AKP's election campaign manifesto in 2002 stated that the Party attributes importance to Turkey's relations with Islamic countries, and would aim to intensify cooperation with these countries as well as the promotion of Organisation of Islamic Conference (OIC) (AK Parti 2002). The second stream within the AKP is the centre-right circles previously represented by DP, AP, DYP and ANAP in Turkish politics. This stream is mostly joined with liberals.

The current AKP government is pursuing a foreign policy of 'strategic depth' which is the name of the voluminous foreign policy book written by the now foreign minister Ahmet Davutoğlu. The starting point of this policy is the argument that Turkey should openly claim its legacy of Ottoman Empire and enhance relations with the regions, which were previously under Ottoman rule but later neglected due to the Republic's policies of Westernisation and Europeanisation. Neo-Ottomanism, on the other hand, is the concept used to characterise the foreign policy preferences of the major right-wing and Islamist political parties, which claim that Turkey's orientation in foreign policy should be towards the Middle Eastern and Islamic countries. In this respect, the foreign policy of the AKP government based on 'strategic depth' should be more encompassing than 'neo-Ottomanism'. Neo-Ottomanism is considered by the bureaucratic and military elite as a challenge to the Western identification of the Turkish Republic. On the other hand, in the traditional Turkish foreign policy, the Ottoman legacy in the Balkans is taken for granted and as something to be preserved and Turkey's policy towards the Balkans openly aims to preserve the Ottoman heritage, whereas any strengthening of relations with the Middle East is immediately questioned as Islamisation of foreign policy.

Davutoğlu explains his views on the Ottoman past as a certain preference for Turkey to make its peace with the Ottoman history, with the awareness of a certain nostalgia felt toward the Ottoman past. This policy envisages a more active role for Turkey in the Balkans and the Middle East and even in Central Asia and presents Turkey as the leading power in these regions and recalls the Pax Ottomanica as opposed to the conflicts that loom in these regions since 1990s. (Uzgel 2001: 514) Thus, Neo-Ottomanism is claimed to symbolise political and cultural tolerance signified by the Ottoman Empire, the promotion of economic ties with the nations of the Balkans, the Caucasus and the Middle East and aims at the creation of a macro-identity among the nations that once shared in the Muslim Ottoman culture (Yavuz 2001: 62–3).

The AKP leaders claim to have gone through a learning process with the previously banning of the Islamist parties and the AKP does not call itself an Islamist, but a Muslim Democrat party, like the Christian Democratic parties of Western Europe (Arman 2006). The foreign policy preferences of the AKP's foreign policy elite, and especially that of Ahmet Davutoğlu, stressed a new understanding of 'neo-Ottomanism' and a distinguished perception of a soft-power status. In his book titled 'strategic depth' (*stratejik derinlik*), Davutoğlu (2007) had criticised the previous Turkish governments for denouncing the ties Turkey should have with its Middle Eastern neighbours. Instead of the traditional perception of threat from almost all of Turkey's neighbours, Davutoğlu suggested a policy of zero-problem with neighbours, which would then enable Turkey to make full use of its geo-strategic location and the historical ties with its surrounding region. Neo-Ottomanism also gained ground by the emergence of a new economic and political elite with the rise of the conservative bourgeoisie, i.e. Anatolian businessmen which established MÜSİAD and in turn demanded of the state to smooth its attitude to religion, increase ties with the Middle Eastern countries and make its peace with the Ottoman past, whereas the Istanbul-based businessmen's association TUSIAD preferred an ideological identification with the West (Yavuz 2001: 49–50).

Tarık Oğuzlu mentions a Middle Easternisation of Turkish foreign policy, which means a greater salience of the Middle East in Turkey's relations with the West. He also argues that Turkey does not have a romantic and emotional approach to the EU and the US any more, but a pragmatic and rational one. Turkey has seen that as chaos and instability in the Middle East continues, it would diminish Turkey's chances of acceding to the Union since the EU does not wish to border conflict-prone regions. So Turkey has attributed a greater importance to the emergence of a stable environment in the Middle East. Secondly, the US occupation of Iraq in 2003 has shown Turkey that the US can be a threat as well as an ally. The situation in Iraq and the security threat diverted to Turkey from Northern Iraq became a major determinant of Turkey's relations with the US. The deterioration of relations with the US coupled with partial suspension of negotiations with the EU created a feeling in Turkey as if Turkey was trying to 'Westernise despite the West'(Oğuzlu 2008).

It is possible to discern the growing importance of Middle Eastern developments in Turkey's security definitions and interests as well as the adoption of a more active and assertive Turkish policy towards the region. Turkish policy-makers have realised that Turkey's interests are not always best served by a western-oriented foreign policy and that her institutional links with NATO and the EU does not grant her a belonging in the Western international community. Hence, Turkey's former policy of 'renunciation of the Eastern identity in order to confirm the Western identity' has been replaced with 'acceptance of Turkey's placement in the West through strengthening of Turkey's links to the East' (Oğuzlu 2008). Additionally the AKP government has been emphasising Turkey's Islamic and Middle Eastern characteristics more often than the previous governments and believes that as an inheritor of the Ottoman Empire Turkey holds a certain responsibility in the international politics of the region. AKP conceptualises a different identity for Turkey than the past governments did, which saw Turkey as a modern secular state with an ideological commitment to the West. For the AKP, Turkey has a Muslim and democratic identity and belongs in the Islamic civilisation, but is compatible with the Western one (Altunışık 2009: 171–94). On such a new ideational basis, Turkey's policy towards the Middle East is increasing being determined by elected politicians rather than by the military (Walker 2007: 32–47), which was the case in the 1990s, and this change reflects on the actual policy performance. The AKP's constituency is more sympathetic to Turkey's Islamic character and its Muslim neighbours.

According to recent research, Turkey has increased its level of trust among Middle Eastern countries in the last couple of years. The Arab countries increasingly perceive Turkey as defending the rights of Palestinians and as a friendly country toward the Arabs, whereas a decade ago, Turkey's increasing ties with Israel was causing concern, Turkey was almost going to war with Syria, and was fighting against the PKK in Iraq. A decade later, Turkey's efforts as a mediating country between Syria and Israel were most appreciated in Syria, despite suspicions on the Israeli side. Through this perspective AKP's policy toward the Middle East have gained it many friends in the region while its relationship with Israel has been deteriorating (Akgün, Perçinoğlu and Senyücel-Gündoğar 2009). Turkey's perception of threat from Islamic or Arab countries has fallen sharply and the government is wishing to see Turkey as 'the' regional power in the Middle East and as a facilitator of conflict resolution in the region, whereas no such acclamation is made with respect to the existing problems in the Balkans. It is easy to see that the intensity of AKP's political and economic relations with Arabic countries outweigh those with Balkan countries. This makes one wonder whether it is the Ottoman heritage in the Middle East or the National View heritage in AKP that makes the government feel more welcome in the region.

Turkish leaders have been most supportive of the Arab spring, the ousting of their former counterparts in countries like Syria, Libya and Egypt and called for the promotion of democratic freedoms in the Middle East. All these calls emphasised Turkey's faith in democratic values and freedoms. However, reflections from within the country show that the AKP government is mostly utilising these values and freedoms for foreign policy and not putting them into immediate practice in its domestic politics.

Values in Turkish Foreign Policy and Discussions on the Shift of Axis

If the changes in the substance of Turkish foreign policy were to be seen as a result of the Europeanisation process, they took some time to gain effect and flourished during the first term of the AKP government due to two reasons. First, a certain amount of time was needed for the change in domestic politics to be reflected onto foreign policy. The declaration of Turkey as a candidate country to the EU signalled that if it was ever to succeed in its EU path, many things in the domestic politics and the foreign policy of Turkey were to change. The change in the power disposition between the civilian and the military actors in the making of foreign policy mainly due to reforms accomplished by the AKP government, as well as the strengthening of civil society, were definitely EU induced. There is also a growing awareness on the side of the Turkish military that the government is to bear the political responsibility of the decisions concerning foreign policy. Second, a significant amount of that change resulted from the world-perception of the new single-party government of AKP, which needed to prove itself worthy of governing the country, in the face of the quite strong domestic scepticism about its undisclosed – Islamist – policy aims. The current foreign policy of Turkey, as explained by the foreign minister Ahmet Davutoğlu (2007), is based on the historical ties of Turkey in its surrounding region and aims at a zero-problem with neighbours. The AKP's preference for keeping up to the EU accession aim and promoting relations with the Middle Eastern countries based on the conceptual premises of the 'strategic depth' doctrine prove to be, in practice, the continuation of foreign policy á la Ismail Cem (2000) that stressed Turkey's dual identity and belonging in both Europe and the Middle East. Nevertheless, some of the changes in foreign policy is the result of a certain inclination of the AKP government to develop ties with Islamic countries, and especially with those in the Middle East, eventually at the expense of severing ties with Israel, which strengthened questions about a 'shift of axis' in Turkish foreign policy due to certain doubts in both domestic and foreign circles concerning the pro-Islamist background of the party leaders.

The discussions in 2010 on the shift of axis of Turkish foreign policy were closely linked with the performance of Turkey at the UN Security Council. This debate started before Turkey's term at the UNSC with Ömer Taşpınar and Philip Gordon's (2006, 2008) works that focused on the question 'Who Lost Turkey?' and emphasised the rising nationalism and xenophobia in Turkey. They claimed that this was a result of Turkey's disenchantment with the unilateralist policies of the George W. Bush administration in the Middle East that disregarded the rising terrorist activities that stemmed from Northern Iraq. It resulted in the loss of trust of Turkey in its closest ally. Turkey's distancing itself from the EU was seemingly a result of the stalling of negotiations due to the Cyprus problem but was actually a result of the policies of France and Germany that favoured a privileged partnership short of full membership for Turkey. The simultaneous distancing of Turkey from both the US and the EU raised suspicions about the loss of Turkey for the West. On the other hand when compared with the unilateralist polices of the US under the George W. Bush administration that was mainly disrespectful of international law and organisations, Turkey's new policies of zero-problems with its neighbours made Turkey seem much more 'European'.

The incoming Obama administration has started a process of reconciliation with Turkey as it did with the rest of Europe and also with the Middle East (Obama 2009a, 2009b). At the same time, the principles upheld by the Obama administration can be expected to prevent Turkey from going back on a tendency to disregard international law and pursue unilateralist policies in its foreign relations as could have been inspired by the former US administration in the absence of an EU accession process. It can also be expected that Turkey give more serious thought to becoming a party to the ICC or becoming more involved in the prevention of climate change in the pre-accession process.

However, the 'no' vote by Turkey in June 2010 regarding further sanctions against Iran or its stance in the Israeli-Palestine conflict do not result from the 'wrong' policies pursued by the US or the EU. With respect to the sanctions against Iran, it is possible to say that Turkey perceived more threat from a future US intervention in Iran than from a prospective nuclear Iran. Turkey's 'no' vote regarding sanctions against Iran has not resulted in a domestic criticism of the government's policy. None of the political parties in Turkey define Iran as an enemy or its nuclear capabilities as a threat, despite the fact that Iran was a major source of threat perception in the 1990s due to its aims of regime exportation to Turkey. All political parties, on the other hand, agree that a US intervention in Iran or the intensification of the conflict between Iran and the West is a major source of instability in Turkey's vicinity. At least part of this perception is induced by the fact that despite all previous intelligence reports, no WMDs were found in Iraq, but the country ended up in irreparable turmoil after the US intervention. Turkish policy-makers may be questioning the ability of Iran's nuclear programme, despite the latter's strong wish to be able to acquire nuclear technology capable of producing nuclear weapons. Apart from this perception, calling president Ahmadinejad a 'friend' (Guardian 2009) may be an act that is attributable only to the personal feelings of AKP leaders which have definitely played into the perceptions of a shift of axis in Turkish foreign policy. On the other hand, the incessant efforts of Turkey as a member of the UN Security Council to reconcile Western fears of Iran and the finding of a solution to the problem of Iran's nuclear capabilities is actually an act in search of peace and stability, which is one of the major aims of the EU in the international arena, as well. For these reasons, Turkey's 'no' vote in the UN Security Council right after Turkey and Brazil had concluded a swap agreement with Iran in June 2010 should be seen as part of a strategy on the Turkish part to preserve the ability to negotiate with Iran as a mediator in the future (Apakan 2010).

Another incident to contribute to debates about the shift of axis of Turkish foreign policy is its deteriorating relations with Israel and the growing importance of the Palestine problem in Turkey's policy towards the Middle East. The policies of Israel in the last decade has caused a deep resentment in Turkish public opinion and have previously resulted in similar exclamations by the former Prime Minister Bülent Ecevit on 'commitment of a genocide by Israel' (BBC News 2002). Thus, AKP is not the only government in Turkey to react against Israeli policies. While there is a big international concern about the nuclear capabilities of Iran, the nuclear weapons capacity of Israel to go undisputed is not only a sign of Western hypocrisy in the eyes of the Middle Eastern peoples, but also a contradiction in the EU's Barcelona Process that foresaw a Middle East free of WMDs. The mentioning of this fact by the AKP government and the consistency of the arguments of the government have resulted in the questioning of the unconditional support Israel enjoyed in the international arena and succeeded in finding its reflections in the Obama administration (Obama 2011) – though quite limited. Such a policy based on principles and consistency of arguments rather than one favouring the usage of hard-power or complying with existing power relations is actually quite a change of behaviour in Turkish foreign policy.

Conclusion

In December 2009, Turkey completed its tenth year as a candidate country without a certain timeline for eventual membership, as this chapter is going into print, it is into the thirteenth. There are many problems ahead for Turkey's accession to the Union and not all of them stem from Turkey. The EU itself seems to be rather undecided about what it wants to do regarding its relationship with Turkey. Under such circumstances it is unfortunately quite a valid question to ask whether these changes in Turkish foreign policy are sustainable without an EU membership prospect. The future trend of Turkish foreign policy rests on two major pillars. One of them is definitely the EU and the future (and the nature) of the relationship between Turkey and the EU. The second pillar is the US. What the US upholds in its global foreign policy and its policy towards Turkey is the other determinant of the future Turkish foreign policy. As the US policy became more unilateral and less concerned over the protection of human rights, Turkey amazingly found itself to uphold these values, rather than following the US example under George W. Bush. As the new Democratic Party administration in the US aims to re-gain the upper-hand in the international promotion of the values such as democracy, protection of human rights and international law, Turkey may feel the need to abide by them even more strongly, especially when the US administration considers Turkey as belonging in the West rather than in the Middle East, which was the case during the previous administration that labelled Turkey as a moderate Muslim country.

Turkey's relations with the Middle East seem to be the most enhanced during the almost nine years of AKP government from November 2002 until October 2011. It is for certain that Turkey does not perceive the same amount of threat from the region as it used to in the 1990s, despite the increase in instability of the region after the US intervention in Iraq in 2003.

Overall, it is possible to say that Turkish policy-makers have adapted to the fact that Turkey is acting in a new European environment now. It needs to accomplish certain specific goals as to the finding of a solution to the Cyprus problem and a policy change towards Armenia. It needs to converge its policies towards the Middle East with those towards Europe and not end up facilitating the visa regime towards the Middle Eastern countries while it will have to comply with Schengen border control standards during the pre-accession process. On this latest incident, it is possible to see that the government is making cost-benefit calculations between easy and attainable goals in the Middle East and the difficult and costly goals towards Europe. The loss of credibility of the EU membership perspective since 2006 is playing into the hands of Euro-sceptics at this point to uphold other values and targets instead of the long-term European one. The freedom of movement between European countries is one of the most successful tools of building a European identity. The restriction on travel of Turkish citizens in Europe, but its facilitation into the Middle Eastern countries can be a future determinant of where Turks feel more at ease, in Europe or in the Middle East. Soner Çağaptay (2007) draws attention to this fact, foreign policy pursuit being not only an outcome of identity, but also a major input into building of a future identity.

The increasing predominance of the AKP government's Middle East policy over other items on the foreign policy agenda has raised questions about a 'shift of axis' in Turkish foreign policy away from the West and towards the Middle East. It is certain that due to its political background, the AKP government would want to enhance relations with the Middle East. However, its party programme reflected aims concerning both the Middle East and EU accession. The party leaders often make remarks about the convergence of their policies towards the West and the Middle East or the Muslim world. Their vision for Turkey is one that links these regions and they want Turkey to be given importance in both of these regions due to the position it holds in the other one. As the prospect of Turkey in the EU grows weaker, Turkish foreign policy under the AKP government becomes more pre-eminent in the Middle East since it is no longer balanced by a strong European perspective. Especially since 2008, there is a decreasing level of alignment with the EU's CFSP statements. The regular reports of the European Commission on Turkey reveal that in 2007 Turkey aligned itself with 98 per cent of CFSP statements, in 2008, with 88 per cent, in 2009 77 per cent, in 2010 74 per cent and according to the 2011 report published very recently Turkey aligned itself with only 48 per cent of the CFSP statements (European Commission 2007, 2008, 2009, 2010, 2011). These numbers show that Turkey is distancing itself from EU positions more frequently and presenting more of an independent attitude that need not necessarily clash with that of the EU, but that does not support it either. The example of Turkish Europeanisation then links with the wider theoretical debates on the possibility of Europeanisation without a membership perspective.

References

Aggestam L. 2004. Role identity and Europeanisation of foreign policy: a political-cultural approach, in *Rethinking European Union Foreign Policy*, edited by B. Tonra and T. Christiansen. Manchester: Manchester University Press, 81–98.

AK Parti. 2001. *Party Programme*. [Online]. Available at: www.belgenet.com/parti/program/-ak_1.html and www. akparti.org.tr [accessed: 16 August 2009].

AK Parti. 2002. *Election Campaign Manifesto*. [Online]. Available at: http://www.belgenet.com/-secim/bildirge/akp2002-html [accessed: 16August 2009].

Akgün, M., Perçinoğlu, G. and Senyücel-Gündoğar, S. 2009. *Ortadoğu'da Türkiye Algısı* (Perceptions on Turkey in the Middle East). Istanbul: Tesev.

Altunışık, M.B. 2009. Worldviews and Turkish Foreign Policy in the Middle East. *New Perspectives on Turkey*, 40 (Spring), 172–6.

Apakan, E. 2010. *Explanation of Vote by H.E. Ambassador Ertuğrul Apakan, Permanent Representative of Turkey at the 6335th Meeting of the Security Council (Non-Proliferation/Iran)*. 9 June. [Online]. Available at: http://turkuno.dt.mfa.gov.tr/ShowSpeech.aspx?ID=1133 [accessed: 25 May 2011].

Aras, B. and Polat R.K. 2008. From Conflict to Cooperation: Desecuritisation of Turkey's Relations with Syria and Iran. *Security Dialogue*, 39(5), 495–515.

Arman, M.N. 2006. Refah Partisi ve Refah-Yol Koalisyonunun Dış Politika Yönelimleri (The Welfare Party and the foreign policy orientation of the Welfare-True Path coalition), in *Uluslararası İlişkiler ve Türk Siyasal Partileri* (International Relations and Turkish Political Parties), edited by N. Doğan and M. Nakip. Ankara: Seçkin Yayıncılık, 333–44.

Bakır, B. 2007. Necmettin Erbakan, in *Türk Dış Politikasında Liderler* (Leaders in Turkish Foreign Policy), edited by A.F. Demir. İstanbul: Bağlam Yayınları, 343–438.

BBC News. 2002. *Turkey Accuses Israel of Genocide*. 4 April. [Online]. Available at: http://news.bbc.co.uk/2/hi/europe/1911609.stm [accessed: 25 May 2011].

Börzel T.A. and Risse T. 2003. Conceptualizing the Domestic Impact of Europe, in *The Politics of Europeanization*, edited by K. Featherstone, C.M. Radaelli. Oxford: Oxford University Press, 57–80.

Cem, İ. 2000. *Turkey in the 21st Century*. Nicosia: Rustem Publishing.

Çağaptay, S. 2007. *Secularism and Foreign Policy in Turkey: New Elections, Troubling Trends*. The Washington Institute for Near East Policy. Policy Focus no: 67.

Davutoğlu, A. 2007. *Stratejik Derinlik: Türkiye'nin Uluslararası Konumu* (Strategic Depth: The International Location of Turkey). 23rd Edition (first edition: 2001). İstanbul: Küre.

Ekengren, M. and Sundelius, B. 2005. Sweden, in *Foreign Ministries in the European Union*, edited by B. Hocking and D. Spence. Hampshire and New York: Palgrave Macmillan, 238–49.

European Commission. 2007. *Regular Report on Turkey's Progress Towards Accession*. SEC (2007) 1436. Brussels.

European Commission. 2008. *Regular Report on Turkey's Progress Towards Accession*. SEC (2008) 2699. Brussels.

European Commission. 2009. *Regular Report on Turkey's Progress Towards Accession*. SEC (2009) 1334. Brussels.

European Commission. 2010. *Regular Report on Turkey's Progress Towards Accession*. SEC (2010) 1327. Brussels.

European Commission. 2011. *Regular Report on Turkey's Progress Towards Accession*. SEC (2011) 1201. Brussels.

General Affairs Council Meeting. 2005. *Negotiating Framework Document*. 3 October. [Online]. Available at: http://ec.europa.eu/enlargement/pdf/turkey/st20002_05_tr_framedoc_en.pdf [accessed: 26 May 2011].

General Affairs Council Meeting. 2006. Brussels. 11 December. [Online]. Available at: http://www.consilium.europa.eu/uedocs/cms_data/docs/pressdata/en/gena/92122.pdf [accessed: 25 May 2011].

Gordon, P. and Taşpınar, Ö. 2008. *Winning Turkey: How America, Europe and Turkey Can Revive A Fading Partnership*. Washington DC: Brookings Institution Press.

Gordon, P. and Taşpınar, Ö. 2006. Turkey on the Brink. *The Washington Quarterly*, 29(3), 57–70.

Grabbe, H. 2006. *The EU's Transformative Power*. Hampshire and New York: Palgrave Macmillan.

Guardian. 2009. *'Iran Is Our Friend' Says Turkish PM Recep Tayyip Erdoğan*. 6 October. [Online]. Available at: http://www.guardian.co.uk/world/2009/oct/26/turkey-iran1 [accessed: 25 May 2011].

Hocking, B. and Spence, D. 2005 (eds). *Foreign Ministries in the European Union*. Hampshire and New York: Palgrave Macmillan.

Hyde-Price, A. 2004. Interest, Institutons and Identities in the Study of European Foreign Policy, in *Rethinking European Union Foreign Policy*, edited by B. Tonra and T. Christiansen. Manchester: Manchester University Press, 99–113.

Larsen H. 2005. *Analysing the Foreign Policy of Small States in the EU: The Case of Denmark*. Hampshire and New York: Palgrave Macmillan.

Manners I. and Whitman R. 2000. Introduction, in *The Foreign Policies of European Union Member States*, edited by I. Manners and R.G. Whitman. Manchester: Manchester University Press, 1–16.

March, J. and Olsen, J. 2004. The Logic of Appropriateness. *Arena Working Papers* WP 04/09. [Online]. Available at: http://www.arena.uio.no/publications/working-papers2004/papers/wp04_9.pdf [accessed: 25 May 2011].

Miles, L. 2005. *Fusing with Europe? Sweden in the European Union*. Aldershot: Ashgate.

Milliyet. 2008. *Rehn: Artan Rolün Teslimi* (Rehn: Acknowledgement of the Increasing Role). 19 October. [Online]. Available at: http://www.milliyet.com.tr/Siyaset/HaberDetay.aspx?aType=-HaberDetayArsiv&ArticleID=1005016&Kategori=siyaset&b=&ver=66 [accessed: 22 October 2008].

Obama, B. 2009a. Remarks by President Obama to the Turkish Parliament. 6 April. Available at: http://www.whitehouse.gov/the-press-office/remarks-president-obama-turkish-parliament [accesssed 25. May 2011].

Obama, B. 2009b. Remarks by the President on a New Begining. 4 June. Available at: http://www.whitehouse.gov/the-press-office/remarks-president-cairo-university-6-04-09 [accessed: 25 May 2011].

Obama, B. 2011. Remarks by the President on Middle East and North Africa. 19 May. Available at: http://www.whitehouse.gov/the-press-office/2011/05/19/remarks-president-middle-east-and-north-africa [accessed: 17 October 2011].

Ohrgard, J. 2004. International Relations or European Integration: Is the CFSP Sui Generis, in *Rethinking European Union Foreign Policy*, edited by B. Tonra and T. Christiansen. Manchester: Manchester University Press, 26–44.

Oğuzlu, T. 2008. Middle Easternization of Turkey's Foreign Policy: Does Turkey Dissociate from the West? *Turkish Studies*, 9(1), 3–20.

Schimmelfennig, F. 2004. *The Impact of EU Democratic Conditionality in Central and Eastern Europe: a Qualitative Comparative Analysis*. Paper to the Second Pan-European Conference Standing Group on EU Politics, Bologna,

24–26 June 2004. Available at: http://www.jhubc.it/ecpr-bologna/docs/230.pdf [accessed: 25 May 2011].

Tonra, B. and Christiansen, T. 2004 (eds). *Rethinking European Union Foreign Policy*. Manchester: Manchester University Press.

Tonra, B. 2001. *The Europeanisation of National Foreign Policy: Dutch, Danish and Irish Foreign Policies in the EU*. Aldershot: Ashgate.

Uzgel, İ. 2001. Balkanlarla ilişkiler (Relations with the Balkans), in Türk Dış Politikası (Turkish Foreign Policy), Vol II :1980–2001, edited by B. Oran. İstanbul: İletişim, 481–523.

Uzgel, İ. 2009. AKP: Neoliberal Dönüşümün Yeni Aktörü (AKP: the new actor of the neo-liberal transformation), in *AKP Kitabı: Bir Dönüşümün Bilançosu* (The AKP Book: The Balance Sheet of a Transformation), edited by İ. Uzgel and B. Duru. Ankara: Phoenix, 11–39.

Walker, J.W. 2007. Learning Strategic Depth. Implications of Turkey's New Foreign Policy Doctrine. *Insight Turkey*, 9(3) 25–36.

Yavuz, M.H. Değişen Türk Kimliği ve Dış Politika: Neo-Osmanlıcılığın Yükselişi (The changing Turkish identity and foreign policy: the rise of neo-Ottomanism), in Türkiye'nin Dış Politika Gündemi: Kimlik, Demokrasi, Güvenlik (the Foreign Policy Agenda of Turkey: Identity, Democracy, Security), edited by Ş. Çalış, İ. Dağı and R. Gözen. Ankara: Liberte, 35–63.

Chapter 11
Turkey's Cyprus Policy:
A Case of Contextual Europeanisation

Alper Kaliber

Introduction

Throughout its long-lasting history the Cyprus question has always referred to a thick (in)security signifier for Turkish foreign and security policy (FSP) elite. The FSP establishment in Turkey has always placed special emphasis on the geo-strategically vital location of the island of Cyprus for the country's defence and security. The Cold War conception of security, which draws on politics of military power balancing and clashing conflicting national interests, has long dominated Turkish and other conflicting parties' policies on the Cyprus question. This entrenched security outlook has often confined the Cyprus dispute to the realm of bilateral Greek-Turkish relations and has implied that the real threat for Turkey has been Greece itself (Kaliber 2005, 2009). Furthermore, the casting of the Cyprus issue as one of national security in Turkey has severely constrained democratic debate and capacity of subsequent governments to intervene in the substance of the existing policies in domestic politics.

However, from the late 1990s on, there occurred mainly two dramatic shifts in Turkey's security outlook on Cyprus paving the way for radical reorganisation of Turkish policies on the issue in the 2000s. First, regionalism has steadily gained prominence in mapping out Turkey's security outlook on Cyprus since the 1990s. Even if Greece has not completely disappeared as a source of insecurity, the emphasis shifted from Greece toward the Eastern Mediterranean as a new regional context of Turkey's threat perceptions and strategic calculations. Turkish policy-makers began to make more frequent references to the 'Eastern Mediterranean' with a constellation of new strategic and security connotations. Secondly, issues of energy security and economic interests have been incorporated into Turkey's strategic outlook on Cyprus. The proximity of the island to the oil rich Middle East and its critical location within the new routes of oil transportation stretching out from the Caucasus to Europe has incorporated the issue of energy security into Turkey's new calculations on the Cyprus question (Kaliber 2009).

The analysts of Turkish FSP often tend to explain these dramatic shifts only by making reference to the policies and discourses of the Justice and Development Party (*Adalet ve Kalkınma Partisi* (AKP)) governments that have been in power continuously since November 2002. The scholarly analyses on the issue refer to AKP's policies as a rupture or 'U turn' from or historical alteration of the conventional state line maintained since the 1950s (see among others Çelenk, 2007, Tocci 2007, Kirişçi 2009). When the support for the Annan Plan and subsequent referenda on the island as well as the current bi-communal negotiations between the leaders of Turkish and Greek Cypriot communities are considered, it is fair to suggest that AKP has become the most important actor inducing change in Turkey's Cyprus policy. However, a more accurate and historically informed account suggests that the shifts in Turkish policies can fully be captured only when they are contextualised within the series of internal and external developments. These developments include increasing involvement of the EU in the Cyprus conflict, the UN-led peace initiatives accelerating in the 2001–2004 period, changing characteristics of Turco-Greek relations (albeit to a limited degree) in the post-1999 era and the historical changes occurring in Turkish and Turkish Cypriot domestic politics.

This historical account does not deny that the AKP has become the most influential agent behind Turkey's comprehensive policy changes on Cyprus. Yet, it suggests that the strategic outlook and the security lexicon accompanying and even legitimising these policies hardly represent a historical rupture from the conventional Turkish state line. Rather than representing a historical departure, these policy shifts denote a 'radical reorganisation' of Turkish policies on Cyprus. The incorporation of energy security issues and intermingling of economic interests and security concerns have not begun with the AKP era and have been articulated not only by the current FSP establishment in Turkey. Furthermore, in its most revisionist period, Turkey did not avoid mentioning the substance of her conventional Cyprus policies which are the geostrategic importance of the island for Turkey, security of Turkish Cypriots, and non-recognition of the Greek controlled Republic of Cyprus (RoC) until a viable solution has been reached. The presence of nearly 30,000–40,000 troops on the island is still one of the main elements of Turkish policy.

The chapter by considering, but without focusing on these, aims to discuss the impacts of Europeanisation as a normative/political context on Turkey's Cyprus policy. It is a widespread conviction among the students of Turkish foreign policy that despite its radical reorganisation, the impact of Europeanisation on Turkey's Cyprus policies has been very limited. When considering that Turkey still does not implement requirements of the Additional Protocol and keeps its ports closed to Cypriot ships and planes, and that Turkish-EU relations still remain hostage to Cyprus, it seems that this is an observation hard to object to. Yet, one should note that the radical reorganisation of Cyprus policies in the late 2003–2004 period has been possible mostly due to requirements of Turkey's integration into the EU-Europe. Therefore, the current intervention argues that the impact of Europe is better understood if it is conceptualised as contextual and contingent rather than being limited.

The scholarly analyses on Turkish foreign policy largely depart from the mainstream definition of the term Europeanisation as a top-down process of domestic change and adaptation to the EU model. To this understanding, when EU policies, rules and norms are not properly diffused into domestic structures, the impact of Europeanisation remains limited. Yet, this approach does not explain why Europeanisation has deeply transformed Turkey's Cyprus policies in the 2003–2005 period, while its impact remained almost marginal in ensuing years. This chapter argues that the impact of Europeanisation in a given society is heavily conditioned by the extent of and the ways in which Europe is used as a political/ normative context by domestic actors. Europeanisation penetrates into domestic politics, if and when these actors use the European context as a 'mobilising political instrument' (Malmborg and Strath 2002: 4) to promote their political agenda. Change through Europeanisation occurs 'not simply because it is imposed from the outside, but also because it interacts with domestic developments on the inside' (Tocci 2005: 79). Unlike the mainstream and procedural understandings, this chapter does not conceive Europeanisation as a top-down or bottom-up process. It conceptualises Europeanisation as a context from within which national-domestic and European level actors act and speak to their audiences. It also develops an analytical distinction between EU-isation and Europeanisation: EU-isation as a formal *process* of alignment with the EU's institutions, policies and legal structure and Europeanisation as a wider socio-political and normative context.

Departing from such a conception, this chapter suggests that the extent to which Europeanisation has penetrated into Turkish policies has largely been determined by domestic political actors in Turkey. It argues that when the ruling AKP elite needed Europe to consolidate their position within Turkey's domestic power politics, they mobilised Europeanisation as a political/normative context: a context whereby they can frame and justify their reformist agenda in domestic and foreign policy issues. Making references to the European norms, values and expectations were in turn instrumental to problematise the conventional Turkish foreign policy paradigm and the Cyprus policy, which is often defined as pro-*status quo*, passive and counter-productive. For the AKP, commitment to the EU-induced reforms was the most effective means to legitimise and consolidate its governing power 'vis-à-vis the international community and secular establishment in Turkey' (Tocci 2005: 80). Yet, in the subsequent period, due to a complex constellation of internal and external factors, Europeanisation has retreated as a context influencing Turkey's Cyprus policies. The mainstream literature on Europeanisation often considers domestic actors only 'as mediators' of the European impact. However, as I will try to indicate with respect to the Cyprus case, domestic actors are not 'mediators', but creators of Europeanisation.

Against this backdrop, this contribution first examines the main tenets of the current scholarship on Europeanisation. Secondly, it unpacks the distinction it has made between EU-isation and Europeanisation and relocates the latter within a broader sociological terrain. It then moves on to examine how Europeanisation has been utilised by the ruling elite for the radical reorganisation of Turkish policies on Cyprus. The chapter also analyses recent developments in Turkish-EU-Cyprus relations as well as the ongoing bi-communal peace negotiations between the Cypriot leaders. It concludes by outlining possible implications of different scenarios in the Cyprus conflict for Turkish-EU and Turco-Greek relations.

Europeanisation as a Normative/Political Context

The common denominator in most usages of the term Europeanisation is its definition as a 'process of change and adaptation which is understood to be a consequence of the development of the European Union' (Ladrech 2001: 1). It denotes an EU-induced process of domestic change and adaptation to the penetrating 'European values, directives and norms' (Mair 2004: 341, see also Baun et al. 2006: 252ff., Börzel and Risse, 2000, Ladrech, 1994). The Europeanisation literature, inspired particularly by the rationalist and sociological variants of neo-institutionalism, tends to explain domestic change in the member and associate countries 'via the institutional goodness of fit of domestic and European arrangements' (Knill and Lehmkuhl 1999: 4, see also Cowles et al. 2001). The degree of misfit between the domestic and European settings determines the intensity of pressure for institutional and policy adaptation exerted by the EU. Misfit is often taken as the exclusive factor inducing Europeanisation of domestic settings (Börzel 1999, Duina 1999, Cowles et al. 2001). Domestic actors are often 'only considered as mediators' of these top-down pressures and no real political role and discretion are recognised to them (Jacquot and Woll 2003: 1).

The rationalist variance of Neo-institutionalism suggests that the elimination of mismatch between domestic and European settings is contingent upon the ability of domestic pro-EU actors to use opportunities and constraints emerging from Europeanisation at the expense of their rivals (Börzel and Risse 2000). According to sociological institutionalism, domestic change occurs when the actors holding social and political capital learn and internalise European rules, norms and institutions so as to redefine their identities and interests (Börzel and Risse 2000: 6). In either case, change through Europeanisation is conceptualised as the successful import of EU norms, principles and institutions as established and even fixed identities to be internalised by the member states. However, these norms, and values claimed to be 'typical of Europe' are always involved in a process of discursive/political reconstruction both at the European and domestic levels. For instance, the norms attributed to Europe and particularly to the EU are subject to constant interpretations during the accession negotiations for full EU membership. European norms 'do not remain stable during the negotiation process, and in fact are often only constructed, or at least made explicit, in this context' (Diez, Agnantopoulos and Kaliber 2005: 3). Therefore, a more sophisticated analysis of Europeanisation should embrace domestic public debates and deliberations where different notions of Europe, its norms and values are negotiated and politically used by domestic actors.

This chapter suggests that to better comprehend the transformative impact of Europe, an analytical distinction is needed between EU-isation and

Europeanisation. EU-isation is conceptualised as a formal process of alignment of the domestic structures with the EU's body of law and institutions. The most radical and manifest impacts of EU-isation can be observable during the accession negotiations. Alignment with and implementation of the *acquis communitaire* is the *sine qua non* and the yardstick against which to measure achieved level of EU-isation. Europeanisation however, rather than being a process, exists as a context embracing all other processes and institutions of European integration as well. It may be understood as a context or situation (Buller and Gamble 2002) where European norms, policies and institutions are (re)-negotiated and constructed by different European societies and institutions and have an impact on them. The more the national and European-level political, bureaucratic and civil societal actors make reference to specific European norms, policies or institutions, the more Europe can be expected to have an impact on domestic policies and political structures. Unlike what Europeanisation literature often implies, domestic actors are not 'mediators', but creators of Europeanisation. Europeanisation exists as a context to the extent that the European norms, values, institutions are incorporated into the public narratives by domestic actors. Thereby, its transformative impact is not procedural and linear, but is contextual, contested and contingent. Yet, it is also true that European level developments (policy-making, the scope of integration and Europe-wide debates) shape perceptions of domestic actors and the political structure within which they react to and make use of this context.

Europeanisation and Foreign Policy

Foreign policy is often considered as the least institutionalised area of European integration, characterised by strong intergovernmentalism and having 'a very limited impact on domestic policy choices' (Hix and Goetz 2000: 6). In the case of foreign policy, Europeanisation manifests itself as 'the emergence of a distinct decision-making culture and the consolidation of standards of appropriate behaviour' (Torreblanca 2001: 3) reorienting domestic security and foreign policy cultures (Smith 2000). European integration creates a new political normative framework allowing national political elites to articulate alternative (post-national, regional) constructions of identity and security. The increasing impact of Europeanisation makes the use of inflammatory nationalist and securitising discourses redundant and even self-defeating. The national elites are encouraged to draw more on 'regional and European in addition to national identifications' (Adamson 2002: 177) in the formulation and conduct of foreign and security policy.

However, as the Cyprus case illustrates, the impact of Europeanisation is often more complicated than assumed in the literature, since it may also trigger counter-nationalist and securitising discourses at the societal and elite levels. Particularly in the issues deemed as national cause, Europeanisation of the FSP may well be perceived as the erosion of national sovereignty and as a threat to national security and interests. Domestic actors commit themselves to European reforms in such issues only when they come to view European norms and values resonate with their political interests or ideological positions (Tocci 2005). When domestic actors perceive the cost of compliance to EU-required or externally imposed reforms to be excessively high, they tend to see EU-isation/Europeanisation as a danger to themselves and to so-called national interests. Hence, it is largely contingent upon willingness and capacity of domestic actors to utilise Europe as a political/normative context to articulate and justify their policy ambitions.

Throughout the long-lasting history of the Cyprus conflict there came several attempts to bring the parties together and 'work towards de-securitization, all of which have so far failed' (Diez 2002: 144). The main factor crippling these attempts was the lack of incentives for the disputants 'to modify the ethno-nationalist rhetoric on which they have constructed their negotiating positions' (Richmond 2002: 129). Mutual and extensive securitisations have created so far a confrontational politics in Cyprus and the parties to the conflict could not find a way of getting out of it. For many, the EU was the only body politic that could provide the political elites in the disputant parties with a set of tangible incentives to refashion their security-oriented policies on Cyprus and to redefine their national interests in a more communitarian manner. Yet, the EU's increasing involvement in the conflict since the RoC's full membership application in 1990, did not induce a significant de-securitising effect. Furthermore, the expectations that Cyprus's full membership would catalyse any peaceful resolution on the island have not yet materialised (Diez 2002: 139, Buzan and Wæver 2003: 369, Eralp and Beriker 2005: 180). It would be useful to glance at the post-2002 developments to better comprehend why Europeanisation has not worked in Cyprus and particularly in Turkey's policies.

The AKP Era and Turkey's New Position on Cyprus

It is fair to suggest that soon after the AKP came to power, the Cyprus issue has increasingly turned out to be an integral part of the internal debates and power struggles in Turkey. From the end of 2002 onward, the Cyprus issue has emerged as one of the main 'discursive battlefields' of the polarisation among the ruling AKP and the opposing state elites. For the AKP reforming Turkey's Cyprus policy was a necessity not only because it failed and proved to be counter-productive, but also it was required by the EU. The EU, which would decide on the beginning of accession talks with Turkey, had established an explicit linkage between the fate of Turkey's EU perspective and resolving the Cyprus problem. Strengthening relations with the EU was an indispensable source of legitimacy for the AKP government blamed for challenging the core premises of the regime in Turkey, i.e. secularism and nationalism. Europe, particularly the EU, was seen as a window of opportunity by the AKP leaders to broaden the political, economic and cultural spaces which were considerably narrowed particularly by the military wing of the bureaucratic apparatus since the late 1990s. Europe transformed into a possibility where some 'authoritarian' aspects of the regime, i.e. the grip of military and civilian bureaucracy on politics can be challenged and eliminated in Turkey (Duran 2004).

A radical reorganisation of the Cyprus policy has been seen as vital both to get the backing of Europe and also to erode the supremacy of the military in the formulation and implementation of FSP in Turkey. The conventional Turkish policy on Cyprus was drawing on a particular conception of national security placing foreign policy beyond normal politics and public debate (Kaliber 2005). To this understanding, vital foreign policy issues may be entrusted only to those cognisant of its peculiar rules and techniques. The casting of the Cyprus issue as one of national security has severely constrained the power and capacity of the political elite to intervene in the substance of the existing policies. It has forced the governments as the political authority to pursue pre-determined policies by remaining loyal to the 'red lines' drawn up by the foreign policy and security bureaucracy (Kaliber 2005). The insulation of the Cyprus issue from public debate in Turkey has reinforced the power and hegemonic status of the bureaucratic apparatus, which 'consider themselves as the ideological guardian of the state (Cizre and Yeldan 2002: 17).

Soon after it came to power in November 2002, AKP 'saw an opportunity in the rapid settlement of the Cyprus issue as a means of strengthening its domestic political power through an international success' (Çelenk 2007: 360). Cyprus has been instrumental for AKP both to challenge the conventional state policies and to gain the needed support of the external actors most notably the EU and the US. In the 2003–2004 period, the AKP leaders mobilised Europe and Turkey's European vision to publicise drastic policy shifts on Cyprus. They began to make references to European norms and expectations to express Turkey's new policies and to persuade the international community about Turkey's willingness to reach a viable solution. Europe in general and the EU in particular have become a common reference point increasingly referred to in domestic debates on the Cyprus question. Hence, Europeanisation in this period has deeply impacted the public and policy discourses in Turkey as a normative/political context.

Yet, the Cyprus issue has also been extensively mobilised by the nationalist opposition to criticise the AKP government blamed as selling out one of Turkey's 'national causes'. The increasing involvement of the EU in the issue was exploited by nationalist circles in Turkey to create a sense of emergency about the future of Turkish Cypriots and Turkey's geostrategic interests in the island. Given the then explicit and strong support of Turkish society to the EU perspective, directly targeting the government's pro-EU reforms was politically risky for the opposition. However, the Cyprus issue, which has been vulnerable to nationalist agitation, has always constituted a relatively easy ground for questioning and disempowering the governments in Turkey. Thus, it took some time for AKP cadres to translate their reformist rhetoric into a substantive policy shift on Cyprus which could only occur gradually 'over the course of 2003 and 2004' (Tocci 2007: 65).

As a matter of fact, direct negotiations had already resumed between the leaders of the Turkish and Greek Cypriot communities (Denktaş and Clerides respectively) in late 2001 without bearing any fruit. It was in November 2002 that the first AKP government was formed and the first version of the 'Annan Plan' was made public. The plan foresaw a bi-zonal bi-communal federal structure for the reunified Cyprus based on political equality of two constituent states in northern and southern parts of the island. During late 2002 and early 2003 new versions of the plan were prepared and published in line with the objections and proposals coming from the two Cypriot communities. That the plans were vehemently rejected by Denktaş provided a shield to Greek Cypriot leadership to hide their negative stance towards this UN-led initiative. When the Annan Plan and the notion of submitting it to public vote was rejected by the Turkish Cypriot leader in March 2003, the first AKP government in Turkey avoided criticising him publicly mostly due to inadequate governmental experience and self-confidence. Yet, the then AKP government managed to prevent the Turkish Cypriot side from leaving the negotiation table for good.

Meanwhile, the rejection of the Annan Plan and the referendum triggered mass demonstrations backed by a very large segment of the society in the northern part of Cyprus where the domestic order was 'dominated since 1974 by nationalist parties (in particular by Rauf Denktaş)' (Tocci 2007: 65). When the Republican Turkish Party (CTP) won the parliamentary elections in December 2003, AKP had already consolidated Turkey's new position on the Cyprus conflict. During the election campaign CTP leaders extensively mobilised the European context and they referred to its institutions, norms and values to promote their political agenda. The Annan Plan was presented as the key to integrating into Europe, seen as the only gateway for Turkish Cypriots. In January 2004 Turkish Prime Minister Erdoğan stated that Turkey would accept the negotiations for the settlement of the Cyprus issue on the basis of the Annan Plan. Turkey also accepted that the UN Secretary General Annan would have the last say on the matters upon which Turkish and Greek Cypriot sides fail to compromise (Çelenk 2007). The fundamental objective of Turkey's new activism was to enable a solution before 1 May 2004, the date when the Greek Cypriot-controlled RoC would become an EU member.

The fifth version of the plan shaped by the bi-communal negotiations resuming in February 2004 and subsequently by Annan's interventions was brought to the referenda in both parts of the island on 24 April. For the bulk of Turkish Cypriots, the Annan Plan was symbolising the end of political uncertainties and impasses, the collapse of the *status quo* dominated by Turkish nationalist leader Denktaş, the restriction of Turkey's influence over Turkish Cypriot politics and eventually EU membership. Therefore, the plan which was wholeheartedly defended by the liberal and left political parties, intellectuals and civil society organisations was approved by 65 per cent of Turkish Cypriots. But the then Greek Cypriot leadership which had already guaranteed EU membership 'turned against the plan' (International Crisis Group 2009), supported strongly by the international society and the EU in particular. In the Greek Cypriot part of the island the plan was deemed unacceptable and as an existential threat by nationalist left and right to the survival of the RoC and was presented as a foreign intervention. In fact both

Turkish and Greek Cypriots had already accepted bi-zonal bi-communal federation as the basis of negotiations in High Level Agreements of 1977–79. A furious campaign conducted particularly by Tasos Papadopulos resulted in the rejection of the UN-led initiative by 76 per cent of Greek Cypriots. He cherished the hope that the RoC, which achieved to join the EU as the sole representative of Cyprus, would have all means in hand to do a much better agreement after accession: a better deal where Turkey's guarantorship rights are substantially eroded and the Greek Cypriots' sense of security *vis-à-vis* Turkey is better satisfied.

Different reactions given to the Annan Plan in both parts of the island opened a new chapter in the long-lasting history of the Cyprus conflict. For the first time the Turkish side gained the moral high ground in the international arena as a party who favours the solution even if this is not translated into concrete political changes. Soon after the referenda on 26 April 2004, the EU promised to take some measures to mitigate the 'isolation' of the Turkish Cypriots, i.e. the Green Line regulation facilitating direct preferential trade for Turkish Cypriots with the EU member countries and financial aid worth €259 million. Yet, all EU efforts to ease the economic isolation were blocked by the RoC government as they would serve to confirm the consolidation of the Turkish Republic of Northern Cyprus as a separate entity. Greek Cypriot leaders were also tempted to see Turkey's membership negotiations as leverage to exert pressure on Turkey and to obtain Turkey's eventual recognition of the RoC. In December 2004 to get membership talks started, Turkey accepted the signing of a protocol extending its 1963 Association Agreement to the ten new members, including RoC, which it does not recognise. However, the Turkish government after signing the additional protocol to the EU-Turkey association agreement in July 2005 immediately declared that opening up its airports and ports to Greek Cypriot vessels and aircrafts would not amount to the recognition of the RoC.[1] The EU strongly criticised this declaration and called upon Turkey to lift the restrictions on all EU member states, recognise all EU members and normalise its relations with all of them.[2]

The Turkish government, with the aim of breaking the deadlock on the issue, announced a Cyprus Action Plan on 24 January 2006 foreseeing the simultaneous opening of Turkish ports and airspace to Greek Cypriot commercial traffic and opening of the ports in northern Cyprus to international trade as well as of the Turkish Cypriot Ercan airport to international flights.[3] Turkey also called upon the UN to host multiparty negotiations to finalise the plan towards finding a comprehensive settlement of the Cyprus problem. Yet, even if the Action Plan was

---

1   Turkey's declaration is accessible at http://www.mfa.gov.tr/declaration-by-turkey-on-cyprus_-29-july-2005.en.mfa.

2   The EU's response can be read at http://www.auswaertiges-mt.de/diplo/en/Europa/Erweiterung/-TuerkeiErklaerung.pdf.

3   The press statement about Turkey's Cyprus Action Plan by the then Foreign Minister Abdullah Gül can be accessed at http://www.mfa.gov.tr/new-initiative-by-turkey-on-cyprus.en.mfa.

assessed as a positive step by some European states, it failed to create momentum toward resolution largely due to Greek Cypriot objections. There were not enough incentives to persuade the Greek Cypriot leadership, who have believed that time is on their side, to return to the negotiating table under the auspices of the UN's good mission. As Turkey kept its ports closed to Greek Cypriot traffic, in December 2006 the European Council, 'under pressure from the Republic of Cyprus' (International Crisis Group 2009), decided to suspend accession talks with Turkey in eight chapters. The Council also stated that it would not 'close the other chapters until Turkey fulfils its commitments under the additional protocol' (Council of the European Union 2006). The December 2006 European Council furthermore asked the European Commission to review the developments in particular for the next three years understood as a new deadline for Turkey. Eventually half of the 35 chapters (see Introduction for details) in Turkey's accession negotiations was blocked as they were associated with her non-compliance with the Additional Protocol.

The hopes for the settlement of the Cyprus problem revived when the 2008 parliamentary elections in southern Cyprus resulted in the victory of 'pro-solution' Christofias. Throughout the history of the conflict for the first time pro-settlement politicians who were also sharing 'more common ground than any of their predecessors' (International Crisis Group 2009) simultaneously were assigned leadership by their respective communities. On 21 March 2008 Christofias and Talat declared their enthusiasm to re-launch UN-mediated reunification talks and two months later they drew up the basic parameters which would guide the negotiations: 'bi-zonal' 'bi-communal' federation with a single international personality, but consisting of Turkish and Greek Cypriot 'constituent states' that will be of politically equal status.[4] Turkey expressed a strong support to the negotiations which started on 3 September with the understanding that the plan would be put in referenda in both parts of the island. The first round of intensive talks that ended in August 2009 focused on the following issues: power sharing and governance, compensation of properties, the representations of the new state within the EU, coordination of federal economy and its institutions, the internal boundaries of two constituent states, security and guarantee issues, and the status of settlers, most notably those coming from Turkey (International Crisis Group 2009).

The second round of bi-communal negotiations came to a halt due to Turkish Cypriot elections in April 2010 where Talat lost to Derviş Eroğlu known as a hard-line nationalist. Yet, this did not lead to the breakdown of the negotiations and Eroğlu expressed his willingness to remain at the table for a possible solution. There still exist thorny issues where the parties seem to be far away from an agreement, i.e. continuation of the 1969 guarantorship system, the structure of the federal state, the compensation of properties, territory issues and the status of Turkish settlers. According to the Turkish political leadership, Turkey is still

---

4   See the joint statement issued after the Christofias-Talat meeting on 23 May 2008 accessible at http://www.mfa.gov.cy/mfa/mfa2006.nsf/All/EFE2ADBC7F4092EBC22574 5500288A96?OpenDocument.

committed to re-unification in accordance with the basic parameters of the Annan Plan, however it does not need to take further steps since Turkey had already done everything it could do for a solution. The current Turkish position is not to implement the Protocol unless the trade sanctions on northern Cyprus are lifted as the EU had promised. Thus, even if an impasse in Cyprus will badly affect Turkey's EU accession, foreign policy elite is 'far less engaged over Cyprus than previously' and also in preparations of Plan B in case of a deadlock in the settlement talks (International Crisis Group 2009).

Freezing the peace initiatives would also mean freezing of Turkey's accession negotiations as there will be no new chapters to open for Turkey in the near future. As David Hannay (2009) aptly puts it, if the *status quo* on the island persists, neither Turkey can join an EU of which Greek Cypriot controlled RoC is already a member, nor Turkey 'rebuffed by the EU' could offer a deal that Greek Cypriots could accept. That Turkey's accession talks grind to a standstill would also deprive the Greek Cypriot leaders of the most powerful mechanism at hand which could persuade Turkey to a 'better solution' for themselves. If the current bi-communal negotiations fail to produce an agreement, the most optimistic scenario for Cyprus could be to find a way of simultaneous implementation of the Additional Protocol by Turkey and a set of measures by the EU easing Turkish Cypriots' economic and cultural isolation. Given the Greek Cypriots' strong objections to that and presence of some EU members exploiting Cyprus to derail Turkish accession, it will not be easy for the EU to take initiatives in that direction.

The recent statements by senior Turkish politicians further complicate the relations within the Turkey-Cyprus-EU triangle. Soon after the AKP won a third consecutive term in June 2011 elections in Turkey, foreign minister Davutoğlu called upon Turkish and Greek Cypriot leaders to agree on the parameters of the solution and put them to referenda in early 2012 (Spiegel Online 2011). However, this seemingly constructive proposal was overshadowed by his other words uttered in a rather threatening mode: 'If the Greek Cypriot side stalls negotiations and takes over the presidency of the European Union in July 2012, this means not only a deadlock on the island, but also a blockage, a freezing point in Turkey-European Union relations' (Reuters 2011), Davutoğlu said in a news conference. Turkish Prime Minister Erdoğan reiterated the threat to freeze relations with the EU during the RoC presidency (July–December 2012) and sent strong signals about returning to 'old' policies of a two-state solution. He also blamed the EU for treating Turkey in a 'wrong' and 'dishonest' manner (*Hürriyet Daily News* 2011). These declarations by Turkish policy-makers reveal that Europeanisation is currently far from being a normative/political context influencing Turkish policies. They are also indicative of the fact that the current government does not feel the same level of dependency on EU perspective to consolidate its power and legitimacy in domestic politics.

Conclusion

This chapter has discussed the impact of Europeanisation on Turkey's Cyprus policies as a normative/political context where domestic actors are the principal creators of Europeanisation. The students of Turkish FSP often converge on the idea that this impact has so far remained limited. Even if this observation vindicates a part of the truth, it does not reveal why Europeanisation had a more transformative impact in different periods, while has less or no impact at other times. The literature on the Europeanisation of the Cyprus conflict and Turkish policies largely depart from the mainstream definition of the term Europeanisation as a linear process of domestic change and adaptation to the EU. Yet, this chapter suggests a more sociological approach where Europeanisation is conceptualised as a normative/political context rather than a process: a context the impacts of which are largely shaped by actions and discourses of domestic political and social actors. This reconceptualisation allows us to better comprehend the nature of European impact on Turkey's Cyprus policies, which is contextual and contingent rather than being only limited.

It is also proposed that European level developments overwhelmingly influence the ways in which domestic actors react to and make use of Europe. Hence, whether Europeanisation would have a determining impact on Turkish policies also depends on actions and discourses of European level actors shaping normative, ideational, and institutional structure of Europe-Europeanisation. Ongoing discourses of several European leaders questioning Turkey's place in Europe would continue to weaken the context of Europeanisation for Turkish society and politics. 'Lack of a clear and consistent EU strategy and commitment' (Tocci 2005: 77) to Turkey's full membership strengthens the conviction in many strands of Turkish society that Turkey will never join the EU. This is a phenomenon which renders references to European norms, values and expectations to reconfigure Turkish policies on Cyprus more difficult for political actors in Turkey. Therefore, it seems that at least at the current juncture, we are far from the days when Europeanisation has manifested itself as a thick context transforming the ways in which the Cyprus question has been debated in the country.

Unlike the dominant academic discourse, this chapter defended the notion that the AKP governments' Cyprus policies do not represent a historical rupture or 'U turn' from Turkey's conventional line on the issue. This does not mean to deny the AKP's agency in making comprehensive policy shifts possible. Yet, these dramatic shifts sticking to the substance of well-established Turkish policies may better be defined as a 'radical reorganisation' rather than being an alteration *en masse*. Some recent statements (July 2011) by senior Turkish policy-makers signal a reversal to the policies of the 1990s, even one may say, the rewinding of this radical reorganization. For instance, Turkey's minister for EU Affairs Egemen Bağış publicly mentioned the creation of two independent Cypriot states and 'annexation of the TRNC to Turkey'[5] amongst the possible outcomes when bicommunal negotiations are doomed to fail.

Apparently, the fate of Turkey's accession talks 'riddled with obstacles and uncertainties' (Tocci and Diez 2009: 1) is tightly linked to that of protracted Cyprus conflict. The opening of these talks could have been perceived and used as an opportunity by all parties for the reunification of Cyprus. A reunified Cyprus that has close ties with Turkey would not only clear a bulk of obstacles in her way to Europe, but would also contribute substantially to her ambitions of being a peace-promoting 'soft power' in its surrounding regions. Yet, the probability that 'EU-Turkey relations may become the next victim' (Tocci and Diez 2009: 1) of the Cyprus conflict is not less feeble than the pre-2003 period.

On the other hand, Turkish-EU relations are not the only area where the implications of breakdown in bi-communal peace talks could be observed. Failure to resolve the Cyprus dispute would prevent the EU from fully benefiting from NATO's military capabilities, damaging the EU's objective of becoming a substantial security actor. Failure would also inflict stability and security in the Eastern Mediterranean, which is very close to oil-rich and the geo-strategically important Middle East. When the RoC unilaterally started offshore oil and gas drilling in south of the island in September 2011, Turkey's fierce reactions and retaliatory actions followed suit. Further complicating the conflict in the Eastern Mediterranean, the drilling US-based company 'is 30 per cent owned by Israeli interests' (International Crisis Group 2012) and the drilling field is partly in Israel's exclusive economic zone. This means that the conflict on oil drilling bears the potential to escalate into a major crisis in the regionOn the other hand, Turkey's objectives of becoming an energy hub and an active player in its surrounding regions would also be weakened by an unresolved Cyprus question. That the tension prevails in the Eastern Mediterranean because of the Cyprus conflict would threaten the present and future projects for transporting Caspian oil and natural gas to Europe. Furthermore, any progress toward the settlement of Cyprus will be a very big step for Turkey to achieve its foreign policy goal of normalising relations with all her neighbours.

The survival of the Cyprus dispute would have a destabilising and deteriorating impact on the Turco-Greek relations as well, which are characterised by a fragile rapprochement in recent years. In 1999 Greece drastically changed its policy of blocking Turkey's way to Europe and became one of the most vigorous protagonists of her integration to the EU. Both countries supported the Annan Plan and the subsequent referenda held in Turkish and Greek parts of Cyprus in April 2004. The softening of the securitising tone in their discourses *vis-à-vis* each other, careful management of tensions (Rumelili 2007: 707) and sophistication of monolithic perceptions (Keridis 2001: 14) are among the manifestations of rapprochement between the two. Yet, as Ifantis and Aydın (2004: 1) suggest, what still exists 'is a very disturbing potential for escalation which can lead to a more serious crisis

---

5   Interview to Cypriot daily *Kıbrıs*, 3 March 2012.

with alarming destabilising effects at a regional level'. In that sense any tension in Cyprus may still monopolise Turco-Greek relations and reverse the fragile rapprochement.

If the current stalemate in the Cyprus question persists, this may lead to the beginning of a new process where some steps are taken by Turkey and Turkish Cypriots to enhance the international identity of the Turkish Republic of Northern Cyprus. Any steps in this direction would undoubtedly trigger renewed tensions in the Turkey-Cyprus-EU triangle and further slow down Turkey's integration into the EU. However, I beg to differ with the view that the current bicommunal negotiations constitute the last chance for re-unification of Cyprus. So long as Turkey's EU perspective is alive and the two Cypriot communities are adamant to live together, there would always be new opportunities for a lasting, peaceful solution. Nevertheless, one should consider the fact that each time the parties will have fewer reasons to trust each other, less incentives to negotiate and will be more fatigued by the endless negotiations.

References

Adamson, F.B. 2002. Democratisation in Turkey, EU enlargement and the regional dynamics of the Cyprus conflict: past lessons and future prospects, in *The European Union and the Cyprus Conflict: Modern Conflict, Postmodern Union,* edited by T. Diez. Manchester: Manchester University Press, 163–80.

Baun, M, Dürr, J. Marek, D. and Saradín, P. 2006. The Europeanisation of Czech politics: the political parties and the EU referendum. *Journal of Common Market Studies*, 44(2), 249–80.

Börzel, T.A. 1999. Towards convergence in Europe? Institutional adaptation to Europeanisation in Germany and Spain. *Journal of Common Market Studies,* 37(4), 573–96.

Börzel, T.A. and Risse, T. 2000. When Europe hits home: Europeanisation and domestic change. *European Integration online Papers (EIoP)* [Online], 4(15). Available at: http://eiop.or.at/eiop/-texte/2000-015.htm [accessed: 23 July 2007].

Buller, J. and Gamble, A. 2002. Conceptualising Europeanisation. *Public Policy and Administration*, 17(2), 4–24.

Buzan, B. and Wæver, O. 2003. *Regions and Powers: The Structure of International Security*. Cambridge: Cambridge University Press.

Çelenk, A. 2007. The restructuring of Turkey's policy towards Cyprus: the justice and development party's struggle for power. *Turkish Studies*, 8(3), 349–63.

Cizre, Ü. ve Yeldan, E. 2002. *Turkey: Economy, Politics and Society in the Post-Crisis Era*. International Development Economics Associates (IDEAs). [Online]. Available at: http://www.networkideas.org/feathm/jul2002/Turkey. pdf [accessed: 18 August 2011].

Council of the European Union. 2006. Press Release. 2770th Council Meeting General Affairs. Brussels, 11 December, 16289/06 (Presse 352). [Online]. Accessible at: http://www.consilium.-europa.eu/ueDocs/cms_Data/docs/ pressData/en/gena/92122.pdf [accessed: 29 November 2011].

Cowles, M., Caporaso, J. and Risse, T. 2001. *Transforming Europe: Europeanisation and Domestic Change*. Ithaca NY: Cornell University Press.

Diez, T. 2002. Last exit to paradise? The European Union, the Cyprus conflict and the problematic 'catalytic effect', in *The European Union and the Cyprus Conflict*, edited by T. Diez. Manchester: Manchester University Press, 139–62

Diez, T., Agnantopoulos, A. and Kaliber, A. 2005. Introduction in file: Turkey, Europeanisation and civil society. *South European Society & Politics*, 10(1), 1–15.

Duina, F.A. 1999. *Harmonizing Europe: Nation States within the Common Market*. New York: University of New York Press.

Duran, B. 2004. Islamist redefinitions of European and Islamic identities in Turkey, in *European Integration and Turkey*, edited by M. Uğur and N. Canefe. London: Routledge, 125–46.

Eralp, D.U. and Beriker, N. 2005. Assessing the conflict resolution potential of the EU: the Cyprus conflict and accession negotiations. *Security Dialogue*, 36(2), 175–92.

Hannay, D. 2009. Cyprus: the costs of failure. Centre for European Reform Briefing Note. [Online]. Available at: www.cer.org.uk/pdf/bn_cyprus_1sept09. pdf [accessed: 21 November 2010].

Hix, S. and Goetz, K.H. 2000. Introduction: European integration and national political systems. *West European Politics*, 23(4), 1–26.

Hürriyet Daily News. 2011. Turkish PM slams EU, threatens to freeze ties. 19 July. [Online]. Available at: www.hurriyetdailynews.com/n.php?n=turkish-pm-slams-eu-threatens-to-freeze-ties-2011-07-19 [accessed: 21 July 2011].

Ifantis, C. and Aydın, M. 2004. Introduction, in *Turkish-Greek Relations: The Security Dilemma in the Aegean*, edited by C. Ifantis and M. Aydın. London: Routledge, 1–17.

International Crisis Group. 2009. Cyprus: reunification or partition. Europe Report, No 201. [Online]. Available at: http://www.crisisgroup.org/home/ index.cfm?id=6330&l=1 [accessed: 2 August 2010].

International Crisis Group. 2012. Aphrodite's Gift: Can Cypriot Gas Power A New Dialogue?. Europe Report No. 216. [Online]. Available at: http://www. crisisgroup.org/en/regions/europe/turkey-cyprus/cyprus/216-aphrodites-gift-can-cypriot-gas-power-a-new-dialogue.aspx [accessed: 9 June 2012].

Jacquot, S. and Woll, C. 2003. Usage of European integration – Europeanisation from a sociological perspective. *European Integration online Papers (EIoP)* [Online], 7(12). Available at: http://eiop.or.at/eiop/texte/2003-012a.htm [accessed: 25 July 2010].

Kaliber, A. 2005. Securing the ground through securitized 'foreign' policy: the Cyprus case revisited. *Security Dialogue*, 36 (3), 297–315.

Kaliber, A. 2009. Re-imagining Cyprus: the rise of regionalism in Turkey's security lexicon, in *Cyprus: a Conflict at the Crossroads*, edited by T. Diez and N. Tocci. Manchester and New York: Manchester University Press, 105–23.

Keridis, D. 2001. Domestic developments and foreign policy: Greek policy towards Turkey, in *Greek-Turkish Relations in the Era of Globalisation*, edited by D. Keridis and D. Triantaphyllou. Dulles, VA: Brassey's, 2–18.

Kirişçi, K. 2007. The Kurdish question and Turkey: future challenges and prospects for a solution, *ISPI Working Paper*, No. 24. [Online]. Available at: www.ispionline.it/it/documents/wp_24_2007.pdf [accessed: 16 June 2011].

Kirişçi, K. 2009. Turkey's foreign policy in turbulent times. *Chaillot paper*, No 92. [Online]. Available at: http://www.iss.europa.eu/fr/publications/detail-page/article/turkeys-foreign-policy-in-turbulent-times/ [accessed: 1 July 2011].

Knill, C. and Lehmkuhl, D. 1999. How Europe matters. Different mechanisms of Europeanisation. *European Integration online Papers (EIoP)* [Online], 3(7). Available at: http://eiop.or.at/eiop/-texte/1999-007.htm [accessed: 21 March 2010].

Ladrech, R. 1994. Europeanisation of domestic politics and institutions: The case of France. *Journal of Common Market Studies*, 32(1), 69–88.

Ladrech, R. 2001. Europeanisation and political parties towards a framework for analysis. *Keele Political Parties Research Unit (KEPRU) Working Paper* [Online], 7. Available at: www.keele.ac.uk/depts/spire/research/KEPRU/Working_Papers/KEPRU%20Paper%207.pdf [accessed: 13 May 2011].

Mair, P. 2004. The European dimension. *Journal of European Public Policy,* 11(2), 338–9.

Malmborg, M.A. and Strath, B. 2002. Introduction: the national meanings of Europe, in *The Meaning of Europe*, edited by M.A. Malmborg and B. Strath. Oxford and New York: Berg, 1–26.

Reuters. 2011. *Turkey Says EU Ties Will Freeze If No Cyprus Solution.* 13 July. [Online]. Available at: http://www.reuters.com/article/2011/07/13/us-turkey-eu-idUSTRE76C23D20110713 [accessed: 21 July 2011].

Richmond, O. 2002. The multiple dimensions of international peacemaking, in *The European Union and the Cyprus Conflict*, edited by T. Diez. Manchester: Manchester University Press, 117–36.

Rumelili, B. 2007. Transforming conflicts on EU borders: the case of Greek-Turkish relations. *Journal of Common Market Studies*, 45(1), 105–26.

Smith, M.E. 2000. Conforming to Europe: the domestic impact of EU foreign policy cooperation. *Journal of European Public Policy*, 7(4), 613–31.

Spiegel Online. 2011. *German Conservatives Welcome Turkey's EU Threats.* 20 July. [Online]. Available at: http://www.spiegel.de/international/europe/0,1518,775490,00.html [accessed: 21 July 2011].

Tocci, N. 2005. Europeanisation in Turkey: trigger or anchor for reform? *South European Society and Politics*, 10(1), 73–83.

Tocci, N. 2007. *The Missed Opportunity to Promote Reunification in Cyprus.* Cyprus Policy Centre. [Online]. Available at: www.cypruspolicycenter.org/dosyalar/nathalie.doc [accessed: 9 June 2011].

Tocci, N. and Diez, T. 2009. Introduction, in *Cyprus: a Conflict at the Crossroads*, edited by T. Diez and N. Tocci. Manchester and New York: Manchester University Press, 1–14.

Torreblanca, J. 2001. Ideas, preferences and institutions: explaining the Europeanisation of Spanish foreign policy. *Arena Working Papers*, 26(1). [Online]. Available at: www.arena.uio.no/events/-papers/torreblanca%20europeanisation%20of%20spanish%20foreign%20policy.pdf [accessed: 9 September 2010].

Chapter 12

Europeanisation and Migration and Asylum Policies in Turkey

Catherine Macmillan

Introduction

Justice and Home Affairs (JHA) has been one of the EU's fastest growing policy areas in recent years. With the securitisation of migration and asylum in the EU, especially following the events of 11 September and the subsequent terrorist attacks, there has been increased pressure on the candidate countries to act as the 'gatekeepers' of the EU. This is particularly true in the case of countries with large borders, such as Poland or Turkey. Such reforms are wide-ranging, and are often politically and economically costly. However, Turkish adoption of the JHA *acquis* has been relatively slow when compared with that of the Central and Eastern European countries (CEECs), including Poland.

This chapter, then, uses Schimmelfenning and Sedelmeier's 'External Incentives' and 'Social Learning' models in an attempt to explain the relative lag in the Europeanisation of Turkey's migration and asylum policies. According to the first model, the candidates adopt EU rules on the basis of a 'cost-benefit' calculation, in which the promise of full membership is the most important incentive for reform. The second model argues that a candidate country adopts EU rules if it views them as appropriate in terms of collective identity, values and norms. While the two models may be compatible, however, empirical evidence suggests that the 'External Incentives' model provides a better explanation for Europeanisation in the case of the candidate countries due to the importance of conditionality in the accession process. Thus, it is suggested here that the relative weakness of EU conditionality in the Turkish case may explain its slow rate of Europeanisation in this area.

Europeanisation in the Candidate Countries: A Theoretical Basis

Europeanisation, broadly speaking, refers to the domestic consequences of the process of European integration. Thus, in Europeanisation, European-level developments are the explanatory factor while changes in the domestic system of government are the dependent variable (Olsen 2003: 343). As Radaelli points out, students of Europeanisation have searched for its effects on governance, institutionalisation or discourse. However, all three frameworks deal with domestic change, they are not mutually exclusive, and most authors consider them in combination (Radaelli 2004: 6–9).

While the term 'Europeanisation' is normally used in relation to the member states, the question of Europeanisation has also been examined in the case of the candidate countries. However, an important difference is that there is likely to be a higher rate of policy Europeanisation in the candidate countries, and it is more likely to be of a top-down nature, due to the EU's intensive use of conditionality in the accession process. In addition, EU institutions cannot rely on treaty-based sanctions in the case of the candidate countries but must use softer instruments such as conditional incentives, normative pressure or persuasion. On the other hand, there is increased monitoring of compliance in the case of the candidate countries (Sedelmeier 2006: 2).

As in the case of Europeanisation in the member states theoretical accounts based on new institutionalism have been dominant in studies of the candidate countries. These have been based primarily on rationalist institutionalist and constructivist or sociological institutionalist accounts. In the case of the candidate countries, studies contrast the use of conditionality as a strategy employed by rationalist institutionalist approaches with norm-based convergence as a result of social learning, based on sociological institutionalism (Sedelmeier 2006: 3), although empirical studies suggest that rationalist institutionalist approaches provide a more suitable explanation as conditionality is the dominant mechanism of the EU's influence (Sedelmeier 2006: 19). These two approaches, however, are not necessarily contradictory, and may be complementary (Sedelmeier 2006: 10). Schmmelfenning and Sedelmeier (2005: 13–20) have further developed the theoretical basis for the study of Europeanisation in the candidate countries by constructing models based on the rationalist institutionalist and sociological institutionalist approaches respectively. These models, termed the External Incentives model and the Social Learning model, are described below.

The External Incentives Model

The External Incentives model focuses on the effects of conditionality in the accession process, and begins from the standpoint that the adoption of EU rules will be absent if the EU does not set them up as conditions or rewards. Rule adoption on the part of the candidate countries increases with the determinacy of the rules (their clarity and binding status). Moreover, rule adoption depends on the size and speed of the rewards. Thus, the promise of enlargement should be more powerful than that of association, and rewards perceived as short term more powerful than distant ones. However, even if accession is still distant, intermediary rewards such as pre-accession support or the opening of accession negotiations can have a positive impact according to this model (Schimmelfenning and Sedelmeier 2005: 10–13)

The credibility of conditionality is an important factor according to this model. Conditionality has most impact on rule adoption if the candidates are confident that they will receive the reward if they adopt the required conditions, and they must also be convinced that the reward will be witheld if the conditions are not fulfilled. Moreover, there must be little internal EU conflict over conditionality and the EU should be able to monitor the candidate country effectively.

In addition, the compatibility of EU conditionality with that of other organisations is important. There should also be little cross conditionality, referring to a situation where other organisations offer similar benefits at lower adjustment costs. In contrast, if other international actors offer the government additional benefits for fulfilling the same conditions (parallel conditionality) or make their rewards conditional upon prior fulfillment of EU conditions (additive conditionality) the likelihood of rule adoption is increased (Schimmelfenning and Sedelmeier 2005: 13–16).

Finally, the external incentives model argues that rule adoption is determined by the size of domestic adoption costs and their distribution among domestic actors. Thus, the likelihood of rule adoption decreases with the number of veto players (including the government) incurring net adoption costs (opportunity costs, welfare, and power losses) from compliance. However, if conditionality is credible, adoption costs and veto players are likely to influence the timing of rule adoption rather than whether rules are adopted (Schimmelfenning and Sedelmeier 2005: 216).

The Social Learning Model

The social learning model is based on social constructivism. Thus, in contrast to the rationalist model, it assumes logic of appropriateness. From this perspective, then, the EU represents a European international community which is bound together by a specific collective identity and set of values and norms. According to this view, then, whether a candidate country adopts EU rules or not depends if it views those rules as appropriate in terms of collective identity, values and norms; it is not dependent on conditionality. The EU may either persuade the government of its legitimacy or it may seek to convince social groups and organisations, which then lobby the government. Therefore, rules adopted through social learning are much less contested domestically than those adopted through conditionality (Schimmelfenning and Sedelmeier 2005: 219). However, if only the relevant actors are persuaded, these actors will seek to adopt and implement EU rules but may founder when faced with opposition from unpersuaded actors (Schimmelfenning and Sedelmeier 2005: 18–19).

The legitimacy of EU rules is undermined by definition in the case of the candidate countries as non-member states do not participate in defining EU rules. However, rules are likely to be perceived as more legitimate if the EU takes into account the concerns and special needs of the applicants in question than if it simply demands their adoption without discussion. Moreover, legitimacy is likely to be improved if the EU relates its rules to higher principles and general international standards. Thus legitimacy in the case of EU accession is problematic as the candidate countries have to adopt the *acquis* in its entirety. In addition, legitimacy will tend to be damaged if there are conflicting rules from other relevant international actors, but improved if these actors back up EU rules (Schimmelfenning and Sedelmeier 2005: 18–20).

Identity is another important factor in the social learning model, which argues that rule adoption will increase the more the target government and society identifies with the EU and shares its norms and values. In addition, resonance is another factor which determines rule adoption according to the social learning model. Resonance can be defined as domestic factors that facilitate or inhibit persuasion. For instance, rule adoption is more likely if a policy area is new or if domestic rules have been delegitimised, or if domestic and EU belief in 'good policy' and rules are compatible. However, rule adoption decreases if domestic rules conflict with the EU *acquis* and if they enjoy high and consensual domestic legitimacy (Schimmelfenning and Sedelmeier 2005: 19–20).

The authors argue that, although the two approaches are not mutually exclusive and may be complementary (Sedelmeier 2006: 3), the External Incentives approach is more suitable to explain candidate country Europeanisation due to the use of conditionality in the accession process (Schimmelfenning and Sedelmeier 2005: 10–13). Thus, the hypothesis of this chapter is that, without completely discounting the importance of social learning, the external incentives model can best explain Turkey's rule adoption in the area of asylum and immigration.

Conditionality in Turkey's Accession Process: How Credible?

According to the External Incentives model, the goal of membership has to be perceived as realistic. If there is considerable doubt in a candidate country, then, that it will be accepted as a member even if it does carry out the required rule adoption, its will to carry out a sometimes arduous series of reforms will decrease. On the other hand, there must also be a fear of rejection if reforms are considered to be inadequate, as overconfidence in eventual acceptance can also undermine the pace of reform.

While Turkey was excluded as a candidate for EU membership in the Luxembourg council of 1997, its candidacy was accepted two years later at the Helsinki council of December 1999. Notably, the Helsinki Council Decision stated that 'Turkey is a candidate state destined to join the Union on the basis of the same criteria as applied to the other candidate states' (Duyulmuş 2008: 17). After an energetic period of reform under the first AKP government, the decision was taken at the December 2004 Brussels Council to open accession negotiations with Turkey the following year.

The Negotiation Framework adopted by the European Council in October 2005 reflects these concerns, emphasising the 'open-ended' nature of the negotiations. The Negotiation Framework states that 'while having full regard to all Copenhagen criteria, including the absorption capacity of the Union, if Turkey is not in a position to assume in full all the obligations of membership it must be ensured that Turkey is fully anchored in the European structures through the strongest possible bond' (European Council 2005: 11). Thus, the possibility of alternative outcomes, such as a privileged partnership is suggested in the document, and the EU's absorption capacity is emphasised (Duyulmuş 2008: 28). This differs not only from the Negotiation Frameworks of the countries which acceded to the EU in 2004 and 2007, but also from that of Croatia, which was issued on the same date as Turkey's (Aydın 2006: 6).

Moreover, the suspension of negotiations on eight chapters in 2006 over Turkey's refusal to open its harbours and airports to Cypriot shipping, and the French government's announcement in December 2007 that it opposed the opening of five specific chapters as they were expressly linked to full membership has further weakened Turkey's confidence that it will be accepted as a full member of the EU even if all conditions are fulfilled. Thus, according to the External Incentives model, it is expected that, costs being equal, the EU's influence on Turkey will be reduced during the negotiations. This is in contrast to the CEECs' experience, where EU influence was boosted as they felt more secure that they would be accepted as full member states on condition that they completed the required reforms. EU-imposed conditionality is therefore unlikely to have so much salience in Turkey until it becomes more secure about, and supportive of, eventual full membership.

This can perhaps account for the dramatic fall in domestic support for Turkish EU accession in Turkey. Public support for EU accession fell from around 70 per cent to below 30 per cent between 2005 and 2008 (Kirişçi 2008: 19). This, therefore, translates into a reduction of political will to carry out reforms. Thus, it is argued here that the credibility of conditionality has an effect not only on the external incentives model but also on the social learning model, in that it can affect 'we feeling' or identification with the EU.

Clarity of Conditionality and Accession Costs in the area of JHA: A General Overview

The JHA *acquis* has posed considerable difficulties for the CEE candidate countries in the late 1990s and early 2000s as well as for Turkey. Firstly, this has been one of the fastest-developing policy areas in the EU. From a largely intergovernmental policy following the Maastricht Treaty, supranationalisation in this area has progressively increased since the Amsterdam Treaty. Thus, JHA is, in effect, a *moving target* for the candidate countries as the *acquis* that they are expected to adopt is itself constantly developing. However, despite this growth and development, the basis of the JHA *acquis* has been relatively clear since the Amsterdam Treaty, and particularly after the publication of the Schengen *acquis* in 1999, before which it was not well defined (Grabbe 2006: 115). It has been summarised as follows:

- The adoption of entry control systems, including professionalisation and demilitarisation of border guards, technological improvement and collaboration with border control corps in neighbouring countries
- The 'Europeanisation' of visa policies, including adoption of the Schengen negative and positive visa lists, the abolition of the granting of visas at border posts and organisational and technological improvement
- The passing of rigorous immigration legislation including the adoption of EU standards of norms and practices on refusal of entry and expulsion, the stipulation of a network of readmission agreements with third countries of origin and transit and improvement of norms and practices on legal immigration (Pastore 2004: 130).

There has generally been a lack of goodness of fit between both the CEECs' and the Turkish border control systems on the one hand and the developing EU *acquis* on the other at the beginning of the accession process. In the case of CEE, while border controls existed during Communist times, these were geared towards exit rather than entry control, and were largely dismantled after the collapse of Communism. In the Turkish case, entry control was also relaxed in comparison with the EU system as part of Turgut Özal's 1980s policies of *rapprochement* with Turkey's neighbours through open borders, while Turkey's asylum system was rather more restrictive than that of the EU. Thus, from the social learning point of view, it can be argued that resonance was lower in Turkey, which had functioning policies in these areas, than in the transition countries of CEE. From an external incentives viewpoint, then, adoption of the *acquis* contained significant costs for both Turkey and the CEECs. The adoption of the Schengen visa system, in particular, is costly for the candidates both in economic terms due to loss of trade and tourism and the cost of setting up a consular infrastructure and in political terms, as it may damage relations with neighbouring countries.

Moreover, the emphasis that the EU has put on the candidate countries' adoption of this part of the *acquis* has been great, resulting from political pressure for immigration control in Western Europe. Both the CEECs, especially Poland, which also has large borders and is an important transit country (Şemşit 2008: 368), and Turkey have been viewed, largely without reason, as potential hotbeds for irregular migrants and asylum seekers aiming to get to the EU, both from the applicant states themselves and as a consequence of transit migration (Pastore 2003: 105). Thus the EU has tended to treat these countries as the EU's 'gatekeepers' (Şemşit 2008: 365, Guiraudon 2004: 160–80), and put great pressure on them to strengthen security at their borders: it is perhaps, then, no coincidence that these accession rounds and the development of JHA have gone in tandem.

Although JHA was one of the most difficult and contentious issues between the EU and the candidate countries, the negotiations on this topic went surprisingly smoothly with the CEECs (Pastore 2004: 131), with Hungary being the first candidate country to close the chapter in November 2001, followed by Cyprus, Slovenia and the Czech Republic a month later. By July 2002, when Poland closed negotiations on JHA, they had been completed by all candidate countries with the exception of Romania, Bulgaria and Turkey, which had not yet begun negotiations (Occhipinti 2004: 197).

In the case of Turkey, in contrast, while the European Commission is preparing its final report on the screening process for Chapter 24 (the JHA chapter), this chapter is not due to be opened in the near future due to the difficulties inherent in this policy area (Kirişçi 2008: 17–18). The following section of this chapter, then, aims to explore the extent and limitations of Europeanisation and of other pressures, both external and domestic, in Turkey's asylum and immigration policies. The first section examines the EU conditions and Turkey's progress in fulfilling them, while the second examines four important stumbling blocks between Turkey and the EU in this area.

Turkey's Adoption of the *Acquis* in the area of Migration and Asylum

EU pressures have certainly played an important part in moving the issue of irregular migration up the domestic agenda in Turkey. Broadly speaking, the EU has demanded that Turkey, as part of its accession process, securitises migration within its borders. Turkey has thus been viewed increasingly as the guardian of the 'South-Eastern gate' of Europe, and is expected to protect it from waves of irregular migration (Kirişçi 2008: 131). However, the EU has not been the only external source of pressure on Turkey to clamp down on irregular migration, although it is almost certainly the major one. Other pressures include individual member states. Notably, in 2002, the British and Spanish leaders Tony Blair and Jose Maria Aznar even went as far as to threaten Turkey with sanctions if they did not co-operate with the EU in this area (Apap, Carrera and Kirişçi 2004: 17). In addition, Italy has repeatedly accused Turkey of violating its international obligations by not controlling its borders and coasts regularly (Özcan 2005: 123).

With the commencement of full-membership negotiations between Turkey and the EU migration has been a key item on the agenda between the EU and Turkey, and the issue of transit migration has been especially emphasised in the Commission's reports on Turkey. The ability of Turkey's state institutions and legal framework to manage migration and asylum flows arriving in the country has been an important area of debate, as have possible areas of co-operation, including external border security, human smuggling and human trafficking (İçduygu 2008: 4).

According to the Accession Partnership, Turkey is expected to implement a number of measures intended to curb transit migration to the EU, including reinforcement of border management with a view to eventually fully implementing the Schengen Convention. This includes increasing Turkey's capacity to fight organised crime, including people trafficking (Mannaert 2003: 11), and the signing of readmission agreements with both neighbouring countries and the EU itself (Apap, Carrera and Kirişçi 2004: 17), the consequences of which will be discussed in more detail below. Moreover, as has been mentioned above, the alignment of

Turkey's visa system with that of Schengen is also intended to reduce transit migration through Turkey (Mannaert 2003: 11).

In consequence, therefore, of changes resulting from Turkey's 2001 National Programme for the adoption of the *acquis* (NP) the Turkish government has been increasingly successful in recent years in controlling illegal transit migration and people smuggling. This results from a combination of factors including an increase in the number of border control staff and sea patrols, tougher laws for people smugglers, as well as the signing of readmission agreements with several countries, and the progressive application of the Schengen visa list (Mannaert 2003: 11).

This progress can also be partly explained by Turkey's participation in the EU's 'twinning' projects in the area of border control and migration management (Gresh 2005: 17–20). The twinning projects, on asylum and immigration and asylum and combatting human trafficking, have involved Austria, Denmark, Germany and the United Kingdom, and have helped to build up Turkey's institutional capacity and develop EU-*acquis* oriented training programmes for officials working in this area. Evidence suggests that these twinning projects have had a 'socialising' effect on bureaucrats and officials (Kirişçi 2007: 26). Although the resulting Action Plan was adopted in March 2005, progress in its implementation has been slow mainly due to the issue of negotiating and signing an EU/Turkey readmission agreement, which is explored in further detail below (Kirişçi 2007: 26).

In the area of asylum, Turkey's adherence to the geographical limitation of the 1951 UN Refugee Convention is also a serious stumbling block. According to this, Turkey only recognises Europeans as refugees, while those coming from outside Europe are classified as asylum seekers. As discussed below, Turkey is unwilling to lift the geographical limitation until it is more confident of its eventual full membership of the EU (Kaya 2009: 23). However, in practice, at least until the early 1990s, Turkey showed flexibility in accepting refugees from other regions on a temporary basis. Despite this, as a result of various refugee crises from the late 1980s to the early 1990s, Turkey introduced the relatively strict 1994 Asylum Regulation, according to which asylum seekers originally had to register with the police within five days on pain of deportation (Mannaert 2003: 9).

Moreover, the Regulation effectively put status determination entirely into the hands of the Ministry of the Interior, reducing the role of the United Nations High Commission for Refugees to that of settling abroad those asylum seekers whose status had been accepted in Turkey. During its first few years of implementation, Turkey was heavily criticised by Western governments and human rights groups, which resulted in it extending the registration time and in closer co-operation with the High Commission on status determination. Although co-ordination between these two mechanisms has improved considerably, according to the EU it needs to be improved still further in order to avoid ambiguity (Mannaert 2003: 21).

Other reforms required by the EU include the enactment of an asylum law by Parliament as current legislation, based on the 1994 Regulation and the 2006 circular, lacks a statutory base. Although no draft bill has yet been submitted to Parliament, the deadline for completion has been brought forward in the NP from

2012 to 2011 (Kaya 2009: 10). In addition, a professional single authority must be established, as well as an independent evaluation board for appeals. A building for this authority is planned to be completed by 2010, while a training academy for its staff is to be set up by 2011. By contrast, there is no deadline for setting up the board of appeals which, according to the NP, is to be evaluated within the perspective of full membership (Kaya 2009: 10).

Stumbling Blocks in Turkey's Adoption of the Migration and Asylum *Acquis*

Border Control

Turkey, due to its geographical position, is an important country of transit migration. The difficulty of controlling such migration is compounded by the length and nature of Turkey's borders. According to a 2000 report published by the Turkish Security Department Directorate on Smuggling and Organised Crime, for instance, there are 13 major points of entry between Turkey's borders with Georgia, Armenia, Iran, Iraq, and Syria and ten on the Aegean and Mediterranean Sea coasts (Özcan 2005: 126). Thus, due to the Turkish government's difficulty in controlling these borders and the relative ease of entering the country illegally, Turkey does, to a certain extent, welcome co-operation with the EU on this issue (Gresh 2005: 8). Indeed, it has made some progress in modernising its border crossing points in recent years (European Commission 2009: 75).

At present, the sea borders are controlled by the coastal guard, while the land borders are controlled by the army and gendamerie. One of the main requirements of the JHA *acquis* which Turkey is expected to implement is the replacement of the current border-control system by an integrated civilian, professional border control unit which would be situated within the Ministry of the Interior. There is, then, considerable institutional misfit between Turkey and the EU *acquis* in this area.

After initial scepticism on the part of Turkish officials, this proposal is largely welcomed by Turkey, which sees it as contributing to national security, although Turkey prefers to implement this gradually due to the huge effort and financial cost that such an undertaking would incur. This has been supported by a twinning project, completed in 2006, which resulted in an Action Plan adopted by the Turkish government. However, the Action Plan has been criticised for a lack of detail concerning the form and timeline of its establishment (Apap, Carrera and Kirişçi 2004: 17–20).

This lack of progress can be explained by concern on the Turkish side over instituting a 'civilian' border control unit on the grounds that Turkey's eastern borders are vulnerable to infiltration by terrorist groups, and due to the unrest and violence in Iraq. Moreover, Turkey has argued for substantial financial support from the EU as the EU will eventually benefit from these measures, while the EU provides only limited financial aid as it expects Turkey to meet the costs as part of its accession process (Kirişçi 2007: 21–2). Thus, although there is some domestic support for reform in this area, the large costs, both political and financial, coupled with the lack of a secure promise of full membership of the EU have resulted in 'stalling' on the part of Turkey, which has postponed the implementation of this area of the *acquis* until 2014, when presumably its perspective of accession to the EU will become clearer.

Readmission Agreements

The conclusion of readmission agreements, both with third countries and with the EU, is proving problematic in itself for Turkey. Firstly, third countries may have little incentive to sign readmission agreements with a country like Turkey – they have potentially little to gain and much to lose from such a situation. In addition, taking the example of the Greek/Turkish readmission agreement, these may be open to abuse. In this case, Greece has sometimes been tempted, for instance, to push boats of migrants back into Turkish waters or release them, allowing them to escape into Turkey (Tokuzlu 2005: 342–3). For these reasons, then, progress in concluding bilateral readmission agreements has been slow, and so far have been concluded only with Greece, Kyrgyzstan, Romania, Syria and Ukraine (Kaya 2009: 8) although negotiations are underway with several other countries (European Commission 2009: 75).

The requirement for Turkey to sign a readmission agreement with the EU poses problems of its own. As has been pointed out, due to Turkey's geographical position, it is a destination for many asylum-seekers and irregular migrants, many of whom intend to get to the EU. The implementation of such an agreement, then, in the absence of adequate arrangements for burden-sharing, may also contribute to Turkey's effectively becoming a buffer-zone for unwanted migrants and asylum seekers otherwise destined for the EU. This would not only put undue strain on Turkey's financial resources but would also prevent some genuine asylum seekers from making claims in the EU (Frantz 2003: 14–15).

Moreover, the fact that Turkey is the only candidate country which has been asked to conclude a readmission agreement with the EU itself during its accession process has had a negative effect on trust in the EU and the accession process among Turkish officials. It it has cast doubt on the EU's motivation to eventually accept Turkey as a full member, which has resulted in the Turkish military in particular being against the signature of a readmission agreement with the EU (Kruse). For these reasons, negotiations on the Turkey-EU readmission agreement were blocked in 2006, although Turkey has recently agreed to reopen them (European Commission 2009: 77).

Visa Policy

One of the most important areas of the JHA *acquis* that the candidate countries are required to adopt is the Schengen visa system and negative visa lists. As in the case of the CEECs, this involves a significant degree of upheaval on the part of Turkey as there is considerable misfit between the Turkish and Schengen visa systems. Prior to Turkey's EU candidacy the Turkish visa system was generally liberal in nature. This was part and parcel of President Turgut Özal's attempts to improve relations with neighbouring countries, both in the Black Sea area and the Middle East, and those countries which share a linguistic and cultural heritage with Turkey, mostly located in Central Asia and the Caucasus (Derviş et al. 2004: 51).

As a result, Turkey has a three-tier visa policy. Nationals of the above groups of countries have usually been able to enter Turkey visa free for periods of up to three months, while those of the majority of other states simply needed to acquire a moderately priced 'sticker' visa at the airport. Relatively few countries' nationals needed to apply for a visa through the Turkish Consulate before entering the country (Derviş et al. 2004: 51).

While the sticker visa system has had advantages, particularly regarding Turkey's foreign policy, it has been argued that the resulting ease of entering Turkey for the nationals of many countries has contributed to a rise in illegal immigration, particularly by nationals of ex-Soviet republics or other ex-Communist neighbouring countries (Apap, Carrera and Kirişçi 2004: 27–8). Throughout the 1990s, particularly as a consequence of the arrival in Turkey of a considerable number of sex workers principally from the ex-Soviet Union and other parts of Eastern Europe who were often victims of people trafficking, both the Turkish authorities and the general public began to press for a tightening of the visa regime. This led, in some cases, to an increase in the price of a visa to 20 dollars and the requirement to show a certain amount of hard currency on entering the country (Kirişçi 2003: 131).

Therefore, pressure for change to the Turkish visa system has come from inside Turkey itself as well as from the EU. Thus, there are some advantages in applying the Schengen negative visa regime from Turkey's point of view. It should allow Turkey to increase its control of irregular migration, as many migrants enter Turkey legally and then become 'overstayers'. For the same reasons, it should also help Turkey to clamp down more successfully on human trafficking (Apap, Carrera and Kirişçi 2004: 25).

However, the adoption of the Schengen visa *acquis* is also likely to imply some negative externalities for Turkey and its neighbours. Firstly, evidence from the CEECs accession process indicates that trade with neighbouring countries is likely to be disrupted as a result, with negative consequences for both sides' economies. Tourism in particular could suffer, especially if visas issued by a consulate are imposed on Russian citizens, for instance, as Turkey has been a prime destination for wealthy Russians. They may be put off coming to Turkey if a lengthy process, possibly including a long trip, was necessary in order to obtain a visa. In addition, judging from the experience in CEE, the imposition of Schengen-type visas on citizens of neighbouring countries may also be detrimental to bilateral political relations. While Turgut Özal first allowed visa-free entry for visitors from neighbouring countries in order to improve Turkey's bilateral relations with its neighbours, then, the imposition of the Schengen visa regime is likely to achieve the opposite effect (Apap, Carrera and Kirişçi 2004: 27–8).

Thus, adoption of the *acquis* has been slow in this area. Indeed, after imposing visa restrictions on six Gulf states in 2002 and 13 geographically distant countries in 2003 (Tokuzlu 2005: 345), Turkey has considerably slowed its adoption of the Schengen negative visa list despite the fact that it was supposed to be implemented by 2005 according to the NP. Indeed, Turkey has recently removed the visa requirement for several countries from the Schengen 'blacklist', indicating a reversal of Europeanisation in this area. Turkey has, however, been more active in implementing the less controversial positive visa list, having concluded visa exemption agreements with several Latin American countries, the Czech Republic and Andorra in 2006 (Kirişçi 2007: 37–8).

Moreover, the Commisson's proposal of a visa-facilitation programme for Turkey in exchange for signing a readmission agreement may also have negative consequences for Turkish-EU relations as these agreements have normally been offered to third countries, such as Russia, Ukraine and the western Balkan countries. Such a proposal, therefore, has raised doubts in Turkey about whether the EU really views Turkey as an eventual member and partner or as just another third country (Kirişçi 2008: 50).

Thus, although pressure for reform in this area has, to a certain extent, come from domestic sources as well as EU conditionality, reform is highly costly. This is not balanced by strong conditionality credibility; indeed the fact that Turkey is still itself on the Schengen 'blacklist' and the proposal of a visa facilitation programme tend to further undermine Turkish faith in eventual full membership.

The Geographical Limitation

In addition to the conclusion of readmission agreements with the EU and third countries perhaps the most controversial change that Turkey is required to make to its asylum policy is to lift the geographical limitation included in the UN Agreement on Refugees. While, according to the Agreement, Turkey is only responsible for granting full refugee status to those fleeing from events in Europe, the EU expects Turkey to extend this to refugees originating from other parts of the world (Derviş et al. 2004: 50). This is, however, not unique to Turkey: other candidate countries such as Hungary, have been required to do the same during the accession process (Apap, Carrera and Kirişçi 2004: 25).

In Turkey officials are reluctant to implement the readmission agreement with the EU and lift the geographical limitation on the UN Agreement for Refugees for fear that the country may become a buffer-zone for irregular migrants and unwanted asylum-seekers who would otherwise be destined for the EU. If Turkey adopts these areas of the *acquis*, it will automatically become a safe third country and, as it will also frequently be a first country of entry, will have to deal with potentially large numbers of asylum seekers otherwise destined for the EU (Tokuzlu 2006: 368). This would be exacerbated especially in the case of a mass influx of refugees, a situation which Turkey has experienced twice in the recent past (Kaya 2009: 16).

Thus, burden sharing is at the top of the agenda in meetings between EU and Turkish officials regarding asylum reform, and is also mentioned in the NP (Kaya 2009: 15), which states that burden sharing 'should both include the financial burden and refugees/asylum seekers according to parameters such as [the] national income and population density of countries (Government of Turkey 2008: 49). Thus, Turkey is ready to lift this limitation if the EU provides financial support and accepts a certain number of refugees who have applied for asylum in Turkey. In this context, then, according to the NP, a proposal for lifting the geographical limitation may be presented to Parliament in 2012 in line with the completion of Turkey's negotiations for accession (Kaya 2009: 15–16).

Conclusions

In conclusion, Europeanisation has been slower in this area in Turkey when compared to the CEECs. This can be largely explained by the fact that, unlike those of the CEECs, Turkey's accession negotiations are 'open-ended'. Thus, conditionality is less credible as Turkey has no firm promise that it will eventually become a full member and is therefore less willing to carry out costly reforms, especially those that it perceives as making it into a 'buffer zone' for unwanted migrants and asylum seekers, until it has a firmer promise that it will eventually accede to the EU if reforms are completed. The empirical evidence, then, largely bears out the external incentives hypothesis in this case, with some reservations.

Despite several important setbacks, Turkey has made considerable progress in aligning its immigration and asylum policies with those of the EU. In line with EU demands, it has 'toughened' its migration policies and begun to 'soften' its asylum policies. In these cases, EU pressures have combined with other pressures, including those from the USA, individual European states, pressure from NGOs and domestic public opinion. It appears that the threat of sanctions by the USA in the area of human trafficking and from individual EU states in the area of general migration control have been particularly powerful when combined with EU conditionality.

Moreover, socialisation appears to have played an important role, most notably through the twinning projects. However, in the absence of sufficiently credible conditionality, this is insufficient to allow rule adoption in the more politically or economically costly areas, identified as the 'stumbling blocks' of readmission agreements, visa policy, border control and the geographical limitation. In line with the external incentives hypothesis, then, more credible conditionality is needed if the EU is serious about Turkey carrying out these reforms.

References

Apap, J., Carrera, S. and Kirişçi K. 2004. Turkey in the area of freedom, security and justice. *CEPS EU-Turkey Working Paper* [Online], 3. Available at: http://www. ceps.be [Accessed 14 February 2005].

Aydın, S. 2006. *Seeking Kant in the EU's relations with Turkey*. [Online]. Available at: http://www.tesev.org.tr/UD_OBJS/PDF/DPT/AB/seeking%20kant_ SON_07.12.06.pdf [Accessed 20 July 2010].

Derviş, K., Gros, D., Emerson, M. and S. Ülgen. 2004. *Çağdaş Türkiye'nin Avrupa Dönüşümü* (European Transformation of Contemporary Turkey). Istanbul: Doğan Kitap.

Duyulmuş, C.U. 2008. *Europeanisation of Minority Rights in Turkey*. Paper to the 7th Biennial Conference of the European Community Studies Association-Canada (ECSA-C): The Maturing European Union, Edmonton, Alberta, 25–27 September 2008.

European Commission. 2009. *Regular Report on Turkey's Progress Towards Accession*. [Online]. Available at: http://ec.europa.eu/enlargement/pdf/key_ documents/2009/tr_rapport_2009_en.pdf [accessed 29 November 2009].

European Council. 2005. *Negotiating Framework – Conclusions of Luxembourg Summit*. [Online]. Available at: http://ec.europa.eu/enlargement/pdf/st20002_05_ tr_framedoc_en.pdf [accessed: 7 May 2010]

Frantz, E. 2003. *Report on the Situation of Refugees in Turkey: Findings of a Five-Week Exploratory Study*. [Online]. Available at: academia.edu/ElizabethFrantz/ Papers/624205/Report_on_the_-Situation_of_Refugees_in_Turkey_Findings_ of_a_Five-week_Exploratory_Study_December_2002_-January_2003 [accessed: 15 July 2007].

Government of Turkey. 2008. *National Action Plan for the Adoption of the EU Acquis in the Field of Asylum and Immigration*. [Online]. Available at: http:// www.ir.metu.edu.tr/iom/pdf/tr3.pdf [accessed: 27 May 2010].

Grabbe, H. 2006. *The EU's Transformative Power: Europeanisation through Conditionality in Central and Eastern Europe*. London: Palgrave Macmillan.

Gresh, G. 2005. Acquiescing to the *acquis*: combating irregular migration in Turkey. *Insight Turkey*, 7(2), 8–27.

Guiraudon, V. 2004. Immigration and asylum: A high politics area, in *Developments in the European Union 2*, edited by M.G. Cowles and D. Dinan. Hampshire: Palgrave Macmillan, 160–80.

İçduygu, A. 2008. Rethinking irregular migration in Turkey: some demo-economic reflections, *CARIM Analytic and Synthetic Notes*, 2008/72.

Kaya, İ. 2009. Reform in Turkish asylum law: adopting the EU *acquis*? *CARIM Research Reports*. 2009/16.

Kirişçi, K. 2003. *Justice and Home Affairs Issues in Turkish-EU Relations*. Istanbul: Tesev.

Kirişçi, K. 2007. Border management and EU-Turkish relations: convergence or deadlock? *CARIM Analytic and Synthetic Notes*. 2007/03.

Kirişçi, K. 2008. Managing irregular migration in Turkey: A political-bureaucratic perspective. *CARIM Analytic and Synthetic Notes*. 2008/61.

Kruse, I. 2006. *The EU's Policy on Readmission of Illegal Migrants*. Working Paper Series Max Planck Institute for the Study of Societies. [Online]. Available at: http://socsci2.ucsd.edu/~aronatas/-scrretreat/Kruse.Imke.pdf [accessed 27 June 2007].

Mannaert, C. 2003. Irregular migration and asylum in Turkey. *New Issues in Refugee Research Working Paper*, No. 89. Available at: http://www.unhcr.org/research/RESEARCH/3ebf5c054.pdf [accessed: 5 March 2005].

Occhipinti, J. 2004. Police and judicial co-operation, in *Developments in the European Union 2*, edited by M.G. Cowles and D. Dinan. Hampshire: Palgrave Macmillan, 181–99.

Olsen, J. 2003. Europeanisation, in *European Union Politics*, edited by M. Cini. Oxford: Oxford University Press, 333–48.

Özcan, M. 2005. Turkey's possible influences on the internal security of the European Union: the issue of illegal migration, in *European Union with Turkey: the Possible Impact of Turkey's Membership on the European Union*, edited by S. Laçiner, M. Özcan and İ. Bal. Ankara: International Strategic Research Organisation.

Pastore, F. 2003. Aneas's route: Euro-Mediterranean relations and international migration, in *Migration and the Externalities of European Integration*, edited by S. Lavenex and E. Uçarer. Maryland: Lexington, 105–24.

Pastore, F. 2004. Visas, borders, immigration: formation, structure, and current evolution of the EU entry control system, in *Europe's Area of Freedom, Security and Justice*, edited by N. Walker. Oxford: Oxford University Press, 89–142.

Radaelli, C. 2004. Europeanisation: solution or problem? *European Integration Online Papers (EIoP)* [Online], 8(16). Available at: http://eiop.or.at/eiop/texte/2004-016a.htm [accessed: 20 February 2009].

Schimmelfenning, F. and Sedelmeier, U. 2005 (eds). *The Europeanisation of Central and Eastern Europe*. New York: Cornell University Press.

Sedelmeier, U. 2006. Europeanisation in new member and candidate countries. *Living Reviews in European Governance* [Online]. Available at: http://www.livingreviews.org/lreg-2006-3 [accessed: 18 June 2009].

Şemşit, S. 2008. Transformation of migration policies in Poland and Turkey in the EU accession process: Europeanized and/or securitized? *CEU Political Science Journal*, 04/2008.

Tokuzlu, L. 2005. Turkey: the legal dimension of migration. *Mediterranean Migration 2005 Report*, edited by P. Fargues. Robert Schuman Centre. [Online]. Available at: http://cadmus.eui.eu/bitstream/-handle/1814/3294/AR2005CARIM.pdf?sequence=1 [accessed: 20 April 2010].

Tokuzlu, L. 2006. *Non-refoulement Principle in a Changing European Legal Environment with Particular Emphasis on Turkey, a Candidate Country at the External Borders of the EU*. Unpublished PhD Thesis. Istanbul: Marmara University.

Conclusion

Çiğdem Nas and Yonca Özer

Europeanisation is linked with the evolution and deepening of the European integration process and the formation of EU institutions and decision-making structures. While a great portion of public policies are being formulated and legislated at the EU level, EU institutions and policy-making functions increasingly permeate domestic settings. The boundaries between sub-national, national, and supranational levels are becoming more permeable and blurred. While this process takes place, it may be possible to discern both a top-down effect emanating from the EU level to the national level and a bottom-up effect where member states may upload their norms, values, policies to the EU system. At the same time, transnational relations may also be considered as part of the process of Europeanisation whereby not only goods, capital, and people but also ideas, norms, methods, institutions may make a horizontal impact between member states aided by the coordination of the EU.

As argued in Chapter 1, with the recent enlargement process of the EU towards Central and Eastern European countries not only member states but also candidate and associated states are undergoing a Europeanisation process with the growing importance and international presence of the EU. The EU was able to influence the political processes, democratic mechanisms, policy-making structures and actors' preferences in such states by way of a policy of political conditionality and the implementation of a detailed and phased pre-accession strategy. The tying of the goal of EU membership – or in the case of associated countries the conclusion of a preferential trade or a similar agreement – to the completion of certain criteria and the recognition of the EU as a model of reform created the 'transformative impact' of the EU. The EU aided this process by acting as both the 'mentor' and the 'critic', facilitating the reform process by providing financial, administrative and moral support and by vocally criticising the conditions in a country that is contravening the EU template.

The case of Turkey constitutes an interesting example in studying the impact of Europeanisation on candidate countries. This case differs from the case of some Central and Eastern European states whose membership was supported not only on functional grounds but also on the grounds of cultural and ethical considerations. Turkey is the 'rebuffed candidate' whose European credentials were put to question after the decision to open accession negotiations was taken. While the EU submitted a road map to Turkey by way of the progress reports, accession partnership documents and negotiation framework document, leaders of two member states told Turkey that the end of this process may not be membership after all but some other type of relationship. This situation would not nullify the Europeanisation effect on Turkey. However, the weakening of the conditionality mechanism could retard the Europeanisation process.

It would also be misleading to assume that Turkey is a totally unique case. Similar trajectories were experienced during the accession of Britain, Spain and Poland to the EU. While Charles de Gaulle unilaterally challenged the UK's suitability for EC membership, Spain's accession process was also wrought with difficulties due allegedly to Spain's eligibility for membership and ability to implement the EU *acquis*. The accession of Poland on the other hand was problematised in several member states by referring to the threats to jobs that could emanate from free movement of Poles inside the EU. The case of Turkey may be quite similar. Yet, it is also quite specific in the sense that public opinion surveys tell us that only 31 per cent of the total EU population support Turkey's membership to the EU.

While Turkey is seen as somewhat of a controversial candidate to join the EU, it has been undergoing a Europeanisation process at least since the mid-1990's when the last phase of the association was reached and the customs union decision of the Association Council entered into force. The law of the economy started to Europeanise, followed by the constitution and laws governing the political system, rights and freedoms. In the meantime, EU candidacy also acted as a stimulus for change and realignment between different political forces in Turkey. Those groups that wanted change and reform legitimated their values and norms on the basis of the EU criteria. While desire for better governance and more democracy was a generally held concern in Turkey at least since the 1980 coup and due to the limitations of the 1982 constitution, the pace of reform accelerated after the 1999 Helsinki European Council declaring Turkey to be a candidate country. In line with the Westernisation tradition that influenced the reform process during the last centuries of the Ottoman Empire, constitutional amendments and harmonisation packages were passed one after another between 2001 and 2004 with the aim of fulfilling the Copenhagen criteria so that the European Council would set a date for the start of accession negotiations with Turkey. It was really hard to resist this process of alignment to the EU, since the carrot of EU membership was a very strong incentive and leverage to justify the legislative reform.

At this juncture, it was also of critical importance that the Justice and Development Party that came to power in 2002 in a landslide electoral victory adopted the goal of EU membership in its programme. Coming from Islamic roots, the party's predecessors were against EU membership. The AKP on the other hand was a modern version of the Islamic current and successfully mixed a conservative world view with a neoliberal approach to public policy and a pragmatic and populist approach to politics in general. The AKP's message to the new Turkish middle class and lower classes was that there was nothing wrong with being a pious Muslim and it does not necessarily bar you from enjoying the fruits of the consumer society. You can wear your headscarf or go to Friday prayer and at the same time have a prestigious place in society. You can be whatever you like – a politician, businessman, university teacher, judge etc. Thus the AKP came to power both as a source of change and reorientation of the political, judicial and administrative system in Turkey but also had a role to play in the global sense as a new model of a moderate Islam that could be a source of inspiration for Muslim-majority States.

The AKP's grasp of the value of the EU clearly showed the rupture with former Islamist parties and it was used by the AKP cadres to relieve pressures that could prevent the party from establishing its hegemony in the system. This would be the military and civil bureaucracy that viewed the Islamic roots of the party as a source of danger for the Republican regime. The EU card also meant that influential liberal intellectuals gave support to the AKP legitimising further the power of the AKP and making it more difficult for its opponents to question the legitimacy of the Party.

Throughout this process, Europeanisation can be depicted in different domains and levels, i.e. at the level of the state, political parties and society, in norms, values, legislation, policy-making, bureaucracy and related actors. This book was an attempt to put under speculation the different issue areas and sites of Europeanisation in Turkey. While Europeanisation is an ongoing process despite the slowing down of the accession negotiations, its impact may be varied depending on the issue area.

Regarding Europeanisation of identity, Chapter 2 states that the process has been going on since at least the Helsinki European Council which declared Turkey as a candidate country. The adoption of the goal of EU integration as a permanent policy preference even during times of military rule or interim regimes and the all-party support to EU reforms after 1999 shaped Turkey's general identification with the European model, instigating a slow but steady social learning process in the political system. Even as the EU enlargement process loses credibility in the eyes of the Turkish elite and public, the norms and values symbolised and preached by the EU continue to influence the expected normative understanding, value judgements and mindset of political and societal actors. Thus a Europeanisation of identity is not contrary to a 'regionalisation' of Turkish identity since Turkey's value as a model country in the Middle East is related to its Europeanisation.

The acceleration in Turkey's democratisation after 1999, as Chapter 3 concludes, can be explained within the context of Turkey's Europeanisation process through a credible and strong conditionality which combined with the favourable domestic conditions that led to a significantly low number of veto players with significant net costs of compliance. By the same token, after the opening of accession negotiations during which this political pressure has weakened and membership perspective has lost its certainty and credibility, along with the high number of veto players with significant net costs of compliance, Turkey's Europeanisation through political conditionality has decelerated. The deceleration of Turkey's accelerated democratisation has taken place not only in terms of upgrading existing rules and legislation in line with the EU's norms but also regarding implementation of the adopted norms. Turkey has been suffering implementation problems regarding the EU's democratic rules since it adopted those rules under the influence of membership incentive rather than social learning. Formal rule adoption motivated by membership incentive has caused domestic resistance and poor implementation in the absence of effective conditionality. The EU's democratic rules have not been able to be internalised through the EU's persuasion or socialisation strategies.

In case of constitutional Europeanisation in Turkey, Chapter 4 states that Europeanisation is generally referred for justification of political agendas which do not fully comply with values of constitutionalism or which bundle European friendly items with those representing the priorities, passions and ideologies of ruling majorities although specific amendment packages may be regarded as serving the aims of constitutional Europeanisation. The chapter concludes that Europeanisation regarding real sense constitutionalism is not sufficient in the absence of sincere motivation for constitutionalism on the part of the government and in the absence of proper replacement of eliminated provisions with real liberal-democratic values and instruments of constitutionalism in spite of the fact that even the most contentious constitutional amendments eliminated anti-democratic or disputed provisions and, therefore, provided a degree of improvement. The chapter accordingly reaches the conclusion that 'failure of deliberate and planned action of real sense constitutionalism is the main factor slowing down the democratic consolidation as well as Europeanisation in Turkey'.

Regarding Europeanisation of Turkish civil society, Chapter 5 states that several linkages and networks, which have been established since 1999 between civil society actors in Turkey and the EU, have promoted a socialisation process for civil society organisations. However, the level of cooperation among CSOs in Turkey is still low although the EU has transformed the activities of civil society through engagement of its institutions and programmes with civil society organisations. The EU has exercised its transformative power on Turkish civil society particularly in legal terms through the conditionality mechanism. But, there are still many problems in the implementation of the law. Overall, Chapter 5 concludes that the current impact of civil society in Turkey is still not as much as the impact of civil society in EU member states.

Regarding the area of minority protection, Chapter 6 finds that Europeanisation is significant in both the daily life of the citizens of Turkey and in legal and behavioural adoption between 2002 and 2004, which has been pursued since 2008. The implementation of the rules adopted in previous years has intensified since 2008 although the legal reforms recently launched by the government are unsatisfactory. The chapter explains this relatively instable process between 2002 and 2010 with its ups and downs through sequential impact of EU conditionality and the government's policy dissatisfaction with previous minority policies acting as a pioneer for change.

Chapter 7 explores the issue area of women's rights and gender equality in Turkey with reference to second-wave feminist movement. The chapter notes the legal progress made in this area with such reforms as the adoption of a new civil code that took a more egalitarian approach to the family status of women. The chapter discusses the role of women's organisations formed after the 1980s as main agents of change in this realm. The efforts of these organisations drew attention to the plight of women in Turkish society and problematised the deficiencies in women's rights and their subjugation in terms of gender roles. The 'gender mainstreaming' norm developed within the EU provided an important source of inspiration that mobilised women's organisations. The chapter concludes that a bottom-up process of Europeanisation may be observed in this issue area whereby the independent women's organisations were the primary local actors that facilitated the process.

Social policy is another area on which the Europeanisation effect is weak. According to Chapter 8, 'at best, "Europe" is used as a legitimisation device for policies conceived and designed at the national level and with domestic political priorities in mind'. The result is an approximation of some social policy structures to those in other EU states. However, this tends to be more the result of the policy design chosen rather than policy transfer mechanisms at work. While for most of the issue areas analysed in this book incredible membership incentive is assessed as responsible for the limited Europeanisation, the limited Europeanisation on social policy in Turkey is explained with references to weakly-developed EU social policy, the demonstrated weaknesses of the soft coordination approach in introducing substantial policy change and the related neglect of social policy as a major item in pre-accession negotiations.

Regarding environmental policy, even Turkey's international commitments arising from being a party to many international environmental regimes since the 1970s have not so far provided a smooth process for approximation of EU environmental *acquis*. High financial and administrative burdens of full compliance with EU environmental *acquis* clearly challenge development priorities in Turkey. The low credibility of EU membership perspective further complicates the compliance leading to serious implementation and enforcement problems. Chapter 9 finally points out that Europeanisation of Turkish environmental policy often oscillates between inertia and low change depending upon both the credibility of EU conditionality and a number of external factors such as international security concerns and economic gains.

Another issue area on which the Europeanisation effect is assessed in this book is Turkish foreign policy. Turkish foreign policy under the AKP government becomes more dominant in the Middle East in the absence of a strong European perspective although the AKP's leaders often make remarks about the convergence of their policies towards the West and the Middle East or the Muslim world. Accordingly, Chapter 10 concludes that there is a decreasing level of alignment with the EU's CFSP statements particularly since 2008. Indeed, the numbers referenced in this respect in the Commission's regular reports on Turkey's progress show that Turkey is distancing itself from EU positions more frequently and presenting more of an independent attitude.

With respect to Turkey's Cyprus policy which is cast as a national security issue, Chapter 11 concludes that the AKP-led change does not represent a historical rupture or 'U turn' from the conventional state line. The chapter does not deny the

AKP's agency in making comprehensive policy shifts possible. But these dramatic shifts are defined as a 'radical reorganisation' rather than being an alteration as a whole. The chapter contextualises Europeanisation 'as a normative/political context rather than a process: a context of which the impacts are largely shaped by actions and discourses of domestic political and social actors'.

In the areas of migration and asylum, as concluded in Chapter 12, Turkey has made considerable progress in aligning its immigration and asylum policies with those of the EU although Europeanisation has been slower in this area in Turkey when compared to the CEECs. Migration policies have been 'toughened' and asylum policies began to be 'softened' in line with EU demands. However, rule adoption is insufficient in the more politically or economically costly areas of readmission agreements, visa policy, border control and the geographical limitation.

There are also a number of general conclusions that may be drawn from the chapters in this volume. Firstly, the contributors to the volume applied the external incentives and social learning models developed by Schimmelfennig and Sedelmeier to analyse the Europeanisation effect in various issue areas. It is generally upheld that the external incentives model could be applied to explain Europeanisation following the Helsinki European Council up until the start of accession negotiations. The promise of opening accession negations once Turkey fulfils the political aspects of the Copenhagen criteria and the reiteration by the European Council in 2002 that the EU 'will open accession negotiations with Turkey without delay' if the European Council decided in December 2004 that 'Turkey fulfils the Copenhagen criteria' created strong incentive for Turkish governments to act and initiate a comprehensive political reform process. The existence of a clear deadline, well-structured guidelines with regard to the political criteria and strong political will on the part of the EU to abide by its promises with regard to Turkey's candidacy led to a credible EU perspective for the country.

This would not mean much, however, if it were not for the mobilisation of domestic actors in pursuit of EU membership. Almost all the contributions to this volume attribute much importance to the alignment and realignment of domestic political and civil society actors with regard to Europeanisation. The EU incentive influences political and societal actors both through social learning and interaction processes and by putting its weight behind those actors that demand and mobilise for reform or are able to shift their positions in this direction. The AKP, an offshoot of the Islamist Welfare Party that was ousted from government by 28 February 1997 decisions of the National Security Council, was established in 2001 by a reformist group within the Party that aimed to reach a synthesis between liberal values and social conservatism. The 2001 financial crisis led to a widespread disillusionment in the society regarding the coalition government headed by Bülent Ecevit. All the coalition partners were left out of the Parliament by the electorate in the 2002 elections that carried the recently-established AKP to power. This quite radical shift in the political landscape facilitated the rise of a new actor in Turkish politics that effectively seized upon the EU dimension and employed it as a source of legitimacy to expand its room for manoeuvre in the system and successfully challenge forces opposed to it, above all the military. Thus the transformative impact of the EU was felt in Turkey mostly through its influence on power configurations and alignments in the system.

Europeanisation in this period was largely observed in the 2001 and 2004 constitutional amendments and the eight harmonisation packages that were passed through Parliament with all-party support. The EU perspective also gave a boost to civil society actors that saw the opportunity to liberate themselves from excessive bureaucratic procedures and scrutiny of State authorities. Turkish political and societal actors have been debating Turkish democracy, human rights and the 1982 Constitution since the 1980s. Reformist groups, especially liberals questioned the state-centric system that restricted rights and freedoms in Turkey. These demands and yearnings were mostly delayed or rebuffed by the bureaucratic and military elite that usually legitimated their tutelary role in the system by referring to questions of security. Securitisation of the Kurdish problem and Islamic political currents in Turkey provided a source of legitimacy to the State elite that could be employed to also erect barriers to the authority of elected governments and Parliaments. The EU candidacy instigated a process of desecuritisation creating a suitable environment for democratisation and effective enjoyment of rights and freedoms by Turkish citizens.

The start of accession negotiations was the culmination of this intensive reform period when Turkey was rewarded by the EU. However, from the start the negotiation process was full of inherent contradictions due to the cautious language used in the negotiation framework document and the realisation of the EU membership of Greek Cyprus representing the whole island in 2004. Turkey was mostly disappointed that Greek Cyprus could join the EU after rejecting the Annan plan for reunification of the island and the EU did not take any measures to end the ongoing international isolation of Turkish Cyprus. Moreover, the application of sanctions against Turkey by the 2006 European Council decision to suspend eight chapters of the *acquis* added further to the disillusionment in Turkish politics and society based on the realisation that opening accession negotiations did not mean a smooth path towards membership.

After 2006, the pace of Europeanisation slowed down due to the above-mentioned changes in the EU approach to Turkey and Turkey's understanding of the EU. The coming to power of Nicholas Sarkozy in France and Angela Merkel in Germany also had a major factor on the EU impact on Turkey. The third major development had to do with the financial crisis, the failure of Greece due to sovereign debt, and the fact that the EU could not remedy the situation despite consecutive summit meetings. Countries such as Greece and Ireland which were given as examples of EU success in the past were now on the verge of debt crises. This situation also devalued the EU in the eyes of the Turkish public and government. Turkey increasingly started to define its international standing with relevance to surrounding regions especially the Middle East. During this period, while the EU continued to persist as a background factor since Turkey did not drop its claim for EU membership, the loss of credibility concerning the EU incentive for reform was deeply felt and observed.

In the meantime nationalist backlash with regard to the fast pace of political reforms surfaced between 2005 and 2007 in the form of an opposition to the AKP government and liberal intellectuals. The widespread protests against the holding of a conference on the Armenian question at the Bilgi University in Istanbul and the assassination of an Armenian intellectual Hrant Dink in 2007 attested to a resentment to further democratisation that was to be found not only in society at large but more seriously among groups within state security institutions such as the military and police as well as the judiciary. This period witnessed a polarisation in the society and political system between supporters of the AKP and liberal intellectuals on the one hand, and both left-wing and right-wing groups that viewed the AKP as a threat to the secular character and/or integrity of the State.

As the credibility of the EU faded, the second AKP government that came to power in 2007 moved to replace the void by seeking a regional role of leadership for the country making use of systemic changes in the global system and the power vacuum that emerged across Turkey's southern borders with the demise of the Saddam regime, the ongoing strife among ethnic groups in Iraq and failure of the USA to restore order and the approaching retreat of American forces from the region – which actually took place by the end of 2011. During this period the EU mostly had a nominal value as a supranational organisation that Turkey could one day become a member of. The ambiguity about the timing and even the probability of membership and the internal problems of the EU led to the EU dimming in the background. At the same time the Turkish government asserted its autonomous foreign policies with regard to its approach to Israel and Iraq and distanced itself from the West. After 2010, the discourse of major political figures such as President Abdullah Gül, Prime Minister Erdoğan, and chief negotiator Egemen Bağış increasingly began to take on an incriminating tone against the EU. They emphasised Turkey's economic success as opposed to the deep crisis in the Eurozone, and criticised the EU for applying double standards and being insincere towards Turkey mainly due to a racist mentality. Egemen Bağış more recently regularly talks of this racism disease that the EU is inflicted with and offers Turkey's tolerance as a cure while Abdullah Gül's reference to the EU's condition as 'miserable' in a recent visit to the UK made the headlines. Not only did the EU's credibility weaken with regard to the membership perspective, its legitimacy in terms of representing a model of democracy, welfare, human rights and freedom also declined.

This periodisation of Europeanisation since 1999 attests to a declining effect of the EU in terms of being the driving force of reforms and change and influencing the context in which politics takes place in Turkey. It should also be noted however that the demand and search for greater democracy in Turkey is still present and a sizeable majority of civil society actors look upon the EU as an external incentive for democratisation. In policy areas such as environment, food safety or social policy the EU still embodies norms, rules and practices that could shed light on

Turkey's socio-economic development. Turkey's EU narrative is still not finished and more time is needed for both the EU and Turkey to sort out their differences and make decisions with regard to the final destination of accession negotiations. Throughout this process, it is possible to observe inertia, and even backlash in some sectors such as human rights reforms or social policy in Turkey's Europeanisation process. However, faced with a Middle East in a transition process towards freedom where the only alternative is an untenable theocratic regime in Iran or an authoritarian regime in Saudi Arabia, Turkey's only option is to keep its connection with the EU and employ the EU anchor as an external incentive for reform and change. In the context of drastic decline in the support of the Turkish public for EU membership that further undermines the potential for using EU accession as a legitimisation device, the attitude of the EU about how the rest of the accession process would advance has a vital importance. Considering particularly the latest developments around a new constitution the Turkish government needs the EU to facilitate this hard process through a strong and credible membership incentive. Otherwise, as Chapter 10 suggests, the Turkish example of Europeanisation requires 'wider theoretical debates on the possibility of Europeanisation without a membership perspective'.

Index